ECONOMIC AND DEMOGRAPHIC CHANGE
IN PREINDUSTRIAL JAPAN

Economic and Demographic Change in Preindustrial Japan 1600-1868

BY SUSAN B. HANLEY AND
KOZO YAMAMURA

PRINCETON UNIVERSITY PRESS
PRINCETON, NEW JERSEY

TO
JOHN WHITNEY HALL
FRIEND AND MENTOR

CONTENTS

TABLES AND FIGURES

TABLES

PREFACE

This book took much longer to be completed than was first hoped. The major reasons include the initially overambitious goal set by the authors, each author's substantial overestimation of the other's ability to compromise gracefully, and both authors' tendency to suffer from chronic self-imposed distractions.

Hanley's interest in Tokugawa demography began more than a decade ago when she wrote a graduate seminar paper on the subject at the suggestion of John W. Hall. The premise of the paper was that, if the economy was growing, abortion and infanticide could not have been widely practiced and the official population records must therefore have contained omissions which grew larger over time. But this problem was not to be easily resolved, and thus she decided to follow up this initiation into demography by going into village studies. These first efforts resulted in a dissertation (Yale, 1971), but her quest for village documents continued. More evidence brought more problems and, since there is no end in sight to this research, she is here reporting her progress to date.

Yamamura came to Tokugawa economic history in 1968, when he spent a year at the Harvard East Asian Research Center where he had the good fortune to spend many hours discussing Japanese economic history with E. Sydney Crawcour and Henry Rosovsky. Dissatisfied with the basically Marxist interpretation of Tokugawa economic history by most Japanese scholars, he made a reexamination of Tokugawa economic history his goal.

The authors met at seminars on the Japanese economy held each month on the East Coast and at a history seminar guided by Professor Hall. Each realizing that the other's research interest complemented his own, a decision was made to collaborate. Though the fruitfulness of their collaboration is not theirs to judge, the authors believe that this study has benefited from it, fully justifying the high cost of communication between two not-so-reticent authors trained in different disciplines.

Throughout the study, Hanley provided the demographic input and Yamamura the economic. While both authors contributed in one way or another to every chapter, the final division of labor followed these lines. In retrospect, what each believed to be unwelcome intrusions to his respective responsibility by the other proved to be highly valuable in prodding *kenken-gōgō-to* fuming authors to improve their work.

A part of this study has been previously published in condensed form and the authors are grateful to the publishers for permission to use the material here. Kozo Yamamura laid out the basic framework and much of the analysis of Morioka in an article entitled "Toward a Reexamination of the Economic History of Tokugawa Japan, 1600-1867," published in *The Journal of Economic History*, Vol. 33, No. 3 (September 1973), pp. 509-546. Some of the content of Chapters Three and Four was jointly published as "Population Trends and Economic Growth in Pre-industrial Japan," in D. V. Glass and Roger Revelle, eds., *Population and Social Change* (London: Edward Arnold Ltd., 1972), pp. 451-487. Chapter Eight originally appeared in Hanley's "Fertility, Mortality and Life Expectancy in Pre-modern Japan," *Population Studies*, Vol. 28, No. 1 (March 1974), pp. 127-142. And some of the material on the village of Fujito was published by Hanley in "Toward an Analysis of Demographic and Economic Change in Tokugawa Japan: A Village Study," *The Journal of Asian Studies*, Vol. 31, No. 3 (May 1972), pp. 515-537.

The authors would like to acknowledge the considerable financial assistance that made this study possible. Susan Hanley is grateful for a Fulbright-Hays Fellowship in 1968 for study in Japan and for a Foreign Area Fellowship for study both in Japan and this country. Both authors were recipients of a National Science Foundation grant for this study. They are particularly indebted to the East-West Population Institute of the East-West Center in Honolulu where they spent the academic year 1971-1972 as research associates, and to Paul Demeny, the director, who was responsible for inviting them and providing them with a large amount of research assistance. Finally, the authors would like to thank the Japan Program at the University of Washington, which supported this study in its final stages.

The authors would like to thank the many scholars who aided them in this study by providing data, criticizing chapters, solving troublesome problems involving use of the data, and helping in many other ways. Only a few can be mentioned individually here, but among those without whom this study would not have been possible in its present form are John W. Hall and Hayami Akira.

Professor Hall guided Hanley's doctoral dissertation and her training as a historian, and in addition generously provided much of the material for Okayama. She is also deeply indebted to Professor Hayami for initiating her into village studies ("hysterical demography" as he terms it), for generous help in locating material, and for guidance in reading handwritten documents and in analyzing the data. She is grateful to Samuel Preston for suggestions that substantially improved Chapter Eight. Yamamura would like to thank Nathan Rosenberg who, through his insightful comments, helped improve the basic economic framework of this study.

Both authors would like to express their appreciation for assistance with materials and helpful suggestions to Professors Taniguchi Sumio, Fujino Tamotsu, Sakudō Yōtarō, Shimbō Hiroshi, Iwamoto Yoshiteru, and Naitō Jirō (who supplied the records for Numa). The authors are grateful to Hayami Akira, Gilbert Rozman, James I. Nakamura, Mary C. Brinton, and Sister Margit Nagy, C.D.P., all of whom read the manuscript in its entirety and offered numerous suggestions that were helpful in the rewriting. Thanks are also due to Inoko Hiroko, Ikeda Akiko, and Akimoto Hiroya for research assistance. Finally, Hanley would like to acknowledge a special debt to Haru Matsukata and Edwin O. Reischauer for encouraging her initial interest in Japan, and to Hugh T. Patrick, who taught her that economics can be interesting.

ECONOMIC AND DEMOGRAPHIC CHANGE
IN PREINDUSTRIAL JAPAN

CHAPTER ONE

Introduction

Our knowledge of economic growth and demographic change in Tokugawa Japan is so limited that scholars specializing on the eighteenth and nineteenth centuries not only have not arrived at a consensus but also disagree fundamentally even on basic questions such as: Was the economy growing during the second half of the Tokugawa period? Did the population increase after the beginning of the eighteenth century? Was the living standard of the peasant rising? Most Japanese scholars answer these questions in the negative, arguing that during the last century and a half of the Tokugawa period the economy failed to grow—*teitai* (stagnation) is the term most frequently used. Neither did the population increase; in the traditional view this was both because of the ravages of severe famines and because of a deterioration in the living standard of the peasants resulting from "exploitation" by a few large landholders in each village and by the ruling samurai class.

Several quotations from the works of Japanese and Western scholars illustrate their gloomy view. Nomura Kanetarō, a well-known economic historian, wrote in 1953:

> Thus during the second half of the Edo period, life in the villages became increasingly distressing. Small peasants as a rule could not balance their household budgets and were barely able to maintain a subsistence level of life only because of the communal cooperative organization of the extended household [*ie*].[1]

Kodama Kōta, an acknowledged doyen of Tokugawa economic history, said in 1957:

> [Tokugawa peasants] had little to spare. We can assume that medical and entertainment expenditures were out of the question. Therefore, no savings were made and this meant that neither technological improvements nor capital accumulation was possible. Such peasants suffered starvation no sooner than a drought or a flood fell upon them.[2]

3

A widely used Japanese college textbook informed students during the 1960s that:

> The Temmei famine [of the 1780s] is said to have claimed the lives of one million peasants. The population failed to increase because of the frequent famines and stagnation in the productive capacity of the economy.[3]

An essay contained in a book published in 1971, edited jointly by two study groups of Japanese historians, concluded:

> In the Kanto and Tohoku regions especially, the peasants' ability to bear the burden of taxes declined. With the excessively burdensome taxes imposed after the Kyōhō period [1716-1736] as the cause, a pervasive trend emerged: peasants sold their land out of desperate poverty and left agriculture. Frequent harvest failures and famines also were important contributing causes of the general impoverishment and reductions in the number of peasants.[4]

These views reappear in some college textbooks used in the United States. George Sansom's widely used three-volume text states:

> The Bakufu did not interfere when merchant capital was invested in agriculture, but here they were on unsafe ground, for the commercial methods applied to purchasing the produce of the farms were obnoxious to the villages. The merchants fixed the price they were willing to pay at such a low level that the peasants for the most part found that the more they produced, the less they earned in terms of cash. . . . There is no doubt that . . . the rapid growth in an agrarian society of a commercial economy . . . weighed heavily upon the peasants.[5]

And in another American textbook, published in 1972, we read that:

> The peasantry was the segment of the society that supported the national economy and endured hardships and miseries in silence. The expanding money economy was affecting them most adversely and, after the Genroku era [1688-1704], as the Bakufu and the daimyō faced growing financial difficulties, the plight of the peasants appeared to worsen as they were taxed even more heavily.[6]

4

In contrast to the dominant view expressed in these quotations, however, an ever growing number of Japanese specialists and some Western scholars are presenting evidence and interpretations that are clearly in conflict with the majority view. Among the Japanese scholars, Andō Seiichi has gone so far as to state rather bluntly that:

> Ordinarily, it is assumed that the peasants suffered increasing poverty because of an increasing tax burden levied upon them by their masters who were in deteriorating financial circumstances. But if the rulers had had sufficient power to transfer their financial difficulties to the peasants, they would not have suffered the difficulties which they experienced.[7]

According to Ito and Kawana, the life of the peasant, from whom the ruling class was unable to extract more taxes, was steadily improving:

> By the end of the eighteenth century . . . even the [peasants living in] mountainous villages were beginning to eat *mochi* [rice cakes] with sugar in them . . . the life of the commoners was visibly improving. What brought about such an improvement? Even for the smallest peasants, it had become impossible to live by just paying the rice tax and providing all they needed by themselves. They had to produce what they could sell for cash. . . . The need for cash was no longer limited to the upperclass peasants. And, once cash came into the villages, it became the motive force for improving the living standard of all.[8]

But by far the most open challenge to the traditional view has been issued by Hayami Akira, the unquestioned leading scholar in the study of Tokugawa population:

> [In Tokugawa Japan] both the output per acre and per man rose. The economy did not merely expand, retaining the same productive structure; it grew accompanied by qualitative changes—it developed. . . . The economic development of the Tokugawa period was not slow by the standards of preindustrial societies. . . . A vicious circle of poverty was cut, and a new chain of growth was formed: increases in productivity, the formation of a surplus, a rise in the living standard, the accumulation of capital, and then back to increases in productivity.[9]

5

Among the Western scholars, Thomas C. Smith, author of a number of studies on the Tokugawa economy, stated after analyzing records from villages in Kaga *han* and other domains:

> Add to urban growth an increase throughout the population in per capita consumption of food and fibers such as unquestionably took place, and one is forced to conclude that there was a very sizable increase in the productivity of agricultural labor. There was also an increase in crop yields; on individual fields for which we have production data it ran as high as 112 per cent in fifty years.[10]

And, in his well-known essay on the growth of Tokugawa commerce, E. Sydney Crawcour made it amply clear that his description of commerce reflected "rising agricultural productivity," which met the needs of the "free-spending citizens."[11]

While the number of scholars who question the dominant view has clearly been growing, especially during the past fifteen years, they have not succeeded in changing, let alone deposing, the majority view. The reason is that while the predominant view is based either explicitly or implicitly on the Marxist framework of analysis, scholars questioning the well-established interpretation of the majority do not yet possess an overall, unifying analytical framework of their own with which to replace the Marxist framework of analysis. The results, therefore, have provided only a partial critique of the long-standing majority view, the presentation of a series of disjointed pieces of evidence questioning the orthodox interpretation or, even worse, attempts to include contradictory facts and interpretations in studies that are still basically dependent on the Marxist view of Tokugawa economic and demographic change.[12]

Given the state of the frontiers of research in this area, Fairbank, Reischauer, and Craig, the authors of a respected textbook, trod very carefully when answering the questions of what happened to the economy and the peasants in the second half of the Tokugawa period. They indicated their knowledge of the latest research findings:

> The Japanese population grew with the economy but not as rapidly. It stood at about 30 million at the time of the first census in 1721, which is thought to have been a 50 per cent increase over the estimated 20 million for 1600 and was well above the

population of any European country at that time. In the second
half of the Tokugawa period the population grew hardly at all,
despite a continued, even if slower, growth of the economy. As
a consequence, there was a clear rise in living standards throughout the Tokugawa period, even for the peasantry. What had once
been luxurious city ways became commonplace in the countryside too. Thus during these centuries, the Japanese economy
outpaced the population.[13]

But the authors were also aware that the orthodox view still pre-
vails, and thus very skillfully wove this into their discussion:

> Despite generally improving economic conditions, however, the
> economic position of large parts of the peasantry seems to have
> deteriorated during the second half of the Tokugawa period.
> This was reflected in the rising number of famines and also of
> "peasant uprisings," which usually were peaceful demonstra-
> tions against increased taxes or misgovernment and turned to
> violence only late in the period. The root cause of this situation
> seems to have been a growing imbalance in the distribution of
> rural wealth.[14]

John W. Hall, an eminent Tokugawa specialist, clearly believes that
life was getting better in Tokugawa Japan:

> During the last century of the Tokugawa period it was not pop-
> ulation that outstripped production, but the reverse. . . . Signs
> of affluence were plentiful. . . . One of the most obvious signs
> of economic growth in Tokugawa Japan was to be seen in the
> general improvement of the standard of living of the four
> classes. Evidence of better housing, clothing, food, and more
> entertainment and leisure was everywhere apparent after the
> middle of the seventeenth century.[15]

On the other hand, Hall dealt with the evidence on peasant unrest
and rural poverty by relying on the esssentially Marxist explanation of intraclass economic polarization in the villages:

> The "economic problem" of the late Tokugawa period was more
> a matter of differentials in regional development and of the un-
> equal distribution of wealth. At the village level it was as much
> as anything the spread of landlordism and commercial activity
> which led to the breakup of the traditional village economy and

to many of the social dislocations which troubled the authorities. . . . Village society began to separate out at two levels, at the top a small group of wealthy, partially commercialized, families and at the bottom the general run of tenant and part-time cultivators and laborers. The differential development of Tokugawa economy, in which the economically underprivileged may well have found conditions unbearable may help explain why evidence of agricultural commercialization and signs of affluence could coexist with a heavy incidence of peasant uprisings.[16]

But if the number of those who found life unbearable was significantly large (enough to have been the cause of the lack of population growth), who was purchasing the increasing variety of goods made available in the villages? ("Economic surplus made possible numerous secondary activities such as moneylending or the manufacture of *sake, shōyū* (soy sauce) or textiles."[17]) And Hall leaves the question of Tokugawa population growth unanswered: "This leveling off of Japanese population has never been adequately explained,"[18] but one cannot fault him for this statement, as it is a fair assessment of the scholarship to date.

Clearly, the problem faced by both Reischauer and Hall in the textbooks quoted above was how to integrate the large amount of contradictory evidence into a comprehensive explanation of economic, demographic, and social change in the Tokugawa period when the only model available—explicit or implicit—was the essentially Marxist framework used by Japanese scholars. But a better understanding of economic and demographic change during the Tokugawa period is more important than simply clearing up the remaining puzzles over contradictory evidence. Greater knowledge of these subjects will assist and enhance our understanding of the rapid industrialization that followed the Meiji Restoration. It will provide important non-Western input useful in the continuing search for answers to the relationship existing between economic and demographic changes in premodern societies, and will add knowledge crucial for the better understanding of political, social and other aspects of Tokugawa history.

Thus, the purpose of this book is to reexamine the Tokugawa economy with the aid of an analytical framework based on modern, as opposed to Marxist, economic theory, and to investigate demographic changes and their relationship to economic change. Three basic hypotheses are tested in this book: The first is that the economy grew throughout the entire Tokugawa period, though slowly by modern standards, and unevenly. The second is that the rate of economic growth tended to exceed the rate of population growth even in the poorer regions, thus raising the living standard of the large majority of the population throughout the Tokugawa period despite major famines. The third is that population growth was controlled by a variety of methods, ranging from deliberate individual control to pressures arising from tradition or social custom, and that the major reason for such control was to enjoy a rising standard of living, even in those areas that lagged in economic growth. That is, population control for the purpose of maintaining a subsistence standard of living was rare and mostly limited to brief periods during severe famines.

In testing these three hypotheses, we will also attempt to answer the following questions:

1. To what extent are the Tokugawa statistics on population and grain output reliable? Can they be considered at the very least indicative of relative growth rates to be used for comparative purposes?

2. Was the effective tax rate on the peasants rising or falling?

3. How much evidence is there on productivity changes in agriculture and in manufacturing? What effect, if any, did productivity changes have on wages and on the tax base?

4. Why did the centers of commerce and manufacturing shift from the largest urban centers to the rural areas? Which groups created the demand for the products produced in the rural areas?

5. What patterns of demographic behavior resulted in the population trends of the eighteenth and nineteenth centuries? Were the seemingly low rates of population growth due to high mortality or low fertility or to a combination of the two?

6. To what extent are the seemingly stationary population trends in the eighteenth and nineteenth centuries due to the effects of famine? How significant were the famines?

7. How much deliberate population control took place? What were the primary methods used? Were abortion and infanticide the primary methods, or were social controls such as late marriage perhaps more important?

8. Was there a labor shortage in Tokugawa Japan or was labor in excess supply? Why did people move? How much did migration to the economically prospering areas affect population trends?

To ensure that our analyses of economic and demographic trends are consistent with our answers to the above questions and many others that will arise in the course of our discussion, we have constructed an analytical framework of economic and demographic change in Tokugawa Japan. In testing our hypotheses on the economy, and thus our framework, we shall rely primarily on evidence provided by Japanese and Western scholars, by scholars who support as well as those who oppose the traditional view. Given the scope of the subject and the nature of the evidence, our testing of the economic aspects had to be limited. Our selection was the Kinai region and the domains of Morioka and Okayama. We believe that one of the major goals of our study will be accomplished if others interested in Tokugawa Japan are persuaded to add their studies on a domain or a region to support or reject the hypotheses we offer.

In defending the demographic aspects of our hypotheses and several propositions that are derived from them, we go a step further than in the testing of the economic aspects. Within the limits imposed by the time-consuming nature of the research and by the availability of the data sources, we present a considerable amount of new quantitative evidence generated from heretofore unused original village sources. Though we must acknowledge the pioneering research of several Japanese scholars, especially Nomura Kanetarō and Hayami Akira, we believe that our evaluation of various patterns of fertility, mortality, nuptiality, family size, population composition, life expectancy, birth intervals, and migration add revealing insights to those already provided by Hayami and others. More importantly, we believe these insights provide support for the hypotheses advanced in our reexamination of the Tokugawa economy and are useful in further studies of elusive causal relationships between economic and demographic change in preindustrial societies.

This study is divided into two basic parts. The first part is concerned with national and regional (at *kuni* and *han* levels) economic growth and demographic changes. In Chapter Two we present what we believe to be the esssential aspects of the Marxist interpretive framework used by many Japanese scholars, followed by the basic analytical framework we have used in this study. An analysis of the national aggregate population data and an assessment of their reliability follow in Chapter Three. Chapter Four contains a general overview of economic change and a first approximation of the interrelationships existing between population changes and economic growth. In Chapters Five, Six, and Seven we examine economic and demographic changes in three economically distinct regions of Japan. The Kinai region represents the most economically advanced areas of the country and is itself considered the most advanced. Morioka *han* exemplifies the most "backward" domains and is located in the region hardest hit by famine, the Tohoku. Okayama *han* is an example of a relatively advanced domain in western Japan and, because three of the four villages studied in depth were located here, a domain-wide discussion of economic and demographic changes was considered essential for providing the village studies with perspective.

The second half of this book contains the results of microstudies at the village level that reveal population patterns and demographic behavior, including responses of the people to changing economic and demographic conditions. Population trends, including fertility, mortality, and life expectancy, are the focus of Chapter Eight, while the factors affecting population growth—especially famine, infanticide, and social factors—are examined in Chapter Nine. An in-depth study of the village of Fujito in Okayama is presented in Chapter Ten. Chapter Eleven contains a comparison of the demographic findings in this book with the results of other studies on the Tokugawa population and with studies done on other countries just prior to industrialization, particularly in Europe. The conclusion will summarize what we believe to have been the basic patterns of economic and demographic change, outline the interrelationship of these changes in Tokugawa Japan, and examine the implications of our findings with regard to the rapid industrialization and modernization of Japan following the Meiji Restoration of 1868.

CHAPTER TWO

The Framework of Analysis

The traditional interpretation of Tokugawa economic history leaves the non-Marxist with many questions unanswered. It is in an attempt to resolve seemingly contradictory evidence and create a coherent picture of the economic and demographic changes in Tokugawa Japan that we offer here a new framework as an alternative to the Marxist interpretation. But first we will present what we believe to be the essential aspects of the basically Marxist framework adopted, often implicitly, by the majority of Japanese scholars. We do this in order to illustrate the reasons for the pessimistic tone that pervades much of the Japanese literature, the scarcity or virtual absence of quantitative evidence useful in testing hypotheses derived from modern economic theory, and the continued adherence to the traditional interpretation. We will then present the analytical framework to be used in this study, together with hypotheses and propositions that are derived from, or are analytical extensions of, the framework. The hypotheses and propositions will be tested in succeeding chapters.

THE DOMINANT JAPANESE VIEW
OF THE TOKUGAWA ECONOMY[1]

In summarizing the Japanese view, it is important to stress at the outset that most Japanese scholars make two crucial analytical assumptions: The first is that "the question of distribution" (who gets how much at whose cost) is much more important than "the question of growth" (how or whether total output grew). The other often implicit, but consistently made, assumption is that commercial transactions leave one party worse off and the other better off. Most of the Japanese literature on commerce is difficult to understand without an awareness of this "zero-sum" view of commercial transactions.[2]

Using these ideologically oriented assumptions, Japanese historians interpret the seventeenth century as the period in which

12

the Bakufu and the daimyo established the *honbyakushō* system, a system of "independent peasants." The *honbyakushō* were peasants who cultivated an amount of land sufficient to enable them to perpetuate their economic existence and therefore to continue to pay taxes in rice.[3] The ruling class, understandably, made concerted efforts to create *honbyakushō* whenever possible by various means, including reclamation, since this was the most efficient method by which to reduce the number of small landholders and the landless, neither of whom, according to this view, were economically viable. They therefore paid taxes only through the *honbyakushō* under whom they worked. Village leaders were appointed to make sure that all *honbyakushō* fulfilled their tax obligations. The decrees prohibiting the sale and subdivision of land, issued from 1643 on, were measures to perpetuate the *honbyakushō* system. Within this system, which was geared to the "exploitation" of the peasants, the Bakufu and the daimyo proceeded during the seventeenth century to increase the amount of cultivated land in order to widen their tax base.

The system, however, contained a "contradiction"[4] within itself. The ruling class was soon joined by village leaders in its efforts to reclaim land. These village leaders were large landholders who were able to wield the power vested in them by the ruling class as tax collectors to obtain the corvée needed for reclamation projects. The *honbyakushō*, already burdened by high taxes, could ill afford the added corvée. Unable to support the increased burden, the *honbyakushō* began to abscond, and numerous conflicts arose between the village leaders and the peasants, causing the amount of tax revenue to decline or, at best, to fluctuate. At this point the foundation of the *honbyakushō* system began to weaken. In the words of a popular college textbook, which went into its third printing in 1971:

The reason why the agricultural policy of the Bakuhan power took the form of reclamation was simply that it increased tax revenues. However, it was inevitable for such an agricultural policy to magnify the contradiction involved. The contradiction lies in the fact that the interests of those larger landholders who reclaimed land and those of smaller landholding peasants who wanted to improve their economic status were diametri-

13

cally opposed. The contradiction appeared in the forms of extremely unstable tax revenues and widespread absconding but was most evident in the misery the peasants suffered during famines.[5]

While this contradiction threatened the *honbyakushō* system, another, no less serious, contradiction—the increasing commercial activities within "the rice-based Tokugawa feudal economy" —emerged to erode the foundations of the entire Bakuhan system. The tax rice had to be marketed, and the growing urban centers where the samurai class resided had to be supplied with daily needs. Commerce, therefore, was a necessity for the Bakufu and the daimyo. As long as commerce was necessary, the ruling class chose to permit its growth under the control of, and preferably for the benefit of, the samurai class. This was the beginning of the so-called *ryōshu keizai taisei*, whereby each ruler attempted to maximize his control over the economy of his domain. Under this system, the domain granted to a small number of wholesalers privileges that permitted them to conduct business, frequently on a monopoly basis, in exchange for *myōga-kin* ("thank-money"). Another aspect of the system was the attempt by daimyo to become monopsonists of selected products from their own domain. But, most important, commerce was limited to urban centers, that is, castle towns and a few large population centers within each domain. The increased revenue in the form of thank-money was welcomed by the daimyo, whose needs for cash were large because of the *sankin kōtai* requirement (residence in Edo in alternate years) imposed on them by the Bakufu.

As the seventeenth century progressed, commerce gained momentum in the major cities of Osaka and Edo and in many castle towns. Thus, the effects of the zero-sum nature of commerce were increasingly felt. The daimyo who required cash, principally for *sankin kōtai* purposes, had to exchange large quantities of goods for cash in Osaka. The Osaka merchants dealing in large quantities of goods accumulated huge profits at the expense of those with whom they traded. The increasing poverty of the retainers of both the Bakufu and the daimyo began to be noticeable by the mid-seventeenth century, an inevitable consequence, according to this view, of the developing cash-based economy.

However, despite the contradictions emerging in villages and in cities, on balance the economy of the seventeenth century was characterized by continued growth. Because the tax base was increasing, the ruling class could enjoy more of the amenities of urban life, and the zero-sum nature of commerce had not yet offset the benefits resulting from the increasing tax revenues. Though some authors are unwilling to say so, most do admit that on balance the peasants benefited too. The increase in output resulting from increased productivity and land reclamation tended to outpace the tax burden for the century. The new *honbyakushō* system, combined with a century of peace following the war-torn previous centuries, added security to the peasants' lives and motivated them to produce more. The increasing tax and corvée were onerous and even ruinous for some, but the economy was growing at a rate sufficient to permit the peasant population to expand steadily during the seventeenth century. The emerging merchants, though still under the control of the ruling class, found their balance sheets in the black even after paying thank-money. Thus, it was possible for the century to end with a period known for its flourishing economy and its gay and even luxurious life in urban centers: the Genroku period, from 1688 to 1703.

The Genroku period, however, represented the peak of the Tokugawa centuries in more ways than one. By the Kyōhō period (1716-1735), it was clear that the precarious balance of the Genroku years had shifted. Commerce had developed rapidly up to the first decades of the eighteenth century, and the dependence of the ruling class on commerce—"involvement in a cash-based economy"—had increased, while samurai control over commerce had begun to slip away. At the same time it was becoming evident that further reclamation was possible only at a sharp increase in cost. The Bakufu and the daimyo began to shift the burden of their economic difficulties onto other classes. Taxes were raised on the peasants, thank-money was increased, and merchants were forced to accept default-prone loans more frequently. Even daimyo retainers, who suffered increasingly from the effects of their dependency on the cash-based economy, found part of their stipends "borrowed" by their lords. By the mid-eighteenth century, according to the prevailing view, the economy was clearly changing from bad to worse for most people. To describe the Japanese view of the economy during the last century of the Tokugawa period, it will be convenient to follow the practice of the Marxist literature and examine the economic difficulties experienced by each class.

According to the Marxist view, the ruling class suffered "increasing poverty" because of their ever-increasing dependence on markets over which they had ever-decreasing control. Expenditures rose rapidly for a variety of reasons, ranging from costly riparian works to military expenses incurred during the nineteenth century in response to threats from Western powers. Peasants, already overburdened with taxes and suffering from famines and the advance of commerce into the villages, could be made to yield more taxes only at the risk of inciting revolts, to which desperate peasants were resorting with increasing frequency. There were also limits to "borrowing" from already poverty-stricken retainers and to forcing loans from the big city merchants, who had their own problems in coping with the competition emerging in the countryside. There is no shortage of stories about daimyo who mortgaged ten years of their tax revenues or about low-level samurai who starved to death.

Also, according to the Marxist literature, the life of the peasants grew steadily worse. The ruling classes were aware that they were approaching the limits of their exploitation of the peasants but could not prevent themselves from making more demands on them. Beginning with the tax reforms of the Kyōhō period (1716-1735), the peasants' tax burden rose almost continuously. The motto of the tax collectors was said to be: "Leave the peasants only enough to let them survive to produce more, but not enough to live on," or "from peasants, as from sesame seeds, more can be had if they are squeezed harder."

The peasants suffered from more than high taxes. By the mid-eighteenth century, commerce had begun to invade the villages "with the vigor of the running tide." This new phase of the Tokugawa economy began with the rise of the *zaikata* merchants (literally, merchants in the countryside). These were merchants in rural towns and other nodes of the agricultural population, who bought agricultural cash crops from peasants and sold to them the numerous commodities coming from all parts of Japan in increasing quantities. At this point, according to the traditional Japanese interpretation of history, the zero-sum effects of the commercial trade began to exert a negative effect on the peasant. Hard-pressed peasants selling cash crops resorted to borrowing or to selling their land and becoming agricultural laborers, tenant farmers, peddlers, or emigrants to the cities in search of a living. What Japanese economic historians call the "disintegration of the peasant class" was now under way. The large landholders were acquiring more land, while an increasing number of peasants were pushed to the edge of subsistence.

The process of the "impoverishment of the villages" was hastened by three major famines and frequent poor harvests. The famines were severe enough to result in death by starvation of from 10 to 20 percent of the total peasant population in some regions, and the poor harvests only accelerated the process that commerce and high taxes had begun. Invariably cited as evidence of the degree of agricultural impoverishment are the practices of abortion and infanticide to which the peasants resorted, and the increasing number of peasant revolts—made in circumstances of desperation and, in most cases, in opposition to tax increases. Under the circumstances, it was inevitable that the total peasant population should "stagnate."

But who were the rural merchants who must have prospered on the gaining side of the zero-sum commercial activities? Many were large landholders (usually referred to as the gōnō, wealthy peasants) who were able to aggrandize their landholdings by acting as village entrepreneurs and moneylenders. Some leased their land to tenants and others became full-time merchants and moneylenders but, given the desperate condition of the peasants, all made handsome profits. Also, in the nineteenth century, especially in the region around Kyoto and Osaka, additional profits could be had by the larger landholders who were able to take advantage of the increasingly capital-intensive cultivation of cash crops, which typically they marketed themselves. The profits then were reinvested in moneylending and in commerce, in other words, in taking advantage of desperate sharecroppers. By the early decades of the nineteenth century, the power of the rural merchants was such that the urban merchants (who had been weakened by their own rigid guild system, noncompetitive monopolistic behavior, and frequent forced loans of huge magnitude) were no match in competing for market shares and profits.

However, neither the rural merchants nor the gōnō were exempted from the effects of the "feudal contradiction." The very prosperity of the gōnō depended on the existence of a class that could be exploited. Dispossessed small landholders or tenants hopelessly in debt were no longer sources of further profits. As the *gōnō*, in their capacity as merchants, wished to obtain cash crops from peasants, they needed peasants who produced such crops. However, as the *gōnō* expanded their economic activities, further exploiting the peasants, they eventually weakened them to the point where they could no longer be exploited. "Herein lies the limitation imposed on the *gōnō*. And, because of this limitation, the *gōnō* remained to the end merchant moneylenders,"[6] without ever being able to blossom as capitalists in a capitalist economy.

In sum, the Marxist view of the Tokugawa economy maintains that: (1) Though the economy grew during the seventeenth century, it stagnated during the last century and a half of the Tokugawa period. Some scholars have observed a seemingly rapid growth of commerce during the last few decades of the Tokugawa period, but this observation is often ignored or glossed over in assessing the economic performance of the second half of the Tokugawa period as a whole. (2) Peasants, consisting of no less than 80 percent of the population, existed to be exploited by the ruling class and by the *gōnō*. The peasants' living standard tended to deteriorate during the eighteenth and nineteenth centuries because of commercialization and an increased tax burden. (3) The samurai class suffered increasing financial hardship because of the development of commerce. (4) The *gōnō*, in a position to exploit peasants most effectively in their capacity as landowners, moneylenders, and rural merchants, grew rich at the expense of urban merchants and peasants. In essence, the Tokugawa economy after the seventeenth century was seen by the Marxist as generally bleak. An overwhelming majority of the population suffered from heavy taxation, commercialization, crop failures, and exploitation by the *gōnō*. The oppressed majority struggled unsuccessfully and the struggle was to continue even after the Meiji Restoration, which ushered in a period of "absolutist capitalism" with its new capitalist oppressors.

Many questions remain unanswered in the minds of Western scholars who read through the voluminous Japanese works expressing various versions of the traditional view just summarized. Major questions are: Can we ignore the evidence of a rising living standard for the peasants, which slips through even in the most ideologically oriented studies? If a rising living standard was being enjoyed by a small number of *gōnō*, at most a few in each village, how could they consume most of the increasing output made available by the growth of rural commerce that the traditional scholars agree took place? Why does so little quantitative evidence exist demonstrating that the effective tax burden on the peasants rose? Are we to ignore all the quantitative evidence of rising wage levels for agricultural labor and for wage earners in towns? Were the famines in fact as severe as they would have had to be to produce the devastating consequences on the economy and population claimed by many Japanese scholars? How reliable are the official data on the population and the rice output cited by many Japanese scholars in support of their view? The list of questions could be much longer, but these samples are sufficient to indicate our dissatisfaction with the Marxist framework of analysis. We shall now present a new analytical framework which, hopefully, is capable of answering these and many other questions while accommodating the quantitative and qualitative evidence we have.

AN ALTERNATIVE FRAMEWORK

The analytical framework presented here, unlike the Marxist model, will yield testable hypotheses and can be used to evaluate recent non- and contra-Marxist findings. For the sake of analysis, let us assume that the Tokugawa economy consisted of two major regions and that the economy of each region can be analyzed in two relatively distinct time periods. The model for Region I was based on the characteristics of the Kinai (the area around Osaka and Kyoto) and areas in western Japan (especially the Chugoku region). Region II was drawn from the Tohoku region in northeastern Honshu and parts of Kyushu. The early time period corresponds roughly to the seventeenth century, and the later period to the remainder of the Tokugawa years. It should be remembered that the following description of each region constitutes a model and that, given the diversity of economic and demographic patterns in Tokugawa Japan, one can expect to find many minor and even major variations with its application to any specific area. The Kinai and part of the Tohoku region will be examined closely in Chapters Five and Six, which will present empirical support for these two polar cases of our analytical framework.

Partly through increased productivity and partly because more rice paddies and upland fields were created by reclamation, agricultural output increased steadily in Region I during the early period. The productivity increase resulted from improved irrigation techniques and agricultural implements, more efficient use of land through increased double cropping, more productive methods of rotation, and other improvements.

The peasants' own motivation to increase both productivity and the cultivated acreage is crucial in explaining both the increased agricultural output and the savings necessary to take advantage of technological developments. This motivation was strengthened as the private ownership of land was more securely established. The *honbyakushō* system, which began to develop in the pre-Tokugawa years, was important because it provided a legal framework that significantly contributed toward the establishment of the private ownership of land by individual peasants.[7] The daimyo, many of whom had secure domains of their own for the first time, were also eager to reclaim land because they were assured of capturing the gains resulting from it. Also, many resource-consuming irrigation and water control projects within each domain became profitable because the daimyo domains were sufficiently large and politically secure to benefit from economies of scale.

Commerce and manufacturing activities in Region I increased during the period, in part for similar reasons. The establishment of law and order significantly reduced the cost of enforcing contracts, and the efforts and expenditures of the ruling class to protect and encourage these activities were justified by its ability to capture the resulting gains. The most important reason for the growth of commerce and manufacturing was, however, an increase in "domestic" demand from within Region I itself and in the demand for Region I's exports by Region II, "export" demand. The increase in domestic demand reflected the steadily rising living standard of the population resulting from increasing agricultural productivity, the gains due to increasing specialization, and a larger scale of transactions and production in commerce and commercial agriculture. The export demand came mostly from the ruling class of Region II in the form of imports through Osaka or Edo and expenditures connected with the *sankin kōtai*, both those involved in the journey of the daimyo and his retinue (mostly through and to Region I) and the expense of maintaining a residence in Edo and providing for his family and his retinue. These expenditures accounted for a large proportion of the cash revenue of any domain.

While the exports stimulated commercial and manufacturing activities in Region I, they had the effect of transferring Region II's demand for commercial and manufactured goods to Region I and consequently Region II was deprived of the essential stimulus needed for the development of commerce and manufacturing there.[8] This transfer of demand was due not only to the *sankin kōtai* system but also to the fact that, by 1600, Region I already enjoyed a considerable relative advantage over Region II in terms of ability to provide desired goods and services. It had relatively more advanced technical and institutional capabilities and transportation and communication facilities, and a higher degree of urbanization (thus specialization). These relative advantages were strengthened during the early Tokugawa period by the export demand.

No less important in characterizing Region I during the early as well as late Tokugawa period is the comparative lack of rigor with which political authority was exercised. Authority was less rigorously applied in Region I than in Region II for a number of reasons: Most of the *tenryō* (the Bakufu territory) was in Region I, and this territory, though centrally located, tended to be geographically fragmented and also highly urbanized, making rigorous controls on commerce difficult to enforce. But the Bakufu was also less inclined to strictly regulate commerce and industry, finding that the *tenryō* yielded more revenue if commercial activities were allowed to increase. Thus, the tax burden tended to be lighter in territory directly controlled by the Bakufu for a combination of reasons, including the facts that, during the early period, the Bakufu was financially sound and tax revenues from the nonagricultural sectors relatively large. These characteristics of control in Region I meant that a greater proportion of revenue was left in the hands of the peasants, merchants, and artisans, who were able both to enjoy a higher standard of living than their counterparts in Region II and to allocate part of these higher incomes to capital investment.

In contrast, Region II was less productive, less urbanized, and for the most part less favored climatically (more typhoons or a colder climate, for example). The daimyo in this region were able to establish more effective control at the local level because they usually controlled a geographically contained unit, which meant that control over commerce was more feasible than in Region I. And with commerce and industry less developed, they typically tried to tightly control these activities through monopolies and monopsonies. Often located far from Edo, the daimyo in Region II faced even higher expenses related to the *sankin kōtai* and in many cases were forced to levy higher taxes on their less productive land than their counterparts in Region I. Thus, Region II was less developed than Region I at the outset of the Tokugawa period, and the system of government set up by the Tokugawa House favored, though in many ways accidentally, the continued development of Region I over Region II.

During the late Tokugawa period, the economic growth of Region I was further accelerated. Agricultural productivity continued to rise because of the increased use of fertilizers, a gradual increase in the number of farming units approximating the optimum size under the conditions emerging in both factor and product markets, and a constant improvement in agricultural implements and management. Because of the reallocation of land and labor to increasingly more profitable cash crops, the total real value of agricultural output rose steadily, despite the fact that reclamation was proceeding at a slower pace in the late Tokugawa period than in the earlier one.

Commercial and manufacturing activities grew even more rapidly than agriculture in Region I during the late Tokugawa period. This growth reflected both the rising living standard in Region I and the continuing export demand from Region II. The productivity of both capital and labor rose in the nonagricultural sectors, as it did in agriculture, because of increasing economies of scale, technological advances, and the continued development of financial, marketing, and other related economic institutions and of increasingly more efficient transportation and communication facilities.[9] While the rate of the growth of the export demand may have slowed due to "import substitution," which became possible because of the gradual development of nonagricultural activities in Region II, the level of income reached by the population in Region I allowed for an increasing proportion of it to be spent on the goods and services of the nonagricultural sectors—a demand more than sufficient to offset the possible decline in the export demand.

As Region I has been discussed vis-à-vis Region II, much of what occurred in Region II is clear by inference. During the early Tokugawa period, agricultural output and productivity rose in Region II, but at a slower rate than in Region I, though reclamation was also vigorously carried out by the daimyo in this region. Commercial and manufacturing developments lagged behind those in Region I because of the difference in initial conditions, the relatively lower initial income level of the population, and the shift in demand for goods and services to Region I. The initial disadvantages in terms of historical, geographical, and institutional factors for the nonagricultural sectors of this region were significant, and the degree of urbanization achieved was considerably less than in Region I. The lower level of income reflected the slower rate of increases in productivity arising from slower rates of capital accumulation, institutional development, and improvements in the quality of labor resulting from specialization; unfavorable climatic conditions; and the relatively stronger daimyo, many of whom were *tozama*. More effective tax collection and more rigid enforcement of the *han* monopolies and monopsonies in Region II tended to leave less in the hands of commoners. The commoners also had to bear what seems to have been a larger burden of the Bakufu exactions, which were levied more frequently in Region II because the daimyo were *tozama*, and which were more onerous because the standard of living was lower.

Agricultural productivity continued to rise during the late Tokugawa period in Region II for the same reasons it did in Region I. However, the rate of growth of the total real value of output was slower in this region because of a lower rate of growth in productivity and a limited allocation of land and labor for cash crops (for reasons of a limited and slowly growing demand, the relative unprofitability caused by the efficient monopsonistic practices of the daimyo, and climatic limitations). More frequent poor harvests and more severe famines than in Region I also contributed to the relatively slow agricultural growth. These factors caused the living standard to be lower in Region II than in Region I during the late as well as the early Tokugawa period. The relative effectiveness of the daimyo of this region in collecting taxes helped maintain this pattern.

However, during the late period, commerce and industry did become increasingly more important, reflecting slow but continuing increases in the standard of living. Over time, even the daimyo of this region became less efficient in collecting taxes, and the peasants benefited here too. The taxation of commerce and manufacturing perhaps continued to be more effective than in Region I, but even Region II daimyo faced increasing difficulties in capturing the surpluses generated by the growing activities in non-agricultural sectors.[10]

Despite poor harvests and a number of famines, on balance the living standard in Region II rose, and thus rural commerce and manufacturing developed in this region too. Famines and poor harvests had a negative effect on population growth, but the population increased nevertheless. Here, too, out-migrants from the villages were underenumerated and the slow growth rate of population can be at least partly attributed to the desire of the people to raise their living standard. Infanticide was undoubtedly practiced, but its importance in the trend of changes in population has been highly exaggerated, as was the severity of the famines in contemporary reports.

Underlying the preceding explanation of the economic changes in the latter half of the Tokugawa period are two crucial hypotheses. The first is that the political ability of the ruling class to tax away increasing "surpluses" declined during the eighteenth and nineteenth centuries in both regions. The peasants found that, because of rising productivity, the fixed or even slightly rising nominal tax rate left them with rising incomes. There were more cash crops, and these provided wider latitude for tax avoidance and evasion than rice did. The *jōmen* system, which was ill suited for capturing productivity gains and which encouraged corruption by officials, helped peasants rather than hurt them. In commerce and manufacturing, tax collection was even less efficient. The most prevalent methods of tax collection—fixed taxes, license fees, bidding for the privilege of doing business, and even self-assessments by merchants—led to a relatively low effective tax rate.

The second hypothesis is that the total peasant population did not stagnate but rather grew slowly during the eighteenth and nineteenth centuries. The slow growth of population was caused not by desperate peasants who were forced to resort to infanticide, but primarily by the preference (though often through social coercion) of people to increase their standard of living by limiting the number of children they raised. This they did by socially accepted and institutionalized methods, including abortion and even infanticide, delayed marriage, and other practices that resulted in population control.

Scholars are agreed that Japan's population rose rather rapidly during the seventeenth century. The growing economy increased the demand for children, and the end of the civil wars plus the trend for family servants to be made into tenant farmers and marry rather than be kept single caused an increase in marriages. Thus, with an increase in the demand for children during this century and with demand exceeding supply, social controls over fertility were loosened and the birth rate rose as the proportions married increased.

At some point, however, varying in time by region and even by village, an additional increase in children was seen to amount to an economic burden by the villagers, and they found themselves with more children than they wanted. Shortly after this occurred, social controls were tightened and, in addition, individuals began to limit their own fertility. The best known of the latter measures are abortion and infanticide, but the birth rate is also known to have declined in a village where male migration for employment was common. In any case, the birth rate started to decline.

The imputed preference of the rural population for small families during the latter half of the Tokugawa period can be explained, we believe, by several factors. One is the familiar "demonstration effect." The peasants had ample opportunity to observe the lifestyles of their betters in close proximity, and such opportunities increased as interregional and village-town mobility grew in the eighteenth century. Observing how the well-off commoners in both the villages and towns were living compared to the samurai whose incomes were not rising, the rural population took less and less seriously the dictum "to live as befitting one's social status." We also speculate that an active desire to improve the living standard in Tokugawa villages originated in the same sociopsychological and cultural mold that continues to serve today as a partial, but significant, explanatory factor of Japan's rapid industrial growth.[11]

A second factor in limiting children—and families—within a village in order to increase consumption per capita was not the mere desire for a better life but the social necessity of "keeping up with the Jones's" which, in Tokugawa as well as in modern Japan, was a virtual necessity rather than a preference. At the top of village society, the leaders had to maintain a certain level of wealth in order to preserve their relative economic position in the village and to be able to meet the emergency needs of the villagers and the social obligations necessary to preserve their social status. If they had numerous children to provide for, within a generation or two the family's wealth could be dissipated and its status lost. The same was true for farmers with a larger than average holding and, for all farmers who had hopes of climbing the status ladder, having to support a large number of children could only prove detrimental to achieving the family's goals. Those at the bottom of village society could not afford to feed many mouths if they were to see a rise in their economic and social position, nor could they afford to incur the displeasure of those in the village who would be the providers of aid in emergency situations. In the village society, and given the Japanese social tradition, it would be very difficult for any family dependent upon farming for a living to go against the consensus of the village community. And added to village social pressure was the weight of government regulation, which in many domains forbade the alienation of land or parceling beyond a certain point to ensure viable farm units and thus a maximum tax revenue.[12]

If the preceding hypothesis is correct, it clearly implies that long-accepted population data compiled by the Bakufu and the daimyo are to a great extent unreliable and that the effects of famines, mostly reported by contemporaries on the basis of impressions and second-hand reports, are highly exaggerated. During severe famines within a limited region, infanticide as an act of desperation, and death from starvation, undoubtedly took place. But we shall argue that while famines may have been responsible for slowing the population growth in certain areas during years of crop failures, they do not account for the low rates of growth throughout the nation for the century and a quarter for which we have national data.

An important implication of the foregoing discussions and hypotheses is that the growth of rural commerce and industry can be explained in terms of the rising living standard of the population in and around the areas largely responsible for this growth (places to which labor moved from agriculture) and, more importantly, by the rising real income level of the agricultural population in general. In this framework, the decline of the major urban centers during the late Tokugawa period in Region I can be explained in terms of an unchanging or only slowly rising (relative to the villages) living standard (demand) of the samurai class whose ability to share in the increasing total output became limited. The decline can also be related to the difficulties that any monopolistically inclined guild system experiences when the demand for its products is either stable or declining and it faces strong competition from merchants outside the system who enjoy an increasing demand for their goods.

Another significant implication of our alternative explanation of Tokugawa economic growth is that what Japanese economic historians call "the disintegration of the peasant class" was, in the main, the outcome of the peasants' efforts to improve their standard of living. While granting that some peasants were forced off the land by personal misfortune, high taxes collected by some *daikan* (local magistrates) and several financially hard-pressed daimyo, and by famines in some regions, we believe that most peasants who left the land did so to become either part- or full-time merchants or wage earners in order to obtain higher incomes. That is, we are asserting that the peasants left the land, in most instances, attracted by higher wages in cities and nearby urban centers or to realize a larger income by part- or full-time trading. The basic difference between our view and the Marxists' on the occupational and geographical mobility of the peasants is that we attribute the mobility to the peasants' desire to increase their income, while the Marxists believe that the peasants left the land because they were forced to by the ruling class who demanded an increasing amount of taxes, by the merchants and the *gōnō* who exploited them, or by the crop failures that pushed them to "the edge of starvation."

We would, in fact, go so far as to argue that the living standard of the peasants rose during the last century and a half of the Tokugawa period thanks to increasing agricultural productivity, to their ability to react to the changing economic conditions (occupational and/or geographical mobility, changes in the mix of crops they planted, by-employments, etc.), and to the population control they practiced. We also suggest that changes in the landholding

27

pattern and the size of the farming unit were products of the peasants' rational responses to the changing conditions in both factor and product markets and especially to the rising costs of labor. Therefore, these changes, brought about to optimize the uses of resources, were not due to the polarization of the peasant class resulting from intensified exploitation by *gōnō* and the ruling class. The changes increased the productivity of resources used in agriculture, thus contributing to the increase in the living standard of the peasants.

What our analytical framework implies is also significant in terms of the successful industrialization that followed the Meiji Restoration. Our model suggests that, since both the total output and per capita income were rising during the second half of the Tokugawa period, the economy was able to generate both the capital required for industrialization and sufficient demand for new products during the crucial first decades of industrialization. A mid-nineteenth century economy in which the per acre yield of rice was as high as in most Southeast Asian nations in the 1950s cannot be considered a "backward" economy. The Tokugawa peasants did not "endure hardships and miseries in silence" nor can we say that their "plight appeared to worsen as they were taxed even more heavily." Industrialization in the Meiji period was possible because the Tokugawa economy was not stagnating, but growing.

THE ALTERNATIVE FRAMEWORK IN DIAGRAMS

To summarize the description of this framework of analysis, let us restate it with the aid of the following diagrams, which are helpful in visualizing the interrelationships of the variables presented. Figure 2.1 illustrates the relative changes in the growth of population and the economy in Regions I (western Japan) and II (northern Japan) respectively. Figure 2.2 indicates how these changes took place and what the various interrelationships are.

In Figure 2.1, both (a) and (b) represent logarithmic values for R, E, TP, and $\widetilde{TP}$. R represents the total output of rice and other grains, while E stands for economic activity—that is, manufacturing and commercial activities added to R, the basic agricultural output. TP refers to the total population of the region, and $\widetilde{TP}$ to an adjusted population figure where we consider TP to be incorrect. The axes refer to quantity and time (t). Lower case (r and p) indicates rate of change.

In Figure 2.1 (a) we see that the rate of growth of grain output for Region I is greater than the rate of growth of the population during the beginning of the Tokugawa period. Other economic activities are not considered to have contributed significantly to the total income of the region and thus are not added here. During the

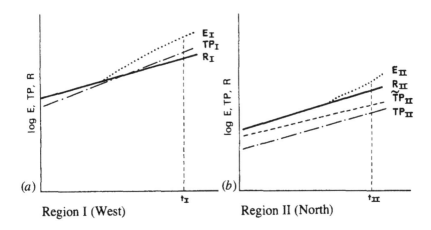

Region I (West)   Region II (North)

Figure 2.1: Hypothesized Relative Changes in Total Population, Grain Output, and Nonagricultural Economic Activity

second half of the Tokugawa period, the relationship of the rates of growth of population and grain output are the reverse of what they were earlier because more and more of the land once used for grain was being used to raise cash crops such as cotton, rapeseed, tobacco, and indigo, among others. That is, the economy was growing because the growth rates of cash crops and of commercial and manufacturing activities more than compensated for the decline in the grain output. The growth rate of total economic activities was larger than that of the total population, resulting in an increase in per capita income.

In Region II, Figure 2.1 (b), the growth rates of grain output were larger than the population growth rates throughout the Tokugawa period but, as we shall argue in the following chapter, the official population figures show a growth rate slower than in fact occurred and, to adjust for errors in the figures, $\widetilde{TP}$ has been added.

However, the difference between the official figures and our estimate of the population growth rates tends to diminish over time. While nonagricultural economic activities became important in Region II later than in Region I, they increased significantly from the mid-Tokugawa period on, as is well established.

A comparison of (*a*) and (*b*) as drawn shows that $r_1 < p_1$ (i.e., the growth rate of rice output was less than that of population) but, because of the differences in the rates of increase and levels of the contributions made by E_I and E_{II}, the per capita income of Region II (E_{II} divided by $\widetilde{TP}_{II}$ at t_{II}) is smaller than E_I divided by TP_I at t_I. The distance between TP_{II} and $\widetilde{TP}_{II}$ may vary by location within Region II, but the diagram is drawn to show that the per capita income in this region was always lower than in Region I.

The hypotheses contained in Figure 2.1 imply that in neither of these two regions of Japan were population limits reached, and that the poverty of Region II was only relative to the prosperity of Region I. Moreover, in Region I, E_I grew more quickly than TP_I to assure a rise in per capita income in spite of $r_1 < p_1$. We need not argue that the living standard in Region II necessarily rose, but only that it was most likely that the per capita output of rice remained at least relatively constant while E_{II} increased over time.

Expanding our framework to account for changes in productivity, labor mobility, population growth, and interregional trading, we can present the framework as follows in Figure 2.2. In (*a*), which applies to Region I, A_o refers to agricultural output, M_o to the output from the manufacturing and commercial sectors (the nonagricultural sectors), L_a to labor in agriculture, and L_m to labor in the manufacturing and commercial sectors.

In Region I, agricultural productivity increased over time, and this increase is shown as the shift from A_i to A_{ii} in the fourth quadrant where each of these curves indicates total agricultural output while labor (L_{ai}) in Period I and (L_{aii}) in Period II are combined with relatively fixed resources.[13] The output of the commercial and manufacturing sector is likewise shown as M_i and M_{ii} in the second quadrant. The slopes of the A and M curves show the marginal productivity of labor, and L_a and L_m with time subscripts (i and ii) indicate the amount of labor in each sector in each period. The total labor force is the sum of OL_{ai} and OL_{mi} for

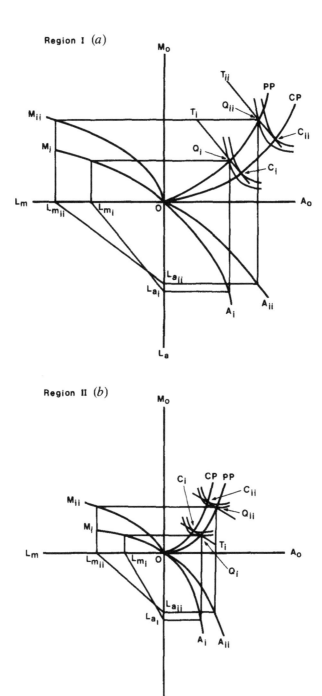

Figure 2.2: A Model of Tokugawa Economic Growth and the Rising Living Standard

Period I and the same with time subscript ii for Period II. The slopes of the line joining OL_a and OL_m with the same time subscripts indicate the proportion of labor in each sector during each period.

The curve PP in the first quadrant for Region I indicates the production path of the region and CP the consumption path. The region consumed C_i and C_{ii} mixes of agricultural and commercial-manufacturing outputs in each period respectively, and these mixes are on higher indifference curves than Q_i and Q_{ii} (quantities produced). That is, this region traded on the trade possibility lines T_i and T_{ii} from Q to C in each period (sold M_o to buy A_o). Obviously, the level of consumption attained in Period II was higher than that obtained in the earlier half.

In tracing the changes over time for Region I, an increasing proportion of the increasing total population is seen entering the nonagricultural sector and the absolute number in the labor force in agriculture declined. But, because productivity was increasing, agricultural output (A_o) did not decline. In (a), the marginal productivity of labor in the nonagricultural sector at points L_{mi} and L_{mii} is higher than that in the agricultural sector at points L_{ai} and L_{aii}. This is the reason for the migration from the agricultural to other sectors, though the commercial and manufacturing sectors began to shift from the urban centers during the latter part of the period to the countryside because the guild-dominated and only slowly growing (or even declining) urban sectors were unable to compete with the growing commercial and manufacturing sectors outside the cities.[14] The declining or nonincreasing demand in the urban centers may have caused the marginal productivity of labor to be lower than in the rural areas because the commercial and manufacturing sectors in the urban centers may have operated at a point closer to the origin on the M_{ii} curve than did their competitors in the rural areas.

Figure 2.2 (b) for Region II differs from (a) for Region I in several respects. First, the absolute level as well as the amount of increase in labor productivity from the early to the latter half of the period was smaller than in Region I. Second, the population increased more slowly than in Region I. Third, the living standard in both periods was lower than that prevailing in Region I. And, last, because Region II's commercial and manufacturing sector developed slowly, the region was an importer of the products of this sector and exported agricultural output: that is, the positions of *CP* and *PP* were the reverse of those in Region I. However, a larger proportion of the total population was in the nonagricultural sector in Period II than in Period I, which had the effect of reducing the absolute number of people in the agricultural sector. Again, as in Region I, the living standard rose over time because of increases in productivity in both the agricultural and the nonagricultural sectors. The relative positions of *C* and *Q* in both periods reflect the gains accruing to both regions from specialization in production.

The difference in the political strength of the daimyo in the two regions was reflected in the standard of living and in labor mobility. The relatively more effective daimyo in Region II were able to tax both the agricultural and the nonagricultural sectors more efficiently than either the daimyo or the administrators of the *tenryō* in Region I. This meant that the rate of increase in income for the producers (the peasants and those in the commercial and manufacturing sectors) was slower in Region II than in Region I.[15] This does not necessarily imply that the ruling class enjoyed a higher income in Region II than in Region I, since the rate of increase in agricultural productivity and in commercial and manufacturing activities was lower in Region II.

The slower growth rate of the producers' income in Region II (caused by the slower growth in productivity), combined with the loss of demand to Region I plus domain monopolies and other manifestations of the strength of the daimyo, caused the nonagricultural sector in Region II to grow more slowly than it did in Region I. This meant that the "pull" factor in migration, that is, the demand for labor by the nonagricultural sector in Region II, was weaker here than in Region I. However, the "push" factor may well have been stronger in Region II because the more efficient system of taxation there meant that the rate of growth in agricultural productivity was slower. The relatively strong daimyo in Region II attempted to retard the flow of labor from agriculture to other sectors, and their attempts were more successful than those of the daimyo in Region I. The supply curve of labor to the nonagricultural sectors, therefore, can be said to have been less elastic in Region II than in Region I.

It will be easiest to explain and elaborate our hypothesis concerning the motivations for limiting population growth if we use the following diagram adapted from Richard Easterlin's "An Economic Framework for Fertility Analysis."[10] (See Figure 2.3.) We are measuring the hypothetical number of surviving children per thousand population, where C_f indicates the total number of surviving children if all women married as soon as they were capable of bearing children and bore all the children they could. Infant mortality is not included, but it is assumed for lack of evidence of changes in either fecundity or infant mortality in Tokugawa Japan that both were constant over time. C_d is the desired number of children within the society, and this number rises over time as the economy starts to grow in the seventeenth century, and then tapers off. C_s is the number of children who would be born if the only controls regulating fertility were social controls, such as customs concerning who married and at what age. During this first period the number of children who actually survived (C), coincided with C_s as social controls were the only controls over fertility.

At some point, however, before the maximum was reached, an additional increase in children was seen to amount to an economic burden by the villagers, and they found themselves with an excess supply of children, indicated by the shaded area on the diagram. This occurred at point m in time. Shortly after this occurred, social controls were tightened and, in addition, individuals began to limit their own fertility, which is indicated by point h. The birth rate started to decline, and the number of surviving children fell well below what it would have been had social controls been the only force limiting births. The number of children averted who would have survived had no individual controls been in effect is indicated by the area labeled R on Figure 2.3.

As the average number of children approached the minimum needed to ensure the continuation of family lines and to supply needed labor in the village (about three to four per couple who ever bore children), the number of children born and the number of children desired came to be stabilized over time. Figure 2.3 shows an excess of surviving children over desired children but, given the fact that the number of children per 1,000 population (rather than per couple) is being measured, and that famines and economic recessions reoccurred during the second half of the Tokugawa period, it is possible that for some places, in some periods, the number of surviving children fell below the number of desired children. In any case, we are hypothesizing that these two

34

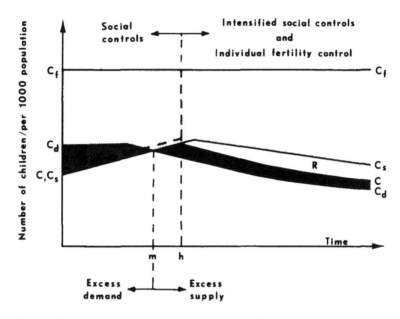

Figure 2.3: A Framework of Analysis for Tokugawa Fertility Change

C_f = number of surviving children without social or individual controls (close to fecundity minus infant mortality)

C_s = number of surviving children where only social controls limit fertility

C = actual number of surviving children

C_d = desired number of children

m = point at which supply for children begins to exceed demand

h = point at which individual fertility regulation begins

■ = unwanted children, excess of actual number of children over desired number

□ = number of children averted by social controls

■ = excess demand for children, i.e., fewer children are born and survive than are desired

$\boxed{R}$ = number of children averted by individual fertility controls

35

lines were very close and possibly identical at times. Naturally, any given couple may have had fewer or more children than desired. Also, the lines have been smoothed out; in reality the number of surviving children would probably fluctuate because of the composition of the population, because of tighter or more relaxed social and individual controls in response to economic conditions, and because of changes in mortality. Evidence for this will be presented in Chapters Eight to Ten.

We have not indicated actual years on the time axis of Figure 2.3 nor have we indicated the actual number of children on the Y-axis because of the diversity of patterns of population and economic change among regions and even among villages in the same region. Probably most of the country was in the excess demand area during much of the seventeenth century, and certainly almost every region was well past point h by the nineteenth century. It is readily conceivable that some economically lagging villages began the Tokugawa period to the right of point h, while some of the villages created on reclaimed land may have been left of point m even in the nineteenth century. What should be kept clearly in mind is that Figure 2.3 presents only a highly generalized trend of changes on a nationwide basis, and is not intended to represent the experience of any specific region or village.

Finally, let us put into theoretical terms the reason people desired fewer children during the second half of the Tokugawa period. As the economy grew, farming became increasingly commercially oriented, and the rural villages were gradually woven into a highly monetized and consumption-oriented society, people began to choose to "trade off" additional children for goods and services or the accumulation of wealth needed to improve or maintain their standard of living and their status within village society. This is equivalent to saying that if a graph were drawn the line connecting the tangencies between the indifference curves representing various levels of income and the slope indicating the rate of wealth-children substitution would be curved backwards to the Y-axis that measures the quantity of goods (X-axis measures children). The situation described is analogous to the backward-bending supply curve of labor. Why the peasants' indifference curves were so tilted to bring about his backward-bending phenomenon has been discussed earlier in this chapter, and evidence will be provided in Chapter Nine.

We will now proceed to test the hypotheses presented in this chapter to determine if the alternative framework set up here can be used to explain the changes in economic development and in the population of Tokugawa Japan. In the next chapters we will analyze national aggregate data on both the economy and population before going on to examine several regions individually.

CHAPTER THREE

Aggregate Demographic Data: An Assessment

In some respects Japan has better data on its premodern population than any other country in the world. With an awareness of the importance of statistics and a degree of bureaucratic control unusual in a premodern government, the Tokugawa Bakufu carried out at various times surveys of the national population by province. The legacy of these surveys is ten extant sets of population figures for the commoner population dating from 1721 to 1846 and a large number of the yearly village population registers that formed the basis for the nationwide count. In this chapter we will present an analysis of the aggregate data.

Although the raw data for the Tokugawa period can be considered very good for a premodern nation, attempts to make systematic use of them have only just begun. Until the 1960s the field of historical demography was dominated by three names, Honjō Eijirō, Sekiyama Naotarō, and Takahashi Bonsen, and the classic studies—and just about the only studies—were made by these scholars.[1] The writings of these three scholars and many who accepted their findings stress "stagnation" (*teitai*) of the population during the latter half of the Tokugawa period, chiefly on the basis of the national aggregate figures, which fluctuated around 26 million during the last century and a half of the Tokugawa period. For the Tokugawa period as a whole, the consensus is that a major population increase occurred during the seventeenth century, following the peace brought about by the Tokugawa hegemony, and that population limits were reached in the first quarter of the eighteenth century. Thereafter the population remained more or less stationary, in large part due to at least three major famines and a great many local disasters, resulting in what are now termed mortality crises. According to the dominant view, a second major factor restraining population growth was the limitation on births through the abortion and infanticide practiced by all classes of Japanese society in response to dire economic distress.

Both Honjō and Sekiyama dealt with the national aggregate figures on the Tokugawa population, though Sekiyama contributed an analysis of the population by region and used various other data available to try to explain the trends seen in the aggregate data. Takahashi's major interest lay in the reasons for population decline, primarily in the Tohoku region, the area hardest hit by famine and natural disaster. Though these scholars confined themselves to descriptive studies of aggregate statistics with little or no attempt to analyze the data statistically, the impressionistic view of the Tokugawa population that they present has become the stereotyped staple of the historical literature on Tokugawa Japan.

Then, in the early 1950s, Nomura Kanetarō—a leading scholar of Tokugawa economic history—began seriously to question whether the traditional view of the Tokugawa population was accurate. He refused to accept an "impossible" discrepancy between the last Bakufu figures and the census figures of 1872, and he distrusted the Bakufu data because the *han* reported their populations "as mere formalities," especially during the late Tokugawa period, and because he believed some *han* data to have been falsified. Like Sekiyama,[2] he pointed out that, for the last Bakufu data to be accurate, one must assume that population grew at a rate that was not possible. Thus, he concluded that the population figures for the second half of the Tokugawa period may have been underestimated and the effects of abortion and infanticide overstated in the literature.[3]

Instead of stopping here, however, Nomura formed a group at Keiō University to undertake a more rigorous analysis of the basic source of population data, the *shūmon-aratame-chō* (religious investigation registers), which recorded the people by temple or village. Unfortunately, this promising start was cut short by Nomura's death while he and his students were analyzing their first village data, that of Kōmi village in Mino province.[4] In the 1960s, however, Nomura's student, Hayami Akira, took up the analysis of the Tokugawa population through these religious investigation registers. Hayami, stimulated by the work of French and English demographers on parish registers, adapted the method of analysis known as family reconstitution to the Japanese demographic sources. To date, a number of villages have been analyzed by Hayami and his group at Keiō, and the work continues.[5] These studies provide revealing insights into various patterns of fertility,

39

life expectancy, nuptiality, family size, population structure, life expectancy, birth intervals, migration, and family composition.

Although the village studies have increased our knowledge of demographic change at the local level in some parts of Japan, the scale of this time-consuming research is still small and thus, for aggregate data at the national level, we are still left with the Bakufu statistics. Let us now turn to an assessment of these data, starting with a brief history of the methods by which they were obtained.

THE HISTORY OF THE
TOKUGAWA POPULATION SURVEYS

The first aggregate population figures for Tokugawa Japan date from 1721. In that year the Shogun Yoshimune issued edicts requiring that the number of "farmers, merchants, townspeople, shrine-priests, temple-priests, [and] temple-priestesses" be recorded.[6] Also recorded were the *eta* and the *hinin* (the outcasts). Only the samurai, their families, and their attendants were exempted from this enumeration. The age at which children were to be included was left to the discretion of the individual daimyo and past customs of the *han*.[7]

In 1726 another edict was issued similar to that of 1721, but this one stipulated that thereafter there were to be population surveys made regularly every six years even though no future instructions be given.[8] Just how many of these censuses were taken is not entirely clear, but the surveys resulted in at least nine additional nationwide enumerations of the population for which the figures still exist for the years 1750, 1756, 1786, 1798, 1804, 1822, 1828, 1834, and 1846.[9]

These figures for the commoner population of Japan fluctuate around 26 million for the entire period they cover, starting with 26,065,425 in 1721 and ending with 26,907,625 in 1846.[10] The population hit a trough of 25,086,466 in 1786 during the Temmei famine and reached a peak of 27,201,400 in 1828 in the decade just prior to the Tempō famine. Naturally, the totals taken by themselves indicate a relatively stable population from the early eighteenth century to the mid-nineteenth century.

For a preindustrial country to take a census of its citizens who numbered in the millions is quite a feat, but the Japanese had already had considerable experience in census taking by 1721. Literary references to the Emperor Sujin's population survey in 85 B.C. cannot be considered historically accurate, but it is probable that attempts were made to enumerate the Japanese as early as the sixth century A.D.[11] This tradition of census taking probably influenced Yoshimune's decision. For example, Yoshimune ordered his surveys to be taken at six-year intervals, the same interval that had been specified in the seventh century, and the content of the later population records was also similar to that of the seventh century.[12]

Various daimyo took population surveys during the Sengoku period, notably Lord Hōjō in the Kanto region and Lord Takeda of Kōshū.[13] In 1591 Hideyoshi created his *hitoharai*. This was to have been a national population and house survey in which the entire commoner population was to be recorded by class, using the village as the unit of survey. Certainly no nationwide census was taken at this time, but surveys were subsequently undertaken in various domains. The best figures in existence for the early seventeenth century are those for Kokura *han* located in Buzen and Bungo provinces in Kyushu.[14] Lord Hosokawa undertook surveys there in 1609 and 1611, and again in 1622, of the *kokudaka* (the grain output in rice equivalent), the number of houses, the number of people, and the number of draft animals in each village in his provinces. Lord Uesugi of Yonezawa in the Tohoku region made a similar study of his domain.

These early Tokugawa surveys were called *jinchiku-aratame* (which can be translated as an investigation of men and animals). These were a form of the surveys known as *ninbetsu-aratame* (census investigations). In the seventeenth century the surveys were undertaken by individual daimyo on their own initiative, usually for the purpose of determining the resources of the domain in terms of manpower.

But the system that really enabled the Bakufu to undertake a nationwide census in 1721 was the regularly taken survey known as the *shūmon-aratame* (the investigation of religion). The *shūmon-aratame* was begun in the seventeenth century as a means of controlling Christianity and preventing its dissemination throughout the country. One of the measures taken by the Bakufu after making the decision to prohibit this foreign religion, which it considered a threat to state security, was to order all Japanese to become members of a recognized Buddhist sect and to register every year with the temples with which they were affiliated.

The *shūmon-aratame* was first carried out in the 1630s in the areas under direct Bakufu control but, from at least 1671, it was carried out on a nationwide basis, theoretically every year.[15] Despite the fact that Christianity posed no threat from the mid-seventeenth century on, the surveys were undertaken until the end of the Tokugawa period, and many continued until 1872 when the first Meiji census was undertaken. Though these surveys retained in most cases the title of *shūmon-aratame* until 1872, they had in fact become census records many years prior to this. The *ninbetsu-aratame* and *shūmon-aratame* took on the same function and, in most cases, had the same form.[16]

The existence of these two forms of population registration meant that it was fairly easy for a *han* administration to compile total population statistics for the entire domain. In fact the edict of 1721 specifically stated that there was no need for actual surveys to be carried out; to use the results of existing surveys was perfectly permissible.[17] The second edict on this subject stated that the population was to be counted in that year but the method was still left to the discretion of the *han*. Since the *shūmon-aratame* was carried out every year, the simplest way for most daimyo to carry out a population survey was to use the records that already listed every person in each village.

The format for the *shūmon-aratame-chō* had become fairly standard by the Kambun period (1661-1672).[18] The documents usually recorded the names of the head of household, male family members, and unmarried females. The relationship to the head of household and the sect and temple of affiliation were listed for every household. Most extant registers include the ages of everyone recorded. Some *shūmon-aratame-chō* contained additional information, such as the amount of land held, village offices held and special occupations, the wife's original family, dates of marriage, and information on employees, such as where they came from and the term of employment. At the end of the register, the amount of *kokudaka* held by the village, the number of houses, the total population, and the number of draft animals were recorded.

The major differences among various *shūmon-aratame-chō*

seem to have been the age at which children were first listed. In some domains the children were listed from year of birth; others were first included when aged 2 or 3, or even older. But infants certainly posed no threat in terms of subversive religious sects, nor were they of importance if the purpose of the population surveys was to obtain some estimate of the productive population. Thus, in Wakayama *han*, children under the age of 8 were not reported.[19] In most of the country children seem to have been first recorded in the registration that took place in the year after they were born, which meant that they were in their second calendar year of life and thus were listed as "age 2." By Western methods of calculation they were, of course, between a few days and a year old. Where the extant records are village copies of documents that were sent up to the domain, children may be listed in the year they were born, as in the Okayama *shūmon-aratame-chō*. The copies retained in the village were used during the year to update information by adding births and brides and by marking who had died or left the village.[20] Most of the village registers that have survived reveal a conscientious effort on the part of officials to keep the documents reasonably up to date.

The results of these well-enforced population surveys provide a basis for estimating the population of the provinces of Japan plus the commoner population of the country from the early eighteenth century on. The population of the seventeenth century, however, has remained more of a mystery. Estimates of the seventeenth-century population requested by the Shogun and submitted in 1721 by the ten largest daimyo suggested a rapid increase in population prior to the first nationwide enumeration.[21] These figures submitted were, however, "guesstimates" on the part of the daimyo, who had been ordered to estimate the population in their domains seventy to eighty years previously but who probably had little real information upon which to base these estimates.

Yoshida Tōgō was the Japanese scholar who provided the hypothesis for the population in 1600 that was generally accepted for nearly half a century. Since there was a good correlation of population and *kokudaka* in 1721, with both estimated at 26 million, and since the traditional estimate of how much rice it took to feed one person for one year was 1 *koku*, Yoshida extrapolated backward and came up with the hypothesis that the estimated 18.5 million *koku* of grain output in 1600 would have supported a population of approximately 18.5 million persons.[22] Even should the *grain output estimate of 1600 be accurate—and much doubt has* been cast on its reliability—it scarcely forms the basis for estimating the population. Despite the tradition of 1 *koku* for one person for one year, the Japanese themselves did not use this ratio in estimating dietary requirements.[23]

The wide acceptance of Yoshida's estimate of the population in 1600 would mean a population increase of approximately 40 percent from 1600 to 1721 and an annual average growth rate of around 0.3 percent. Thus arose the widespread notion of a fairly rapid population increase during the first century of peace, one that leveled off in the 1720s, stagnating at around 26 million persons.[24]

Hayami considered Yoshida's estimate, the methods on which it was based, and the crucial grain output evidence to have little grounding in fact. He set out to estimate anew the population during the seventeenth century. His first estimate was based on extrapolating linear trend lines from village studies backward to 1600. He arrived at an estimated rate of natural increase of 1 percent for the century, which would have meant a population ranging from 6.2-9.8 million in 1600. Hayami does admit that this estimate is inconclusive, and his data are biased in that they come from villages with known rapid increases in population, mostly from Kyushu. Hayami has since made a second estimate of the population in 1600, again by projecting backward, this time using the eighteenth-century Bakufu figures, and assuming that the population of each of three regions into which he divides Japan tripled over the course of 150 years, with the growth of the most economically advanced region beginning first. Arriving at an average annual growth rate of 0.62, from this he obtained an estimate of 12,273,000 for 1600.[25]

In both sets of estimates, Hayami assumes that the population grew rapidly during the early Tokugawa period, and he cites the Suwa region as evidence that a premodern population can grow at an average rate of 1 percent for as long as a century. However, Hayami offers little supporting evidence to help fill the void created by the lack of data to show why the population as a whole should have grown so rapidly during this century, or century and a half, and then have leveled off. Another major difficulty in accepting Hayami's backward extrapolation is that it means that the population of Japan, estimated by Sawada Gōichi to have been from 5 to 6 million during the eighth century, either completely failed to grow or grew extremely slowly during the nine centuries prior to the Tokugawa period, despite the known growth of the economy from the thirteenth century.[26]

Because no other data exist at present, except for scattered years or brief periods during the late seventeenth century, the discussion of the population in that century will not be dealt with further at the national level. It does seem too much of a coincidence that the first national survey took place precisely in the decade at which Japanese scholars hypothesize the fairly rapid population growth abruptly ended. However, all sources do indicate a rising population in the seventeenth century, the magnitude of which is yet unknown.

AN EVALUATION OF THE RELIABILITY OF THE NATIONAL DEMOGRAPHIC DATA

Even scholars who rely on the Bakufu statistics admit that there are basic flaws in these data. The data can be criticized on a number of grounds. First, the aggregate figures for Japan were obtained by totaling the statistics for the sixty-nine *kuni*. The method of survey differed by region and the persons who were included in the enumeration differed as well. Second, various elements of the population were specifically excluded, notably the samurai and their families, their direct subordinates, and their servants. The proportion of samurai in the population differed by domain, ranging perhaps as high as one-quarter in rare cases, but the usual estimate lies somewhere between 7 and 10 percent.[27] Just how many of their attendants and servants may have been excluded from the count is unknown. However, the most difficult portion of the uncounted population to estimate is the unregistered: those without fixed domiciles, the vagrants and drifters, including the *rōnin* (masterless samurai). This group of persons was largest in the cities and is estimated to have increased in number over time, making any reliable estimates of the initial number or growth over time virtually impossible.[28]

How large the uncounted population may have been can be seen from the difference between the commoner population of 1846, which was 26,907,625 in the official figures, and the entire population of Japan in 1872, reported as 33,110,796 in the first Meiji census.[29] How much of this growth was due to the inclusion of the samurai population in the 1872 figures is still open to some speculation, as even the Meiji government had difficulty in determining who was to be classified a samurai. Estimates range from 5.7 to 10 percent, but the Office of Registry's total of 1,941,239 for all samurai, quasi-samurai, and family members of both groups amounts to 5.86 percent of the population in 1872.[30] With these groups excluded, the first Meiji population estimate would be 31,169,557, leaving no doubt that there was considerable growth of the population between 1846 and 1872 or else considerable underreporting in the Tokugawa surveys, or most likely both.

Two scholars, Sekiyama and Honjō, have provided estimates of the uncounted population in the Tokugawa period, a difficult task at best because of the lack of data. To obtain an estimate of the Japanese population in 1867, Sekiyama added roughly 5 million to the 1846 figure, "guesstimating" a total population for 1867 of 30 to 32 million persons.[31] Honjō made an estimate for various groups excluded from the Tokugawa surveys and obtained a figure of 28.7 to 29.2 million for 1852.[32] Both estimates are based primarily on common sense and an extrapolation backward of the information contained in the 1872 statistics, and can be considered only crude estimates.

All of the scholars who have used the official aggregate statistics have questioned them to some extent. Takahashi was skeptical of the value of the official figures to the point that he included the *kuni* estimates only for the years 1786, 1804, and 1846. According to him, "no supporting evidence has yet been found for the other years."[33] Yet, upon examining regional and local population data included in Takahashi's volumes, one tends to mistrust his judgment as he has included statistics that can in no way be considered accurate.

Honjō, on the other hand, was worried about the accuracy of the first census, that of 1721, because the Bakufu did not require an actual head count for that year but relied instead on existing survey results. He concluded that the 1726 figures must be considered the first reliable census results, though his argument seems to be superfluous since the results of the two surveys were so close and since so many persons were excluded in any case.[34] Sekiyama, while devoting a large part of his books on population

46

to probable omissions, double counting, and other factors that would bias the statistics, accepted the official figures as they appeared in Katsu Kaishu's *Suijinroku*.[35]

The reliability of the Tokugawa figures in even approximating the commoner population has been questioned. Hayami has bluntly stated that the figures obtained from the Bakufu surveys "cannot be called very significant."[36] Neither he nor anyone in his research group has made any attempt to make adjustments in these figures, preferring to build case studies because they feel that these will lead to a more reliable assessment of the Tokugawa population than a manipulation of the existing figures.

Thus, while Hayami's group has largely ignored the official statistics, none of the authors who accept them in one form or another has made much of an attempt to examine how accurate they may be. One of the original objectives of this study was to rectify this omission. The plan was to analyze the *kuni* data against local or domain data and all the information we could gather from various quantitative and nonquantitative sources, estimate what the figures should have been for various *kuni* and, on the basis of these estimates, make adjustments in the national aggregate data, thereby providing a more accurate estimate for population trends in Tokugawa Japan.

After several years of research, this goal was abandoned with much reluctance. Reliable population data exist for few domains and, in most cases where they do exist, the geographical boundaries of the domain are not those of the *kuni*, making any accurate comparison impossible. If we had attempted to adjust the national figures on the basis of the few corrections we could make, our estimates would probably have been as dubious as those Hayami made based on population changes in Kyushu.

A second approach would have been to extrapolate backward from the Meiji population and adjust at least the totals for 1846 in order to arrive at a better approximation of population growth in the Bakumatsu years. This approach, too, was abandoned due to the controversy over the Meiji population estimates and the abundance of estimates we could have chosen from in making our extrapolation.[37] Scholars studying the Meiji population cannot agree on the nature or the extent of the demographic transition during early industrialization in Japan. Demographers believe the first reliable population figures to be those of the 1920 census, and have used various methods to extrapolate backward to derive fertility and mortality rates for the 1870s, nearly half a century before. Since the basic argument is over fertility and mortality rates, and over whether the rise in the growth rate of the Meiji population was due to a rise in fertility or a fall in mortality, any attempt to extrapolate trends back into the Tokugawa period would introduce even greater biases in the estimates than already occur for the early Meiji period. Thus, we have basically joined Hayami in his stand that new and more accurate estimates of the Tokugawa population must await the results of many more case studies and analyses at the regional level.

The preceding observations, however, do not mean that we believe the aggregate *kuni* figures should be rejected. Even a cursory examination of these figures reveals that the basic trends they show are consistent with much of the supporting evidence that exists on population. Nationwide declines are seen in known periods of famine, and the extent of the decline is generally in line with the contemporary assessment of the severity of the famines in various parts of the country. The basic trends are also consistent with the evidence on economic change and with the results of a variety of local and case studies, which will be examined and reported at length in succeeding chapters. Nor are we saying that it is not possible to evaluate to some extent the reliability of the Bakufu figures.

To try to evaluate the Bakufu figures, let us examine the population data available for two *kuni*. If we compare the Bakufu data on these *kuni* with data held by the domains, we find indications that the national aggregate data may have underenumerated the Tokugawa population by more than just the samurai population and unregistered city people. These two examples suggest that the aggregate data may include only the rural commoner population of Japan, and exclude city dwellers.

First let us look at data for the province of Bizen, which constituted most of Okayama *han*. The *kuni* totals from the Bakufu figures cited in Sekiyama are approximately the same for three dates as the aggregate population figures for the eight districts of Bizen (not including the population of the castle town of Okayama). These figures are shown in Table 3.1.

The second example is that of Kōchi *han*, which was geographically identical to Tosa province. The Bakufu figures for Tosa are smaller by 40,000-50,000, or nearly one-tenth, than the Kōchi *han*

Table 3.1

A Comparison of Population Figures Available for Bizen

	Bakufu Totals on Bizen	Bizen District Totals from Okayama Data	Bizen District Totals Plus Castle Town
1721	338,523	338,513	368,809
1798	321,221	320,795	342,013
1834	318,647	318,207	338,380

Source: The Bakufu official totals are from Sekiyama, *Kinsei Nihon no jinkō kōzō*, p. 139. The total for the eight districts of Bizen for 1721 is from the *Ryōchi tahata chōbu ninzu-chō* and for 1798 from the *Ninzū aratame-chō*, in the possession of the Okayama University Library, Okayama, Japan. The district total for 1834 is from the *Ninzū-chō* and is quoted in Taniguchi Sumio, *Okayama hansei-shi no kenkyū* (A study on the history of the administration of Okayama domain) (Tokyo: Hanawa Shobō, 1964), pp. 460-461. The castle town figures added to the Bizen district totals were obtained from the *Tome-chō* for the year 1798 and from the *Okayama shishi* for the two remaining years. The castle town figure for the year 1834 is actually the figure for 1838, the year for which there were data closest in time to 1834. The castle town figures are quoted in Taniguchi, *ibid.*, pp. 465-466.

annual data. The Tosa figures are shown in Table 3.2. There is nothing to indicate why the figures compiled by the domain differ so markedly from the Tosa figures in the national aggregate series, but the discrepancy is around 10 percent, approximately the difference between the Bizen figures with and without the castle town included. Sekiyama is unclear as to whether urban populations are included in his discussion of the aggregate figures,[38] but the above examples suggest that they are not. Bolstering our argument are the castle town population data for a number of domains which, combined with estimates of population in other urban cen-

Table 3.2

A Comparison of Population Figures Available for Tosa

	Bakufu Totals for Tosa	Domain Totals for Tosa
1721	351,547	404,573
1750	368,192	408,417
1756	372,766	418,365
1786	392,597	432,203
1798	399,702	440,362

Source. The Bakufu totals are from Sekiyama, *Kinsei Nihon no jinkō kōzō*, p. 139. The Tosa data were obtained from Takahashi Bonsen, *Nihon jinkō-shi no kenkyū* (A study of the history of the population of Japan), Vol. 2 (Tokyo: Nihon Gakujutsu Shinkōkai, 1955), pp. 229-235.

ters in the domains, suggest that urban population in the domains in the Tokugawa period, or at least the population of the castle towns, may have been about 10 percent of the rural commoner totals.[30] If we added approximately 10 percent as urban population to the aggregate totals, then the Bakufu totals would climb to a figure more nearly comparable with the 1872 statistics, which include the entire population of Japan, rural and urban, commoner and samurai.

The skepticism shown by some Japanese scholars toward the official Tokugawa population data together with various kinds of evidence suggesting that the data are unreliable seem to cast serious doubt on the usefulness of the statistics in further analysis. The authors, however, consider this source of data extremely important. First, it provides the only source of population figures on a nationwide level, even if these are to be taken only as an indicator of demographic changes. Since these were the statistics used by the Bakufu and since all were compiled by the same method so far as we know, the official figures can be expected to reflect at least the basic trend of actual changes. Second, this source can provide some indication as to how applicable changes and patterns seen in scattered villages may have been to Japan as a whole. Third, as the basic unit for compiling the nationwide figures was the village register, it may at some time become possible through analysis of village data to prescribe adjustments to be made in the Bakufu statistics and thus make them even more valuable than they are at present. But, even unadjusted, the nationwide population figures can be useful if used cautiously, for they were not compiled haphazardly.

AN ANALYSIS OF THE
AGGREGATE DEMOGRAPHIC DATA

An examination and analysis were made of the official statistics on the Tokugawa population using the figures as quoted in Sekiyama.[40] The results are to be found in Tables 3.3 through 3.8. Although it might be possible to make adjustments for some of the figures, consistency was considered to be of more value in assessing general demographic changes than having accurate figures for one or two *kuni* for one or two years. The results of the analysis must thus be considered only an indication of demographic changes within Japan rather than actual values of such changes.

Table 3.3 lists the total commoner population for Japan as a whole and for each of the sixty-nine *kuni* for three separate years: 1721, 1846, and 1872. The figures for the first two years are from the Tokugawa surveys while the 1872 figures are from the first Meiji census. Also included is an index of the 1846 figures using the 1721 figures as its base.

Table 3.4 lists the annual average growth rates between each of the years for which there are statistics, from 1721 through 1872. The 1846-1872 growth rates were also included to show the jump between the Tokugawa and Meiji figures.

Table 3.5 contains linear regression equations calculated for the total commoner population and the population for each of the *kuni*, both for the period 1721-1872 and for the period 1721-1846.[41] Since there is some indication that the underreporting of population may have increased over time due in part at least to a breakdown of controls over population movement, and since the 1872 data are certainly more reliable than those of 1846, the 1872 figures were included in the first trend line calculated. The second included only the population surveys undertaken during the Tokugawa period, and this trend line may therefore be a better indicator of demographic change during the period (unless underreporting significantly increased over time), because the figures on which it was based were all obtained by the same method.

In the trend lines for the period 1721-1872, the regression coefficients (slopes) of 53 *kuni* and the total were significant at least at the 0.10 level and, of these 53, regression coefficients were significant at the 0.01 level for as many as 40 *kuni*. All but 8 of the 53 significant slopes were positive, and there were only 3 negative slopes significant at the 0.01 level. In the trend lines for the Tokugawa period only, 1721-1846, the regression coefficients of 56 *kuni* and the total were significant at least at the 0.10 level, and of these, 36 were significant at the 0.01 level. When the 1872 data were excluded, the number of statistically significant negative slopes increased, as is to be expected. However, only 17 out of the 56 significant slopes were negative, and only 8 of these were significant at the 0.01 level. Figure 3.1 shows the regional distribution of the signs of the slopes.

The following broad conclusions can be made from these

Table 3.3

The Population of Japan by Kuni

No.	Kuni	1721	1846	1872	$\frac{1846}{1721} \times 100$
	TOTAL	26,064,425	26,907,625	33,110,825	103.24
1	Yamashiro	564,994	452,140	429,030	80.0
2.	Yamato	413,331	361,157	418,326	87.4
3.	Kawachi	243,820	224,055	237,678	91.9
4.	Izumi	218,405	197,656	209,174	90.5
5.	Settsu	809,242	763,729	729,443	94.4
6.	Iga	95,978	91,774	97,164	95.6
7.	Ise	543,737	499,874	585,988	91.9
8.	Shima	31,856	40,693	37,439	127.7
9.	Owari	554,561	653,678	727,437	117.9
10.	Mikawa	416,204	431,800	482,931	103.8
11.	Tōtōmi	342,663	363,959	414,928	106.2
12.	Suruga	245,834	286,290	368,505	116.5
13.	Izu	96,650	115,197	149,749	119.2
14.	Kai	291,168	310,273	360,068	106.6
15.	Sagami	312,638	303,271	356,638	97.0
16.	Musashi	1,903,316	1,777,371	1,943,211	93.4
17.	Awa 1. (Bōshū)	115,579	143,500	154,683	124.2
18.	Kazusa	407,552	360,761	419,969	88.5
19.	Shimo-osa	542,661	525,041	645,029	96.8
20.	Hitachi	712,387	521,777	648,674	73.2
21.	Ōmi	602,367	541,732	576,564	89.9
22.	Mino	545,919	583,137	660,896	106.8
23.	Hida	67,032	86,338	98,378	128.8
24.	Shinano	693,947	794,698	919,115	114.5
25.	Kōzuke	569,550	428,092	507,235	75.2
26.	Shimotsuke	560,020	378,665	498,520	67.6
27.	Tōhoku[a]	1,962,839	1,607,881	2,294,915	81.9
28.	Uzen-Ugo	877,650	912,452	1,191,020	104.0
29.	Wakasa	86,598	77,183	85,487	89.1
30.	Echizen	367,652	353,674	461,032	96.2

Table 3.3 (Continued)

No.	Kuni	1721	1846	1872	$\frac{1846}{1721} \times 100$
31.	Kaga	206,933	238,291	403,357	115.2
32.	Noto	152,113	186,970	262,486	122.9
33.	Etchū	314,158	403,121	615,663	128.3
34.	Echigo	932,461	1,172,973	1,368,428	125.8
35.	Sado	95,748	102,265	103,098	106.8
36.	Tamba	284,893	280,947	295,359	98.6
37.	Tango	125,276	154,308	160,932	123.2
38.	Tajima	149,732	173,573	187,086	115.9
39.	Inaba	122,030	127,797	162,842	104.7
40.	Hōki	132,981	177,420	194,158	133.4
41.	Izumo	222,330	309,606	340,042	139.3
42.	Iwami	207,965	239,963	259,611	115.4
43.	Oki	18,133	26,208	28,531	144.5
44.	Harima	633,725	594,560	635,791	93.8
45.	Mimasaka	194,226	165,468	215,602	85.2
46.	Bizen	338,523	310,576	331,878	91.7
47.	Bitchū	333,731	346,927	396,880	104.0
48.	Bingo	321,008	360,832	456,461	112.4
49.	Aki	361,431	553,708	667,717	153.2
50.	Suō	262,927	435,188	497,034	165.5
51.	Nagato	212,124	261,100	330,502	123.1
52.	Kii	519,022	499,826	613,925	96.3
53.	Awaji	105,226	122,773	164,939	116.7
54.	Awa 2.	342,386	448,287	586,046	130.9
55.	Sanuki	334,153	433,880	559,712	129.8
56.	Iyo	504,045	599,948	775,974	119.0
57.	Tosa	351,547	461,031	524,511	131.1
58.	Chikuzen	302,160	346,942	441,175	114.8
59.	Chikugo	266,426	299,041	391,535	112.2
60.	Buzen	248,187	249,274	304,574	100.4
61.	Bungo	524,394	470,875	562,318	89.8
62.	Hizen	609,926	713,593	1,074,460	117.0
63.	Higo	614,007	755,781	953,037	123.1

Table 3.3 (Continued)

No.	Kuni	1721	1846	1872	$\frac{1846}{1721} \times 100$
64.	Hyūga	211,614	247,621	376,527	117.0
65.	Ōsumi	112,616	99,212	256,816	88.1
66.	Satsuma	149,039	241,797	549,440	162.2
67.	Iki	19,993	27,005	33,010	135.1
68.	Tsushima	16,467	16,904	29,684	102.7
69.	Ezo	15,615	70,887	120,873	454.0

[a]Tōhoku refers to the *kuni* of Iwaki, Iwashiro, Rikuzen, Rikuchū, and Mutsu.

Source: Sekiyama Naotarō, *Kinsei Nihon no jinkō kōzō* (The population structure of Tokugawa Japan) (Tokyo: Yoshikawa Kōbunkan, 1958), pp. 137-139. Figures for the years 1750, 1756, 1786, 1798, 1804, 1822, 1828, and 1834 are on the same pages.

Table 3.4

Annual Average Population Growth Rates by *Kuni*, 1721-1872 (percent)

No.	*Kuni*	1721-1750	1750-1756	1756-1786	1786-1798	1798-1804	1804-1822	1822-1828	1828-1834	1834-1846	1846-1872	1721-1846
	TOTAL	-0.02	0.10	-0.13	0.13	0.10	0.21	0.37	-0.08	-0.05	0.80	0.025
1.	Yamashiro	-0.27	0.15	-0.13	-0.45	-0.40	0.11	0.67	-0.32	-0.65	-0.20	-0.179
2.	Yamato	-0.34	-0.28	-0.30	-0.19	-0.16	0.09	0.49	0.16	0.03	0.57	-0.108
3.	Kawachi	-0.18	-1.88	-0.02	0.49	-0.24	0.72	-1.50	0.08	-0.03	0.23	-0.067
4.	Izumi	-0.17	1.42	-0.57	0.36	0.27	0.09	0.27	-0.13	-0.39	0.22	-0.079
5.	Settsu	-0.02	0.78	-0.17	0.06	-0.35	0.01	0.45	-0.32	-0.35	-0.18	-0.046
6.	Iga	-0.17	-0.53	-0.24	-0.17	-0.09	0.36	0.44	0.24	0.23	0.22	-0.036
7.	Ise	-0.13	-0.12	-0.27	-0.02	-0.05	0.21	0.12	0.06	-0.00	0.61	-0.067
8.	Shima	0.23	0.09	0.27	0.32	-0.32	0.36	0.21	0.39	-0.24	-0.32	0.195
9.	Owari	-0.01	0.68	0.11	0.14	0.02	0.23	0.38	-0.07	0.12	0.41	0.131
10.	Mikawa	0.03	0.25	-0.05	0.09	-0.13	0.21	0.10	0.02	-0.16	0.43	0.029
11.	Tōtōmi	-0.09	0.39	-0.10	0.49	-0.46	0.67	-1.13	-0.02	0.07	0.50	0.048
12.	Suruga	0.84	-3.75	-0.11	0.20	0.26	0.76	-1.08	-1.08	1.00	0.97	0.122
13.	Izu	0.29	0.02	0.45	-1.35	3.37	0.39	-0.49	1.67	-1.89	1.01	0.140
14.	Kai	0.23	0.33	-0.12	0.10	-0.64	-0.12	4.91	-3.44	-0.22	0.57	0.051
15.	Sagami	-0.02	-0.28	-0.30	-0.07	0.05	-0.17	1.17	0.26	0.26	0.62	-0.024
16.	Musashi	-0.25	0.03	-0.29	0.20	-0.12	0.13	0.23	-0.03	0.30	0.34	-0.054
17.	Awa 1. (Bōshū)	1.09	-2.35	-0.32	0.55	-0.07	0.27	0.14	0.44	-0.06	0.29	0.173
18.	Kazusa	0.37	-0.55	-0.41	-0.43	-0.19	0.12	-0.45	0.08	-0.08	0.58	-0.098
19.	Shimo-osa	0.15	-0.06	-0.52	0.02	-0.20	-0.74	2.87	-3.56	2.22	0.79	-0.026
20.	Hitachi	-0.29	-0.36	-0.74	-0.36	-0.24	0.11	0.01	-1.35	1.10	0.84	-0.025
21.	Ōmi	-0.16	-0.04	0.06	-0.68	-0.17	0.25	-0.29	-1.13	0.47	0.24	-0.085
22.	Mino	-0.08	0.32	0.08	0.11	0.07	0.31	0.30	-0.06	-0.34	0.48	0.053
23.	Hida	0.26	0.59	0.13	0.15	0.49	0.52	0.29	0.43	-0.69	0.50	0.202
24.	Shinano	-0.04	0.49	0.08	0.22	0.12	0.22	0.40	0.23	-0.14	0.56	0.108
25.	Kōzuke	0.04	0.11	-0.35	-0.14	-0.56	-0.47	0.26	-0.45	-0.45	0.65	-0.228
26.	Shimotsuke	-0.04	-0.63	-0.68	-0.42	-0.36	-0.13	-0.83	-1.57	0.84	1.06	-0.313
27.	Tōhoku[a]	-0.23	-0.27	-0.48	0.13	0.14	0.16	0.29	0.10	-0.42	0.37	-0.160
28.	Uzen-Ugo	-0.13	-0.15	-0.14	0.48	0.33	0.24	0.66	-0.09	-0.26	1.02	0.031
29.	Wakasa	-0.36	-0.07	0.07	-0.10	0.08	0.30	0.32	-0.06	-0.74	0.39	-0.092
30.	Echizen	-0.19	-0.16	-0.13	0.46	0.15	0.33	-0.34	1.30	-0.98	1.02	-0.031

Table 3.4 (Continued)

No.	Kuni	1721-1750	1750-1756	1756-1786	1786-1798	1798-1804	1804-1822	1822-1828	1828-1834	1834-1846	1846-1872	1721-1846
31.	Kaga	-0.07	0.67	-0.36	-0.17	0.34	0.62	0.02	0.75	0.28	2.02	-0.115
32.	Noto	0.12	0.27	-0.74	1.53	0.24	0.80	0.39	-0.03	-0.47	1.30	0.165
33.	Etchū	-0.01	0.01	0.04	0.51	0.40	0.58	1.28	-0.47	0.01	1.63	0.199
34.	Echigo	0.14	0.73	-0.20	0.82	0.30	0.41	0.54	0.46	-0.36	0.59	0.184
35.	Sado	-0.20	0.01	0.02	0.03	0.18	0.54	0.23	-0.02	-0.07	0.03	0.053
36.	Tamba	-0.11	0.34	-0.01	-0.00	0.07	0.15	0.09	0.05	-0.34	0.19	-0.011
37.	Tango	0.24	0.11	0.14	0.32	0.07	0.27	0.28	0.19	-0.26	0.16	0.167
38.	Tajima	0.15	-0.17	0.07	0.33	0.28	0.38	0.15	0.30	-0.50	0.29	0.118
39.	Inaba	0.09	-0.00	-0.04	0.20	0.25	0.17	0.41	0.03	-0.53	0.93	0.037
40.	Hōki	0.20	0.45	0.24	0.58	0.31	0.35	0.55	0.38	-0.62	0.35	0.231
41.	Izumo	0.19	-1.08	0.54	0.40	0.45	0.39	0.47	0.37	-0.15	0.36	0.265
42.	Iwami	0.19	2.77	-0.41	0.66	-0.19	0.27	-0.01	0.49	-0.83	0.30	0.114
43.	Oki	0.15	0.53	0.19	0.49	-0.23	0.67	0.53	0.31	0.16	0.33	0.295
44.	Harima	-0.48	2.17	-0.11	0.02	-0.26	0.09	0.12	-0.35	-0.09	0.26	-0.051
45.	Mimasaka	-0.36	-0.26	-0.30	-0.04	-0.39	0.20	0.09	0.43	0.07	1.02	-0.128
46.	Bizen	-0.16	0.13	-0.04	-0.01	-0.15	-0.00	0.03	-0.01	-0.21	0.26	-0.069
47.	Bitchū	-0.15	0.32	-0.09	0.26	0.07	0.15	0.32	0.17	-0.01	0.52	0.031
48.	Bingo	-0.16	0.23	-0.08	0.31	0.17	0.40	0.45	0.42	0.00	0.90	0.094
49.	Aki	0.32	0.71	0.31	0.66	0.26	0.51	0.51	0.42	-0.37	0.72	0.341
50.	Suō	0.33	0.11	0.56	0.30	0.06	0.57	1.27	0.26	-0.21	0.60	0.403
51.	Nagato	0.23	0.46	0.11	0.14	0.13	0.07	0.50	0.10	0.06	0.91	0.166
52.	Kii	-0.07	0.15	-0.08	-0.46	0.13	0.35	0.27	0.14	-0.34	0.79	-0.030
53.	Awaji	0.06	0.00	-0.03	-0.15	1.26	0.33	0.61	-0.03	-0.05	1.14	0.123
54.	Awa 2.	-0.06	1.26	0.05	0.14	2.08	0.27	0.29	0.19	-0.20	1.03	0.216
55.	Sanuki	0.23	0.26	0.20	0.24	-0.01	0.19	0.51	0.40	0.02	0.98	0.209
56.	Iyo	-0.03	0.29	0.04	0.26	-0.05	0.34	0.33	0.31	0.20	0.99	0.139
57.	Tosa	0.16	0.21	0.17	0.15	0.40	0.44	0.07	0.36	0.10	0.50	0.217
58.	Chikuzen	0.06	-0.07	0.02	0.01	0.27	0.15	0.41	0.30	0.27	0.92	0.111
59.	Chikugo	-0.07	0.15	0.09	0.06	0.32	0.13	0.51	0.79	-0.22	1.04	0.092
60.	Buzen	-0.08	0.77	-0.23	-0.11	0.11	0.08	0.32	0.22	0.07	0.77	0.003
61.	Bungo	-0.08	0.32	-0.35	-0.09	0.05	0.09	0.02	0.05	-0.09	0.68	-0.086
62.	Hizen	0.13	0.39	0.07	0.15	0.92	-0.23	0.43	-0.06	0.17	1.57	0.126
63.	Higo	0.03	0.03	0.13	0.21	0.20	0.39	0.41	0.12	0.14	0.89	0.166

Table 3.4 (Continued)

No	Kuni	1721-1750	1750-1756	1756-1786	1786-1798	1798-1804	1804-1822	1822-1828	1828-1834	1834-1846	1846-1872	1721-1846
64.	Hyūga	0.22	0.02	0.06	-0.02	0.08	0.25	0.14	0.14	0.07	1.61	0.126
65.	Ōsumi	0.54	0.15	-0.17	-0.68	-0.29	-0.33	-0.53	-0.18	-0.32	3.66	-0.101
66.	Satsuma	0.91	0.92	0.49	-0.08	0.20	0.28	0.05	-0.22	-0.22	3.16	0.387
67.	Iki	0.51	0.15	-0.00	0.54	0.26	0.25	0.67	-0.25	-0.06	0.77	0.241
68.	Tsushima	-0.37	-3.53	0.55	-0.21	0.09	1.03	-2.37	2.39	0.09	2.17	0.021
69.	Ezo	1.15	0.62	0.50	0.73	7.64	1.72	0.81	0.71	0.36	2.05	1.210

aTōhoku refers to the *kuni* of Iwaki, Iwashiro, Rikuzen, Rikuchū, and Mutsu. Some of these growth rates do not necessarily reflect accurately the growth of population, due to changes in the method of survey and/or in coverage. For example, the high growth rates for Ōsumi and Satsuma between 1846 and 1872 are due to the inclusion of the samurai population in the 1872 figures.

Source: Calculated on the basis of the figures quoted in the source cited in Table 3.3.

Table 3.5
Trend Lines for the Tokugawa Population by *Kuni*,
1721-1872[a] and 1721-1846[b]

Kuni	*Constant*	Regression Coefficient	R^2
TOTAL	23,717,840.00[a]	30,637.98	0.402*
	25,301,328.00[b]	9,518.50	0.296*
1. Yamashiro	570,358.62	−764.68	0.850**
	566,593.69	−714.47	0.796**
2. Yamato	371,238.56	−58.22	(0.009)
	393,167.44	−350.69	0.414*
3. Kawachi	222,472.81	25.25	(0.007)
	226,644.50	−30.39	(0.009)
4. Izumi	215,657.56	−88.45	(0.169)
	219,010.25	−133.17	0.283+
5. Settsu	841,732.25	−460.39	0.528**
	829,019.50	−290.83	0.361*
6. Iga	87,976.69	2.79	(0.0004)
	91,320.88	−41.82	(0.110)
7. Ise	505,655.75	31.94	(0.002)
	534,396.25	−351.39	0.433*
8. Shima	31,774.62	58.80	0.681**
	30,065.95	81.59	0.965**
9. Owari	509,683.50	1,062.87	0.905**
	523,101.62	883.91	0.951**
10. Mikawa	400,073.25	318.72	0.590**
	410,841.31	175.11	0.624**
11. Tōtōmi	314,813.12	420.08	0.591**
	325,512.62	277.38	0.463*
12. Suruga	232,288.87	416.87	0.242+
	257,064.56	86.43	(0.022)
13. Izu	88,177.86	323.03	0.681**
	90,485.56	292.25	0.576*
14. Kai	285,353.37	327.86	0.238+
	292,388.50	234.06	(0.112)
15. Sagami	290,190.87	75.86	(0.020)
	310,697.87	−197.65	0.273+
16. Musashi	1,753,755.00	−43.79	(0.0004)
	1,829,405.00	1,057.77	0.289+
17. Awa 1.	125,352.50	132.07	0.241+
	127,892.81	98.19	(0.120)
18. Kazusa	430,429.81	−387.89	0.274+
	452,034.06	−676.04	0.667**
19. Shimo-osa	525,999.37	−155.96	(0.010)
	582,012.37	−903.03	0.436*
20. Hitachi	644,718.87	−1,065.94	0.296+
	728,967.06	−1,922.84	0.801**
21. Ōmi	591,754.06	−328.68	0.316*
	607,631.06	−540.45	0.663**

Table 3.5 (Continued)

Kuni	Constant	Regression Coefficient	R^2
22. Mino	504,452.44	733.45	0.780**
	516,085.19	578.31	0.742**
23. Hıda	62,113.77	205.72	0.913**
	62,451.82	201.21	0.882**
24. Shınano	626,519.56	1,349.21	0.838**
	649,765.50	1,039.17	0.902**
25. Kōzuke	603,121.31	−954.63	0.670**
	622,354.81	−1,304.45	0.919**
26. Shimotsuke	563,632.31	−1,171.76	0.464*
	616,026.94	−1,870.58	0.918**
27. Tohoku[c]	1,727,413.00	253.73	(0.003)
	1,928,595.00	−2,429.53	0.593*
28. Uzen-Ugo	746,740.69	1,589.75	0.485**
	812,350.44	714.69	0.400*
29. Wakasa	79,882.87	13.30	(0.028)
	81,156.00	−3.69	(0.002)
30. Echizen	320,475.19	473.02	0.368*
	343,209.50	169.81	(0.140)
31. Kaga	130,063.19	929.29	0.448*
	173,634.25	348.16	0.413*
32. Noto	134,972.31	489.00	0.413*
	151,641.37	266.68	(0.205)
33. Etchū	219,794.19	1,559.49	0.644**
	268,811.50	905.72	0.788**
34. Echigo	823,495.50	2,731.38	0.850**
	852,349.56	2,346.54	0.816**
35. Sado	87,174.69	95.24	0.552**
	86,998.63	97.59	0.488*
36. Tamba	276,799.00	84.84	0.394*
	278,322.75	64.52	(0.235)
37. Tango	121,598.56	250.25	0.946**
	120,173.87	269.25	0.954**
38. Tajima	141,689.00	267.64	0.873**
	141,444.25	270.90	0.839**
39. Inaba	112,496.00	187.28	0.554**
	119,460.12	94.39	0.599*
40. Hōki	121,525.56	450.38	0.927*
	119,669.44	475.14	0.920**
41. Izumo	189,922.00	869.21	0.952**
	190,158.31	866.06	0.935**
42. Iwami	215,199.62	287.60	0.497**
	213,257.75	313.50	0.469*
43. Oki	15,407.77	73.03	0.953**
	15,623.40	70.16	0.938**
44. Harima	601,557.81	58.93	(0.013)
	610,811.69	−64.49	(0.014)

Table 3.5 (Continued)

Kuni	Constant	Regression Coefficient	R^2
45. Mimasaka	169,419.44	9.28	(0.001)
	186,542.37	−219.09	0.550*
46. Bizen	330,412.50	−79.04	0.228+
	336,196.56	−156.18	0.794**
47. Bitchū	302,970.62	349.66	0.520**
	315,938.87	176.70	0.433*
48. Bingo	265,228.00	743.69	0.592**
	289,544.31	419.38	0.590*
49. Aki	302,643.19	1,969.13	0.964**
	312,769.75	1,833.95	0.963**
50. Suō	211,759.06	1,576.50	0.968**
	215,649.25	1,509.82	0.957**
51. Nagato	192,994.56	573.80	0.746**
	207,900.44	374.99	0.976**
52. Ku	480,252.06	329.59	(0.166)
	509,816.81	−64.73	(0.026)
53. Awaji	87,389.50	300.21	0.608**
	95,340.81	167.49	0.691**
54. Awa 2.	272,059.19	1,444.78	0.819**
	297,207.62	1,109.37	0.858**
55. Sanuki	289,574.56	1,167.90	0.794**
	316,172.31	837.16	0.988**
56. Iyo	419,721.56	1,407.00	0.655**
	463,596.81	821.82	0.842**
57. Tosa	310,416.87	1,082.75	0.931**
	321,116.94	940.04	0.955**
58. Chikuzen	262,678.12	654.57	0.557**
	287,990.75	316.96	0.746**
59. Chikugo	225,342.25	632.80	0.602**
	247,366.81	339.05	0.765**
60. Buzen	229,644.06	188.92	(0.194)
	245,941.31	−28.45	(0.032)
61. Bungo	501,957.69	−94.28	(0.017)
	531,365.69	−486.51	0.698**
62. Hizen	510,672.75	1,964.92	0.506**
	597,396.75	808.24	0.886**
63. Higo	513,748.62	1,876.98	0.759**
	558,469.06	1,280.52	0.899**
64. Hyūga	176,570.37	685.19	0.487**
	208,101.19	264.65	0.930**
65. Ōsumi	94,060.00	330.94	(0.115)
	134,704.06	−211.14	0.526*
66. Satsuma	87,201.18	1,650.51	0.533**
	155,694.95	736.97	0.842**
67. Iki	18,602.63	69.01	0.877**
	19,577.39	56.00	0.920**

Table 3.5 (Continued)

Kuni	Constant	Regression Coefficient	R^2
68. Tsushima	10,199.82	60.25	0.338*
	13,702.78	13.53	(0.113)
69. Ezo	−14,598.63	633.54	0.834**
	−4,421.00	497.80	0.864**

Note: The levels of significance for the coefficients of determination at $n = 11$ and $n = 10$ are indicated as follows: ** for 0.01, * for 0.05; and + for 0.10. Those in parentheses are not significant.

[a]The first set of numbers for the total and for each kuni is for the 11 observations from 1721 to 1872.

[b]The second set of numbers is for the 10 observations from 1721 to 1846, with the Meiji data for 1872 eliminated.

[c]Tohoku refers to the kuni of Iwaki, Iwashiro, Rikuzen, Rikuchū, and Mutsu.

Source. Calculated on the basis of the figures quoted in the source cited in Table 3.3.

tables: First, between 1721 and 1872, the population of Japan as a whole showed a distinct upward trend. The average annual growth rate for the entire period was 0.16 percent. If the periods affected by nationwide famines and the years from 1846 to 1872 are deleted, the average annual growth rate is still slightly under 0.20 percent. However, this percent growth rate was the net result of the averaging of various regional differences in the pattern of growth. (See Table 3.6.) Excluding Ezo (Hokkaido), which experienced steady in-migration, the annual average rate of growth for the entire period varied widely between −0.18 percent and +0.86 percent.

The growth rates for the nation as a whole varied by period as is shown in Table 3.7. The only periods in which the growth rate

Table 3.6
Frequency Distribution of Annual Average Kuni Growth Rates, 1721-1872

Rate of Growth (percent)	Negative	0.00-0.10	0.11-0.20	0.21-0.30	0.31-0.40	Over 0.40
Frequency (no. of kuni)	10	12	18	15	7	7

The kuni (provinces) of Japan

1 Yamashiro
2 Yamato
3 Kawachi
4 Izumi
5 Settsu
6 Iga
7 Ise
8 Shima
9 Owari
10 Mikawa
11 Tōtomi
12 Suruga
13 Izu
14 Kai
15 Sagami
16 Musashi
17 Awa (1)
18 Kazusa
19 Shimo-osa
20 Hitachi
21 Omi
22 Mino
23 Hida
24 Shinano
25 Kōzuke
26 Shimotsuke
27 Tōhoku (kuni of Iwaki,
   Iwashiro, Rikuzen,
   Rikuchū, and Mutsu)
28 Uzen-Ugo
29 Wakasa
30 Echizen
31 Kaga
32 Noto
33 Etchū

34 Echigo
35 Sado
36 Tamba
37 Tango
38 Tajima
39 Inaba
40 Hōki
41 Izumo
42 Iwami
43 Oki
44 Harima
45 Mimasaka
46 Bizen
47 Bitchū
48 Bingo
49 Aki
50 Suō
51 Nagato
52 Kii
53 Awaji
54 Awa (2)
55 Sanuki
56 Iyo
57 Tosa
58 Chikuzen
59 Chikugo
60 Buzen
61 Bungo
62 Hizen
63 Higo
64 Hyūga

65 Osumi
66 Satsuma
67 Iki
68 Tsushima

The regions of Japan

Kinki – 1-5, 21, 36-38, 44,
   52, 53
Tōkai – 6-15
Kantō – 15-20, 25, 26
Tōhoku – 27, 28
Tōsan – 14, 22-24
Hokuriku – 29-35
San' in – 39-43
San'yō – 45-51
Shikoku – 54-57
Kyūshū – 58-68

N

Note: Due to the lack of
statistical reliability of the
data on Ezo (Hokkaidō),
this region was not included
on the map

$\oplus$ = Positive regression coefficient significant at the 0·01 level
$+$ = Positive at the 0·05 level
$\ominus$ = Negative at the 0·01 level
$-$ = Negative at the 0·05 level

Figure 3.1: Significant Population Trends by *Kuni*, 1721-1872

Table 3.7
Average Annual Growth Rates for Japan by Subperiod

Year	1721-1750	1750-1756	1756-1786	1786-1798	1798-1804	1804-1822	1822-1828	1828-1836	1836-1846	1846-1872
Total Growth Rate	−0.02	0.10	−0.13	0.13	0.10	0.21	0.37	−0.03	−0.05	0.08

for the country as a whole was negative were those during which major nationwide mortality crises occurred: the Kyōhō famine of the 1730s, the Temmei famine of the 1780s, and the Tempō famine of the 1830s. However, a high number of negative growth rates for nearly every period appears when a frequency table is made for *kuni* growth rates by rates and periods (Table 3.8). And Table 3.4 reveals that negative growth rates occurred in different parts of the country at different times. It might be concluded in comparing Table 3.8 with Table 3.7 that the Tempō famine was slightly more widespread over the country than was the Temmei famine, as is evidenced by a larger number of negative and smaller growth rates in the period 1834-1846 than in the period 1756-1798. The country as a whole, though, experienced its largest negative growth rate, −0.13 percent, during the period 1756-1786, a period which included a large number of regional famines and the terminal date of which was during the Temmei famine. The effects of the Kyōhō famine, which took place during the period 1721-1750, appear to have been widespread also. Since the growth rate for the final period is distorted by the inclusion of previously excluded groups of the population in the 1872 survey, the only obvious period of steady population growth took place from 1804 to 1828, after the eighteenth-century famines and prior to the Tempō famine.

The foregoing analysis would seem to confirm the pessimists' view that the Tokugawa population failed to grow because of recurring famine. However, let us take another look at these same data. Of the 10 subperiods in Table 3.7, only 4 had negative growth rates and 3 of the 4 were under one-tenth of 1 percent. Thus in 6 of the subperiods the population was growing, and on the average by a larger rate than it was falling in periods of negative growth. Furthermore, if we return to Figure 3.1, we find that almost all of the statistically significant negative growth rates for

63

Table 3.8
Frequency Distribution of *Kuni* Growth Rates by Rate-Class and by Subperiod

Period	Negative	0.00-0.10	0.11-0.20	0.21-0.30	0.31-0.40	0.41-0.50	Over 0.50
1721-1750	36	6	10	8	3	0	6
1750-1756	22	9	9	5	7	3	14
1756-1786	38	13	8	2	1	3	4
1786-1798	23	8	10	8	6	5	9
1798-1804	26	11	10	9	6	2	5
1804-1822	8	7	12	14	13	2	13
1822-1828	11	9	6	10	7	10	16
1828-1834	26	9	7	7	7	7	6
1834-1846	42	11	5	5	1	1	4
1846-1872	3	1	2	9	5	6	43

the entire period 1721-1872 are in the northeastern section of Japan, with the exception of three *kuni* in central Japan around the Kyoto-Osaka area. In contrast, almost every *kuni* in western Japan sustained statistically significant increases in population over the period as a whole, whether the terminal date used is 1846 or 1872.

The major problem in analyzing the significance of these findings is how to assess the decline in the population of the *kuni* in which the major metropolises were located.[42] The tremendous growth of cities, both in size and number, from the late sixteenth century through the seventeenth should be considered a topic of major importance in the history of this period. Sekiyama estimates that the total urban population must have reached 3.7 to 3.8 million, or about 12 percent of the total population if we estimate it to have been about 30 million.[43] Gilbert Rozman, who is engaged in comparative research on premodern urbanization, is clearly impressed with the growth of Japan's cities during the Tokugawa period:

> While China stood out in total urban population, Japan was the more dramatic case. With 3 per cent of the world's population, Japan in the late eighteenth century contained more than 8 per cent of the people in cities of more than 10,000. It is likely that Japan was the only large-scale premodern society outside of Europe with more than 10 per cent of its population in cities of this size. Moreover, the sudden increase in Japan's urban population in the century and a half prior to the 1700s may well have had no parallel in world history before industrialization.[44]

The significance of the rapid growth of cities containing in the neighborhood of one in ten of the country's population should not be underestimated. But the authors of this work believe an analysis of Tokugawa cities must be left to a separate study. First, demographers are in unusual agreement in their skepticism of the population data that we do have for Japan's premodern cities. In addition to the people who, lured by employment opportunities, swarmed to the cities without proper authorization from the authorities, and who thus more often than not went unregistered, the samurai and their attendants were excluded from the city registers. Thus, statistics on the size of the city populations and even on whether they grew or declined often are at best "guesstimates."

The cities also affected the rural population surrounding them. It is likely that most premodern cities had higher death rates than birth rates, both because of the composition of the population and because of health conditions within the cities themselves. Thus, in order for their population even to be maintained, they needed an influx of people from the countryside.[45] Though the amount of evidence is still minute, it now seems likely that the death rate was higher for people who had had experience working in the cities, even if they returned to their native villages.[46] Metropolitan populations and the areas surrounding them are therefore likely to show somewhat different demographic patterns from the rest of the country. Because of the lack of evidence at present on urban populations, and because our data are the Bakufu statistics on what can be assumed to be the rural commoner population at the national level and rural village data at the local level, we will be dealing primarily with the rural population in this study.[47]

Thus if we put aside for the moment an assessment of the regions with the largest urban populations, we find that, with the exception of Tohoku, the population in Japan grew during the period 1721-1846 (see Table 3.9). Growth ranged from nearly 7 to just under 27 percent for the 125-year period but, even in the region with the lowest growth rate, it meant that in 1846 almost 7 more people had to be fed for every 100 who were fed in 1721. And it is likely that the growth is severely underestimated for west-

Table 3.9
An Index of Tokugawa Population Growth by Region
(1721 population = 100)

Region	1846	1872
Kinki	93.50	99.75
Tōkai	106.65	115.36
Kantō	86.63	100.98
Tōhoku	88.73	122.72
Tōsan	110.11	127.56
Hokuriku	117.57	153.06
San'in	124.81	140.05
San'yo	120.25	143.09
Shikoku	126.82	159.66
Kyūshū	113.78	161.72

Source: Taken from a table on p. 141 of Sekiyama, *Kinsei Nihon no jinkō kōzō*. For a list of the *kuni* included in each region, see p. 140.

ern Japan if 1846 is used as the terminal date, because the jump
was so much larger between the figures for 1846 and 1872 for
these four regions than for the other six, suggesting considerable
underestimation even in the farm villages since these four regions
tended to be less urbanized than much of the rest of Japan. Even
though the figures for 1872 are inflated by the inclusion of samurai, the 42 percent jump in Kyushu's population between 1846 and
1872 is scarcely accounted for by samurai who, even in Satsuma,
are estimated to have comprised no more than 25 percent of the
population, which was three to five times the national average. The
addition of children in domains that excluded them from the *shūmon-aratame-chō* still would not create the growth seen in Table
3.9.

Looked at from this perspective, it seems difficult to draw the
conclusion that the population in the second half of the Tokugawa
period "stagnated." Granted that growth was undoubtedly slower
during this century and a quarter than during either the seventeenth century or the Meiji period, on balance the population grew,
despite famines and other disasters. And what may have been of
equal significance in the long run is the fact that the balance of the
population began to shift toward the west during the latter half of
the Tokugawa period. Because of the growth of the four western
regions and losses in the north and in the central urban areas, the
percentage of the population living in western Honshu (San'in and
San'yo), Shikoku, and Kyushu grew from around 28 percent in
1721 to over 32 percent in 1846 and nearly 35 percent by 1872.

Thus, instead of merely concluding that the population stopped
growing in the latter half of the Tokugawa period, we need to assess demographic change by area. The regions containing the
largest cities become something of a puzzle: were the cities declining in population and draining off the population of the surrounding countryside in addition, or was the underregistration so serious
by the nineteenth century that it affected even the sign of the
growth rate, making a stable or even slightly growing population
seem negative? We do not even know whether the population of
these three cities was included in the Bakufu totals for the *kuni*
in which they were located. But population change in the rest of
Japan becomes less of a mystery if not all regions are analyzed
together. When we eliminate the regions containing the major ur-

ban centers, we find that population continued to grow during the latter half of the Tokugawa period, even if at a rate that seems very slow by twentieth-century standards.

This slow rate of growth of the rural population and even slower rate for the nation as a whole meant that, with the growth of the economy, the per capita income began to rise, making possible the development of a surplus. Deane and Cole believe that low average rates of population growth for nearly three centuries in England, while total output was known to have been growing at a faster pace, were an essential ingredient in her successful industrialization.[18] Japanese population was undoubtedly growing at a slow rate, and in the next chapter we shall provide evidence for the argument that the Tokugawa economy continued to grow even during the eighteenth and nineteenth centuries, creating a consequent rise in the living standard and a surplus in the hands of many.

CHAPTER FOUR

Economic Growth: A General Perspective

Before presenting case studies of three regions, let us summarize here various indications on a nationwide level of increasing economic activities, a rising living standard, and other changes hypothesized in our analytical framework presented in Chapter Two. Since by far the most important contributor to total output was agriculture and the largest total output of this sector was rice, we will begin with an examination of the increase in the output of rice and other grains (measured in rice equivalent) and with a comparison of the rates of growth of these major grains with the population growth rates examined in the preceding chapter.

Many Japanese economic historians begin their examination of the Tokugawa economy by citing the estimate of 18.5 million *koku* for the total rice output for the early seventeenth century. This figure, however, is based on untested assumptions and subjective estimates and is no more useful than the numerous "guesstimates" for total national rice output advanced by some Japanese economic historians on the basis of their limited regional case studies.[1]

This means that the only national data that can be deemed worthy of analysis for the purpose of obtaining an indicator of the growth of output are the results of three national surveys conducted by the Bakufu in 1645, 1697, and 1829.[2] These surveys were said to have been conducted with varying emphases on assessing increases in arable land and in productivity, correcting for previous underreporting of various kinds, and adjusting for changes made in the standard measures of land in the late seventeenth century.[3]

However, it is most unlikely that the Bakufu was able to obtain data that were adjusted for various types of underreporting, and thus it is more reasonable to assume that the correspondence between the real yield and reported yield diverged, perhaps increasingly so as time went on. The daimyo became less able to share in the rising output resulting from increases in productivity, especially during the latter half of the Tokugawa period and, in addition, the daimyo had good reason to underreport to the Bakufu as the *ad hoc* demands for contributions and military services depended on the economic status of each domain. A case in point is the output data for Satsuma, which were precisely the same for 1829 as for 1697. Of course, it was not very likely that domain officials knew the real output of grain in their own domain, as the assessment of yields tended to be fixed and often lagged considerably behind the increase in real output due to increases in productivity. If these notes of caution are kept in mind, the results of the Bakufu surveys will be useful at least in indicating the general trend of changes in output by *kuni*. Table 4.1 contains the Bakufu data[4] along with the results of the survey made by the Meiji government in 1873[5] and the average annual growth rate of output that we computed for each of the subperiods between the surveys and for the entire period 1645-1873.

The annual average growth rate calculated for the grain output, which was 0.12 percent for the period 1645-1873 and almost 0.12 percent also for the period 1645-1829, is undoubtedly smaller than it must in fact have been. First, even should the 1645 figures be fairly accurate, the 1873 data are almost certainly underestimates. The *Tōkei nenkan* (Statistical yearbook) of 1886, in its section on agricultural statistics, warns that "it is extremely difficult to obtain reliable statistics because people . . . conceal the truth and because measurement techniques have not been sufficiently improved."[6] Although James Nakamura initiated an intense debate among economists in the early 1960s through his argument that the early Meiji statistics contain serious underestimation, virtually all scholars who took part in the debate agree that some underestimation occurred and that the 1873 figures should be readjusted.[7]

Second, this low growth rate during the Tokugawa period of about 0.12 percent is clearly in conflict with what is known of increases both in the cultivated area and in agricultural productivity. Although much of the data are in the form of case studies, there exist numerous descriptions and sample data attesting to continuous land reclamation, irrigation projects, and the conversion of marsh and forest into arable land. As will be shown in later chapters, numerous sources document the creation of *shinden* (new fields), and the changes they brought to the Tokugawa village economy.[8]

Though the all-important information on the amount of arable created by *shinden* is lacking, there are fairly reliable data on the

Table 4.1

Grain Output (*Koku*) and Annual Average Growth Rates by *Kuni*

	1645	G.p.a. 1645-1697	1697	G.p.a. 1697-1829	1829	G.p.a. 1829-1873	1873	G.p.a. 1645-1873
TOTAL	24,553,757	0.10	25,876,392	0.13	30,558,917	0.11	32,008,292	0.12
1. Yamashiro	215,982	0.07	224,257	0.02	230,131	-0.08	222,265	0.01
2. Yamato	459,380	0.16	500,497	0.00	501,361	-0.02	497,404	0.03
3. Kawachi	264,952	0.08	276,329	0.05	293,786	-0.00	293,708	0.05
4. Izumi	159,326	0.03	161,692	0.05	172,847	-0.02	171,295	0.03
5. Settsu	375,478	0.09	392,707	0.05	417,391	-0.00	416,521	0.05
6. Iga	100,540	0.00	100,540	0.07	110,090	0.02	110,917	0.04
7. Ise	585,065	0.11	621,027	0.11	716,451	-0.01	714,376	0.09
8. Shima	20,061	0.00	30,061	0.05	21,470	-0.24	19,279	-0.02
9. Owari	483,432	0.15	521,480	0.03	545,875	0.77	764,976	0.20
10. Mikawa	350,888	0.17	383,413	0.15	466,080	0.03	472,373	0.13
11. Tōtomi	280,696	0.30	328,651	0.09	369,952	0.02	372,878	0.12
12. Suruga	191,315	0.49	247,437	0.01	250,530	0.01	251,865	0.12
13. Izu	79,653	0.10	83,991	0.00	84,171	-0.04	82,690	0.02
14. Kai	245,298	0.06	253,023	0.16	312,159	-0.00	311,502	0.10
15. Sagami	220,617	0.30	258,216	0.08	286,719	0.03	290,469	0.12
16. Musashi	982,327	0.33	1,168,613	0.07	1,281,431	0.00	1,282,000	0.12
17. Awa 1. (Bōshū)	92,641	0.03	93,886	0.01	95,736	-0.00	95,641	0.01
18. Kazusa	n.a.	n.a.	391,113	0.06	425,080	0.01	427,313	n.a.
19. Shimo-osa	444,829	0.47	568,331	0.14	681,062	0.01	685,027	0.19
20. Hitachi	840,048	0.14	903,778	0.08	1,005,707	-0.20	921,629	0.04
21. Ōmi	832,122	0.01	836,829	0.01	853,095	0.01	857,757	0.01
22. Mino	609,718	0.11	645,010	0.06	699,764	0.10	729,831	0.08
23. Hida	38,764	0.26	44,469	0.18	56,602	0.03	57,243	0.08
24. Shinano	548,600	0.22	615,818	0.17	767,788	0.03	779,462	0.15
25. Kōzuke	515,215	0.27	591,834	0.06	637,331	-0.01	635,766	0.09
26. Shimotsuke	568,733	0.35	681,702	0.09	769,905	-0.02	761,523	0.13
27. Tōhoku	1,431,060	0.76	2,124,941	0.23	2,874,236	0.10	2,999,417	0.32
28. Uzen-Ugo	965,674	0.30	1,126,247	0.11	1,295,322	0.35	1,514,186	0.20
29. Wakasa	85,099	0.07	88,281	0.02	91,018	0.02	91,767	0.03
30. Echizen	682,182	0.01	684,271	0.01	689,304	0.00	609,243	0.01
31. Kaga	422,957	0.07	438,281	0.07	483,665	0.11	508,609	0.08

Table 4.1 (Continued)

	1645	G.p.a. 1645-1697	1697	G.p.a. 1697-1829	1829	G.p.a. 1829-1873	1873	G.p.a. 1645-1873
32. Noto	225,006	0.12	239,208	0.11	275,369	0.24	305,482	0.13
33. Etchū	592,415	0.06	611,001	0.21	808,008	0.19	877,760	0.17
34. Echigo	611,960	0.56	816,775	0.25	1,142,555	0.01	1,149,017	0.28
35. Sado	24,812	3.19	130,373	0.01	132,565	0.04	135,095	0.74
36. Tamba	289,829	0.02	293,445	0.08	324,136	0.04	329,465	0.06
37. Tango	123,175	0.30	143,624	0.02	147,614	0.01	148,002	0.08
38. Tajima	129,069	0.02	130,673	0.08	144,313	0.06	148,147	0.06
39. Inaba	149,539	0.25	170,728	0.03	177,844	0.22	195,632	0.12
40. Hoki	170,254	0.26	194,416	0.09	217,990	0.32	251,067	0.17
41. Izumo	253,597	0.21	282,489	0.05	302,627	0.13	320,709	0.10
42. Iwami	139,401	0.04	142,499	0.14	172,209	0.13	182,136	0.12
43. Oki	11,601	0.09	12,165	0.02	12,559	0.00	12,562	0.03
44. Harima	562,291	0.02	568,517	0.10	651,964	0.03	660,557	0.07
45. Mimasaka	186,500	0.63	259,353	-0.02	252,099	0.09	262,333	0.15
46. Bizen	280,200	0.06	289,224	0.28	416,581	0.01	418,960	0.18
47. Bitchū	236,691	0.61	324,455	0.09	363,915	0.05	371,441	0.20
48. Bingo	248,606	0.30	289,878	0.06	312,054	0.03	315,511	0.10
49. Aki	265,071	0.08	276,678	0.09	310,648	0.02	313,164	0.07
50. Suō	202,787	0.00	202,787	0.67	489,428	0.27	552,160	0.44
51. Nagato	166,623	0.50	216,623	0.47	404,853	0.28	458,143	0.44
52. Kii	398,393	-0.00	397,668	0.08	440,839	0.02	444,162	0.05
53. Awaji	70,186	0.01	70,428	0.24	97,164	0.77	136,637	0.29
54. Awa 2.	186,753	0.07	193,862	0.25	268,894	0.31	307,732	0.22
55. Sanuki	173,554	0.14	186,394	0.34	291,320	0.15	311,064	0.26
56. Iyo	400,271	0.13	429,163	0.05	460,997	-0.10	442,079	0.04
57. Tosa	202,626	0.54	268,486	0.16	330,026	0.99	510,572	0.41
58. Chikuzen	522,512	0.12	556,981	0.12	651,782	-0.06	633,434	0.08
59. Chikugo	302,089	0.18	331,497	0.09	375,588	0.81	536,841	0.25
60. Buzen	231,680	0.32	273,801	0.23	368,913	-0.01	366,948	0.20
61. Bungo	378,592	-0.05	369,540	0.09	417,514	0.22	459,184	0.08
62. Hizen	561,437	0.04	572,284	0.16	706,470	-0.05	691,444	0.09
63. Higo	572,980	-0.03	563,787	0.06	611,920	0.75	851,237	0.17
64. Hyūga	288,589	0.14	309,954	0.07	340,128	0.47	418,142	0.16

Table 4.1 (Continued)

	1645	G.p.a. 1645-1697	1697	G.p.a. 1697-1829	1829	G.p.a. 1829-1873	1873	G.p.a. 1645-1873
65. Ōsumi	170,828	0.00	170,843	−0.00	170,833	0.97	261,793	0.19
66. Satsuma	315,251	−0.00	315,005	0.00	315,005	0.06	323,483	0.01
67. Iki	15,982	0.24	18,072	0.45	32,742	0.15	35,042	0.34
68. Tsushima	123,711	−0.00	123,611	0.13	146,023	n.a.	n.a.	n.a.

Source: The figures on grain output in *koku* (rice equivalent) are from Kikuchi Toshio, *Shinden kaihatsu* (The reclamation of fields) (Tokyo: Shibundō, 1964), pp. 223-225. The annual average growth rates (G.p.a. or growth per annum) were calculated on the basis of these figures.

number of *shinden* created during the subperiods of the Tokugawa rule.[9] Compared to 28 *shinden* known to have been created from 1551 to 1600, 243 *shinden* were created during the first fifty years of the Tokugawa period (1600-1650). This increase was partly made possible by the fact that Japan was completely at peace for the first time in several hundred years. With the reclamation of land strongly encouraged by the Bakufu and various domains, *shinden* reached a peak of 434 during the period 1651-1700. The amount of reclamation carried on during the eighteenth century fell sharply, probably because all of the land readily and economically reclaimable under existing technology had been reclaimed. The first half of the century recorded 182 *shinden* and the last half 142. But, during the last sixty-eight years of the Tokugawa period (1801-1868), the number of *shinden* created rose to 788 because of technological development and the Bakufu's near-desperate efforts to widen its tax base.

The types and sizes of *shinden* varied widely by period and by region. The *shinden* created during the nineteenth century were usually smaller in size and less productive than the earlier ones. Also, *shinden* in the Kyushu, Chugoku, and Shikoku areas were more numerous and tended to be larger in size than those found in the Tohoku or Kanto regions.[10]

The following comparison may be useful for gaining some impression of the total magnitude of the arable area added by *shinden*, though the two surveys are not strictly comparable. The survey of 1873 put the total arable area at 4,126,771 *chō* of paddy and upland fields. If we compare this with the oft-cited estimate of about 2.06 million *chō* for the beginning of the Tokugawa period, we can conclude that the amount of land reclaimed during the Tokugawa period doubled the size of the total arable area.[11] As the best land was reclaimed first, with the passing of time the productivity of the newest *shinden* tended to be lower. However, if the arable area did in fact double or nearly double, then the annual growth rate of the grain output cited earlier (0.12 percent) is less than half of what the data on arable land suggest.

Another reason why the low annual growth rate is difficult to accept is that few (including Marxist) scholars deny that agricultural productivity increased throughout the Tokugawa period. Most Japanese scholars, who explain the increasing economic difficulties of the peasants in terms of exploitation by the ruling class, the merchants, and the *gōnō*, are explicit in recognizing increases in productivity on the strength of their own case studies. Thus, college textbooks generally following the Marxist view of the Tokugawa economy include such statements as "agricultural productivity rose after the mid-Tokugawa period, and agriculture developed visibly as commercial agriculture too expanded,"[12] or "by the mid-Tokugawa period, commerce began to expand nationwide on the strength of peasant agriculture. Though there were differences in speed by region, in some regions such developments began as early as the Genroku period. The increase in agricultural productivity was the cause of such developments. The power of the peasants who could now sell their surplus products began to destroy the foundation of the feudal economy."[13] And even *Kōza Nihon-shi*, after listing numerous changes in agricultural techniques, stated that "we can summarize two common denominators of these changes. One is that, in commercial agriculture, technological improvements more suitable for larger scale production were made . . . the other was a more intensive use of labor which increased productivity. The latter especially was a common characteristic found in the technological improvements relating to the production of major grains."[14]

Numerous case studies support these observations. But let us leave to later chapters a discussion of the findings made by such scholars as Furushima, Naitō, Takeyasu, Shimbō, Hayama, and others, and note here only that they argue persuasively that the Tokugawa agricultural output and productivity as a whole grew more or less consistently throughout the entire period.[15] And all of these Japanese scholars bear out Thomas Smith's carefully researched findings, based on Kaga *han* and eleven villages scattered around Japan, that "the productivity of land was generally rising."[16] Specific examples of technical innovations, improvements in agricultural management, increased variety and productivity of agricultural implements and seeds, and other changes are presented in Chapters Five through Seven.

Though still keeping in mind the preceding *caveat* that the Bakufu data on grain output are incongruent with our knowledge of increases in the arable area and productivity, let us now examine the growth rate of the grain output by *kuni* in comparison to the population growth rates presented in Table 3.4 of the preceding chapter. The results are to be seen in Figure 4.1. When the

The kuni *(provinces) of Japan*

1 Yamashiro	34 Echigo	65 Osumi
2 Yamato	35 Sado	66 Satsuma
3 Kawachi	36 Tamba	67 Iki
4 Izumi	37 Tango	68 Tsushima
5 Settsu	38 Tajima	
6 Iga	39 Inaba	*The regions of Japan*
7 Ise	40 Hōki	Kinki — 1-5, 21, 36-38, 44,
8 Shima	41 Izumo	52, 53
9 Owari	42 Iwami	Tōkai — 6-15
10 Mikawa	43 Oki	Kantō — 15-20, 25, 26
11 Tōtomi	44 Harima	Tōhoku — 27, 28
12 Suruga	45 Mimasaka	Tōsan — 14, 22-24
13 Izu	46 Bizen	Hokuriku — 29-35
14 Kai	47 Bitchū	San' in — 39-43
15 Sagami	48 Bingo	San'yō — 45-51
16 Musashi	49 Aki	Shikoku — 54-57
17 Awa (1)	50 Suō	Kyūshū — 58-68
18 Kazusa	51 Nagato	
19 Shimo-osa	52 Kii	
20 Hitachi	53 Awaji	
21 Omi	54 Awa (2)	
22 Mino	55 Sanuki	
23 Hida	56 Iyo	
24 Shinano	57 Tosa	
25 Kōzuke	58 Chikuzen	
26 Shimotsuke	59 Chikugo	
27 Tōhoku (*kuni* of Iwaki,	60 Buzen	
Iwashiro, Rikuzen,	61 Bungo	
Rikuchū, and Mutsu)	62 Hizen	
28 Uzen-Ugo	63 Higo	
29 Wakasa	64 Hyūga	
30 Echizen		
31 Kaga		
32 Noto		
33 Etchū		

N

Note: Due to the lack of statistical reliability of the data on Ezo (Hokkaidō), this region was not included on the map

⊕ = Growth rates of rice output exceed those for population by at least 0·1%
+ = Growth rates of rice output exceed those for population by 0·05–0·1%
◎ = Virtually identical rates, differing less than 0·05%
⊖ = Growth rates of population exceed those for rice output by at least 0·1%
— = Growth rates of population exceed those for rice output by 0·05–0·1%

Figure 4.1: A Comparison of Signs and Relative Magnitudes of Annual Average Growth Rates of Rice Output (1645-1873) and Population (1721-1872)

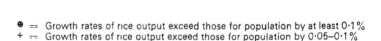

annual average growth rate of rice for a *kuni* for the period 1645-1873 exceeded that of population by at least 0.1 percent, that *kuni* is marked ⊕ on the map, and if by less than 0.1 percent by +. The signs ⊖ and − conversely indicate those cases in which the rate of population growth exceeded that of rice. In several cases, where the growth rates of rice and population were identical or virtually so (the difference either way being less than 0.05 percent), the *kuni* are marked ⓞ.

When Spearman's rank correlation coefficients were calculated between growth rates of rice and population, the results were 0.208 for rice (1697-1829) and population (1721-1828) and 0.226 for rice (1829-1873) and population (1828-1872). When the coefficient was calculated for the entire period, for rice (1697-1873) and for population (1721-1872) a higher coefficient was obtained, 0.408, which one would expect over the long run in a predominantly agricultural economy.

Questionable though the data are, they are significant in analyzing variations in the relative rates of growth of population and grain output per *kuni*. The regions of Kanto, Tohoku, and the environs of Osaka, Kyoto, and Nagoya, which showed population trends ranging from positive but statistically insignificant to statistically significant and negative in Figure 3.1, are the very regions showing positive signs in Figure 4.1. The reverse holds true for those regions in western Japan and the region sandwiched between Nagoya and Edo, which have negative signs, indicating that the rate of increase in the rice yield was falling behind that of population growth.

The Tohoku region, known for its famines and used by Japanese historians as an example par excellence of peasant misery in Tokugawa Japan, showed a surprising increase in the per capita output of rice. Several explanations are possible. The famines may not have been so severe as much of the literature would have us believe, or both the economy and the population were sufficiently resilient to recover from famines within a short time. Or, famines may have curtailed population growth in certain periods without adversely affecting the long-term productivity of the land and, when the worst of a famine was past, labor productivity would rise, thus creating a rising per capita output over time. In Chapter Six we shall examine Morioka *han*, considered one of the most economically backward in the region, in search of answers to this possible discrepancy (within the framework of the Marxist analysis) and in an effort to shed more light on the reliability of the data we used in preparing Figure 4.1.

No less important is our finding that for much of western Japan the official statistics of the Bakufu indicate a per capita decrease over time in the output of essential grains. The inference that the standard of living fell, however, is unwarranted, and most Japanese scholars would be quick to stress the probable underreporting of output by the large *tozama* domains in this region—witness the Satsuma figures—and the growth of the economy, especially during the second half of the Tokugawa period. Thus, one interpretation of Figure 4.1 is that economic activities other than the growing of rice and other grains became important over time. If one followed the orthodox Marxist interpretation, one would say that the rate of increase in population contributed to the economic difficulties of the peasants, because any surpluses earned from commercial crops and nonagricultural activities were taxed or exploited away from them. And many Japanese scholars also tend to argue that the growth of nonagricultural output was an indication of the increasing poverty of the peasants, who had to rely on such activities in order to subsist. However, our view, based on the large body of regional evidence, is that total regional economic activities (as a proxy for regional gross production) grew at a rate faster than that of population growth, and that the per capita income of the peasants in western Japan rose steadily even throughout the last century and a half of the Tokugawa period.

That commerce—trading in increasing amounts of commercial crops, processed agricultural products, handicrafts, various industries (iron, other metal products, salt, cotton and silk goods, etc.), and rice—contributed to the growth of the Tokugawa economy and the rise in the living standard of its population is beyond dispute. Even in the words of a Japanese historian who argued that "the lot of the peasants always hovered between life and death,"[17] the growth of commerce was all important in Tokugawa Japan:

> Like it or not, the feudal lords were forced to ride a new horse—newly developing commerce—changing over from the old one—an economy based on rice. Naturally, the growth of commerce changed the peasants and transformed the villages. During the Genbun period [1736-1740], those areas shipping

cotton to Osaka consisted of Tamba, Kawachi, Yamashiro, Yamato, Izumi, Settsu, Hōki, Bitchū, Bizen, Aki, Sanuki, and others.[18]

Though the western part of the nation, with Osaka as its commercial entrepôt, figured more importantly in Tokugawa development than other parts of the country, commerce grew nationwide and the growth rate accelerated during the second half of the Tokugawa period. The products traded steadily increased over time, and major goods traded by the early eighteenth century were rice, cotton, rapeseed oil, *sake*, silk, fertilizer (dried fish cakes), salted and dried marine products, a variety of mineral products, draft animals, vegetable dyes, and literally scores of the regional *meisan* (products associated with a region and known for their quality).[19]

The center of commercial activities gradually shifted from the major urban centers such as Osaka and Edo to the outlying areas during the eighteenth century. However, prior to this shift, the trade network had become well established, integrating the whole nation into a unified market. In the face of a developing transportation network and improving communications (relating to price differentials and market opportunities), the efforts of some of the daimyo to restrict trade for their own gains were decreasingly successful.

The expansion in trade contributed to regional specialization. For example, sugar, pottery, tallow wax, flint, and straw matting were widely produced in Kyushu; paper, salt, lumber and cotton came from Shikoku; white paper, indigo, carrots, silver, and iron were among the major products marketed in western Honshu. The Kansai was famous for mandarin oranges, cotton and leather products, umbrellas, fish fertilizers and oil, and masonry products. Specialty goods were fewer in the Tohoku region, where rice was listed as the major item produced, though Kōfu grew grapes, Morioka had its iron and Toyama was noted for its medicine.[20] And as our regional studies in Chapters Five through Seven will make abundantly clear, the growth of trade enabled the capturing of gains resulting from economies of scale, and it promoted capital investment and technological changes for improving the productivity of agricultural and manufacturing activities directly and indirectly stimulated by the growing commerce.

An excerpt from a summary of a study on eighteenth-century commerce by Yagi conveys the trend of the period well:

In the early eighteenth century, the commercial production . . . of rapeseed and rice increased, second only to cotton. Areas specializing in cotton emerged, as did areas growing rapeseed and rice. In the second half of the . . . century, as rapeseed and cotton became important commercial crops, the processing of these crops began to spread from the towns into the villages that grew them. . . . Towns continued to grow as centers of distribution and processing . . . even after the villages also entered these activities. What happened from the seventeenth through the eighteenth centuries was the geographical expansion of these commercial activities.[21]

Paralleling the growth of commerce (and also as evidence of the growth itself), economic institutions continued to be developed, facilitating and contributing to the gains realized from trade. The institutional development achieved was impressive by almost any standard. Highly sophisticated banklike institutions, led by the "Big Ten" money exchangers (*jūnin ryōgaeya*) of Osaka and Edo, developed after the beginning of the eighteenth century to substantially reduce the costs and risks of interregional trade. These institutions had self-imposed quasi-reserve requirements to assure sound operations, and they performed many services that modern banks were to render after the Meiji Restoration. Though they did not accept deposits, they issued their own bills, drafted exchange bills, issued promissory notes, speculated in both spot and future prices of gold coins and gold and silver bills, and functioned as important centers of economic information.[22]

Reflecting and enhancing the growth of commerce were other important institutions such as *fudasashi* (rice-jobbers), a rice market that functioned as a commodity market for rice (trading both on spots and futures), warehousing and forwarding agents in all major shipping points, and the inns catering to traveling merchants. Descriptions of these institutions, found readily in numerous Japanese sources and several works in English, lead readers to conclude that any economy with such institutions must have been highly commercialized and prosperous. What is important here are the contributions made by these institutions in increasing trade at decreasing transactions costs, in other words, both the traders and the economy as a whole reaped increasing gains from the development of these institutions.

A secular increase was seen in the real income level of both wage earners and farmers and, although this increase occurred unevenly and gradually, it signifies the more productive use of labor and a growing economy. The more productive use of labor was achieved by the reallocation of labor, either on a full- or part-time basis, from agriculture into commercial and manufacturing activities. Also contributing to the rise in real income was a labor shortage in agriculture, which caused landholders to compete for the labor remaining in agriculture by paying higher wages or offering better contractual terms to tenant cultivators. Implicit in this analysis is a continued growth in the productivity of labor, both in the agricultural sector (as already noted) and in the commercial and manufacturing sectors.

To demonstrate that the statements contained in the preceding paragraph are justified in the virtual absence of time series data on real wages and farm income, let us here present a diagram to show the analytical relationships among labor mobility, the labor shortage in the agricultural sector, increases in productivity in both the agricultural and nonagricultural sectors, and the rising income level of the peasants, all of which can be verified by an abundance of evidence. Since direct and indirect evidence is presented in Chapters Five through Eleven to support the points made here, Figure 4.2 is offered only as an explanatory sketch of how these changes affected one another.

If we assume that a regional labor market was in equilibrium at the outset, given the marginal productivity of agriculture (I_a) and manufacturing (I_m) with OA units of labor in agriculture and OB units in manufacturing, the equilibrium wage level (marginal physical product of labor) was P, assuming competition in the labor market, an assumption that becomes increasingly tenable over time during the Tokugawa period. Suppose then that the productivity of labor rose over time in both sectors as indicated by II_a and II_m (the line declines more sharply than I_m to indicate the increased use of capital) and that the population increased in both sectors: in agriculture from OA to OF, and in manufacturing from OB to OD. Given the changes in the productivity of labor, the demand for labor in both sectors would rise to OC and OE respectively, if the wage level remained unchanged. However,

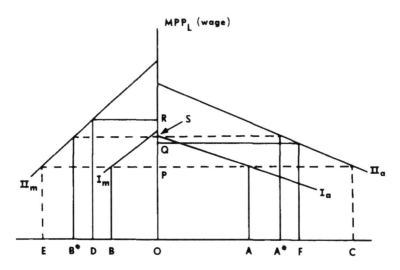

Figure 4.2: A Model of Relative Wages and Labor Mobility Between the Agricultural and Nonagricultural Sectors

since the supply of labor increased less than was needed to meet this demand, the wage level *in the absence* of labor mobility would be Q in the agricultural sector and R in the manufacturing sector.

With a wage differential between these sectors, the labor market is in disequilibrium, that is, agricultural labor in the amount of A^*F will move to the manufacturing sector, thus increasing the labor in manufacturing from OD to OB^* ($A^*F = DB^*$). After this shift in labor from a low productivity sector (agriculture) to a high productivity sector (manufacturing) is complete, a new equilibrium results with the wage level at S, OA^* units of labor in agriculture, and OB^* units of labor in manufacturing.

Following the foregoing analysis, in order to show that the real wages of wage earners were rising and that the living standard of the peasants was improving, we need only demonstrate that: (1) the labor available for agriculture declined (partly due to out-migration to the cities and partly—perhaps more importantly in most domains—due to the participation in by-employments by peasants still in the village); (2) a labor shortage occurred in the agricultural sector; (3) productivity in manufacturing rose (increases in agricultural productivity have been argued and increases in commercial productivity can be inferred from our earlier descriptions); and (4) the labor markets in both sectors were competitive. Before examining the evidence presented in later chapters, the general validity of these four statements can be demonstrated with little difficulty.

Descriptive evidence showing that labor moved from agriculture to nonagricultural activities and from villages to towns and cities is abundant in the form of case studies, as Marxist scholars have long been accumulating this evidence in order to demonstrate that peasants were "forced out" of agriculture.[23] As the problem of peasant migration into the cities became increasingly serious, especially during the eighteenth century, the Bakufu and the *han* resorted more and more to decrees prohibiting peasants from leaving their villages but, for the most part, these were clearly unenforceable.

Perhaps more important in quantitative terms than the number of peasants who left the village was that the increase in peasant by-employments was seriously draining agriculture of labor. The Bakufu's effort to curtail and then to limit the trend was unavailing. For example, by the mid-nineteenth century, a village of 180 households in Gōshū (Shizuoka) examined by Harada had 27 households specializing in the weaving of cotton cloth and "several times more" this number engaged in part-time weaving. The list of the by-employments in another village included eighteen different occupations ranging from "petty trading" to the "squeezing of oils." Harada concluded that by-employments were of a type that could be called "petty trading or family industry" and that were carried on for the purpose of augmenting family income.[24]

Another excellent study on the expanding by-employments was made by Smith.[25] His findings on the Kaminoseki region of Chōshū *han* during the last several decades of the Tokugawa period clearly show the importance of by-employments even in this part of Honshu not especially known for its commerce. The proportion of the nonagricultural income in the fifteen districts for which Smith obtained data from a *han* survey ranged from 23 to 83 percent with a mode of 55 percent (which also was the regional average). After rejecting the possibility that farm income might have been underestimated, Smith advanced another possible explanation for the observed high proportion of nonagricultural income, which was that productivity was higher in nonagricultural economic activities than in agriculture. That is, finding that "non-agricultural income was larger than one would expect from the proportion of non-farm families in the population alone, and in most districts between 2 and 7 times larger," he wrote of this differential:

> The lowest differential in any district . . . is probably near the actual ratio, and it corresponds fairly closely to figures from other preindustrial societies and to the ratio that may be inferred from a comparison of non-agricultural wages with the average income of farm families from farming. Such comparisons suggest an average productivity ratio, on a man-day basis, of about 1.5 to 1, or on an annual basis . . . of 2.47 to 1.[26]

In short, Smith's study on Kaminoseki and his descriptions of by-employments elsewhere effectively show that more and more peasants were engaging in by-employments, that is, ceasing to be full-time cultivators, because it was more remunerative to do so.[27] As we shall see in Chapter Six, this was true of even the poorest regions in Tokugawa Japan.

Evidence that a labor shortage existed in the agricultural sector in the Tokugawa period can also be easily obtained and, ironically, this evidence is frequently found in the writings of Japanese scholars who maintain that the economic well-being of the peasants was deteriorating during the second half of the Tokugawa period. In addition to such indirect evidence as Bakufu and *han* decrees prohibiting peasants from moving to cities because arable land remained uncultivated, direct evidence comes from all parts of Japan, often in the form of landowners who lament that their servants are less respectful of them and "prone to feigned illness," and of complaints of rising wages by the large landholders and the authorities. In the late eighteenth century a man from Saga in Kyushu wrote: "The peasants, who are expected to live a simple life and work assiduously on the land, are leaving the land to become merchants whose life is easier," and "repeated pleading by the authorities had no effect because the peasants had learned the more pleasant ways of the townspeople."[28] Even in the north, contemporary sources in Sendai and Tsugaru *han* observed that "because agriculture yielded only meager returns, many chose to be merchants for high wages. Agricultural workers are becoming much harder to find and land remaining unattended has increased."[29] As we shall see later in this study, the problem was even more acute in the economically advanced regions of the Kinai and Okayama, and as early as the early eighteenth century. What was happening is clear even when expressed in the Marxist framework:

> When a shortage of persons developed in the farm villages, not all the arable could be cultivated with equal intensity because the tax rates were high and fixed [sic]. Since the lords' finances depended primarily on the tax rice, this created difficulties for them. Thus, they prevented the peasants from leaving the villages, prohibited free planting [i.e., of crops other than rice] and banned the sale of paddies. However, by the time of the eighth shogun, Yoshimune, a decree [encouraging the planting of mulberry trees, weaving, and other activities between the peak periods to "assist the daily needs of clothing and food"] had to be issued. . . . The commercialized economy, by making rice into a commercial crop, was causing the rapid disintegration of the villages.[30]

The mura-meisai-chō (records) of a village in Musashi stated all this in simple terms: "Of late, both peasants and servants are extremely scarce in number. Wages are rising and the paddies are uncultivated. Caught between higher wages and the higher costs of fertilizers, it is difficult to remain in farming."[31]

The evidence necessary to show that the productivity of labor was rising in manufacturing is found in the increasing use of capital, in the expanding unit size in manufacturing activities, and in scattered wage data. According to a study made by Shinobu, an innovation in weaving the famous Nishijin cloth "made production far more efficient" than before, and an increasing number of persons were engaged in this industry, which employed only a few in 1742 but more than 700 by the end of the 1750s. Noting this development, Naramoto, who belongs to a faction of Marxists who date the beginning of "manufacturing in the strict sense of the term" from the Tokugawa period, wrote:

> Manufacturing contributed in the taking of steps toward the modern age. Tasks were divided and simplified. Because of this, anyone could engage in them, and no special skill was required. This helped to expand the market and liberate peasants from the land.[32]

The century from 1750 to 1850 saw the growth of large-scale manufacturing establishments and large wholesalers. In the textile industry a variety of woven goods was developed that matched the famous Kiryū Nishijin-ori and cloth from Ashikaga in technology. These firms were on such a scale that they were in fact "manufacturing establishments with their own workshops." South of Edo, soy sauce, *sake*, and Japanese vinegar were produced on a large scale. By 1821 the soy sauce produced in Choshi and Noda "accounted for 1,230,000 barrels (*taru*) out of the 1,250,000 barrels imported annually by Edo."[33]

Because of the existence of these and many other examples from across the nation, some Japanese historians stress the development of *manu* (from manufacturing, and signifying by the early nineteenth century the appearance of economic organizations representing a post-feudal, capitalistic, stage of the economy, with wage labor and a large scale of production). A recent textbook, after describing large establishments in various regions, concluded the section by saying that "these budding manufacturing establishments . . . contributed to an increase in labor productivity."[34]

That the labor markets, both in the agricultural and in the non-agricultural sectors, were competitive by the beginning of the eighteenth century, if not before, is beyond dispute and is assumed by all Japanese economic historians. Well-known works describe the competition among *sake* brewers for labor, which resulted in bidding up wages; wage competition and the competition in contract terms among employers of agricultural labor, and the changes in labor contracts from a multiple-year employment agreement to annual, monthly, and even daily payments during the last 200 years of the Tokugawa period; both agricultural and manufacturing employers being forced to tolerate increasingly "unruly and disobedient employees"[35] in an effort to retain their services; the increasing inability of the samurai class to offer competitive wages to their servants; and complaints of merchants in the nineteenth century that their employees were becoming disloyal because higher wages alone were enough to make employees leave their present employers.[36]

However, the most eloquent evidence to date of an increasingly fluid and competitive labor market is found in Hayami's calculation of the average duration of employment for agricultural *hōkōnin* hired on annual contracts in eight Kanto villages. Hayami's results showed that the average duration of employment was 6.8 years for the period between 1651 and 1675 and then steadily declined to 2.2 years by the period 1701-1725. This, however, was not the end of the visible trend because the average duration fell by the period 1826-1850 to a mere 1.1 years, only slightly longer than the usual minimum contracted.[37]

The preceding discussion by no means suggests that direct evidence for a rising standard of living for wage earners and peasants is totally absent, as there exists a fair amount of wage data and descriptions noting—explicitly or implicitly—an improvement in the living standard. Much of this evidence is found in the writings of Japanese economic historians, often those who are strongly committed to the Marxist interpretation of the Tokugawa economy. These writers usually explain the contradiction between their thesis of increasing misery and their evidence of a rising living standard by arguing that the rising taxes and the famines quickly negated all signs of improved living standards and that the higher living standard was enjoyed only by a select group of the rural rich.

Here, let us cite evidence of a rising living standard from regions that will not be examined in the following chapters. First, T. C. Smith, in concluding his study on by-employments, wrote:

> Contemporaries in the latter half of the Tokugawa period were aware that trade and industry were growing and living standards among the farm population improving, and some observers explicitly linked these trends to by-employments. An Akita headman wrote in 1825 that some sixty years ago his father had begun raising silk-worms, the first person in his village to do so; after some years of technical failure his operation became highly profitable and others followed his lead. At the time of writing he could say: "Every family in the village without exception works at sericulture in the intervals of farming, thereby earning more income."[38]

And in describing the economy of Tokugawa Japan in the 1860s, he added the following which, in its tone, contrasts sharply with the dismal view of the last decades of the Tokugawa economy presented by many Japanese scholars:

> It would probably be a mistake to think of Tokugawa Japan as a very poor country, even by contemporary European stand-

ards. Western observers during the second half of the Tokugawa period were widely impressed by the amount of travel and shipping they saw, the condition of the main roads, the variety and abundance of goods for sale, the state of technology (though not of science), the spread of literacy, the size and public order of towns and cities, the excellence of farming, and the general well-being of the population. Even as late as the 1860's Sir Rutherford Alcock, an acute observer by no means blind to the faults of the Japanese, who thought their officials were deficient in moral sense and their painting and music laughable, had high praise for the economy.[39]

Among Japanese scholars, Hayami and Sano, both of Keio University, present us with useful quantitative examinations of wages. Hayami, on the basis of his examination of the wages of the *hōkōnin*, which we have referred to earlier, concluded that the real wage level of these persons in Kanto villages rose steadily after the Genroku period. In his own words: "The price of rice and the prices of other goods undoubtedly rose between the beginning of the seventeenth century and the early nineteenth century, but not by as much as did wages. . . . The *hōkōnin* enjoyed better conditions."[40] Sano, who examined the wages of construction workers in Edo and the cost of living index for the period between 1830 and 1894, clearly demonstrated that the real wages of construction workers rose during the last decades of the Tokugawa period.[41] The fact that these careful studies are ignored by most Japanese economic historians is indicative of the strength of the traditional view of the Tokugawa economy.

Much quantitative evidence on rising wages and incomes is found in case studies and local histories, which usually consist of a comparison of data over a few years, or over several decades within a small geographical area, or for a specific type of person. But when they are examined and considered *in toto*, they convey the unmistakable fact that real wages were rising and that the income of the peasants was increasing throughout the Tokugawa period, including the supposedly stagnating latter half. In Chapters Five through Seven we will present some of these data.

Also useful in demonstrating the improving living standards of the majority of the Tokugawa peasants are the repeatedly issued Bakufu and *han* decrees prohibiting "luxurious" expenditures by the peasants. Local histories contain example after example of sumptuary decrees, and the frequency of their issue was clearly on the increase during the latter half of the Tokugawa period. These include: detailed restrictions on the size and methods for constructing peasant dwellings (Kanazawa *han*, 1668); restrictions on clothing and household furniture (Sendai *han*, 1677); restrictions on the types of lumber that could be used for building farm houses (Aizu *han*, 1711); restrictions on matting and other "luxuries" for furnishing peasant houses (Fukuoka *han*, 1733, 1760, 1769); restrictions on rainwear and footgear for those aged less than 70 (Shōnai *han*, 1812); restrictions on the type of cloth to be used for kimono and on colors (limiting them to inexpensive dyeing processes) (Ogaki *han*, 1829); restrictions on clothing, prohibitions of ivory and silver in women's hair ornaments (Kishiwada *han*, 1765); and the prohibition of "overly decorative clothing," gold, silver and ivory decorations, and foods "which are beyond those fitting their station in life" (Yanaga *han*, 1735, 1776).[12]

Topping all these decrees, however, was the one issued in 1788 to local magistrates by one of the highest-ranked Bakufu officials, Matsudaira Sadanobu, which read:

> For long it has been the custom among peasants to wear simple clothing and tie their hair with straw. However, of late, they have become accustomed to luxuries and forgetful of their status. They wear clothing befitting those of higher status and use oil and *motoyui* [made usually of cloth] to tie their hair. They now use umbrellas and *kappa* [raincoats made of waterproof cloth] in the rain instead of straw hats and *mino* [rain covers made of straw]. As expenses rise because of all this, villages decline and people leave the villages. . . . The peasants should at no time forget their station in life. For peasants to engage in trade or for villages to have hairdressers is to be disrespectful. Henceforth, all luxuries should be avoided by the peasants. They are to live simply and devote themselves to farming.[13]

Despite these admonitions, the peasants went on to acquire more goods than their fathers had. Ogyū Sorai (1666-1728) was clearly opposed to what he saw as an "increase in consumers which has come about because there are no regulative institutions." As an example he pointed out that the country people who migrated to Edo stopped wearing home-woven hemp and cotton garments and eating inferior grains and began to "eat *miso*, warm themselves at wood-burning fires, buy clothes to wear, drink fine *sake*, and equip their houses with *shōji*, covered ceilings, . . . tatami mats and mosquito nets which they did not have in the country."[44] Had Sorai seen Japanese life a century later he would have been sure he was witnessing the demise of society as he felt it should be: not only were commoners copying the life of their betters in the cities but—even in the rural villages of Okayama, for example—people were buying perfumes, cosmetics, candies, linen, and furniture and other goods imported from other domains throughout the islands.[45]

CHAPTER FIVE

The Kinai

THE SETTING FOR ECONOMIC GROWTH

The Kinai refers to the region composed of the five *kuni* or provinces of Izumi, Kawachi, Settsu, Yamashiro, and Yamato. It is not large; a circle twenty-five miles in diameter drawn around Osaka encompasses 85 to 90 percent of four of the five *kuni* and about 40 percent of Yamato, the more developed and urbanized part. Here, we will limit our discussion to this small circle, which includes the ancient capitals of Nara and Kyoto and excludes the mountainous part of Yamato.

Despite its size, the economic importance of the Kinai in Tokugawa Japan is beyond dispute. Because the region included the Imperial residence for nearly a millennium before the appearance of the Tokugawa Shogunate, and because it is blessed with fertile plains, ready access to the sea, highly developed networks for river and land transportation, and a mild climate, the Kinai by 1600 was economically far advanced in comparison to the other regions of Japan. While Edo was no more than a fishing village in the late sixteenth century, Kyoto, Nara, Sakai, and many smaller urban centers of the region had seen centuries of commercial and agricultural development, and Osaka had grown rapidly during this century. By 1600 the Kinai contained the largest enclave of highly urbanized and commercialized centers of economic activity. It contained the most developed economic institutions and transportation facilities, the highest agricultural productivity, the most skilled manpower to produce the most advanced processed and handicraft goods, and a sizable and economically responsive merchant class.

No less important in characterizing the course of economic growth in the region is the fact that during the Tokugawa period the Kinai consisted of highly fragmented administrative units. About half of the Kinai was *tenryō* land ruled directly by the Bakufu, while the other half was shared by about two dozen daimyo. The *tenryō*, which were scattered about in the region, consisted of Osaka, small urbanized centers, and numerous fiefs given to *hatamoto* (the direct retainers of the Shogun). All of the daimyo domains were small. Nearly a dozen of them were only 10,000 *koku* in *omotedaka* (officially assessed yield), the minimum required for daimyo status, and only a few were as large as 50,000 *koku*. The only domain larger than this was assessed at 74,000 *koku*, but this domain, like the other large fiefs in the region, consisted of scattered holdings: seven oddly shaped areas surrounded by *tenryō* and the holdings of other daimyo. So fragmented was the landholding in the Kinai that a few villages were administered by, and paid taxes to, as many as half a dozen overlords consisting of *hatamoto*, *daikan* (who administered the *tenryō*), and daimyo.[1]

The relative economic importance of the Kinai at the beginning of the Tokugawa period is easily documented. According to the *Kefukigusa*, compiled in 1638 by Matsue Shigeyori, an innkeeper and poet who listed "all the famous local products" in Japan, there were 1,807 well-known products traded interregionally. Of the total, 706, or slightly under 40 percent, were produced in the Kinai alone, compared to the remainder, which were produced by the sixty-one other *kuni*. Matsue attributed 437 items to Yamashiro (which included Kyoto), 126 to Settsu, 72 to Yamato, 43 to Izumi, and 28 to Kawachi (which included Osaka). Among the 706 Kinai items, 132 were "household goods," 124 could be termed arts and crafts, another 124 were agricultural products, and the remaining 326 items were in the following categories: cloth (91), medicine (47), forest products (46), marine products (41), mineral and animal products (35), armor and military equipment (26), "tools used for the production of goods" (26), fuels (13), and "other" (1).[2]

The dominance of Yamashiro was, of course, due to Kyoto, which alone accounted for 287 items. As the city of emperors, court nobles, and many powerful warriors who had large economic resources at their disposal, Kyoto had developed the ability to supply numerous goods in response to the demand on the city's merchants and artisans by its residents.

ECONOMIC GROWTH DURING
THE SEVENTEENTH CENTURY

With the establishment of a peaceful and stable government under the Tokugawa Bakufu, the people in the Kinai began vigorously to exploit the substantial advantages of the region to achieve rapid growth in commerce and manufacturing in the seventeenth century. While the Kinai's advantages at the starting line were decisive factors in the economic growth achieved during this century, growth was even further accelerated by the establishment of new coastal shipping routes and the conscious Bakufu policy to develop Osaka as "the kitchen of Tokugawa Japan," the largest entrepôt of commerce.

Before the shipping routes were established, limitations imposed by the modes of transportation had, in effect, created a bottleneck for the further growth of commerce. For example, rice shipped from the province of Kaga or Echizen, two prominent rice-producing provinces on the Sea of Japan, first had to be sent by sea to Tsuruga or Obama and then some twenty miles by land to the northern shores of Lake Biwa. From there boats carried the rice to Otsu and finally down the Yodo River to Osaka. Thus, when a regular shipping route was opened in 1624 to serve the Osaka–Edo trade, and another regular route was established in 1672 to facilitate the trade between the northern provinces facing the coast of the Sea of Japan and Osaka, the bottleneck was broken, giving the Kinai, especially Osaka with its excellent natural harbor, direct access both to rice and other goods produced in all parts of Japan and to the rapidly growing Edo market. The importance of these sea routes to the growth of the Kinai region, as well as to the nation as a whole, was incalculable because the services of the ships on these routes cost significantly less than earlier methods of transportation. The increasing speed of ships, the establishment of warehousing services, and improved scheduling to avoid sending less than full loads further contributed to the growth of trade, especially in the Kinai.[3]

Another significant factor in Osaka's growth was the policy adopted by the Bakufu toward this city and its satellites. Although there were some exceptions, the policy prior to the Kyōhō period (1716-1735) was basically laissez-faire. The Bakufu and the daimyo in the region did impose various restrictions and encouraged the organization of wholesalers' guilds for taxing purposes, especially during the latter half of the seventeenth century, but the measures adopted were of limited consequence compared to the meddlesome and growth-inhibiting policies of the post-Kyōhō years. In fact, during the early decades of the Tokugawa period, both the Bakufu and the daimyo in the Kinai actively encouraged competition among merchants. Indications of the Bakufu's desire to encourage the growth of Osaka include generally light taxes on merchants and the abolition in 1634 of the land tax on residents of the Osaka *tenryō*. At the time of abolition the annual tax amounted to 178,934 *momme* of silver (or nearly 30,000 *ryō*), and thus its abolition was no minor favor bestowed on the residents but had a significant effect on the growth of commerce.[4]

The merchants responded quickly to the rapidly growing volume of commerce in Osaka. The *kuni-donya* (wholesalers for a province), who dealt in all goods supplied by a specific domain or a region, were gradually replaced by more efficient *tonya* (or *toiya*, wholesalers who specialized by commodity). By the 1670s there were 378 *tonya* covering fifty-four commodities, and the number increased to 5,655 *tonya* dealing in eighty-one commodities by the beginning of the eighteenth century. Part of this increase resulted from the Bakufu policy of encouraging the *tonya* system, but the major impetus for its rapidity came from the increasing volume of trade.[5] Crawcour noted the rapidly changing commercial patterns of the century:

> By about the 1650's, most *han* put the management of their Osaka warehouses into the hands of Osaka merchants, who were then known as *kuramoto*. They usually acted as financial agents (*gin-kakeya*) also and received a salary and various social and economic privileges. When the Osaka banking system was organized in 1670, most of the ten members of the controlling group (*junin ryōgae*) were active as *kuramoto* and/or *kakeya* for the various *han*. None seems to have been prominent before the beginning of the Tokugawa period.[6]

Most indicative of the ability of Osaka to develop highly sophisticated institutional arrangements to facilitate trade and to reduce transaction costs (i.e., costs of doing business) was the appearance of a market for *kome-kitte* (rice-notes) in 1654. Osaka merchants started to use these notes, originally issued as receipts for rice received by warehouses,[7] as cash. And very soon these notes came to be traded by the rice merchants who speculated on the price of rice.

The Kinai villages and towns also changed rapidly as Osaka, the pivot of Tokugawa commerce, grew. While the commanding position this city achieved in the Tokugawa economy owed much to its "rich hinterland"[8] with its ability to produce goods to meet the needs of a growing metropolis, the stimulating effects of trade emanating from Osaka were also a crucial force in transforming the economy of the Kinai. The first visible response took the form of an increase in the acreage planted in cotton, which was already a significant amount by the Sengoku period. A survey made by Yagi of fourteen villages in Settsu, Kawachi, Izumi, and Yamato shows that land allocated to cotton ranged between a low of 20.6 percent to a high of 61.8 percent of total paddy and upland during various periods in the seventeenth century and early decades of the eighteenth.[9] Hayama wrote of a village in Kawachi:

> Though under various restrictions imposed by the Bakuhan system, changes in the agricultural production of Yota village followed the pattern of agricultural villages around Osaka— a trend towards the commercialization of their output. It was not a basically autarkic village which sold limited amounts of surplus. The economic base of this village, if one is to characterize it in simple terms, was goods, mostly cotton, produced for the market. . . . Thirty percent of its paddy and 90 percent of its upland were allocated to cotton by the 1660s and 1670s.[10]

No less visible than the response of the cotton industry was that of the *sake* industry, which in fact led the steadily growing industries in the region. As the demand for *sake* for local consumption rose, reflecting the buoyant economic conditions, the *sake* producers in Kyoto, Ikeda, Itami, and Osaka also found that the demand for their product from Edo and other parts of the nation was rapidly increasing. The well-known superiority of their product helped, but the crucial factors underlying the rise of demand from more distant regions were the sharply reduced costs of transportation, the dependability of shipments, and the cost advantages arising out of economies of scale in production.[11]

By the mid-seventeenth century the *sake* industry had expanded into the *zaigō-chō* (smaller urban centers that "emerged within one or two *ri* of each other")[12] and more and more of the wealthier villagers themselves began to enter the industry. By the end of the century it was not uncommon to find establishments in Settsu,

95

Kawachi, and Yamashiro employing up to 300 men.[13] And, at the turn of the eighteenth century, up to 230,400 *koku* (approximately 11 million gallons) of *sake* were shipped annually to Edo alone.[14]

Another industry worthy of special attention was the processing of oil from cotton and rapeseed. More than 20 percent of the upland in the Kinai was planted in rapeseed, and the region became the leading oil producing center, processing both the rapeseed and cottonseed from its own region and from western Japan. The Bakufu had originally prohibited the planting of rapeseed in uplands in the Kinai because of its desire to maintain a grain-based economy and because taxes on grain were easier to meter than on other cash crops. But the demand for rapeseed oil expanded so fast that in 1643 the Bakufu reversed its policy and began actively to encourage the cultivation of rapeseed in order to moderate the rapidly rising price of lamp oil in Edo.[15]

Close behind cotton, *sake*, and oil in output were soy sauce, vegetables, tobacco, cloth, and myriads of handicrafts and processed agricultural products, which were produced in ever-increasing quantities throughout the seventeenth century. A list made of the major products shipped from Osaka at the beginning of the eighteenth century included, in order of magnitude, *sake*, soy sauce, vegetable oils, cotton cloth and batting, rice, charcoal, fish oil, and salt.[16]

Increases in the living standard, in labor mobility, and in agricultural productivity accompanied the growth of commerce and the commercialization of agriculture. As few would contest this statement when applied to the seventeenth century, let us present here only a few observations, to stress how conditions improved during this century. For example, after intensive examination of a village in Settsu, Shimbō concluded:

> Commercial crops were cultivated and agricultural productivity rose by means of an intensive application of labor. While productivity rose, the amount of tax paid to lords remained virtually unchanged. This meant that the tax burden on peasants declined and a surplus was increasing in the hands of the peasants.[17]

Because of the policies of the Bakufu, the relative lack of political power and administrative ability of the small daimyo, and the known rapid progress of agricultural techniques in this region, this statement would undoubtedly apply to most of the villages in the same region.

With regard to the mobility of labor, Nakabe noted on the basis of her study of villages in Settsu and Kawachi that:

During the Kambun period [1661-1672], large cities and smaller rural and castle towns such as Yodo, Toba, Fushimi, and Takatsuki developed rapidly to form a part of the commercial structure corresponding to the formation of the Bakuhan system. A large number of persons was absorbed by these cities and towns.[18]

Her evidence for this was the difficulty that the samurai class and temples experienced in finding servants "because of their inability to compete with the higher wages" offered by merchant houses, *sake* makers, and rapeseed processors in towns and cities. As far as she could determine, the surplus labor in the villages surrounding these cities and towns had virtually disappeared by the end of the century. The Bakufu and the *han* that officially prohibited the free mobility of peasants apparently chose not to, or were unable to, enforce this policy.

The effects of new employment opportunities and higher wages offered in Osaka and other urban centers and the Bakufu's non-enforcement of antimigration measures were evident in the population data of these cities. According to Arai, Osaka's population rose from 279,000 in 1625 to 360,000 in 1699; Sakudo and Takenaka believe that the population of Sakai rose from between 18,000 and 30,000 in 1532 to approximately 69,300 by 1665. Though no reliable estimates are available for Kyoto, few would question that its population also rose substantially until the second decade of the eighteenth century, when it was probably over 350,000.[19]

Though our discussion of the Kinai economy in the seventeenth century has been brief, when it is read together with numerous Japanese sources that are nearly unanimous in their description of a buoyant Kinai economy at that time, hopefully it leaves little doubt that the economy, stimulated by and in turn stimulating the rapid growth of commerce, reaped increasing gains from commerce, from improved economic institutions, and from the increased productivity of labor.

ECONOMIC GROWTH AFTER 1700

The trends of economic growth in both agriculture and the manufacturing sectors discussed in the preceding section continued throughout the remainder of the Tokugawa period. In the rural towns and villages, the commercialization of agriculture and commercial and manufacturing activities continued to increase, thus requiring more and more labor for cultivating and processing commercial crops.[20] As more peasants engaged in commerce and manufacturing on a part- or full-time basis, the amount of labor available for working the land was reduced. And the increased demand for labor within the rural towns and villages reduced the supply of labor to Osaka and other urban centers, with the effect of forcing urban employers to pay higher wages just to retain a declining absolute number of skilled and seasonal workers. In short, urban employers were finding it difficult to compete for labor because rural manufacturing and commercial establishments, growing larger and more efficient, could offer wages attractive enough to keep the labor for their needs, and because many people preferred to work in or near their villages on a part-time basis in order to make the best use of their labor throughout the year. That is, a combined return for their labor used in agriculture and in by-employments promised a larger total income than what could be earned in urban employment because landholders, who were also forced to compete for labor, offered improved terms of contract to tenant cultivators, and wage levels in by-employments were rising.

While rural commerce and manufacturing grew in size to realize economies of scale and compete more successfully in wresting away the urban merchants' customers in other provinces and in Kinai towns and villages, economic activities in urban centers steadily declined. In contrast to the rural areas, which enjoyed a growing effective demand from the large number of villagers, the urban economy suffered from a stagnant or even declining demand from urban residents (especially from samurai whose incomes failed to rise), from the declining population in urban centers, and from the Bakufu's vacillating policies, which finally sacrificed the interests of the urban guilds in favor of the rural competitors.

The continuing growth of rural commerce and manufacturing made labor scarce, first in outlying towns and then even in the villages. As wages of both day-laborers and contract labor rose further, as tenants received reductions in rent from the landholders, and as the opportunity costs of both the land and own labor of owner cultivators rose, resources in rural areas were used more efficiently than ever before. The size of the unit farmed was rationalized to maximize the returns to the land, and labor, combining various opportunities to realize the highest total income, was more fully used, with the result that total output and per capita income in rural areas continued to rise. Effective demand, as a consequence, rose further, stimulating economic activities in these areas. And an important factor behind all these developments, of course, was the continued scarcity of labor, which is suggested by the slight decline in total population in rural Kinai.

IMPROVEMENTS IN AGRICULTURAL METHODS

Faced with an increasing demand and the rigors of the market, which stimulated the more efficient use of resources, agricultural productivity in both commercial crops and rice increased during the latter half of the Tokugawa period. Though we cannot quantify the contributions made by each factor involved in rises in productivity, we can identify the factors: (1) the availability of a larger variety of seeds bearing higher yields and with variable growing seasons; (2) increased knowledge of rotation; (3) increased knowledge of the use of fertilizers; (4) better preparation of the soil; and (5) improved agricultural tools and irrigation technology. Let us briefly elaborate on how each of these factors contributed to productivity increases.

First, in the Kinai region, the number of varieties of seeds increased to more than 200 by the end of the Tokugawa period. The variety available was significant because:

Peasants chose seeds to increase and stabilize yields. It was important to select seeds which were resilient against unseasonable coldness or insects. . . . Many peasants used a large number of varieties of seeds, that is, chose seeds to distribute risks of yield fluctuations, to distribute labor [more efficiently over a

99

longer planting and harvesting period], and to plant seeds which were most suitable to the types of soils. For example, one Okamoto family, peasants in Kami-Kawarabayashi village in Settsu, planted in 1717 seeds named Kokkoku, Shirakawa, Denpōmichi, Koki-Ishikawa, Ise-Miyage, Yori-Ise, Kogane-mochi, Miyosasuri, etc., but a hundred years later in 1829, this family was planting entirely different seeds. By the Bakumatsu period, the seeds called Ippon-ho and Hodoyoshi, best known for their high yields, had appeared around Osaka. Hodoyoshi was a variety which was later improved and called Shinriki.[21]

As labor became more difficult to obtain in most Kinai villages during the latter half of the Tokugawa period, especially during the planting and harvesting times "when labor costs rose by as much as one-third,"[22] the planting of both early- and later-maturing seeds was economical for farmers, who by doing so could get along with less hired labor because of staggered peak periods. The early-maturing varieties were especially important because household labor could be used to harvest these varieties of rice and after that plant the winter wheat, thus enabling farmers to reduce their hired labor.[23] The region as a whole profited from these seed varieties because the more efficient use of labor in agriculture released labor for other economic activities. Similar improvements occurred in cotton seed varieties as well and were quite rapidly disseminated. As with rice, it was the "better-off peasants who eagerly worked" to improve seeds in order to obtain larger yields.[24]

Knowledge of crop rotation also made steady progress.[25] The following is an example of advice for peasants planting cotton:

> If land is to be used for cotton, the best results are obtained by planting soybeans first and then following with cotton. However, the yield is even better if the soybean–cotton rotation is followed by a year of soybean–rice rotation. . . . If you plant radishes, the cotton tends to have too many offshoots and the yield declines. The planting of wheat before cotton is not advised because it tends to diminish the size of the stalks of the cotton and causes the yield to fall.[26]

Contemporary manuals clearly show that the Tokugawa farmers were experimenting with and adopting new methods of rotation that led to larger yields, and then disseminating their new techniques.[27]

More was also learned about more effective use of fertilizers. In cotton planting, "unlike during the first half of the Tokugawa period when composts and the manure of draft animals and humans were mainly used, during the second half when the knowledge of cotton planting had progressed, more and more fertilizers made of dried fish were used."[28] In Settsu, for example:

Fertilizing began with what one called stick-fertilizing, that is, a hole with a depth of one or two *sun* was made near the roots of the cotton plants every five *sun*, and into the holes pinches of pulverized dried fish or *aburakasu* [rapeseed from which the oil had been extracted] were placed by hand. Then, about 14 or 15 days later, a shallow ditch was made by a plow near the root of the plant, and fertilizers diluted by water were poured into it. The ditch had to be covered immediately. This was called covered fertilizing and the process was repeated again in mid-summer. If it was delayed too long, only the leaves and stems of the cotton grew and the yield was much lower.[29]

In summing up the importance of fertilizers, Furushima, a leading scholar on Tokugawa agricultural techniques, wrote: "The development of agricultural techniques centered around the uses of various types of fertilizers."[30]

Methods of soil preparation also improved as farmers began to realize the desirability of deep cultivation. The necessity of proper irrigation and drainage was stressed in many agricultural pamphlets circulated by the mid-eighteenth century. Some of the advice was detailed, reflecting the knowledge accumulated over time. A pamphlet on cotton planting reads:

From about December, cultivate both sides of the growing stalks of wheat and place there some straw and ashes to soften and enrich the soil. . . . Plant the seeds on the east side of the wheat to reduce the damage to seedlings due to lack of water. . . . Draw air into the soil in winter to kill possible insects and fill the holes made for that purpose with ash.[31]

All aspects of rice culture were taken up by the "three agricultural scholars," Miyasaki Yasusada (1623-1697), Okura Nagatsune

(1768-1844), and Sato Nobuhiro (1769-1850), who seem to have had an inexhaustible supply of advice to the peasants.[32]

Though the Kinai region is credited with the invention of a device to raise water using a series of buckets or a pump (a series of loosely fitting pieces of wood within a wooden or bamboo pipe, and called the *fumiguruma* or *hebiguruma*), increases in the variety and efficiency of agricultural implements as a whole were the result of a nationwide effort. The major innovations of the second half of the Tokugawa period included: (1) the *senba-koki*, a tool to separate the tassels or the grains from the stalks. A dozen or so "teeth" made mostly of iron and sometimes of wood were mounted on a frame (*senba* literally means a thousand teeth); (2) the *sengoku-tōshi* and *mangoku-tōshi*, wooden implements that combined a hand-operated fan and a container that slowly released the threshed rice. The implements separated the grain from the chaff (*sengoku* and *mangoku* mean 1,000 and 10,000 *koku* respectively); (3) the *karausu*, a tool made of baked earth and used in separating husks from grain; and (4) a variety of weeding and cultivating plows, including the famous Bitchū-*guwa*.

The *senba-koki*, "which was invented in response to the labor shortage which developed during the early decades of the eighteenth century," increased the productivity of labor "by at least ten-fold." Because the efficiency of the new tool deprived widows of an important source of income by taking over tasks they had formerly done, it was often referred to as the *goke-taoshi* (the widow killer). The *sengoku-tōshi* and *mangoku-tōshi*, both invented during the 1680s, also increased the productivity of labor "by ten-fold" and the *karausu* enabled a farmer to thresh "4 *koku* instead of 1 as before."[33] The Bitchū-*guwa*, used nationwide by the mid-eighteenth century, were iron plows with two, three, or four prongs, depending on the specific tasks they performed. The most important contribution of this innovation was that this family of plows made it possible to cultivate the soil more deeply with less effort. As the name indicates, this tool was first used in Bitchū (Okayama).[34]

Advances made in irrigation and water control technology during the latter half of the Tokugawa period were also substantial. The well-known *Kōka Shunjū* written by Tsuchiya Matasaburo at the beginning of the eighteenth century reveals that many aspects of technical knowledge related to the damming and distribution of water had changed during the author's own lifetime. As the century progressed, the engineering skills for cutting channels and changing the course of even the larger rivers improved, and the variety of pipes, ducts, and locks rose to meet varying needs under diverse circumstances. Large rivers could now be dammed, and people could depend on water from upstream for irrigating large areas of paddy.[35]

Though no time series data for any large area exist to demonstrate how much these factors raised agricultural productivity, some scattered quantitative evidence may be useful in demonstrating that low rice yields did rise over time. Records kept by the Okamoto family in Settsu show that "during the mid- and late Tokugawa periods when as much as 40 to 50 percent of their total agricultural expenditures were allocated to fertilizers," such as dried sardines, oil cakes, and the ashes from rice straw, their yield per *tan* of rice rose from 0.85 *koku* in the early decades of the seventeenth century to 1.39 *koku* by mid-century, 1.96 *koku* in the 1770s, 2.17 *koku* in the period 1789-1806, and 2.23 *koku* in the 1820s. Takeyasu cites the records of a village in Kawachi where the per *tan* yield of rice averaged 2.8 *koku* during the period 1806-1867, with a high of 2.88 *koku* achieved in 1865.[36] Despite the paucity of quantitative evidence, most Japanese economic historians agree that agricultural productivity in the Kinai led the nation, which as a whole had attained by the end of the Tokugawa period the rice yield per acre reached by most Southeast Asian farmers only a century later.[37]

THE LABOR SHORTAGE AND ITS EFFECTS

What stimulated the improvement in agricultural methods more than anything else was the shortage of labor that resulted from the continued growth of both commercial agriculture and a variety of manufacturing and commercial activities in rural Kinai. This shortage was first felt in the urban centers but soon affected the rural towns and then the villages. Its effects took two principal forms: a relative decline in manufacturing activities in Osaka and other urban centers and a steady increase in wages and in effective improvements in the terms of contract for tenant cultivators.

Descriptive evidence indicating a shortage of labor in both agriculture and the urban centers is abundant. Since the shortage of labor itself in the Kinai during this period is well established among Japanese specialists (though the consequences of improving terms of contract for tenants and a rising living standard are not), let us cite only a few examples.

By the mid-eighteenth century large landholders in the Kinai were beginning to have serious difficulties in obtaining agricultural labor, and Mori wrote of Arakawa village in Kawachi:

> The disappearance of the landholders who had as much as 70 *koku* was due principally to the difficulties encountered, from the 1740s on, in finding sufficient labor and tenant cultivators. . . . Servants (*hōkōnin*) were difficult to find and wages rose noticeably. Even higher wages were being paid. . . . Servants could not be found and daily labor, whose wages were actually even higher, had to be used. Many parcels of paddy were poorly tended.[38]

Because of the labor shortage, we find that from as early as the mid-eighteenth century, many persons were coming to work in some of the Kinai villages, from both nearby and distant villages and even from as far away as Osaka. Furushima and Nagahara found that in 1769 in a Kawachi village called Nishi-Tsutsumi there were 32 servants, of whom 13 were from their own village, 5 from nearby villages, 10 from Osaka, and 4 from other provinces. This finding, of course, is not surprising given the economic decline of Osaka that had begun by this time.[39] In discussing the cotton-growing villages in Settsu and Kawachi during the last century and a half of the Tokugawa period, Wakita went as far as to say that "for anyone with eyes, increases in wages and the shortage of labor were quite evident."[40] As is clear from the above, labor was even more difficult to obtain or retain in the urban centers when the shortage of labor had become so pervasive in the rural areas.

The *sake* industry examined by Nakabe provides a good example of how the labor shortage was experienced in the cities and, as a consequence, how the leadership of this urban industry shifted to outlying towns. As discussed earlier, Osaka, Ikeda, and Itami were, perhaps in that order, the major producers of *sake* during the seventeenth century. However, Itami grew rapidly during the first half of the eighteenth century and began to outproduce both Osaka and Ikeda. Then Itami, in turn, was challenged during the last century of the Tokugawa period by the three districts of Nada in Settsu. Nakabe emphasized the importance of the cost of labor as an explanation for the difficulties faced by Itami:

> Because *sake* was made during the winter . . . labor was recruited from distant stagnating villages which had labor to export during the winter. The polishing of rice necessary for *sake* making was done by villagers from around Itami. However, as cotton processing, the extraction of vegetable oils, and other by-employments increased, a labor shortage occurred and the wages of rice polishers rose sharply. They rose by 40 percent between the Kyōhō and the Kan'en periods [1716-1750].[11]

This increase in wages reduced the competitive ability of Itami, and its *sake* output declined relative to that of Nada. Thus, by the 1840s Itami, despite its better-quality water, "was overwhelmed" by the Nada *sake*-producing districts, which could still count on a supply of labor from the surrounding villages.[42] Not only were the establishments in Nada large and competitive in size[43] but they also were aided by their proximity to the Rokko mountains, which enabled them to harness water power to economize on labor, and to the nearby port of Hyōgo, which was able to supply the rice needed for *sake* making at a competitive price. Nada, which in 1793 had 141 *sake* makers, had 161 by 1837. While only 69 of 141 in 1793 produced 1,000 *koku* per year, 138 of 161 in 1837 were producing over 1,000 *koku*. And the number of establishments producing over 5,000 *koku* increased from 1 to 7 between 1793 and 1837.[44]

Other industries in urban centers also followed the path of gradual decline. As the works by Kobayashi and Wakita in Japanese and by Hauser in English have shown in detail,[45] strong pressure, including a widespread protest movement against the restrictive policies of the urban merchants, brought about a change in Bakufu policy toward rural industry. This change in policy, together with rising wages and the growth of wholesalers and larger establishments, led to a shift from urban centers to outlying towns and even villages in the economic leadership of the processing and trading in cotton, rapeseed, and other products. In the rural areas where "raw material and labor were more easily had" and where "no special disadvantage existed in trading with other provinces," increasingly large rural entrepreneurs could not be prevented from taking the leadership away from their disadvantaged counterparts in Osaka and other urban centers.[46]

Evidence that labor moved in search of higher wages, causing a decrease in the population of urban centers and towns, can also be found in population data gathered by several Japanese scholars. Nakabe estimated that, while Osaka's population grew from 279,-000 to 501,000 between 1625 and 1743, it began to fall as the economic fortunes of Osaka began to ebb. A steady decline in population continued from the mid-eighteenth century. By 1862 its population was only 301,000, which meant a drop of about 40 percent in a little over a century.[47]

Sasaki's recent study of Tennōji village in Settsu is most revealing of the pattern of labor mobility in Kinai. As shown in Table 5.1, the population of this village (adjacent to Osaka and incorporated into it after the Meiji Restoration) rose, though unevenly, up until 1806. Then the trend was downward during the first half of the nineteenth century. The number of the *genan* (male servants) and *gejo* (female servants), mostly employed by households engaged in cotton processing, was significantly larger before 1831, after which it fell rapidly.[48] This pattern, closely resembling what happened in Osaka, simply reflected the economic fortunes of Tennōji village, which was decreasingly able to compete against the cotton processors in villages further removed from Osaka and other urban centers.

Tsuda's work reveals similar mobility trends for the town of Hirano between 1704 and 1858. The town was located about ten miles southeast of Osaka, and Hirano had long been, even in pre-Tokugawa days, an important crossroads with ready access to the Yamato River. The population data, gathered from *yosechō* (records of data collected on households and population), reveals that the town had its largest population during the early decades of the eighteenth century, but after 1732 both the population and the number of households declined sharply. (See Table 5.2.) Tsuda found that the drop of 15 percent in population between 1732 and 1747 was due to increasing competition from emerging rural towns, and another sharp decline of similar magnitude between 1767 and 1797 was due to "the change in the course of the Yamato River and increasing competition in cotton marketing

Table 5.1
Demographic Data for Tennōji

Year	Total Population (1)	Genan and Gejo (2)	Index of (1) 1751 = 100 (3)
1751	446	64	100.0
1754	574	73	128.5
1755	619	77	138.8
1756	588	58	131.8
1757	608	58	136.3
1765	559	61	125.3
1766	567	66	127.1
1767	574	64	128.7
1784	640	87	143.7
1785	640	80	143.5
1788	623	87	139.7
1795	657	93	147.3
1797	655	84	146.9
1798	669	91	150.0
1802	659	87	147.8
1805	749	87	167.9
1806	755	84	163.3
1816	630	72	141.3
1817	624	71	139.9
1831	525	65	117.7
1834	584	31	130.9
1837	528	26	118.4
1838	451	23	101.1
1840	521	23	116.8
1843	454	16	101.8
1845	482	24	108.1
1847	482	19	108.1
1848	485	10	108.7
1849	464	8	104.0
1850	472	10	105.8
1851	478	10	107.2
1852	476	12	106.7
1854	460	11	103.1
1855	438	7	98.2
1856	457	8	102.5
1858	451	5	101.1

and processing from other areas." The total number of the *genin* and *gejo* from outside Hirano also fell steadily from 195 in 1764 to only 5 in 1861.[49]

A study on labor mobility made by Matsuura using *shūmon-aratame-chō* from the village of Hanakuma in Settsu also reveals a pattern of population movement congruent with the patterns

Table 5.2
Demographic Data for Hirano
(index: 1704 = 100)

Year	Town Population	No. of Households in Town
1704	7,936 (100)	2,257
1706	9,210 (116)	2,375
1708	9,099 (115)	2,371
1721	9,029 (114)	2,359
1726	9,222 (116)	2,397
1732	9,003 (114)	2,544
1747	7,827 (99)	2,059
1748	7,888 (100)	2,063
1756	7,946 (100)	2,118
1759	7,965 (100)	n.a.
1761	8,072 (102)	n.a.
1764	7,933 (100)	n.a.
1767	7,986 (101)	n.a.
1797	6,781 (85)	n.a.
1799	6,787 (85)	1,628
1826	6,141 (77)	1,448
1829	6,178 (78)	1,463
1832	6,248 (79)	1,426
1836	6,249 (79)	1,407
1846	6,278 (79)	1,471
1850	6,551 (83)	1,491
1853	6,512 (82)	1,427
1855	6,604 (83)	n.a.
1858	6,700 (84)	1,443

Source: Calculated from Tsuda Hideo, *Hōken shakai kaitai katei kenkyū josetsu* (An introduction to the study of the process of the disintegration of a feudal society) (Tokyo. Hanawa Shobō, 1970), pp. 266-267, 280-281.

seen in the preceding studies.[50] During the period 1792-1868, this village, adjacent to the highly urbanized port of Hyōgo and relatively close to Osaka, was slowly losing its population. The population dropped from about 290 in 1794 to a low around 230 during the 1840s and had climbed back to around 250 only by 1864. (See Figure 5.1.) For most of the period studied the death rate was higher than the birth rate. The death rate was counterbalanced in the years 1792-1825 by a balance of only nine more in-migrants than out-migrants among the population of working age (defined by Matsuura as persons aged 15-50 by Japanese reckoning, i.e., *kazoedoshi*). What slowed the rate of decline in the population from 1826 to 1868 was that in-migrants outnumbered

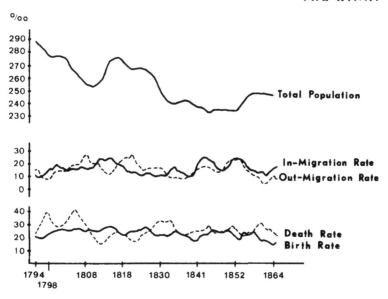

Figure 5.1: The Movement of Total Population, Migration Rates, and Birth and Death Rates in Hanakuma Village. (Source: Matsuura Akira, "Kinsei kōki rōdō idō no ichi keitai," *Shakai Keisai Shigaku*, Vol. 38, No. 6 [February 1973], p. 643.)

out-migrants by forty persons. Many of the migrants were persons who changed their residence either to marry or for adoption, which was often combined with marriage. If we eliminate these from the totals, we find that thirty-two more persons migrated out than came in from 1792 to 1825, but that six more came in than went out from 1826 to 1868. These figures reveal that, prior to 1825, the village proved to be a source of labor for other areas, but during the mid-nineteenth century the village absorbed labor from outside. If the pattern of deaths was at all similar to that found in most Tokugawa villages, then the deaths were most likely among the nonworking population, while the influx of population was among the working, and thus the in-migration was probably not to replace persons who died, but proved to be a net increase to the number of adult workers in the village.

The distribution of places of origin and destinations of migrants in Hanakuma illustrates the general pattern of movement in the

Kinai. In both periods, there is a balance of in-migrants over out-migrants from other places in the same district, from other districts in Settsu, and from other provinces. However, in both periods there is a balance of out-migrants over in-migrants to cities, defined here as Hyōgo, Futatsuchaya, Kobe, and Osaka. And these figures include brides, so that from 1792 to 1825, thirty brides went to urban areas, but only fifteen came from them, and nearly four times as many brides went to cities as came from them between 1826 and 1868. Matsuura concluded that Hanakuma provided a stepping stone for people moving from rural to urban areas, located as it was in the outlying area between the city and countryside. He also found a close correlation between income and mobility: persons with the smallest holdings were the most apt to migrate, and the "main factor of migration was the labor demand in the centers of commerce and industry."[51] We can clearly see the shift in the location of the centers of economic activity through the shift in migration patterns in this village in the late Tokugawa period.

The scarcity of labor in the Kinai economy in the latter half of the Tokugawa period, when labor was apparently highly mobile and productivity was rising, led to a rise in wages and a decline in the effective rents on land. For evidence on the rise in the wage levels, by far the best source is Saitō's work, which is quantitative and which also shows little of the traditional disdain for discussing real wage levels.[52] Though his data are limited to a wage series kept by a village leader in western Settsu for the eighteenth century and various scattered series from other areas immediately surrounding Osaka for the nineteenth century, his work shows clearly that the real wage series (deflated by the price of rice) "continued to rise during the nineteenth century,"[53] was relatively stable during the period 1800-1820, and declined slightly from 1820 to 1868, a period of rampant inflation. The rate of increase in real wages was largest during the period 1730-1770, when the real wage level doubled. The period of most rapid increase in wages was precisely the period when Osaka's population began to decline and when western Settsu villages were increasing their cotton and rapeseed output.

Though the periods covered are shorter, there are many other sources that unmistakably show that the real wage level of agricultural labor in various areas in the Kinai was rising. To cite only the most reliable, we find, first, that Takeyasu discovered in a record kept by a village leader that the wages of daily agricultural labor rose steadily in a cotton-growing village of Kawachi during the nineteenth century. The real wage level also rose as a result of the increasing use of the daily wage to calculate wages, instead of making annual contracts, which had been the prevalent method in the seventeenth century. According to Takeyasu, these data led him to "note anew the relative absence of impoverishment among the daily workers assumed by earlier writers. That is to say, the economic position of daily workers improved as it did for annual workers."[54] Yamasaki discovered, after a careful quantitative examination of wage data in Settsu villages, that real wages rose by about 75 percent between the 1720s and 1820, with more than three-fourths of that increase occurring during the period 1720-1760.[55]

One example of rising wages also demonstrates how dangerous a cursory comparison of wages can be. In Furushima's detailed study of the house records kept by one Imai, a village leader in Kawachi, the author wrote:

> The number employed in 1842 consisted of five male daily laborers, two male employees retained on an annual basis, and four women. The total of eleven persons was considered the equivalent of ten men in the amount of labor performed. The wages for the total hired labor was listed as 800 silver *momme*. . . . This is 80 *momme* per one male labor unit and was the equivalent of the wage paid to the above-average quality of female labor in 1831 . . . the wage must be considered low.[56]

However, a few pages later, Furushima listed additional foods and cash payments made to five daily laborers in 1843:

> But what should be especially noted is 550 *momme* given for pocket money for the daily laborers. Since the wages [800 *momme*] were paid in advance and most likely to the parents of the employees, daily laborers received for themselves an equivalent of 70 percent of the wages which had been paid.[57]

With the food and clothing provided while at work and especially with an additional payment of 550 *momme* of "pocket money" added to them, it clearly is not justified to consider these wages "low." Here we have an example of an employer in a labor-short market who undoubtedly was forced to provide not only daily necessities but pocket money paid directly to the employees in order to obtain and retain labor.

A labor shortage in agriculture should also be reflected in a declining trend for rents charged to tenant cultivators because this was the principal method by which landowners could compete for scarce labor. But, because the majority of Japanese economic historians hold the view that peasants were increasingly exploited, few have examined the changes in effective rent rates, and what studies are available are highly impressionistic and, of course, draw the desired conclusions. It may not be an overstatement to say that the subject was almost taboo for many years.

Fortunately, however, we have for the Kinai Takeyasu's careful study of effective rents.[58] What this study reveals is most significant in rebutting the long-assumed impoverishment of tenant cultivators and in demonstrating that the landowners in Kinai had to compete for labor by offering lower effective rents. Let us follow Takeyasu step by step because of the significance of what he has to say. Based on an examination of the records of nearly two dozen villages in two districts in Kawachi during the second half of the Tokugawa period, Takeyasu stated:

> In reality, the rent was determined on the basis of assessments made annually. This means that the amount of rent recorded [in official village records] and the amount formally agreed upon on signing the tenant contract was not what was paid in fact. . . . The fact that in more than one-half of the villages examined in these two districts such an assessment was made after contracts were signed suggests that, at least after the mid-Tokugawa period, the contracted amount of rent was not paid in most villages examined. Rather, the amount in fact paid was based on an assessed amount which was less than that stipulated in the contract.[59]

But even the assessed rent was not always what was paid:

> The annual assessed rent was the projected rent and it was not necessarily paid in full. There were some arrears, of course. However, even for those who paid, the amount in fact paid could be less than the assessed amount either because of a reduction in the rent base or because of a flat reduction. At times

rent reduced by these means was even further reduced and these additional reductions were given benevolently [by landowners] and were called *yōsha* or *make* [both meaning concessions]. . . . These additional reductions were mostly given individually, but there were cases in which these reductions were given for all tenants in a village as a reward for not falling in arrears.[60]

Takeyasu, who estimated that the actual payment was about 20 percent less than that officially recorded, explained these developments "as an outcome of the constant struggle of tenant cultivators over rent."[61] He also stated that the actual rate was set as "a result of the delicate balance of power between the landholders and the cultivators"[62] as well as by the benevolence of the landholders. While it is easy to understand why Takeyasu, publishing for a Japanese audience, would use these explanations for what he observed,[63] it seems evident that what he uncovered can be best appreciated if we see it as a reflection of pressures on landholders who were increasingly forced to compete with rapidly developing village by-employments for labor.[64] The pressure on landholders continued to mount in the mid-nineteenth century. Takeyasu noted examples of reductions in rent given even when rent was determined on the *jōmen* system (fixed percent of yield without annual assessment) "under which we have long been told no reductions were granted,"[65] and effective reductions through an increased proportion of payment in cash.[66] Takeyasu concluded:

Thus, the fluid character of the rent is generally seen in the reductions given on an annual basis. That the tenant rent was reduced even in 1839, the year of an exceedingly good harvest which was nearly 3 *koku* per *tan* in some villages, leads us to conclude that the reductions in rent occurred without relation to reality [the actual yield of the year]. This indicates that tenant rent functioned as a barometer of the competitive relationship existing between the landowners and the tenants.[67]

Regrettably, numerous other studies on tenant rents are orthodox in approach and of little use for our purpose. However, if we consider officially registered rent as a proxy for the effective rent (and we are justified in doing so if we accept only downward changes as evidence of decline), then we are able to find evidence

113

supporting the general trend of decline in the tenant rates during the second half of the Tokugawa period.

Furushima and Nagahara, examining a rare time series of *mura-meisai-chō* (literally, detailed village records) for villages in the Shibukawa district of Kawachi, discovered that the officially registered tenant rents in the *shinden-mura* (villages created out of newly opened and irrigated paddies) tended to be less than rent in established older villages and that the registered rent declined over time. For example, in Hishiya-shinden, the average rent was 9 *to* in 1760, but it had declined to 7 *to* by 1787. Similar changes were seen for uplands, where rent fell from 8 to 6 *to* during the same period.[68]

There are many more examples for the Kinai of declines in effective rents, but they are only for a small area or cover only a few years or decades. We hope that more Japanese scholars will follow in the footsteps of Takeyasu and examine as carefully as he did the changes in the effective rents paid by tenant cultivators. However, the studies that do exist on the Kinai combined with what we know of other parts of Japan, in such studies as Smith's on the land tax, all indicate that the general trend during the Tokugawa period was for effective rents and taxes to fall, and there is no evidence that the Kinai was an exception.[69]

RATIONALIZATION OF THE
LANDHOLDING PATTERN

The trends of change observed in the landholding pattern in the Kinai during the second half of the Tokugawa period can be briefly summarized as follows: (1) The amount of land cultivated by large landowners employing hired labor declined. (2) Households working an amount of land that could be cultivated primarily by their own family labor increased in number. This change in the size of the holding was achieved through sales and leases. (3) Though the number of households holding too little land to fully employ family labor increased for the Kinai as a whole, the proportion of these households differed significantly from village to village. (4) A small fraction of large landholders increased the amount of land they held up until the last few decades of the Tokugawa period. The process by which these changes took place was necessarily slow and there were many exceptions due to a variety of reasons (personal, unique local market conditions, or political conditions).[70]

We can find any number of examples of these trends. Shimbō found that in a village in Settsu the number of persons holding land yielding less than 1 *koku* fluctuated widely but, in contrast to this, the number of 3-5 *koku* holdings increased over time, while the number of 5-10 *koku* holdings declined.[71] Mori's study of a village in Kawachi shows a distinct trend toward a reduction in the amount of land held by the largest landholders, but farmers with 5-20 *koku* did not reduce their holdings.[72] Kimura, who examined another village in Kawachi (one dependent on major grains), found that a scale of "30 *koku* or 3 *chō* was the upper limit for farm size,"[73] while Takeyasu concluded that in the cotton-growing villages around Osaka, "the superiority of the small scale [in contrast to large-scale landownership] was evident."[74]

Hayama, who analyzed a cotton-growing village near Osaka, wrote: "Labor productivity did not increase even if the unit of farming was enlarged." Thus, one finds in this village with numerous opportunities for by-employments, small-scale farming of from 7 to 10 *tan* per unit. This, according to Hayama, was "a reflection of the owner cultivators' efforts to adapt to local agricultural conditions."[75] And based on many case studies of changing patterns of landholding, Arai concluded that in the cotton- and rapeseed-growing villages in the Kinai, it was "a pervasive phenomenon" for upper and middle "class" owner cultivators to increase while the lower "class" peasants working small plots of land gradually disappeared. More importantly, he noted, "the 5-20 *koku* class of peasant continued to exist without disintegrating" while those working less than 5 *koku* "disappeared" and "the trend of enlarging landownership by the middle and upper class peasants ceased around the Tempō period." That is, while the marginal peasants who were working land suboptimal in scale tended to be bought out by larger owners, the largest owners sold off or leased out part of theirs, but the middle-sized farms, which were economically efficient, remained viable economic units during the period 1740-1840 studied by Arai.[76]

Based on these observed trends and in the light of the preceding discussion of the labor shortage and its effects, we offer the following hypothesis to explain changes in the landholding pattern. These changes occurred primarily because of the peasants' efforts to make the best use of increasingly scarce labor and, more generally, because of the peasants' desire to respond to the changing conditions both in factor and product markets. The reduction in the area of land worked by large landholders and the increase in area worked by others were the results of farmers' efforts over a long period of time to rationalize the size of the farming unit. Large quantities of cotton and rapeseed, both requiring the intensive application of well-motivated labor, were grown in the Kinai. Thus, when wages rose to the point of negating the benefits large farming units realized through the economies of scale in the use of fertilizers and labor and in crop rotation, these units no longer promised greater returns than could be gained by the landholders working a reduced amount of land using less or no hired labor and leasing the remainder to tenants even at a declining rent. For peasants working less than the optimum amount of land for the family labor force they had, the desirability of increasing the size of their farming unit was obvious. However, whether or not a farmer increased the size of his farming unit depended greatly on the availability of attractive alternatives in the forms of part- or full-time by-employments and the market prices of major agricultural products. Also affecting the decision to increase or reduce the size of the farm unit were the tax rates on various commercial crops.

The reason why some large landholders continued to increase their holdings, only to let the land out to tenants was, we hypothesize, because of the lack of opportunities for profitable investments for their accumulated capital. In the Kinai, where the Bakufu and the guilds of Osaka and other urban merchants and producers of manufactured products were successful in protecting their privileged economic interests, the opportunities for investment by the rural rich were limited to the needs of the local or even the village economy. Under these circumstances, the only major investment that the rural rich could make was in land. Attesting to the fact that investments in more land were less than optimum for the largest landholders was the rapid conversion of land into cash by some of these landowners in order to invest in urban commerce and manufacturing during the last few decades of the Tokugawa period, after Bakufu policy changed and the power of the guilds was broken.

Though it remains untested, we offer the above hypothesis only to suggest that the productivity of agriculture was increased by rationalization of the size of farming units in order to make the most efficient use of agricultural inputs, and to show that our examination of the labor shortage and its effects is fully congruent with the observed trends of change in the landholding patterns. Because an extended analysis of this important topic, which has been examined extensively within the Marxist framework of analysis, clearly requires a separate study, our discussion will be limited to the above and to a brief discussion in Chapter Seven on similar trends in Okayama.

THE RISE IN THE LIVING STANDARD IN THE KINAI

As clearly inferred in the preceding sections, we believe the living standard of the Kinai population as a whole rose as the result of increased productivity in both the agricultural and non-agricultural sectors, rising wage levels, a decreasing effective rate of land rent, and the mobility of labor from low to high productivity areas. The purpose of this section is to provide evidence showing that the living standard of the Kinai population continued to rise during the second half of the Tokugawa period, as it did to a lesser degree in other regions.

However, before attempting to make our case, we must first present two additional reasons why we believe that the living standard must have risen: (1) a widely observed decline in the effective rate of the rice tax, and (2) a relatively slow rate of growth in population.

Though no conclusive evidence yet exists, recent writers are more willing to argue that the effective rate of taxes on rice (and other agricultural output) declined during the second half of the Tokugawa period. Nakabe bluntly wrote:

> As the result of demands made by the peasants for lower taxes, the tax rates were reduced. Despite the increasing [economic] difficulties which the ruling class faced, decreased tax rates and the *jōmen* system benefited not only the peasants of Hoshida village, but also those in many Kinai villages.[77]

The *jōmen* system was a fixed-rate tax that dispensed with annual assessments of yields and was used widely beginning in the 1720s,

117

first in the *tenryō* and then in various *han*. Although instituted for the purpose of raising taxes over time, it tended, on the contrary, to reduce the effective tax rate because the productivity of agriculture increased. Mizuhara, who examined numerous rice yield data, found that "the assessed yield tended to change little despite increases in productivity. . . . Often the tenant rent was higher than the assessed yield, and this means that the real yield [by the end of the Tokugawa period] was higher than the assessed yield."[78] Periodic increases in the nominal rate and reassessments of yield tended to come only at long intervals, especially in the Kinai, which was administered by the Bakufu magistrates and the politically weak, smaller daimyo. The relatively low tax rates in the *tenryō* have been well established in various studies and the farmers themselves must have known of them because they frequently demanded incorporation of their land into *tenryō* in order to reduce their effective tax rate. Also, the generally inflationary trend of the late eighteenth and early nineteenth century benefited peasants who were paying more of their taxes in cash and less in kind.[79]

Of course, as the proportion of taxes paid in cash rose, the ruling class made attempts to adjust upwards the nominal amount of cash paid when the price of rice rose, as it did after the 1780s. Such efforts, however, were usually quite unsuccessful because due to the strong objection of the peasants, upward adjustments either lagged or were never made at all. In fact, the Kinai peasants often succeeded in preventing the ruling class from adjusting the cash tax to the increasing price of rice by forcing them to accept a Tokugawa version of a parity price.

> The method which peasants adopted was to insist on paying [the cash tax] on the basis of the average price of rice in the past 5, 10, or 20 years. In 1836 when the price of rice was set [by the ruling class] at 149.537 *momme* per *koku* in Settsu [where usually one-third of the tax was paid in cash], the price agreed upon was 120 *momme* which was not much higher than the 107.599 *momme* which was the average of the rice price during the past five years. In Yamato, [where one-tenth of the tax was paid in cash] the price settled upon was 73.565 *momme*, the mean of the price for the ten-year period between 1827 and 1836, instead of the initially requested 126.944 *momme*.[80]

The effects of a parity price system were significant: surviving records make it clear that, in many administrative units of Kinai, larger and larger proportions of the rice taxes were being paid in cash and rice was becoming an important cash crop for the peasants. Many *han* in the Kinai, led by Amagasaki *han* in the early eighteenth century, began to allow an increasing amount of rice to be sold directly by peasants to *sake* makers and merchants.[81]

Observing the increased sale of rice by peasants for cash and the failure of the ruling class to impose an arbitrary rice price for tax purposes, another scholar wrote:

> The Bakufu and the daimyo, in order to exploit the peasants more, allowed peasants to sell more rice in the market and attempted, at the same time, to set a price [for tax purposes] above the market price. . . . However, from the later decades of the eighteenth century, the peasants succeeded in reducing the price set by the ruling class, i.e., in rejecting the arbitrary will of the ruler. The price set by the rulers was gradually reduced to the market level.[82]

Some authors, aware of the orthodox view on the tax burden and limited by the records, make the point that the tax burden was declining indirectly. Shimbō wrote:

> The tax burden during the latter half of the Tokugawa period remained little changed from the mid-Tokugawa period. . . . The major characteristic of the tax burden of the village was that the tax rate, which was fairly high, remained fixed. . . . The high tax rate did not, by itself, mean a heavy tax burden. If the assessed tax base is small and it diverges significantly from the real yield, the high tax rate does not signify that the actual tax burden was heavy.[83]

Given that Shimbō explicitly discussed the increased productivity of agriculture in the villages he studied, the intent of his words is clear. Or, in the words of Andō:

> The rulers were unable to tax the peasants more, so the former suffered the consequences. That is, the political power of the peasants was not weak. If the rulers increased the tax burden, the peasants could revolt and protest, and they did.[84]

Another important factor contributing to the increases in the living standard in the Kinai was the lack of population growth. Where increases did occur, the rate of increase in population was significantly less than that of the economy. The Bakufu data, presented in Table 5.3, show that in all five provinces of the Kinai population declined between 1721 and 1872, and the decline over the entire period 1721-1846 was sizable: from 2.25 million to less than 2 million.

These data should, however, be considered to give only a general indication of population change because of the weaknesses in the Bakufu data discussed in Chapter Three. Even if we allow for considerable understatement in the data, the growth of population, we believe, was extremely slow. Regrettably, we have no direct evidence with which to quantify the magnitude of the understatement or otherwise to reevaluate the reliability of the data. Thus, the only support we can offer for our view of changes in the Kinai population, other than scattered village evidence, is indirect evidence. The accuracy of the inferences we draw from our study of other regions—especially Okayama, which experienced patterns of economic growth similar to the Kinai—can be tested only when historical demographers unearth and analyze *shūmon-aratame-chō* of sufficiently long time series for some Kinai villages.

While there is much indirect evidence to indicate that the living standard of the Kinai region was rising during the latter half of the Tokugawa period and was high by most standards of a premodern economy, none, by itself, is conclusive. But the numerous examples, both quantitative and descriptive, when taken together all point to a rise in the living standard for most people in this part of Japan. One of the more revealing kinds of evidence on the living standard is the proportion of the persons in a town or village who were engaged, on a part- or full-time basis, in occupations other than agriculture, and also the variety of the occupations found. If the proportion is large and the varieties numerous, we usually have some basis for making an assessment or forming an impression of the living standard of a town or a village.

One example we have is the town of Hirano.[85] From Tsuda's work we learn that in 1705, of the total population of between 8,000 and 9,000, more than 1,000 persons were engaged in occupations other than agriculture on either a full- or part-time basis. Even allowing for the fact that these part- and full-time

Table 5.3
The Population of the Kinai

Year	1721	1750	1756	1786	1798	1804	1822	1828	1834	1846	1872
Kuni											
Yamashiro	564,994	522,626	527,334	507,488	480,993	469,519	478,652	498,296	488,726	452,140	429,030
Yamato	413,331	374,041	367,724	336,254	344,043	340,706	346,319	356,627	360,071	361,157	418,326
Kawachi	243,820	231,266	206,568	205,585	218,102	214,945	244,816	223,747	224,822	224,055	237,678
Izumi	218,405	207,952	226,480	190,762	199,083	202,283	205,545	208,884	207,211	197,656	209,174
Settsu	809,242	803,595	841,981	801,220	806,578	789,857	790,635	812,090	796,439	763,729	729,443
TOTAL	2,249,792	2,139,480	2,170,087	2,041,309	2,048,799	2,017,310	2,065,967	2,099,644	2,077,269	1,998,737	2,023,651

Source: Sekiyama Naotarō, *Kinsei Nihon no jinkō kōzō* (The population structure of Tokugawa Japan) (Tokyo: Yoshikawa Kōbunkan, 1957), p. 137.

merchants and artisans must have served nearby villages as well as Hirano, to have one out of eight or nine persons employed in commerce, the service industry, or the processing of agricultural products, strongly suggests that the community's living standard was relatively high. If not, the population of Hirano and its neighboring villages could not have supported the four silk shops, fifteen tobacco shops, fourteen rice-cake shops, or the twenty-five hairdressers which the Bakufu repeatedly castigated as unnecessary for commoners.

One can justifiably object to the fact that these observations and data are for a town and not a village. Better indicators of the living standard, therefore, might be obtained from calculations of our own based on known facts. How did agricultural day-laborers, considered the most economically marginal workers, fare? According to an actual household record—which from all indications could be considered quite representative, according to Furushima—an average worker in the 1840s had an annual cash income on the basis of twenty working days per month of 160 *momme* paid in advance plus 110 *momme* of "pocket money," a total of 270 *momme* of silver. This does not include at least 100 *momme* worth of food, clothing, and *sake* provided by the employer.[86] This total income corresponds to Hayama's figure that an agricultural day-laborer was paid 1.5 *momme* per day which, on the basis of twenty working days per month, would amount to 360 *momme* per year, without counting food supplied on the days he worked. When the cash value of the food is added, the income would exceed 400 *momme*. (Here we shall not refine the figures by accounting for the 2 *momme* he was paid per day during the peak seasons and the fact that he might have worked fewer than twenty days per month during the winter or supplemented his income by other employment.)

How good was an annual income of 360 *momme* per year during the Tempō period? Except for the three famine years (1836-1838), a *koku* of rice averaged around 75 *momme* and, even assuming our daily laborer bought rice in Osaka, his income would buy about 5.5 *koku*. If 1.8 *koku* per year given to a low-ranking samurai as *fuchi* (support rice, i.e., maintenance) was used as a guide, 5.5 *koku* is better than what three low-ranking samurai received. Many low-ranking samurai with families also lived on between 10 and 30 *hyō*—between 4 and 12 *koku*—of rice. In making such comparisons, we should keep in mind that the samurai, however low their rank, had to maintain prescribed costly social standards (swords, clothing, and required servants in some instances), while agricultural day-laborers were free of such obligations. We should remember also that we are comparing the income of low-ranking samurai and the least economically favored of the peasant class.[87]

How well could a male agricultural laborer earning 360 *momme* per year or 30 *momme* per month live? If he was unmarried, as some undoubtedly were, there is little doubt that his life was an easy one by most standards of the developing nations of today. But what if he had a wife and two children? (Let us examine the case of a family of four rather than the more typical five because we shall ignore any supplementary income earned by his wife, his older children, and him on his "nonworking" ten days per month.) If we assume that the staple in his family's diet consisted of a mixture of rice and wheat in equal parts, as it did for most Tokugawa peasants in the economically advanced regions, his monthly expenditures on staple food would have been about 22.5 *momme* even if we generously allow as much as 1.2 *shō* (0.012 *koku*) per day for the family and assume (though it is highly unlikely) that he paid the market price prevailing in Osaka. The price of wheat was about half that of rice during most of the Tokugawa period.

Since 5 *gō* of rice per day was considered sufficient to cover all needs (food, clothing, etc.) of an adult male, we can safely consider that our allowance of 1.2 *shō* per day for this family would readily cover the costs of vegetables, salt, and other minor requirements along with the grain. This left 7.5 *momme* for occasional fish, clothing, and other expenditures. Very few country people paid rent. Most lived in their own houses, built by the joint effort of villagers at the marriage of the occupant or bequeathed by their parents.

To be sure, the remaining 7.5 *momme* did not go very far. One *shō* of *sake* cost about 1.4 *momme*, the same quantity of lamp oil 3.5 *momme*, and cotton cloth enough to make a kimono cost as much as 6 *momme* at the Tempō prices.[88] If our day-laborer had a family and worked only twenty days per month, his life would not be envied by most. On the other hand, if he had less responsibility, bought staples and other food items at lower prices

(and produced some himself as he most likely did), and worked
all but two days out of a month (as most people in his class did),
then his standard of life could easily have compared favorably
with most of the low-ranking samurai and with many in the developing nations of today.

The farmers who had some land of their own and who probably
engaged in by-employments must have lived better than our agricultural laborer. If our preceding calculations for the least favored
among the peasants reflect reality at all, one starts to doubt the
dismal picture of Tokugawa life painted by many Japanese scholars. We should add that skilled city laborers, such as carpenters
and masons, earned over 3 *momme* per day and it was not uncommon for them to earn over 1,000 *momme* annually.[89] The
authors of *Seikatsu-shi* wrote:

> There are numerous types of historical records for villages in
> the Edo period. Among them, records that vividly show one
> aspect of life are several types of notes of apologies and reports
> written by the peasants to the village leaders. Those who be-
> haved violently as a result of intoxication, men who were rep-
> rimanded for not tending to the paddies, and couples who
> eloped "on the wings of the wind" all left records which bring
> the life of the peasants to our mind's eye. "Living in a fashion
> unbecoming to their station in life" was the cause for many
> letters of apology from nouveau riche peasants. It was pro-
> hibited for common peasants [not the village leaders] to con-
> struct stone gates or to build elaborate entrances to their houses
> but, as the Edo period progressed, these prohibitions became
> harder and harder for the nouveau riche peasants to observe,
> as they had the ordinary desire to live according to their income
> level.[90]

Writing at the beginning of the Meiji period, Takamura Kōun
(1852-1934), a leading sculptor of the Meiji era, recalled the
days of his youth:

> The life of the artisans was simple and easy. If one earned
> about 1 *ryō* 2 *bu* per month, a family of five could live without
> worries. He could drink a *gō* of *sake* in the evening. The wage
> of *geta*-makers and seal-makers [makers of wooden footware
> and wooden seals to be affixed to documents] was 3.5 *momme*;

carpenters and masons, 3.75 *momme*. These were the good days when a dish of noodles was only 18 *mon* [of copper] and *sushi* 8 *mon*. Though the artisans lived in small barrack-like dwellings, all they had to pay was 800 *mon*. And, for that rent, the bald-headed landlords behaved themselves.[91]

Because the living standard of the populace had risen in contrast to the severely strained coffers of the Bakufu, the Bakufu in 1812 issued the little-respected decree prohibiting the production, sale, and use of high-priced cakes, dolls, and sugar; the wearing of costly apparel; the use of gold, silver, and other precious metals and stones for decoration of any kind; and many of the entertainments in Osaka and Kyoto that the Bakufu thought not befitting to the station of life of commoners.[92] Had the living standard of most of the merchants, artisans, and peasants in Kinai been at the level described by many Japanese scholars, no such decree would have been necessary. The point to be stressed is that the living standard of all, from the agricultural day-laborers up, rose during the second half of the Tokugawa period, and that the number of those commoners whose level of consumption offended the Bakufu steadily increased.

CHAPTER SIX

Morioka

Morioka *han*, which presents in many ways a strong contrast to the Kinai region, was selected to represent a less rapidly growing domain for three important reasons. The first is that Morioka, long known for its economic backwardness, has been one of the examples most frequently enlisted to show the harshness of life in Tokugawa Japan. Historians following the traditional pessimistic view of the Tokugawa economy often cite the domain's detailed official population data to show that stagnation in the growth of the population took place as a result of severe famines that occurred periodically in the region.[1] The second reason is the unusual amount of descriptive evidence made available through the efforts of Mori Kahei, who dedicated his life to gathering historical materials on this domain.[2] The last reason is that while most of the recent empirical studies containing findings contrary to the dominant Japanese view have been on areas that would be designated Region I, that is, more urbanized, commercially oriented, and economically advanced regions, Morioka represents a typical Region II domain on which no such empirical studies have yet been undertaken.[3]

Morioka *han*, which included the northern two-thirds of today's Iwate prefecture and about one-third of Aomori, was located on the Pacific side of the northernmost part of Honshu. In terms of size, the domain was one of the largest among the nearly 270 domains, but the arable area comprised less than 10 percent of the total because running through the region are the Ōu mountain range, called "the Spine of Japan" and the Kitakami mountain range, parallel ranges lying in a north-south direction. The climate is as unsuited to rice culture as is the terrain. As it lies between 39 and 41.5 degrees north, the winters are long and during most of three months the temperature is well below freezing.

In contrast to the relatively ineffectual rule seen in the fragmented Kinai, Morioka was administered as a unit, and more effectively, by the House of Nambu during the entire Tokugawa period. The House of Nambu, a political and military power in northern Japan during the war-ridden years of the sixteenth century, had joined forces with Tokugawa Ieyasu at the beginning of the latter's campaign toward national unification. Thus, it was only a matter of course that the Nambu territory be recognized by the Bakufu and the House of Nambu continue to rule.[4]

ECONOMIC GROWTH DURING THE SEVENTEENTH CENTURY

The growth of the economy during the first century or so after 1600 depended mostly on the rice, gold mining, horse breeding, lumber, iron, and marine industries. From the beginning of the Tokugawa period on into the Kyōhō period (1716-1735), the rice output of the domain grew at a steady pace. While the Bakufu-assigned official yield (*omotedaka*) was only 100,000 *koku* for the domain, the taxable yield recorded for the internal use of the domain rose from 205,550 *koku* in 1634 to 226,580 in 1652 and reached 268,160 *koku* by 1735. Thus, the domain's taxable yield increased more than 30 percent during the century between 1634 and 1735.[5]

Though the lack of directly usable data prevents us from making an assessment of the increase in productivity, there is no doubt that some gains resulted from improvements in seeds, agricultural tools, and irrigation and other techniques.[6] The domain made great efforts to increase output through irrigation and water-control projects. As a consequence of these efforts, "agricultural productivity rose well into the mid-Tokugawa period," the *History of Iwate Prefecture* states, "in five [of the ten] districts of the domain," those located in the southern half.[7] Because of the increases in the rice tax resulting from increases in the area in paddy fields and in productivity, and also because of the increases in domain revenue from a variety of economic activities that will be described below, in 1665 the domain was able to increase the stipends to all of its samurai by about 6 percent.[8]

Gold mining was important in boosting the economy of the domain. Though no record exists with which to assess the magnitude of the total output of the mines beyond a domain record stating that the gold output was "very large"[9] during the first century of the Tokugawa period, a few records have survived to tell a partial story of the importance of this industry. We learn, for example, that at least twenty-seven new veins were discovered between 1598 and 1696, and some of these mines were extremely rich: "as much as 70-80 *momme* of gold could be had for every 100 *momme* of earth."[10] In 1645 one entry in the *Nambu han nisshi* (the daily records of Nambu *han*) described a gold mine worked by "about 13,000 miners and carpenters," a mine so rich that one Edo merchant offered 65,000 *ryō* for the right to work it.[11] And we can also establish that at least twenty mines were worked actively during the 1720s and 1730s.[12]

Horse breeding provided an important source of income for the inhabitants in the northern part of the domain. The Nambu horse, well known from the thirteenth century, attracted "a large number of buyers coming from the south—Aizu, Mogami, and the Kanto region—who were willing to pay good prices."[13] Again, no aggregate data are available, but we know that from the beginning of the Tokugawa period the domain maintained nine large grazing grounds and a samurai staff of twenty to supervise all matters relating to horses, including the supervision of sixteen thriving markets specializing in horse trading.[14]

For many people living along the long coastline of the domain and along the Kitakami River, which is still noted for its rich salmon harvests, the first century of the Tokugawa period was one of increasing economic opportunities. The coastal shipping routes, well established by the mid-seventeenth century, made it possible to ship the marine products of the domain to Edo and elsewhere. Increasing quantities of salmon, bonito, abalone, cod, tuna, and a variety of processed marine products were shipped to meet the rapidly rising demand. The increase in coastal activities can only be assessed by the increasing number of ships ferrying these products to Edo and by the amount of taxes paid by the shipowners.[15] Since the tax was paid in the form of competitive bidding for the rights to fish in specific parts of the coastal and offshore areas, increasingly larger bids, shown in numerous examples provided by Iwamoto, indicate the increasing profitability of fishing.[16] By the 1670s bids of 1,000 *ryō* were not infrequent and, while no discernible inflation took place during the following century, by 1757 some bids were as high as 3,500 *ryō*.[17]

In the mountainous regions of the domain, that is, in over three-quarters of the domain, trees of excellent quality were abundant and provided another important source of income. The output of lumber rose rapidly, and permits issued by the domain for cutting trees in units of 10,000 were not uncommon. In 1663 the *Nambu han nisshi* includes an entry to the effect that 3,500 *ryō* were collected from the 10 percent tax on the lumber sold by the Tabe District to a merchant in Osaka. By the end of the seventeenth century the domain had begun to increase its control over the kinds of trees cut and over replanting because "the sales of lumber had reached a huge amount" by this period.[18]

Other economic activities increased during the first century of the Tokugawa period to provide larger incomes for many peasants. The growing and processing of vegetable dyes (mostly indigo) absorbed the labor of many for a few months of the year. Wooden bowls for soup, rice, and a variety of ceremonial uses were made from good local wood, coated with the high quality sumac lacquer of this region, and sold to other domains in growing quantities.[19] The output of salt rose slowly, while that of lead began to increase rapidly after the mid-seventeenth century.[20]

Despite this increase in economic activities in Morioka during the first century of the Tokugawa period, evidence seems to indicate that the effective tax burden on the commoners remained stable, and thus we are justified in assuming that the income level of the population in the domain must have risen.[21] Though there were local exceptions, the effective tax rate on rice does not seem to have risen during much of the seventeenth century. The mean nominal tax rate on rice was 31.72 percent for ten districts of the domain during the mid-seventeenth century, and it stood at 32.77 percent from 1675 to 1682.[22] As these were rates on the assessed yield, the effective rates must have been somewhat lower because of increased productivity and because of "hidden paddies" that escaped assessment.[23]

Because most nonagricultural taxes were fixed by domain policy at 10 percent of the value of the sale of products, with various additional taxes on peasants levied on the basis of a few *ryō* per 100 *koku* of rice, historians of the region consider a total effective tax burden of 50 percent of income to have been the upper limit of taxation. Since there was a variety of economic activities that escaped taxation either partially or completely, 50 percent can be considered too high even as an upper limit for persons whose incomes were generated mostly outside of agriculture.[24] In any

129

event, the frequently mentioned Tokugawa tax rate of "two parts for the samurai and one part for the peasants" was clearly wide of the mark even in this domain, which was known to have had an efficient administration. Noting the increased activities and the generally stable tax rate in the domain, the authors of *Iwate Kenshi* concluded that, "because of the stability gained by society, entertainments such as *sumō* wrestling and village dances became increasingly popular, and visiting Edo *kabuki* players began to draw overflowing crowds everywhere in the domain" during the seventeenth century.[25]

Commerce, however, developed relatively slowly compared to other areas in the country. During the first century of the Tokugawa period, markets were held only three to six times per month even in the urban centers, and in the castle town of Morioka markets were held every day only after the mid-seventeenth century. The bulk of the trading done in the 1660s was by merchants—dealing in *sake*, rice, fish, and oil—who were catering to increasing demand from the samurai class.[26] Despite the slow start of permanently maintained markets, however, trading on market days increased in the larger cities such as Kōriyama, Hanamaki, Tōno, Mihoe, and Hachinohe, reflecting the increase in economic activities within the domain.[27]

A major reason for the relatively slow development of commerce in urban centers was the loss, because of the *sankin kōtai* system, of an important part of samurai demand to areas outside the domain. The samurai took turns in accompanying the daimyo to Edo, and this meant that each samurai had to save a part of his income in preparation for this costly duty. In 1643 the domain began to assess all samurai at 1 *ryō* (1.5 *ryō* after 1653) per 100 *koku* of stipend in order to aid the samurai who accompanied the daimyo. This was called the *moyohi* system.[28] To defray the cost of the retainers' journey to Edo and their living expenses while there, the domain levied special taxes on commoners in an amount estimated at 8,300 *ryō* per year.[29] Of course, the expenses involved in the *sankin kōtai* of the daimyo and his family (including the cost of maintaining a permanent residence in Edo) had to come out of the domain's treasury. The Morioka daimyo's expenses for the required residence in Edo during the seventeenth century are estimated to have been around 30,000 *ryō*, or about 50 percent of the annual cash income of the domain.[30]

Though data limitations make it impossible to estimate the total amount of the demand that shifted to Edo and regions en route, we can be sure that the minimum spent by the daimyo and his retainers to meet the *sankin kōtai* requirement was at least 46,500 *ryō* per year—a total obtained by adding together the 30,000 *ryō* that the daimyo spent out of the domain's revenues, more than 8,000 *ryō* collected from the commoners for the *sankin kōtai*, a special *sankin kōtai* "savings" by the samurai amounting to at least 1,000 *ryō*, and an extremely conservative estimate of 7,500 *ryō* as the sum spent in Edo by the samurai who accompanied the daimyo.[31] This 46,500 *ryō* is an amount that could have stimulated the economy of the domain, especially its commercial and manufacturing sectors, with large multiplier effects. Since one can "guesstimate" the "Gross Domain Product" of Morioka to have been somewhat over 500,000 *ryō* per year, the 46,500 *ryō* lost to the domain's economy through the *sankin kōtai* was significant indeed.[32] What was lost in terms of samurai demand by this domain and others were gains to Edo and to domains on well-travelled routes to and from Edo.[33]

Although the commercialization of agriculture in the villages and the growth of commerce in the castle town of Morioka and other larger nodes of population lagged considerably when compared to those in the Kinai, there is little doubt that the economy of the domain grew steadily because of the increasing economic activities just described. Most Japanese economic historians agree with Mori, who wrote that in the seventeenth century "the domain definitely was not poor," and perhaps even with the official of the domain who reported that "the economy of the domain ranked in the upper tier of the middle group" among all domains.[34]

ECONOMIC GROWTH AFTER 1700

Contrary to the long-held view, we believe that the economy of Morioka continued to grow during the last century and a half of the Tokugawa period and that the major impetus for growth was provided by new "leading industries" and the continued growth of commerce. Rice output stopped growing and gold mining declined, but iron mining and commerce continued to expand, as did lumber, horse breeding, the fishing industries, and commercial agriculture.

The growth, though slower in comparison to that in more advanced domains in western Japan, continued as a trend and brought about predictable changes. Despite the political strength of the Nambu daimyo, it became increasingly difficult to prevent peasants from becoming part-time or full-time merchants or wage earners in the expanding mining and other industries. Because of continued economic growth, the same sequences of interrelated economic reactions experienced in the Kinai were also set in motion in this domain. Labor was drawn to nonagricultural activities by higher wages; the lower supply of labor in the villages improved the bargaining power of even the most marginal peasants; and the living standard of commoners rose.

As the eighteenth century progressed, and especially by the early nineteenth century, even the effective bureaucracy of the domain could no longer check the consequences of economic growth. Attempts to tie the peasants to the land became gradually less effective, and the peasants, now having more rewarding economic opportunities to pursue outside the paddy fields, increasingly insisted on the freedom to maximize their income. The domain's policy to increase its share of total output by means of domain monopolies and monopsonies was met with fierce resistance, and even with a full-scale revolt, which finally forced the domain to abandon these restrictive measures. When the domain coffers were strained by famines and the Bakufu exactions, which increased during the eighteenth century, the domain could not seek relief from the peasants, who had learned the potential of their political power in removing income-reducing restrictions and impositions, but only from the wealthier merchants, who were becoming increasingly prosperous, and from the samurai, who had no option to refuse. Even in this domain, ruled by a strong daimyo, the inexorable process of economic growth could not be tamed to suit the needs of the ruling class, and the commoners succeeded in keeping an increasingly larger share of the increasing total output.

With the preceding discussion as a guide, let us first describe the outline of economic growth of the domain in the eighteenth and nineteenth centuries and, mindful of the traditional view, turn to argue that: (1) the peasants continued to succeed in resisting the domain's efforts to increase its share in the growing output; (2) the effects of famines, which are supposed to have driven the

peasants to extremes of desperation and starvation, were significantly less than is believed by many Japanese scholars; and (3)
the living standard of the peasants continued to rise throughout
the last century and a half of the Tokugawa period, if more slowly
than in the Kinai and other advanced areas.

The assessed rice output of Morioka in 1837 was 249,575 *koku*,
or nearly 10 percent below that of a century earlier.[35] However,
this decline in output did not signify stagnation in the economy,
but rather the relative unattractiveness of rice cultivation compared to other economic activities. This relative unattractiveness
was due to the relatively low price of rice that prevailed during
most of the eighteenth century in Osaka and other major urban
centers,[36] seemingly increased frequency of poor harvests in the
domain during this period, and the continued effective taxation of
agriculture at a higher rate than that imposed on commerce and
industry.[37] Even peasants who remained on the land began to
devote an increasing proportion of their time to such commercial
crops as beans, vegetables, tobacco, and those from which dyes
and oil were produced.[38]

Competition for labor from industry and commerce increased
over time. The output of the iron industry "began to increase
rapidly to make the name of Nambu iron famous across the
nation."[39] By the last decades of the eighteenth century "a continually growing demand encouraged the growth of the industry,
causing the number of iron works in the domain to increase and
the income of peasants in the mountainous regions to rise by providing them with opportunities to supply charcoal and to rent
out horses for transportation."[40] The surviving records of mining
operations reveal that by the beginning of the nineteenth century
many mines employed up to 200 persons and that nearly 90 percent of the employees were recruited from villages outside the
area and even from outside the domain.[41] In contrast to the
seventeenth-century practice of using off-season peasant labor extensively, the iron mining of this period depended increasingly
on full-time wage labor.[42]

During the nineteenth century, employment also rose in iron-
related industries such as the manufacture of iron pots, fish hooks,
and agricultural tools.[43] The demand for iron both within the
domain and from outside continued to be strong to the very end
of the Tokugawa period.[44] And the growth of this industry had

a considerable impact on the domain's economy. In the words of Mori, who made a detailed study of the industry:

The iron industry, and other related industries which were stimulated by it, became the motivating force in converting the static economy of the mountain villages into a dynamic one. The investment of commercial capital made it possible to gather labor from neighboring areas and the products of the industry were sold widely. . . . For wages, imported polished rice was paid, with the consequence of transforming the diet of peasants who had depended on the produce of upland fields.[45]

The development of the industry stimulated not only directly related industries, but also indirectly related ones such as the making of *tawara* (straw bags) in which to carry the large amounts of charcoal demanded by the iron industry.[46] Mori went so far as to say that the growth of the iron industry "helped commercialize marine products, cocoon-raising, and other activities, and made cheap iron tools available for agriculture with the result of raising agricultural productivity and the living standard in general."[47] Though accurate data on the total labor force engaged in mining (iron and other minerals) and directly related industries do not exist, the total number of workers employed by the industry was undoubtedly a significant proportion of the domain's population. On the basis of the known output of various mining industries at the beginning of the Meiji period, the average output per man estimated from scattered data, and the recorded number of carpenters in the iron industry and gold miners during the seventeenth century, we know that a very high proportion of the domain's population was employed in the mining industry by the end of the Tokugawa period.[48] The economic impact of the mining industry, which employed such a large proportion of the population and which provided employment to others in directly related economic activities, could easily have been as "dynamic" as Mori described.

There is little doubt that the fishing industry also grew during the last century and a half of the Tokugawa period. The quantity of marine products exported from the port of Otsuchi and elsewhere began to increase during and after the Genroku period, that is, around the turn of the eighteenth century,[49] and the industry continued to grow throughout the eighteenth century. During this century, bids made for the right to fish in special offshore areas rose;[50] the Bakufu's permission to ship *tawaramono* (goods in straw bags) directly to Nagasaki in mid-century provided an added boost to fishing; and by the 1760s rural participation in the marketing of marine products had increased,[51] as indicated by the increase in taxes paid by the merchants involved. The Isaba-*donya*, for example, paid as much as 1,000 *kan* of tax per year by the 1780s. The magnitude of this tax is readily apparent when we realize that 1 *kan* usually was equivalent to 4,000 *mon* of copper coins and the average daily wage of day-laborers was about 100 *mon* per day.[52]

The scale of fishing operations expanded and output from the industry continued to rise into the nineteenth century to meet the increasing demand for dried sardines for use as fertilizer in western Japan as well as the demand for other marine products.[53] The profits earned by this industry were large. The records of one Maekawa, a large shipowner, show that by the beginning of the nineteenth century his annual taxes ranged between 1,700 and 3,400 *ryō* with a mean of 2,100 *ryō*. This means that the value of his catches fluctuated between 17,000 and 34,000 *ryō* per year.[54] By the last few decades of the Tokugawa period, *tateami* (standing ocean nets) were beginning to be used, greatly improving the productivity of fishermen,[55] and the size of ships increased with the demand for exports.[56] The output of salt rose *pari passu* with the growth of the fishing industry to meet the demand for preserving with salt the growing number of marine products sent to distant markets.[57]

In the lumber industry, the growing volume of exports had surprised domain officials during the Genroku period, and by 1716 an Osaka merchant was known to have paid the huge sum of 55,000 *ryō* for the right to cut Japanese cypress in the domain. By 1806 one record reveals that 691,530 trees were harvested in one district alone. Thus, "it is not difficult to estimate that the trees harvested in the domain were huge in number."[58] The industry not only helped the domain financially throughout the Tokugawa period, but it also enriched the economic life of the population in general by providing employment opportunities. Important also was charcoal making, which provided by-employments for peasants during the winter months. As the demand for charcoal increased, especially from the iron industry, "peasants were spared the necessity of searching for winter jobs to supplement their incomes."[59]

Horse breeding remained an important industry and the number of horses in the domain rose over time, exceeding 87,000 in 1797. Scattered records from various parts of the domain suggest that during the eighteenth century the average number of horses rose from two to three per horse-breeding household.[60] The income from the sale of horses, which brought as much as 7 or 8 *ryō* and a minimum of 2 to 3 *ryō* per horse,[61] was important both to peasants and the domain. In usual years the domain netted about 20,000 *ryō* in taxes levied on the sales of horses at the rate of no less than 1 *ryō* per head.[62] The supplementary income that peasants earned in the form of fees for transporting iron and other products by horse was also considerable. Horse manure, too, according to Mori, was an important by-product for the peasants.[63]

Other economic activities that helped to augment the income of the peasants included the cultivation of such commercial crops as sumac lacquer, oil-producing plants,[64] tobacco, vegetable dyes, and cocoons. Though these activities did not become as important as those just described, because of the quantity of labor required and the limited or negative comparative advantages vis-à-vis other regions, they nevertheless constituted additional sources of income by helping to make fuller use of less fertile land and of labor around the year.

As industry grew, so did commerce. By the Genroku period the network of markets connecting major nodes of population within the domain had been established, and from then on the merchant class steadily increased in number. By 1738 the proportion of the population classified as merchants was 12.2 percent, while only 7.7 percent were classified as samurai.[65] Though we have no comparable data for later years, there is little doubt that the proportion of merchants increased over time as an increasing number of peasants, especially younger sons in peasant households and small-plot holders, moved into the towns.[66] Of course, the total income generated in commercial activities was larger than the total of the merchant income since many peasants engaged in part-time commercial activities.

While commerce in the castle town of Morioka continued to be dominated by merchants who had originally come from Omi, the domain's efforts to strengthen local merchants were partially successful.[67] Relatively low taxes levied on the smaller local wholesalers helped them grow into the well-known Isaba-*donya*, which specialized in marine and other products.[68] By the late eighteenth century the merchants in rural towns had become the dominant force in a variety of commercial activities, so much so that they were considered "essential to the daily life and production in all regions."[69] By the 1830s, as these activities grew to the point of causing concern among the domain officials as to the effects on the villages (of drawing peasants away from rice culture into commerce and commercial crops), the domain issued a series of decrees to try to limit the activities of these rural merchants, but they seem to have been issued in vain.[70]

CONFLICTS OF INTEREST

As the increasingly market-oriented peasants and merchants in large and small towns succeeded in increasing their incomes, the domain continued to attempt to take a share because its needs were constantly exceeding its tax revenues. The domain had to meet the demands made on it by the Bakufu, but its revenue from the rice tax sharply declined several times during the period (because of major famines), expenditures required for the *sankin kōtai* continued to rise, and the short-run policy of relieving financial difficulties by selling samurai status and the rights to restrict commerce to the wealthier merchants had the long-run effect of reducing domain income. Morioka was only suffering from the problems faced by all other domains; a more general problem was the inherent difficulty involved in assessing and collecting taxes from nonagricultural economic activities, which were becoming increasingly more important than rice culture.

The peasants had good reason for resisting any effort by the domain to increase taxes. As opportunities for them to increase their incomes multiplied, they seemed to become even less willing to accept increases in taxes or restrictions on their market activities. And their efforts to resist the attempts by the domain to increase its share of income was sufficient, in most instances, to thwart such attempts. Their resistance took the form of village uprisings, district-wide revolts, and finally even a domain-wide rebellion. Thus, the domain found it increasingly necessary to shift the burden of its financial difficulties to its samurai retainers and to resort to the short-run expediency of obtaining needed cash from the merchants, who were increasingly able and willing, at a price, to accommodate the needs of the domain.

By the end of the Tokugawa period, the domain was virtually in bankruptcy, and its samurai had suffered a series of reductions in their stipends. The economic plight of the ruling class was due, in large part, to the peasants, who had succeeded in eliminating the restrictions imposed on their commercial activities and in forcing the domain to withdraw most of the tax increases instituted by desperate domain officials during the final decades of the Tokugawa period. Let us now turn to follow the course of events that brought about such an outcome.

The battle lines were already drawn by the early decades of the eighteenth century. The domain was beginning to feel financial hardship because of a large Bakufu imposition in 1708—a contribution of 70,000 ryō was asked to repair Edo castle—and because of other, if smaller, Bakufu demands that followed. To ease the difficulty, the domain sought to increase revenues. It could not raise the rice tax without encountering the fierce opposition of the peasants. Also, rice yields were poor during the first two decades of the eighteenth century and this was part of the reason for the domain's strained coffers. Thus, the domain turned to commerce for more revenue. First it began to enforce its policy, initially adopted in 1645, of tsudome (literally, stopping at the ports, i.e., a domain policy to license all exports at a fee), and in 1727 the number of enumerated products was increased and the policy was enforced more vigorously than previously. The products requiring license now included all of the major domain products, and clauses were added to the tsudome decree specifying severe punishments for violators.[71] Second, the domain imposed new taxes—a head tax and a tax on dwellings—during the 1730s.[72]

While the expanded tsudome policy was not challenged, peasant opposition to the new taxes was immediate. Throughout the southern districts of the domain, several thousand peasants made a show of force and marched into the castle town to present petitions demanding that the new taxes be withdrawn. Surprised by the large number of marchers, especially because the new taxes were small, the head fiscal officer decided to "accept the petition and ordered the new taxes abolished. Though the peasants received a warning not to resort to such tactics hereafter, no one was punished for this uprising."[73]

This, however, was only the beginning of a series of confrontations. In 1753, the Bakufu made another imposition of 70,000 *ryō* "to repair the Nikko shrine," which was followed by an order in 1770 to pay 27,000 *ryō* as the share of the domain "in repairing the Imperial residence in Kyoto," and again in 1781 by a request for an unknown amount to make repairs to rivers, presumably in the *tenryō*.[74] Such large impositions were especially burdensome to the domain treasury because of their timing: the harvest was unusually poor in 1753 and the 1780s was the decade of the famine, which reduced domain revenues sharply.

In 1753, the domain, faced with these Bakufu levies and reduced revenues, imposed a special *ad hoc* cash levy on the peasants. The peasants, already strained by the poor harvest, were quick to protest: "About 100 peasants of Otsuchi began an uprising and marched into Morioka. And there were signs that the uprising was about to spread." Sensing the possibility of widespread peasant resistance, "the domain discontinued the *ad hoc* levy and instead decided to collect the needed cash from the samurai and the rich merchants."[75]

A trend was being established. The domain, invariably facing peasant opposition when it attempted to increase taxes, began to rely on its retainers and the merchants. In 1753 the domain reduced the stipend of its retainers in the over-50-*koku* class by one-third and made an emergency assessment on the merchants according to wealth. During the next thirty years, samurai stipends were reduced five more times, twice to help pay Bakufu impositions and three times in response to the reduced revenues caused by poor harvests and the Temmei famine. Assessments on the merchants also continued. And, in examining the increasing contributions made by the merchants, we learn two important facts. One is that many merchants were becoming increasingly wealthy during this period; the other is that the merchants received a variety of lucrative privileges and samurai status in exchange for meeting these assessments as well as for making contributions to the domain.[76]

Mori, noting the first of these developments, wrote that from the first decades of the eighteenth century, "as the level of con-

139

sumption rose visibly" and "the increased use of cash in villages induced [more peasants to grow] more commercial crops, the market activities increased, giving rise to very rich merchants,"[77] and:

It was after the Hōreki famine [1755-1756] that the merchant class became an important social force in the domain. Both the Izutsuya and the Omiya, merchant houses which had originally come from Omi before the end of the seventeenth century, had accumulated substantial wealth by the beginning of the eighteenth century, and eventually became the leading merchant houses in the domain.[78]

Mori then goes on to list nine major towns, and a dozen leading merchants in these towns, that became important as commerce grew in the outlying areas. The number of rural merchants also rose from the mid-eighteenth century in response to the demand for their services. As Iwamoto noted, village entrepreneurs, including the leaders of the fishing villages (which also were increasingly oriented towards long distance as well as intradomain trade), were also becoming wealthy by Tokugawa standards.[79]

In return for the cash contributions made by these large urban merchants and rural entrepreneurs, the domain responded by giving them samurai status and often the rights to conduct their commerce on a restrictive basis. We do not know the exact number, but the domain had a large number of *kaneage samurai* (samurai by cash contributions). In fact, in 1783 the domain issued a "price list" for the various ranks of samurai status and privileges. For example, the right to wear swords and use a surname was 50 *ryō*; a promotion from the low-ranked *yoriki* to a bona-fide samurai was considerably more expensive at 620 *ryō*.[80]

Monopoly and monopsony rights were granted to some major contributors and a few were made chief economic advisors to the domain bureaucracy, with high samurai status. The domain was in effect selling its political authority for short-run economic gains and rich merchants "were taking advantage of the desperate financial status of the domain to obtain a variety of economic privileges."[81] Such developments resulted in the virtual control, by the second half of the eighteenth century, of the domain's most lucrative monopolistic and monopsonistic practices by "samurai by cash contribution." The domain shared in the profits realized by these merchants, who controlled an increasingly larger volume of trade in lumber, dried marine products, grains, iron products, and others, but the merchants were the real gainers. Though the domain assessed *ad hoc* "contributions" and taxes on trading, its ability and willingness to enforce the tax provisions were declining because of corruption in high places, and because of the difficulty involved in ascertaining the real amount of transactions both within the domain and across domain boundaries.[82] The volume and variety of commerce were so large that by the end of the eighteenth century the enforcement of tax provisions was beyond the power of the domain bureaucracy, and corruption only compounded the difficulties.

Because the domain finances were severely strained by the Bakufu impositions, the reduced rice tax revenues resulting from the Temmei famine, and from the rich merchants' ability to profit themselves at the expense of the domain, in 1795 the domain instituted a series of new taxes and restrictions on trade. The peasants again reacted predictably. That year saw thirteen peasant uprisings at the village and subdistrict levels, and the domain, which was already making a special levy on its samurai at the rate of 3 *ryō* per 100 *koku* of stipend, again was unable to increase revenue. In six of the thirteen uprisings, it is clear from the existing records that the domain rescinded the taxes outright. In the remainder, the records merely say that "peasants numbering 700 came," or that "the peasants were pacified and disbanded." However, that these uprisings probably also ended in success for the peasants is clear when we read the lament of a contemporary high-ranking samurai: "These actions by the peasants deserved the death penalty. However, none was even charged with a crime. Not only in these areas [where these uprisings took place] but in the domain as a whole, the power of the peasants is strong and we [the samurai] are being taken lightly."[83]

As the end of the eighteenth century drew near, the financial fortunes of the domain deteriorated even further because of a new Bakufu imposition. In reaction to the appearance of Russian ships along the coast of Hokkaido, the Bakufu decided to strengthen the defense of the northernmost island. This meant that, beginning in 1799 and for the following sixteen years, Nambu *han* had to spend approximately 240,000 *ryō* to defend the forts in Hokkaido and the northernmost parts of the domain. For this the

Bakufu reimbursed the domain with only 48,500 *ryō*, which meant that the domain had to pay out, on the average, 12,000 *ryō* per annum.[84] And, as if such a heavy burden was not enough to punish the domain, the Tempō famine of the mid-1830s followed, reducing domain revenues substantially for several years running.

Because of reductions in their stipends and increased dependence on the market economy at the cost of increased indebtedness to the merchants, the samurai could ill afford further contributions to the domain treasury. In fact, as a stanza of a popular song of the 1840s described their circumstances, they were unenviable: "These days, they [samurai] no longer have a *haori* [a formal short coat worn over *kimono*]/If they have one, they are missing *hakama* [a formal trouser-like garment]/It is a shame that they borrow without a hope of even paying interest/That is why, though we all know of their misfortune, no one lends them a copper any more."[85] Many a lower-ranking samurai found "poverty, and lack of freedom unbearable," and during the century from 1764 to 1851 as many as twenty committed suicide and nineteen simply "disappeared." At least one samurai was known to have become a successful moneylender after marrying the daughter of a well-to-do peasant.[86]

Using the rich merchants as a source of ready cash had its drawbacks. The limits and high costs of dependence on them was demonstrated by an episode in 1833. In that year, the domain authorized Izutsuya, the largest merchant in Morioka, to circulate its notes as fiat within the domain. The official pretext was to "alleviate the shortage of money" within the domain and to drive out illegal privately minted coins, but the real reason for the authorization was to benefit the domain coffers while allowing the Izutsuya and other collaborating leading merchants in the scheme to profit. However, "this *de facto* note-issuing semipublic bank, with major merchants in Morioka as its officers and the domain's senior samurai as its supervisors,"[87] in no time issued enough notes to cause severe inflation. Though the domain attempted to circulate the notes at face value as they supposedly were legal tender within the domain, their value fell sharply and, only slightly over a year after the date of initial issue, the domain was seen attempting the impossible task of forcing public acceptance of the notes while at the same time refusing to accept them in tax payments. Domain-wide confusion ensued and the whole scheme had to be discontinued under a Bakufu order.[88]

It is evident that, by this time, the domain's forced dependence on a small number of rich merchants had become counterproductive. While the large merchants, enjoying monopolistic and monopsonistic privileges, enriched themselves, aided by the willing collaboration of corrupt high officials, domain finances worsened. All this left only the peasants as potential saviors of the domain's dire circumstances. They, however, proved as unwilling as ever to come to the aid of the domain, and the Tempō famine hardened their resolve. Between 1801 and 1837 twenty-nine uprisings took place, twenty-one of which were clearly directed against either increases in taxes or reductions in peasant income that would have resulted from changing regulations to reduce the prices of commodities bought by the largest monopsonistic merchants. In three of the uprisings the peasants demanded an extension of the terms of debt payments, and the causes of others, while undoubtedly economic in nature, are either unknown or ostensibly political. As Mori lamented, the state of domain finances was such that the domain policy "sank to its lowest," creating a cycle of "new taxes, peasant revolts, and the temporary withdrawal of the new taxes."[89]

However, of these twenty-nine uprisings, only ten of the twenty-one in opposition to increased taxes and only four of the remaining eight ended in a clear peasant victory. No longer could the peasants expect to win; it was clear now that the hard-pressed domain had become an equally determined opponent.[90] The win–loss score of the peasants reflected, more than anything else, the effects of the Bakufu demands and the Tempō famine, which had to be shared both by the domain and the peasants alike.

The peasants, however, refused to accept increased taxes for long. As the domain continued to enforce into the 1840s those taxes and monopolistic-monopsonistic regulations that had survived the test of the 1830s, the peasants became more impatient than ever before and decided to challenge the domain outright. The challenges were to be known in the history of the domain as the Great Peasant Rebellions of 1847 and 1853.[91]

The Rebellion of 1847 was instigated as the result of an emergency cash assessment the domain made on all peasants and merchants. Since the peasants had long been wanting to eliminate the domain's continued monopsonistic policies, the levy was all they needed to begin the largest uprising in its history prior to that time. Though the peasant reaction was the same throughout the domain, the uprising itself began in the largest and commercially most advanced district, which faced the Pacific. The leaders demanded an end to monopsonistic policies, especially those applying to soybeans and salt, and the rescinding of the emergency cash levy. The peasants marched south along the coast and, to the astonishment of domain officials, the number of participants exceeded 120,000. Well organized in groups, the peasants refused to be persuaded to disband. "They burned numerous torches at night. The procession was orderly. It was a well-run uprising which could be compared favorably to the samurai campaigns."[92] The magnitude of the uprising and the threat to cross the domain border—an action that would make the uprising a "federal case" and be certain to bring Bakufu intervention—were enough to force the domain to rescind the cash levy on the commoners of the district *in toto*, and two-thirds of the levy made on all other districts.

The domain's action eliminating or reducing the cash levy quelled the uprising, but the peasants were far from appeased. They had failed to force the end of the domain's monopsonistic policies, which by this time seemed intolerable restrictions standing in the way of increasingly rewarding market activities.

Several futile uprisings involving only a few hundred people followed. The peasants were now fully aware that only a determined major rebellion could bring an end to the domain's policies restricting peasant commercial activities. Thus, in the winter months of 1852 they began to plan for this. When a call to action was issued on May 7, 1853, after plans had been well laid out, the domain was in for a peasant uprising involving the peasants of six districts, or nearly all of the southern two-thirds of the domain.

The demands that the planners drew up included forty-nine grievances, of which forty-five were economic and four were requests to change some high-ranking domain officials. The economic grievances could be grouped under the headings of: (1) the ending of all the monopsonistic practices; (2) the elimination of the recently increased taxes levied to defray the cost of the increased number of the domain officials assigned to enforce the existing tax provisions; (3) the elimination of all the taxes on trade across domain boundaries; and (4) some changes in the method of tax collections, such as evaluating the portion of the rice tax paid in cash at the market price rather than at a low official price. By Tokugawa standards, the demands were sweeping and challenged most of the domain's tax policies.[93]

With these demands in hand, the peasants began their march southward on May 20. Unlike the march of 1847, this one headed toward the domain border, which the peasants intended to cross in order to ensure their success. The marchers rapidly increased in number; within a week they numbered more than 8,000, and by the end of the month the total number of participants exceeded 25,000. The domain officials, not suspecting the peasants' intention to cross the border or the magnitude of the rebellion, reacted slowly. When they realized the true nature and scope of the rebellion, it was too late. The peasants were not to be stopped by the half-hearted attempts of an armed unit sent out by the domain, and the sheer number of marchers overwhelmed the samurai, who had not seen battle for many generations. "When some samurai came to help defend the domain gate at the border, they found that the 50 samurai in charge and their underlings had already fled the post."[94] More than 8,500 peasants therefore had no difficulty in crossing the border into Sendai *han* on June 5.

What followed was a protracted but unsuccessful effort by Morioka *han* to persuade the peasants to return to the domain. The peasants stayed on in Sendai *han*, which gave them necessary provisions, and during this time negotiations were continued between the peasant leaders and the domain of Morioka, with Sendai officials functioning as intermediaries. In the process, Morioka officials learned that the peasants were unshakable in their demands and that, despite the best efforts of the domain officials, the supporters of the rebellion still in Morioka could not be coerced to put pressure on the peasants in Sendai. All through the negotiations, the officials of Morioka were fully aware that the Bakufu could step into the case at any time and, if it did so, there was a risk that the Bakufu would deprive the Morioka daimyo of his fief. The Bakufu had been known to take such action for even less serious signs of "administrative ineptness."

By early July the domain of Morioka had capitulated to the peasant demands. It agreed to the forty-five economic demands but

145

not to the dismissal of high domain officials, as stipulated in the other four. However, the peasants ended up winning total victory because a later order from the Bakufu forced the offending high officials out of office. The victory assured the peasants of their long-hoped-for right to trade without domain restrictions. After the rebellion the domain never succeeded in reimposing the restrictions or any significant measures to increase taxes. Between 1854 and 1870 the domain, now politically discredited in the minds of the peasants, lost all twelve small peasant disturbances and uprisings. These took place in opposition to domain attempts to increase taxes, to the remaining export taxes, to officials who incurred the disfavor of the peasants, to prohibition to the cutting of trees in virgin forests, and to the money-exchangers' guild.[95]

In reviewing the peasant uprisings in the domain, Mori concluded that the majority of them succeeded in realizing their goals; most of them occurred in opposition to increases in taxes or various forms of restrictions on the market activities of the peasants; and more of the uprisings before the 1780s and all thereafter took place in the more prosperous southern districts of the domain.[96] In short, the peasants fought to maintain and increase their incomes, and we can conclude with Mori that in the main they succeeded in achieving their goals. Both the degree of success achieved by the peasants and the fact that these uprisings were more frequent in the more commercially oriented and prosperous southern part of the domain cast serious doubts on the traditional interpretation of them.[97]

Since the famines played direct and indirect roles in contributing to these uprisings and because it is important to establish explicitly that the aim of the latter was indeed to increase the income of the peasants rather than to prevent a further deterioration of living standards, as is often argued in the traditional literature, let us now turn to assess the severity of the famines and to present evidence on the improving living standards of the commoners in the domain.

FAMINES AND THE POPULATION OF MORIOKA

Japanese works on the domains in the Tohoku region (northeastern Honshu), especially Morioka, are replete with descriptions of the extremely dire circumstances during the famines, which

146

supposedly drove the peasants to destitution, infanticide, and even cannibalism. Historians invariably cite the works of Takahashi Bonsen, and their conclusions are clearly at odds, to say the least, with our observations and analysis indicating growth of the domain economy and a rising living standard for commoners. How severe in fact were these famines? And are the observations made by Takahashi and others accurate?

The most frequently cited data are the domain reports on the effects of the famines. According to these reports and the writings of contemporaries, the Temmei famine of the 1780s was possibly the worst ever to hit the region up to that date. The official number of deaths in 1783 reported by the domain to the Bakufu exceeded 64,000: 40,850 from starvation and 23,848 from the pestilence that followed the famine. Contemporary observers reported seeing "corpses strewn all over."[98] The last of the major Tokugawa famines, the Tempō famine, which lasted from 1832 to 1838 with varying degrees of intensity, was also extremely severe in the Tohoku region. One man described it vividly:

> A cat cost 300 *mon*. . . . Corpses were thrown into wells and there was a report of a woman who ate her children. . . . The starving and dead were all over; some chose to stone children to death instead of letting them suffer death by starvation. . . . Robbery, burglary, and stealing in general were the order of the day. . . . Masterless samurai attacked the old and children. The world was without order.[99]

However, if we try to verify the reports of cannibalism, we find that those who reported it were always repeating what someone else had told them. And it is difficult to verify the number of famine deaths by using either aggregate population figures available for Morioka or by figures reported for various areas within the domain.

Several sets of aggregate population data exist for Morioka *han*. Takahashi has figures from 1680 through 1840 (Table 6.1) that are basically the same as those listed in the *Iwate kenshi*, 5, for the years 1736-1816 (Table 6.2). The source is memoranda in the *Han nisshi* (Domain journal), and thus the figures can be considered official records, or at least one version of them. But if the domain was reporting losses in the tens of thousands from the Temmei famine, they were not reflected in this version of the

Table 6.1
Samples from the Official Population Data for Morioka *han*

Year	Total Population	Births			Deaths		
		Total	Male	Female	Total	Male	Female
1680	301,936	–	–	–	–	–	–
1690	299,717	5,788[a] 3,444		2,547	3,886	2,075	1,811
1700	343,499	4,520	2,343	2,177	3,630	1,846	1,784
1710	350,072	8,678	4,872	3,806	6,431	3,557	2,874
1720	366,577	8,741	4,886	3,855	6,770	3,464	3,306
1730	343,031	6,348	3,639	2,709	6,173	3,366	2,807
1740	367,403	7,857	4,568	3,289	5,176	2,870	2,306
1750	358,488	4,740	2,775	1,965	8,930[a] 4,926		4,104
1760	355,935	6,113	3,207	2,906	4,058	2,193	1,865
1770	358,855	6,846	3,544	3,302	6,810	4,376	2,434
1780	357,705[a]	8,215	4,305	3,910	8,225	4,492	3,733
1790	356,987	8,703	4,426	4,277	8,783	4,462	4,321
1803	357,810	11,293	5,761	5,332	11,913	6,487	5,426
1838	351,332	11,237	5,689	5,548	10,817	5,451	5,366
1840	356,269	11,214	5,678	5,536	10,872	5,484	5,388

[a]Total figures do not equal the sum of males and females, as is also noted by Takahashi.

Source: Takahashi Bonsen, *Nihon jinkō-shi no kenkyū*, Vol. 3 (Tokyo: Nihon Gakujutsu Shinkōkai, 1962), from a table following p. 185.

population statistics. The population was either 356,000 or 357,-000 for every year from 1780 to 1790. Furthermore, Takahashi suggested that over 20 percent of the population of the domain died as a result of the Tempō famine of the 1830s, and thus he has difficulty explaining why the domain population rose from 326,262 in 1818 to 351,332 in 1838 and to 357,207 in 1839.[100]

The authors of the *Iwate kenshi* were clearly puzzled by the conflicting data on the effect of the famines in Morioka. They questioned first the figures for the famine of 1756:

In 1755 the harvest was extremely poor because of frost, rain, and low temperatures. As a result, a severe famine began in the fall of that year. Because of this, contemporary sources reported that the total number of deaths from starvation reached 49,597. If we add to this those who died from disease following the famine, the total exceeded 60,000. Over 20,000 horses were also reported to have perished. However, the *han* record stated that the total population in September of 1755 was 358,222 and that of the following year was still in excess of 350,000. If over

Table 6.2
A Comparison of Population Figures for Morioka *han*

Year	Based on Han nisshi	Based on shūmon-aratame-chō
1740	367,403	367,403
1750	358,488	358,388
1760	355,935	301,590
1770	358,736	305,984
1780	357,705	306,110
1781	357,899	306,110
1782	357,650	305,831
1783	357,896	306,077
1784	356,402	245,963
1785	357,029	246,554
1786	356,447	245,972
1787	357,251	246,776
1788	356,617	246,144
1789	357,357	246,882
1790	356,987	246,157

Source: The left-hand set of figures were selected from the "Table on Changes in the Population of Nambu-han" in Iwate-Ken, *Iwate kenshi*, Vol. 5, pp. 655-659. They are originally from the "Ryōnai jinkōko ruichō," the original of which is based on memoranda in the *Han nisshi* (Domain journal). The right-hand set are from Niitobe Sengaku, ed., "Morioka-han kokō enkaku shiryō 'Kyu-Nambu-ryōnai shūmon-aratame'" in the possession of Count Nambu (as of 1934) and are cited in Mori Kahei, "Meiji shonen ni okeru Iwate-ken no ikuji seido," *Shakai Keizai Shigaku*, Vol. 4, No. 1 (April 1934), pp. 75-76.

60,000 persons died, this is strange. For Shizukuishi-dōri, the section of the *han* which was hardest hit by the famine, the *han* record reported 6,101 deaths. But the actual number of the deaths reported in *Shizukuishi saidai nikki* [A daily record of years in Shizukuishi, a record kept by a local magistrate] was only 800 to 900 even including those who died from disease following the famine.[101]

If "a more accurate" source kept by a local magistrate is to be believed, the domain record exaggerated the number of deaths resulting from the famine by a factor of seven (800-900 vs. 6,101).

Again, with regard to the Temmei famine, the magistrate from Shizukuishi-dōri reported that the total number of famine-related deaths in his region, verified by him in the *shūmon-aratame-chō* (religious investigation records), was about 800 as opposed to the 9,310 reported in the domain records.[102] If the actual number of deaths in the hardest-hit region was less than one-tenth of the magnitude reported in the official domain records, a domain-wide total of over 64,000 is scarcely credible.

The compilers of the *Iwate kenshi* were equally skeptical of the data on the last of the great famines, the Tempō. They chose to say only that "the total number of deaths cannot be established though one expects the number was large because of the continued poor and bad harvests."[103] Could it be that one Haruyama Kichisaburō, a samurai who kept a diary during the period, was more accurate in assessing the severity of famine when he judged the crop failures to have been "relatively limited" and the famine to have been "not so severe" because of large quantities of goods brought in "thanks to the developed commerce"?[104]

But if the population figures in the *Han nisshi* do not reflect losses from the Tempō famine, those compiled from *shūmon-aratame-chō* do. (See Table 6.2.) The latter show a drop from 358,222 in 1754 to 301,686 in 1755 and a loss in the decade 1750-1760 of 15.8 percent of the domain's population. Similarly, the population fell by over 60,000 between 1783 and 1784, representing a loss of 19.6 percent. Thus, according to the figures compiled from the religious investigation records, the total population of the domain dropped by 33 percent during the half century from 1740 to 1790, in contrast to a fall of only 2.8 percent in the set of figures in the *Han nisshi*.

The religious registration data may be more reliable than those in the *Han nisshi* in reporting famine losses if one believes the famine reports issued by the domain. On the other hand, most domains based their regular population reports to the Bakufu on the *shūmon-aratame* records and officials could well have doctored these records at the domain level in order to have the Bakufu believe that the domain was in economic straits and thus unable to bear the burden of additional Bakufu levies. And this set of figures gives precisely the same population, 306,110, for 1779, 1780, and 1781, an unlikely coincidence to say the least.

But if we go back to the *Han nisshi* data, we find more problems of reliability. To begin with, for the entire period (1681-1840) for which data are available, the total domain population for any specific year rarely matches that calculated from the recorded numbers of births, deaths, migrations, and the total population of the preceding year.[105] Second, the total population frequently fluctuated from year to year by more than 3 percent for no apparent reason. For example, the total population in 1731 was smaller by more than 10,000 than that of either 1730 or 1732.

Third, the sex ratio of the domain population invariably fell between a range of 1.1 and 1.2. Such a consistent and abnormal ratio over a period of 160 years is most unlikely because it contradicts both the trends and ranges of the sex ratios found in numerous village studies based on the generally reliable *shūmon-aratame-chō*.[106] It is also curious indeed how Takahashi, who wrote a thick volume on the practice of sex-selective infanticides during the famine-prone latter half of the Tokugawa period, failed to question the constancy of the ratio.[107] Fourth, the means of the crude birth and death rates (20.7 and 19.8 respectively and each with a small variance) that are obtained from the official data are incongruent with the traditional view, which presumes frequent high death rates caused by famines. These rates, however, are comparable to those rates obtained for other regions for which we have much more reliable data. And, finally, the official data show virtually no dip over the years of famines, and it is difficult to believe that there would be so many reports of suffering and deaths had not a fairly large number of people died.

Figures that seem more likely to be accurate than the two sets of domain data already examined, or the domain's assessment of famine losses, are the population data compiled by the domain for internal use—mostly tax and corvée purposes—for the land directly controlled by the domain (*okuradokoro*). (See Table 6.3.) These figures do not include the population residing on and working land distributed as fiefs or the population of the four major towns, including the castle town. The figures show a very slight rise

Table 6.3
The Population Residing on Land Directly Controlled by the Domain of Morioka

1752	286,877
1790	294,336
1818	296,886
1844	297,659

Source: The 1752 and 1790 figures are from *Iwate kenshi*, Vol. 5, p. 676. The figures for 1818 and 1844 were obtained by subtracting the population of the four major towns from the figures on pp. 685 and 708 respectively to get figures comparable to the first two. For 1818 the town population of 29,379 for 1803 on p. 692 was used, and for 1844, the four-town population for 1834 of 28,282 was taken from the same page.

in population from the mid-eighteenth to the mid-nineteenth century, under 4 percent. If these four figures are accurate, they would allow for normal population growth, some out-migration from these rural areas, and moderate losses due to the three major famines.

An analysis of the urban population, that is, the population of the commoners residing in the castle town plus the three other major towns in the domain, reveals nothing to suggest that urban population trends affected the trends of the rest of the domain's population. The commoner population of the castle town grew slowly and steadily from 12,324 in 1683 to 14,120 in 1701 and 16,008 in 1727, and then fluctuated between 15,000 and 16,000 until the 1770s, with the exception of a drop to 12,759 during the period 1758-1762 as a result of the Hōreki crop failures. From the 1770s the castle town population began to grow again, reaching 18,824 in 1803 and 19,505 in 1834, the last year for which urban figures are available. The total for all four major towns followed the same trend, rising from 20,636 in 1683 to just over 24,000 by 1711, then fluctuating around 24,000 for most of the rest of the century, growing to the 25,000 level in the 1770s and 1780s, to over 28,000 in the 1790s, to 29,376 in 1803, and back to 28,382 in 1834. As a percentage of the total domain population shown in Table 6.1, the urban commoner population fluctuated around 6.8 percent from the 1680s through the 1760s, and then rose slowly to just over 8 percent in 1803 and 1834. However, like the other figures for this domain, those for the urban population should be considered indicative of trends only, as the figures occasionally jump back and forth from one year to another, and in general seem to contain all the flaws found in the other official domain statistics.[108]

Whichever set of statistics one chooses to believe, if any, it is unlikely that the Tohoku region, and Morioka *han*, suffered the tremendous population losses the traditional economic historians and demographers would have us believe. First, the 1872 population survey showed an increase of 42.73 percent over the 1846 figures for the five Tohoku provinces facing the Pacific.[109] Although we do not have the figures for Morioka alone because of the changes made in census units, this domain comprised a large part of the Tohoku region and there is no evidence to indicate that developments were much different here from the rest of the region.

It is impossible to believe that the domain of Morioka—or any other in the northeast—grew by this amount in these two and one-half decades, particularly since they were not free from crop failures or poor harvests. Thus, we are on safe ground in assuming that population losses due to famine were far smaller than the domain of Morioka would have had the Bakufu believe.

But there exists a second kind of evidence that is even more convincing than the population data in supporting our view that the effect of the famines has been exaggerated: the abundance of information showing the role played by commerce in mitigating the severity of continued crop failures. Mori, for one, is fully convinced that the samurai quoted above was correct in his assessment, and he himself states:

> Even during the Tempō years, the income generated by the large iron-related industries centered in the Noda and Ono regions and by the commercialized fish oil and fish cake industries on the coastal areas was used to import rice annually, and rice was coming to be consumed as the main staple. The destructive effects of the harvest failures, therefore, were mitigated despite the relatively high frequency of crop failures.[110]

In discussing the effects of the growth of commerce on the severity of the famines, it should be noted that large rice dealers were actively speculating in the changing rice prices by the famine of 1756. And, during both the Temmei and the Tempō famines, the rice merchants held their stock back from sale when they saw the price of rice steadily climbing. These merchants became targets of "criticism, abuse, and even attacks on their warehouses" while the domain authorities "looked the other way."[111] At the time of the Tempō famine such attacks frequently were made on the larger rice merchants, who were thereby persuaded to distribute rice at a lower price or, in some instances, free. During the Tempō famine "the rich merchants of Kōriyama gathered in response to the tension mounting in the air" and decided to distribute rice, cash, and *miso* (bean paste) to about 300 of presumably the poorest in town.[112] Thus, despite the dire picture of the famines drawn by Takahashi and others, the merchants were still allowed to speculate in rice prices and, unlike the famines in a truly subsistence economy, a "social margin" of sorts existed in the warehouses of these merchants even at the depth of the famines.

An obvious question to be asked is why the domain reported the major famines to have been so much more severe than local contemporary witnesses did. Though speculative, a logical answer is the domain's strong and understandable desire to minimize Bakufu exactions. This might explain the discrepancies in the domain statistics: one set was for Bakufu eyes, others were for the domain's own internal use.

But if we have to admit that we cannot resolve the question of whether life was improving or deteriorating in Morioka by population data, we can turn to other sources for evidence of a general rise in the standard of living over the Tokugawa centuries, famines notwithstanding.

THE RISING LIVING STANDARD

Though our evidence for the rising living standard of the commoners of the domain is often indirect and nonquantitative, there is little doubt that the trend of the living standard of commoners was upward during the last century and a half of the Tokugawa period. The famines may have exacted their toll, but their effects on the living standard were neither long lasting nor severe enough to reverse this trend.

It should be stressed at the outset that we do not intend to deny that the major famines had a serious and cruel impact in some years and in a large number of poorer villages. We know that death from starvation did occur and that the undernourished were more susceptible to disease. We also know that the living standard attained by the commoners of the domain, even at the end of the Tokugawa period, was still lower than that enjoyed by commoners in the Kinai and many other parts of Japan. What we wish to argue is only that the living standard of the Morioka commoners continued to rise, as a trend, from the level attained around 1700, and that the traditional view—that the living standard of the Morioka peasants deteriorated during this period—is incorrect.

Because of the acceleration in the growth of commerce during the early decades of the eighteenth century, the signs of a rise in the living standard began to appear and to attract the attention of the domain officials in the towns first. In 1742 a decree issued by the domain to "the artisans and the townspeople," admonished "those who had begun to wear silk" in violation of the long-standing domain policy, and went on to renew the prohibition of the use of silk and other luxuries including "hair styles which do not appear simple and economical."[113]

The improving living standard of urban workers implied by the decree is substantiated by the *Kanjō kōbenki* (Notes on calculations) written by Murai Jinsuke, a Morioka merchant. This rare record tells us that, during the 1760s, the daily earnings for day-laborers were 50 *mon*, for lumberjacks and carpenters 100 *mon*, and for masons as much as 200 *mon*. Since 1 *shō* of polished rice cost only 20 *mon* during the 1760s, these were clearly good wages. If a carpenter worked only 20 days per month, his income per month would buy 1 *koku* of rice, giving him an annual income equivalent to 12 *koku* per year. Even a day laborer, working only twenty days per month, could earn 6 *koku* per year.[114] As discussed in the preceding chapter, these incomes compared favorably with those of lowest-ranked samurai and were not much different from those earned by their counterparts in the Kinai. However, we should not infer from this that the townspeople in Morioka lived as well as those in the Kinai, because the proportion of the total population earning such wages in Morioka must have been smaller than in the Kinai.[115]

Rises in the living standard came also to people who lived outside the towns. In villages that carried on nonagricultural activities, life was undoubtedly becoming easier. A record kept by a magistrate of Noda-dōri informs us that eight salt-making villages in his jurisdiction were given permission to buy over 1,000 *koku* of rice during the month of November 1772. The amount of rice was so large that Mori concluded that "the simple deduction that those who did not produce rice did not eat rice is childish."[116] Clearly chiding Japanese scholars, who often take it for granted that the peasants in the northeast subsisted on inferior grains, Mori went on to say that:

> The mountainous regions of the domain, known to have produced more than 500,000 *kan* of iron per year and to have sold it to all parts of the Ōu region as well as to Edo, Mito, Sōma, and Niigata, imported more than 10,000 *koku* of rice per year. There were many classes of persons who habitually ate rice. . . . They also drank *sake* as a matter of course.[117]

But improvements in the living standard were not confined to the towns and villages engaged in nonagricultural activities. The lot of most of the peasants was also improving because of continued efforts to improve agricultural productivity, more opportunities for by-employments, and the out-migration of peasants to nonagricultural pursuits in towns and other villages. The magnitude of out-migration suggests that higher wages were earned in towns and in by-employments, and this, in turn, helped to raise the wage level in the villages. We can establish that as early as during the period 1712-1752 the number of peasants who worked on land held directly by the daimyo declined from 178,138 to 165,089, despite constant prohibitions, issued by the domain during the period, to restrict peasant out-migration.[118] This was a period free of major natural disasters, and thus the reason traditionally given for the out-migration of the peasants of this domain—the sale of land as a result of debts accumulated as a consequence of natural disasters—is hardly applicable. Though we do not have records on the population cultivating the land held by the samurai of Morioka, if a similar magnitude of out-migration did take place from these fiefs, the total amount of labor lost to agriculture would have been large.

The best evidence for the improvement in the living standard of the peasants during this period is that the number of the poorest in agrarian society—the *nago*—declined. The *nago*, discussed by many Japanese scholars to stress the poverty of the northeastern domains, were landless peasants who cultivated small plots of land owned by landholders and usually lived in detached houses made available to them by the landholders. The *nago* typically provided labor services to the landholders in exchange for the small plot and dwelling. Of the *nago* and other landless peasants in the relatively better-off areas in the domain, Mori wrote:

> The number of marginal peasants in Higashi-Iwai was surprisingly small. According to the *Fūdoki-goyōsho* [an official report on economic and geographic matters] of 1775, marginal peasants existed in 25 of 36 villages. However, most of them were *mizunomi-byakushō* [literally water-drinking peasants, i.e., small tenant cultivators]. There were 216 households in this category, or only 3 percent of the total number of the households. There were only 54 *nago* households of which 47 were

concentrated in one village. Other villages had only one or two such households, clearly indicating that the liberation of the *nago* had been carried out. A similar situation is also found in Kesen. Of the total 1,891 households, there were only 12 *mizunomi-byakushō* and a mere 6 *nago* households. The villages in the districts evidently consisted of the so-called *honbya-kushō* [independent peasants].[119]

Despite the Temmei famine of the 1780s, signs of improvement in the economic circumstances of the domain's commoners continued to increase. By the Kansei period (1789-1800), the practice of eating fresh fish had spread even into mountainous and poorer villages in the domain, and candies made with sugar had begun to be sold widely.[120] By the first decade of the nineteenth century, peasants' clothing had improved noticeably. "The common human psychology of wanting new clothes at the first chance it becomes possible" had begun to "reduce the distinction in wearing apparel by social class."[121] Noting such developments, the domain issued numerous decrees admonishing and prohibiting these "luxuries" and warned the peasants "not to imitate the peasants of the domain of Sendai."[122]

One of the reasons for these developments was an increase in real wages. We find in the *Iwate kenshi* that the median wage for about 120 day-laborers who were recruited to reclaim land in the 1820s in the Ninohe district was 120 *mon* per day. If this data from a relatively less commercialized district in the domain can be considered to indicate the changes in the general level of wages, we must conclude that real wages in the domain had continued to rise, because the price of 1 *shō* of polished rice was only about 30 *mon* during this decade. Thus, a day-laborer who could buy 2.5 *shō* of rice in the 1760s for his day's work was now able to buy up to 4 *shō* for the same amount of work.[123] We believe that this assessment of the change in the real wage is not wide of the mark, since Watanabe's study also shows that persons hired to transplant rice at the peak period were paid as much as 200 *mon* per day, or as much as a skilled mason during the 1760s.[124]

Another reason for the continued improvement in village life was that the peasants now had more opportunities to increase their incomes. The remaining *nago* in most parts of the domain were now able to achieve *nago-nuke* (termination of the *nago* status) with the supplementary cash they were earning in by-employments. "Many were achieving *nago-nuke* because the general level of living was rising,"[125] and even the *nago* who remained full-time cultivators were doing better because landholders were increasingly forced to change their contracts to payments in fixed amounts of cash despite their understandable preference for labor dues.[126] Given that the price level continued to rise during this period, and accelerated after the 1830s, this change in the terms of contract is even more significant.

Small tenant cultivators, who usually fared better than the *nago*, also succeeded in improving their life:

> As nonagricultural activities developed and cash income rose, tenants worked actively to change their contracts so that they could pay off their rent in a fixed amount of cash. Because these tenants could earn cash by raising horses and cocoons, by making charcoal, or by working in mines or as porters, they gradually succeeded in keeping all the output of the land for themselves and paid their rent in cash.[127]

Improvements in the living standard soon went beyond buying more *kimono* or imitating the peasants of the Sendai *han*. A resident of Morioka wrote in the 1830s:

> Everyone has forgotten the righteous way. Now everyone is seeking to profit. . . . In the villages we now have hairdressers and public baths. If you peep into the houses, you see flutes, *samisen*, and drums on display. Those living in rented houses, the landless, and even servants have *haori*, umbrellas, *tabi* [Japanese version of socks], and *geta* [wooden footwear]. When you see these people on the way to the temples, they seem to be better dressed than their betters.[128]

In 1826 a male servant who had completed his contract after some (unspecified) years of service was given a "gift" by his former master consisting of thirty-eight items, the major items including: 3,000 *mon* in copper coins (enough to buy 3 *koku* of polished rice at the market price), 0.6 *koku* of unpolished rice, 3 *koku* of maize, 0.6 *koku* of soy beans, bowls and cups for ten persons, two sets of *futon* (quilted bedding), five tea cups, a variety of agricultural implements, and kitchen utensils.[129] This example, the most meager among several of such lists gathered by Mori, attests to the rise in the minimum standard of life that had become socially acceptable and to the relatively burdensome obligation of employers to supplement the wages of their servants in this manner.

In the urban centers, which had become the object of increasingly frequent domain decrees against "luxuries," we find evidence on the changing level of consumption such as the domain *sake* output in 1833 (after the onset of the Tempō famine). In that year, the castle town of Morioka was allowed to produce "twice as much as was produced in the Bunsei period (1818-1830), despite the fact that the *sake* production must have been controlled" because of the crop failures.[130] We also know from the records kept by villagers and merchants that in the 1850s village retail shops were buying more food items (seaweed, bamboo shoots, and the like) for daily use from wholesalers in Morioka, indicating that commercial activities had expanded even into the daily food items. A record dated 1852 shows that mandarin oranges costing 18 *mon* each and citron (*yuzu*) costing 25 *mon* each were being sold in the towns.[131] There is no shortage of evidence on the luxuries indulged in by the wealthier merchants, but the increasing demand for clothing, *sake*, and other more widely consumed products constitutes important support for evidence of a rising standard of living in the towns.[132]

Perhaps we should add to our brief examination of the changing living standards of the commoners of this domain a revealing paragraph from the work of Mori who, despite the contradictory evidence that he himself unearthed, made an effort to remain a follower of the traditional view:

> The shortage of labor was closely related to the growth of production oriented to the market. And as the development of new industries continued, labor mobility increased. The *nago* became independent and became wage earners. The villages lost agricultural labor, and large-scale farming by landholders became difficult and more paddies had to be leased to the tenant cultivators.[133]

We will be the first to admit that, rather than relying as we have on the works of Japanese scholars who hold the "pessimistic" view, more, preferably quantitative, evidence is needed to establish that the living standard of the commoners of Morioka continued to rise during the second half of the Tokugawa period. However, the fact that the preceding evidence was all obtained from the writings of Japanese scholars who believe that the quality of life deteriorated in the Tohoku region during the eighteenth and nineteenth centuries leads us to believe that further reexaminations of the economy of the domain would provide the further evidence necessary to strengthen the view of economic and demographic development presented in this chapter.

CHAPTER SEVEN

Okayama

The domain of Okayama was selected for inclusion as one of the samples studied here for several reasons, the most important being the rich records available at both the domain and the village levels.[1] Because of the reliability of the local records, three of the four villages whose population trends are analyzed in Chapters Eight through Ten are Okayama villages.

The economically advanced domain of Okayama as a whole belongs to Region I but, inasmuch as it contained a mountainous area in the north that did not share equally in its economic development, it can also be considered a microcosm of Tokugawa Japan. This domain, therefore, is a good example for showing both that the pattern of economic change often varied even within a single domain, and that there were other areas that closely followed the Kinai's path of economic change, though lagging in time. Equally important, Okayama—in contrast to the Kinai and Morioka—represents scores of large, economically above average and politically unified domains ruled throughout the entire period by one daimyo house, which managed to produce competent daimyo generation after generation.

The secure foundation of rule by the house of Ikeda in Okayama was established early in the Tokugawa period, as were the administrations of other large daimyo, such as the Date in Sendai and the Maeda in Kaga. Under Mitsumasa, who governed the domain from 1632 until his retirement forty years later, activist policies were adopted that were to leave their imprint in the years to come. These included the encouragement and support of public works that would result in economic gains for the domain, such as flood control measures and land reclamation; leadership in the cultural and spiritual life of the people through the establishment of schools; and a generally impartial and just administration. John W. Hall has stated that "the outstanding quality which Mitsumasa brought to Bizen was a certain style of benevolent authoritarianism based on Confucian principles of governance."[2] While we make no pretense of examining daimyo and their policies in this study, we believe it is important to keep in mind as we examine Okayama that the quality of administration could and did affect the course of economic and demographic change.

The domain of Okayama was located about 100 miles west ot Osaka, along the northern shore of the Inland Sea between Himeji and Hiroshima. Although composed of several scattered areas, its basic component was the province of Bizen, which included eight districts and the administrative capital, the castle town of Okayama. (See Figure 3.1.) The eight districts comprising Bizen varied greatly in geographical features and size. Five of them either lay along the coast or were accessible to the sea through Kojima Bay. Three of the largest districts, Tsutaka, Akasaka, and Iwanashi, possessed no coastline, but the Asahi River formed the border between Tsutaka and Akasaka, while the Yoshii River divided Iwanashi and Wake, thus giving all of them access to the Inland Sea. The size of the districts tended to be larger than those on the southern, more densely populated, coastal plain.

The domain of Okayama was formally assessed by the Bakufu at 315,200 *koku* throughout the Tokugawa period, giving the Ikeda House status as one of the sixteen largest daimyo.[3] Bizen contributed 289,225 *koku* to the total and land in thirty-six villages in five districts in Bitchū belonging to the domain was assessed at 25,975 *koku*. In addition, when Mitsumasa resigned from office in 1672, *shinden* in Bitchū assessed at 25,000 *koku* were given to his second son, and later another 15,000 *koku* were given as a fief to his third son. The fiefs granted to these sons became branch domains (*shihan*) of the main domain of Okayama. Because of changes that occurred in the land held in Bitchū and the difficulties in dealing in statistics for areas comprising less than one district, our analysis here will be concerned primarily with the eight districts of Bizen. It was, after all, these eight districts that comprised more than 90 percent of the *shuindaka* (formal assessed yield of the domain).

ECONOMIC GROWTH DURING THE SEVENTEENTH CENTURY

Okayama, like the rest of Tokugawa Japan, experienced accelerated economic growth during the seventeenth century. During the first half of the century, reclamation was mostly privately sponsored and on a small scale, but in mid-century, at Mitsumasa's initiative, the domain became actively involved in the creation of new paddies and upland and committed a large amount of its capital to large-scale reclamation and water control projects that benefited entire districts and would have been impossible to carry out by private means. Due to these efforts large tracts of land fronting on the sea in the lower reaches of the three rivers flowing through Bizen to Kojima Bay were reclaimed. By the time these projects, one in Oku and two in Kamimichi, had been completed at the end of the seventeenth century, land capable of yielding more than 100,000 *koku* of grain had been added to Bizen.[4]

In addition to reclamation, the administration carried out a number of large-scale projects that gave Okayama a reputation for engineering and brought important gains to the domain economy. The Kurayasu River was dug to irrigate the newly reclaimed Kurada-*shinden* in Kamimichi. Completed in 1679, it ran for seventeen kilometers and provided irrigation water for an extremely wide area. The Hyakkengawa, also a tremendous engineering feat, was constructed in 1686 as a drainage channel to prevent the castle town from being flooded again as it had been in 1654. It was built across Kamimichi's Oki-*shinden* to the sea, and a large piece of wasteland in Mino was set aside to receive any overflow from the Asahi River to prevent it from directly threatening the castle town. The economic benefits resulting from this project were twofold: the castle town was saved the disruption and expense of floods, and the reclaimed land in Kamimichi was assured an adequate supply of irrigation water.[5]

As significant as the domain's investments of capital and labor were in contributing to the growth of agriculture, there were other no less important reasons for the steady growth of the domain economy. One was the increase in agricultural productivity brought about by improved tools and seeds and the diversification of crops, and the other was the growth of commercial agriculture and commerce. The two, of course, were closely related developments.

Though we lack direct quantitative evidence of a productivity increase on an aggregate level, indirect evidence leaves little doubt of the growth of agricultural productivity during the seventeenth century. A larger variety of rice seeds was becoming available; the use of fertilizers was increasing; and agricultural implements and techniques were continually being improved.[6]

Separated from the Kinai only by the province of Harima, Okayama in all these developments was never much behind the Kinai and in some cases even ahead. The well-known Bitchū-*guwa*, a three- or four-pronged iron hoe, was developed in this area during the mid-century, and the superiority of this innovation was such that it was adopted in the Kinai within a few decades and subsequently in other parts of Japan as well.[7] Okayama was also a forerunner in the use of draft animals, which could be efficiently used on the domain's broad, flat fields. In the period from 1649 to 1665 alone, the number of draft animals in the domain increased by approximately 60 percent, signifying not only a rise in the productivity of agricultural labor but also an ability by villagers to accumulate capital in the form of this valuable agricultural asset.[8]

The surpluses necessary to enable the Okayama peasants to acquire these assets and to make continued capital investments in agriculture were generated by the steady commercialization of farming. Cotton is known to have been cultivated in Kojima by the sixteenth century, and during the seventeenth the output of this crop increased along with that of rapeseed, *igusa* (the kind of rush used for mats), and other cash crops, which were usually more profitable than rice, wheat, or other grains.[9] Attesting to their profitability are the domain decrees in mid-century to assess an additonal 3 *to* of rice if cotton was planted in place of rice and to tax *igusa* at the rate applied to rice paddies of top quality.[10] The increase in taxes apparently did not affect the trend, however, and in 1666 domain records noted that "the upland is now nearly fully planted in rapeseed and wheat is planted less and less."[11] By the Genroku period (1688-1703) it is known that 30-50 percent of the land in some parts of Kojima District was planted in cotton. Because the domain adopted a policy of "letting the peasants do as they please" (*hyakushō katte shidai*)[12] in their use of the land, and because commercial crops were more profitable, the output of these crops continually increased.

The profitability of commercial crops reflected gains resulting from the rapid expansion of commerce, especially with other parts of Japan, through Osaka. In addition to possessing a relative advantage in their fertile plains, excellent irrigation, long and warm summers, and a century of experience in growing cotton and rapeseed, the cultivators of commercial crops in Okayama also benefited from the rapid development of transportation during the seventeenth century. The most important aspect of this was the establishment of the Nishimawari Kaisen, the major shipping route developed during the early decades of the seventeenth century to provide regular services between western Japan and Osaka and then from Osaka to Edo. The ports of Ushimado, Shimotsui, and Saidaiji became increasingly busy entrepôts for Okayama products destined for Osaka for distribution elsewhere, as well as for goods brought in from many parts of Japan. Because the cost of transportation by ship was much lower than by land, the effects of the new sea route in stimulating commercial agriculture and commercial activities in general in the domain were immeasurable.[13]

Both the number and quantity of goods shipped to Osaka rose continuously. The lengthy list of "exports" included "rice, fish, rapeseed, cotton, lumber, oils, salt, beans, and pottery."[14] And, by the beginning of the eighteenth century, the list had grown even longer to include yeast for making *sake,* hats made of rush matting, barrels, leather footgear, tiles, vegetable dyes, nails, spinning wheels, and farm tools (including the Bitchū-*guwa*). Though some local specialty goods such as pottery, hats, and other products could not have been produced in large quantity, others were. For example, in the period 1661-1672, rice was shipped to Osaka in annual amounts of 84,000 *hyō* (or about 33,600 *koku*), which was nearly 10 percent of the total yield of the domain.[15] And a large quantity of salt "must have been sold to other domains" because in the districts of Oku and Kojima the total output in 1708 exceeded many times the quantity that the domain population could consume.[16]

Commerce also grew within the domain itself. If most commercial activities in the villages were still limited to trading with peddlers from nearby towns and the castle town of Okayama, commerce in the castle town, the three port towns, and the ten largest population centers—the latter two groups making up the "thirteen towns" allowed by the domain to produce *sake* on a commercial scale—grew steadily to meet the increasing demand for goods.[17] By 1707 over 10 percent of the population of the domain was classified either as a merchant or artisan or as a *hōkōnin* working in one of the towns in the domain.[18]

Aiding the growth of these towns, and indirectly the economy of the domain, was the busy traffic on the Sanyōdō, the most heavily traveled road in western Japan. Passing through the castle town and along the Inland Sea, this route was used by many western daimyo and their large entourages on journeys to Edo for *sankin kōtai*. The amount of direct economic benefit provided by the traveling daimyo to the post towns is evident in a record from the town of Yakake: "The daimyo of Hagi traveled with 600 to 800 persons and they occupied from 69 to 96 inns. Kagoshima and Hiroshima daimyo required about 60-70 inns. . . . These daimyo paid for the services as they used them."[19] The indirect, stimulating effect on the local economy of the cash spent by these daimyo must have been many times larger than these data suggest.

ECONOMIC GROWTH AFTER 1700

Led by the southern half of the domain, the economy of Okayama continued to grow during the last century and a half of the Tokugawa period. Several serious crop failures occurred, but these had virtually no effect on the unmistakable trend of growth based on further increases in the cultivated area, on the steady rise in the productivity of agricultural factor inputs, a growing output of commercial crops, and the growth of commerce and various manufacturing activities, especially the processing of agricultural products, which involved more and more villagers in the domain.

As in the Kinai, closely interrelated chains of development became readily traceable by the early decades of the eighteenth century. The center of gravity of the domain's economic activities rapidly began to shift away from the castle town of Okayama to the coastal districts, and especially to Kojima. In the south, commercial and manufacturing activities grew steadily on the strength of the ports, the broad, flat fields well suited to major commercial crops, and the growing demand for goods by merchants and peasants whose incomes were rising. In Okayama, as elsewhere, the growth of the economy, accompanied by both socially and individually controlled fertility, caused a shortage of labor and increased returns to labor. And the latter in turn brought about irreversible trends of change in the landholding patterns, in the terms of tenancy, and in the standard of living of the peasants. We shall now turn to describe the major patterns and the effects of the economic growth and demographic changes.

Rice, increasing amounts of which were marketed by the peasants for cash, continued to increase in total output and remained a major factor in the economic growth of Okayama. While the tempo of reclamation slackened in comparison to that of the seventeenth century, new paddies yielding some 54,000 *koku* were added after the beginning of the eighteenth century.[20] The productivity of the existing paddies also continued to rise during this period through the increased application of fertilizers, continued domain and private efforts to improve irrigation, and a variety of other factors, such as more productive seeds and better crop rotation and farm management. Since many of the changes contributing to the increases in productivity were similar to those already described in the chapter on the Kinai, let us add only enough evidence to emphasize the similarities. Commenting on the general increase in the productivity of the paddies, the authors of *Okayama-ken no rekishi* wrote:

> As rice became a cash crop, the yield per *tan* rose sharply. It is known, for example, that in Numa Village in the district of Kamimichi, yield per *tan* rose from about 1.5 *koku* at the beginning of the Edo period to 2.1 *koku* by the mid-eighteenth century. The major reasons for this development of agriculture were the widespread use of dried sardines and *aburakasu* and the use of efficient tools such as the *mangoku* [large wooden thresher] and *tōmi* [Chinese-style winnower]. . . . By the middle of the Edo period, ships loaded with dried sardines were coming in large numbers to the port of Shimotsui and to the villages of Fujito and Amaki.[21]

The most effective incentive for increasing productivity was the domain's tax policy, by which all increases in output due to gains in productivity accrued to the peasant. Before 1720 the sale of any surplus rice by the peasants was illegal, even after taxes had been paid, but after that year all that was needed was permission from the *nanushi* (village head).[22] The further implications of this policy will be discussed later.

In reading a section entitled "Local Repairs" in the *Hōreishū* (A compilation of the domain's laws), we find that the domain constantly involved itself in maintaining and improving irrigation and drainage facilities for the paddy fields and, despite the financial difficulties that the domain experienced, it continued to allocate resources for these local repairs. For example, in 1714, one of twelve years for which we have quantitative data, the domain spent about 3,500 *koku* of rice and wheat combined and over 37 *kan* (37,000 *momme*) of silver for repairs and maintenance in 487 villages. This sum is not one of the largest expended and the year 1714 was free of floods and other natural catastrophes that would have required large expenditures on an emergency basis.[23]

Agricultural productivity also rose because of improved techniques. Seed varieties increased, and the use of both early and late maturing rice seeds enabled farmers to stagger planting and harvesting, and thus make more efficient use of labor. Also, it was discovered in the early nineteenth century that spreading whale oil on the paddy fields was effective in controlling leaf hoppers (*unka*) without harming the crop. This form of pest control was used throughout western Japan and undoubtedly contributed significantly to minimizing losses in crop yields.[24]

The most important contributors to the growth of the domain economy during this period, however, were the commercial crops and the commercial and manufacturing activities related to their processing. Among them, cotton was undoubtedly the most important. As the *Hōreishū* noted in 1803, cotton was planted "everywhere in the villages."[25] Throughout the eighteenth and especially in the nineteenth century, the output of cotton grew, absorbing more and more labor to cultivate, process, and market the crop.

> Centering especially in the area around the castle town, in the *shinden* of Kamimichi, Oku, and Kojima, cotton [planting and processing] expanded in scope. In the five villages of Kōjō-shinden in Kojima, as much as 234 *chō* or about 45 percent of the land was planted in cotton by 1846. . . . It is not difficult to guess the magnitude of the cotton-related activities by the period 1825-1850 when we learn that there were 21 cotton wholesalers in these southern districts.[26]

Peasants planted more and more cotton, finding it an ideal winter crop requiring much less water than rice. As their output increased, they gradually began to get involved in the processing and selling of their product, becoming part-time weavers and merchants of cotton and cotton cloth. And what began as a by-employment to fill slack periods in agriculture grew in time to be the southern districts' major industry, absorbing labor to the point that wage labor had to be brought in from other districts in the domain as well as from outside the domain itself.[27] In the words of the *Okayama shishi*:

> The conditions to make southern Kojima the center of cotton weaving were met. Wage earners came from all parts of the domain and cotton was shipped in from surrounding areas. Weaving, which began on a commercial basis at the beginning of the eighteenth century, grew during the first decades of the century into a large-scale undertaking directed by wholesalers who were adopting the putting-out system. They provided the looms and the necessary materials needed by the weavers. Even factory-like operations using wage-earners were seen.[28]

The domain officials made many futile attempts to slow the growth of cotton-related activities during the nineteenth century, even through the 1850s. Their concern in admonishing peasants from straying from "the real ways of peasants" was, of course, their fear that the rice output would decline as a result of the growth of weaving and trading in cotton.[29] In contrast to rice, which could be easily taxed and was taxed at a higher rate than other crops, the tax rate on woven cotton was only 5 percent of the gross sales value.[30] A lengthy decree issued in 1842 clearly reveals that revenues were the domain's main concern and also shows the extent to which cotton had come to dominate the economic life of Kojima:

> In recent years many have been engaging in weaving of *kokura* and *sanada*. For this reason agriculture has been neglected and the production of rice in the villages has suffered. Despite numerous prohibitions issued against this development, there are still an increasing number of persons who ignore the wishes of the domain and continue to weave *kokura* on a piece-work basis. Therefore, peasants in the district [Kojima] are to take note of the following: Between peak agricultural periods one weaving machine per household is permitted. If the number in the household is large and hands are plentiful, two machines may be permitted but under no circumstances shall more than

169

two machines be permitted within any household. No one is permitted to weave cloth for others. No one may weave using borrowed machines. Even if a person happens to be a former male or female servant he or she shall not weave for the former master. Under no circumstances shall persons be engaged to weave. After the date of this decree even persons from other provinces or other districts should not be engaged for the purpose of weaving. No one should go to towns to be employed as weavers even on a daily basis.[31]

The tone of the decree and the knowledge that many similar decrees preceded this one indicate that the domain was fighting a losing battle. As subsequent events were to prove, this decree, like many before it, was soon evaded and then openly flaunted. As in the Kinai and elsewhere in Tokugawa Japan, the tide of change in the economy away from rice to commercial crops and commerce was hardly to be reversed by strongly worded decrees.

Along with cotton-related activities, salt was another major product that contributed to the continued growth of the southern district. The salt-making industry, which was already substantial by the end of the seventeenth century, continued to increase its capacity into the nineteenth century. Aiding the growth of this industry was the discovery of coal in the hills of Kojima at the beginning of the nineteenth century, and a large quantity of coal was also brought in from the western provinces. Ships "in large numbers came from Owari, Suruga, Ise, Awaji, Settsu, Bitchū, and even from northern provinces" to carry away the salt, the total output of which exceeded 250,000 *hyō* (or 100,000 *koku*) by the 1840s.[32] Tawa, a historian of the industries of the Kojima Bay area, provides a detailed account of Nozaki Buzaemon, a village entrepreneur from Ajino who made innovations in salt-making technology and who operated large-scale salt fields in eight coastal villages in the Kojima and Oku districts. He contributed so much to the domain economy that he was awarded quasi-samurai status (a small stipend and the right to wear swords) by the daimyo.[33]

Next in output to cotton and salt were *shikon* (a vegetable dye, purple blue), used for dying cotton cloth; *igusa*, which was made into mats and sold to Osaka and even to Edo by the nineteenth century;[34] sugar and sweet potatoes, encouraged by the domain; tobacco and the raising of draft animals in the northern districts;

and coastal fishing, engaged in after the mid-Tokugawa period by persons from farming villages as well as from fishing villages.[35] Though the quantitative evidence needed to establish the magnitude of growth of these activities is extremely limited, we do know that up to 200 *chō* were allocated to *shikon* and that its output in 1841 was enough to occupy ninety-seven dyers in Kojima, and that the output of sugar was 140,000 *kin* (184,800 pounds) at about the same time.[36] Only the output of rapeseed, the price of which declined from the beginning of the nineteenth century, appears to have decreased.[37]

Though it is rarely noted in Japanese sources, we must also emphasize that, as in the Kinai, as the output of agricultural and manufactured products increased, so did the gains from trade. Led by Shimotsui and the other port towns, trade with Osaka and elsewhere continued to increase from the high level it had already reached by the end of the seventeenth century. Indicative of the large gains realized from trade was the fact that there were twenty-six wholesalers of cotton products in Kojima alone by the end of the Tokugawa period,[38] and these wholesalers were paying huge *myōgakin* (de facto tax) to the domain. Most of these wholesalers paid about 200 *ryō*, but two in the village of Kami paid 4,000 *ryō* each and one in the village of Hieda approximately 6,000 *ryō*.[39] A tax of 200 *ryō* would have taken several decades for an average agricultural worker to earn, and indicates a total volume of trade amounting to 120,000 *ryō*. A minor daimyo would have been envious of the profits made by just one of these wholesalers.

Although the growth of commerce expanded tremendously from 1700 on, serious attempts to increase the domain's revenues by controlling trade were not made until very late in the Tokugawa period, and even then they were never pushed as vigorously as in Morioka. For example, only in the 1840s did the domain first try to share in the lucrative exports of *kokura*-weave through newly created domain-controlled channels of distribution (buying monopsonistically and selling through designated Osaka merchants). But even this policy was pursued only halfheartedly because "some of the samurai advised against the scheme" and "it was realized that increasing trade [in the absence of restrictions] earned more gold from other domains" to benefit the domain as a whole.[40]

POPULATION AND ECONOMIC GROWTH

Data on changes in the distribution of the population within the domain and its growth rates provide us with further evidence on the trends and nature of Okayama's economic growth as well as providing support for our hypothesis concerning the relationships between the rising income level and the growth rate of the population. The population data aggregated at the domain and district levels, and for the castle town and villages, show that the total population, both of the domain as a whole and of Bizen, reached a peak at the beginning of the eighteenth century that was never exceeded at any time during the last century and a half of the Tokugawa period, and that the center of gravity of the population shifted visibly to the south and to the rural areas, out of the castle town.

On the basis of all the evidence we have on the economy and the activities of commoners within the domain, we can interpret these population trends as follows: First, the distribution of population within the domain shifted because the southern districts were able to offer more employment opportunities than the castle town and the northern districts. Thus, the shift was a result of the growth of rural commerce and the continued expansion in planting and processing of commercial crops in the villages, replicating the pattern that we have already seen in the Kinai. Second, the total population in the domain remained generally stable during the eighteenth and nineteenth centuries, not because of famines or the increasing poverty of the peasants, but because of the desire on the part of the commoners to improve their living standard. In advancing these arguments we must, of course, remain mindful of differences in the rates of growth of the population, and of the pattern and magnitude of migration among the southern districts—even among the villages within a district. In addition to the desire for higher income, there were a variety of social and other reasons for the low rate of population growth in Okayama. As will be made evident in our closer examination of demographic changes in the sample villages from Kojima and Kamimichi in Chapters Eight, Nine, and Ten, we by no means assume that the apparent stability of population can be explained simply in terms of successful fertility control exercised in order to raise the living standard of the villagers.

Beginning with the aggregate data for the domain and for the province of Bizen, which must be used with caution because of discrepancies and inconsistencies discussed in Chapter Three, we note that the population failed to grow after the early decades of the eighteenth century. Table 7.1 contains the data for eight out

Table 7.1
Aggregate Population Figures for the Domain of Okayama
and for the Province of Bizen

Year	Total Population[a]	Index (1665 = 100)	Year	Population of Bizen[f]	Index (1721 = 100)
1665	307,241	100.0	1721	338,523	100.00
1680	317,096	103.2	1750	322,982	95.41
1707	375,724	122.3	1756	325,550	96.17
1738	368,343[b]	119.9	1786	321,627	95.01
1765	357,007[c]	116.2	1798	321,221	94.89
1798	369,778	120.4	1804	318,273	94.02
1804	366,665[d]	119.3	1822	318,203	94.00
1834	367,039[e]	119.5	1828	318,771	94.17
			1834	318,647	94.13
			1846	310,576	91.74
			1872	331,878	98.04

[a]This figure includes both rural and urban populations for the entire domain, including the areas located in Bitchū.

[b]This figure may be lower than it should be if the drop in Mino's population in this year was due to misreporting.

[c]The figure is for circa 1765.

[d]Taniguchi added the urban population of 1812 to the rural population of this year to obtain this figure.

[e]The total was obtained by adding the population of the castle town in 1838 (20,173) to the rural population (346,866).

[f]These figures are only for the eight districts of Bizen as cited in the national aggregate data discussed in Chapter Three.

Source: The total population figures are quoted in Taniguchi Sumio, Okayama hansei-shi no kenkyū (A study of the history of the administration of Okayama domain) (Tokyo: Hanawa Shobō, 1964), p. 458. The figures for Bizen are found in Sekiyama Naotarō, Kinsei Nihon no jinkō kōzō (The population structure of Tokugawa Japan) (Tokyo: Yoshikawa Kōbunkan, 195), p. 139.

of fifteen different years for which domain data exist; only these eight are presented because the other seven either are not comparable or not reliable because of differences in coverage, unclear specification of the reporting unit, or other problems.[41] The domain data in Table 7.1 show a commoner population, including

rural and urban inhabitants, of over 300,000 for these two centuries, rising during the late seventeenth century and then leveling off to between 360,000 to 370,000 for the rest of the period.
It is difficult to make any more precise statement than this because rises and falls of a few thousand may well have been due to
differences in the compilation of figures, and were certainly due to
changes over time as to which villages in Bitchū were included in
the domain. What seems remarkable is the consistency in the figures from 1707 to 1834, despite famines, periods of good harvest,
epidemics, and all the economic vagaries that can occur in the
course of thirteen decades.

The data at the district level show that the apparent stability in
the aggregate population masks widely varying rates of population
change (Table 7.2). While Mino, Kamimichi, and Kojima grew
between 1679 and 1834 by more than 30 percent—the Bizen
average—the other five districts failed to keep pace with the domain average, and Iwanashi and Akasaka even lost population.
The data for Mino clearly contain serious errors because it is
highly improbable that the population more than doubled in the
fourteen years from 1707 to 1721 and then dropped back again
almost to the level of 1707 in the twelve years from 1726 to 1738.
Even discounting the Mino data, we can safely argue that the
southern half of the domain gained a considerable amount of
population, led by Kojima's gain of 75 percent, which was followed by Kamimichi's addition of more than 46 percent.

Table 7.3 makes explicit what is implicit in Table 7.2 by showing the distribution of population in the districts in relative terms
at three points in time. Kojima's share rose from 17 percent in
1679 to 22.8 percent in 1834 and Kamimichi's from 14.3 percent
to 16.1 percent. It is clear from this table that the center of gravity
of the population was shifting southward. Equally obvious is the
declining size of the average landholding per person in Kojima.
Even in the early eighteenth century average landholdings in this
district were the smallest in the domain, and by 1834 Kojima
had 22 percent of the province's population but only 11.1 percent
of the land based on the cultivated area in 1702, there having been
little reclamation during the eighteenth century. This decline in
landholding size took place during the very period when Kojima's
economy was beginning to develop so rapidly, and provides additional evidence to show that the development was not based on

Table 7.2
The Population for the Eight Provinces of Bizen

Year	Mino Figure	Mino Index	Kamimichi Figure	Kamimichi Index	Oku Figure	Oku Index
1679	17,679	100.0	35,021	100.0	42,886	100.0
1707	21,558	121.9	38,094	108.8	46,107	107.5
1721	51,817	293.1	46,293	132.2	50,561	117.9
1726	51,163	289.4	47,456	135.6	51,989	121.2
1738	23,444[a]	132.6	39,021	111.4	48,469	113.0
1798	40,933	231.5	50,782	145.0	44,599	104.0
1834	40,630	229.8	51,354	146.6	44,578	103.9

Year	Wake Figure	Wake Index	Iwanashi Figure	Iwanashi Index	Akasaka Figure	Akasaka Index
1679	30,287	100.0	17,815	100.0	27,224	100.0
1707	34,040	112.4	20,780	116.6	32,478	119.3
1721	35,697	117.9	21,231	119.2	34,156	125.5
1726	36,562	120.7	21,536	120.9	34,688	127.4
1738	35,432	117.0	21,795	122.3	33,651	123.6
1798	32,755	108.1	17,930	100.6	27,839	102.3
1834	32,187	106.3	16,223	91.1	26,073	95.8

Year	Tsutaka Figure	Tsutaka Index	Kojima Figure	Kojima Index	Total Figure	Total Index
1679	31,825	100.0	41,443	100.0	244,180	100.0
1707	39,707	124.8	51,738	124.9	284,503	116.5
1721	42,816	134.5	55,942	135.0	338,513	136.6
1726	43,295	136.0	58,379	140.9	345,068	141.3
1738	42,820	134.5	59,503	143.6	304,135[a]	124.6
1798	37,342	117.3	68,615	165.6	320,795	131.4
1834	34,652	108.9	72,510	175.0	318,207	130.3

[a]The Mino figures are obviously inaccurate for some years, but they have been left unadjusted because it is not yet known just which years are inaccurate or how inaccurate they really are.

Source. The Bizen figures for 1679 and 1834 are from the *Gogungun mononaridaka narabi ni ninzū sono ta* and the *Ninzū chō,* respectively, and are quoted in Taniguchi Sumio, *Okayama hansei-shi no kenkyū,* pp. 460-461. The remaining Bizen figures were compiled from documents from Okayama in the collection of Professor John W. Hall. The 1707 figure is from the *Arinin aratame chō,* that for 1721 from the *Ryōchi tahata chōbu ninzū chō,* and those for 1738 and 1798 from the *Ninzū aratame chō.*

Table 7.3
Percentage of Cultivated Land and Population of Each District
in the Total Bizen Figures

District	Population			Cultivated Land[a]	
	1679	1726	1834	1702	1702 in chō[b]
Mino	7.2	14.8	12.8	12.9	2,803
Kamimichi	14.3	13.8	16.1	18.0	3,893
Oku	17.6	15.1	14.0	12.9	2,790
Wake	12.4	10.6	10.1	9.3	2,007
Iwanashi	7.3	6.2	5.1	7.4	1,605
Akasaka	11.1	10.1	8.2	12.8	2,770
Tsutaka	13.0	12.5	10.9	15.7	3,392
Kojima	17.0	16.9	22.8	11.1	2,393
TOTAL	99.9	100.0	100.0	100.0	21,653

[a]Since the major reclamation projects were carried out in the seventeenth century, the comparison between population and land is more valid than it would otherwise be when data on land are available for only one year.

[b]One chō equals 2.45 acres.

Source: Percentages of population were calculated from the figures in Table 7.2. The land figures are those quoted by Taniguchi, Okayama hansei-shi no kenkyū, p. 330.

increases in land, but on the more efficient use of land and on growing commercial activities.

Two major forces were at work in bringing about the shift in the distribution of population. One was the strong "pull" of employment possibilities in the southern districts, especially in Kojima and Kamimichi where the prosperous port towns and the weaving industry provided ample opportunities for by-employments, and the other was a gradual relative decline in the economy of the northern districts and the castle town, which acted as a "push."

Findings on labor mobility in the villages of Fujito in northwest Kojima, Fukiage adjacent to the prospering port of Shimotsui, and Numa, a small farming village in Kamimichi, are useful in indicating how labor was moving to obtain employment or higher wages.[42] First, in all three villages the number of persons seeking work outside their own village declined over time as the demand for labor within the village rose. All three villages sent persons to work in the castle town through the eighteenth and into the nineteenth centuries but, by the mid-nineteenth century, not a single person from any of these villages is recorded in any of the extant registers as going to work in the castle town. Fujito residents ceased to go to the castle town sometime between 1810 and 1825 (a period for which there are no *shūmon-aratame-chō* for this village), Fukiage residents sometime between 1826 and 1854 (again a gap in the records), and Numa's sometime between 1832 and 1860 (also a gap).

Migration between areas does not show one-way flows; nevertheless, certain patterns can be discerned. Until well into the nineteenth century both Fujito and Fukiage employed more persons from adjacent villages than they sent out to the same areas. By the mid-nineteenth century a few persons from northwest Kojima were still coming to Fujito to work and from southwest Kojima to Fukiage, but virtually no one was going from these two villages to nearby areas. Migration for employment involving Numa was almost all within the district of Kamimichi. However, particularly in the early years when the net immigration figures were high, persons were coming from the northern districts of Akasaka and Iwanashi to work in Numa.

Much of the movement for employment for all three villages was within the village—people going to work in households other than their own. These figures were certainly even higher than are indicated in Table 7.4, as often a member of one household was listed as working in another, but this was not noted in the household in which he was employed. Certainly, hiring within the village on a short-term basis was not entered in the records as it involved no change of address or movement requiring the permission or attention of the authorities. And employing villagers was obviously the most common way of making efficient use of labor resources within the village. Thus, the most striking development involving migration for employment was the drop in migration figures for all three villages in the mid-nineteenth century. The number of persons in Fujito and Numa who went to work in other households in the village dropped almost to zero. Though net immigration for employment in Fujito, for example, remained almost constant in the 1840s and 1850s, it involved the movement of far fewer people than previously.

The trend of population growth in the castle town of Okayama supports our analysis of the pattern of labor mobility presented

Table 7.4
Net Migration for Employment in Sample Okayama Villages

Year	1 Worked outside village	2 Came into village to work	3 Net immigration for employment (2 − 1)	4 Worked within village in household other than own	5 Hired labor within village (2 + 4)
			Fujito		
1775	27	43	+16	7	50
1794	30	26	−4	9	35
1799	28	22	−6	11	33
1804	12	15	+3	14	29
1809	9	15	+6	7	22
1825	8	6	−2	3	9
1830	10	17	+7	3	20
1835	3	7	+4	1	8
1837	2	3	+1	2	5
1841	2	2	0	3	5
1846	3	7	+4	2	9
1852	4	7	+3	4	11
1857	6	12	+6	1	13
1863	8	15	+7	3	18
			Fukiage		
1685	8	4	−4	9	4
1693	11	5	−6	1	6
1700	30	11	−19	0	11
1706	25	13	−12	0	13
1712	26	24	−2	0	24
1727	23	26	+3	0	26
1730	22	37	+15	0	37
1741	38	40	+2	0	40
1773	15	47	+32	3	50
1780	17	30	+13	2	32
1787	15	32	+17	5	37
1797	30	40	+10	4	44
1801	25	41	+16	1	42
1821	26	21	−5	2	23
1826	17	22	+5	2	24
1854	3	3	0	3	6
1860	1	4	+3	0	4
			Numa		
1780	18	35	+17	2	37
1785	23	31	+8	5	36
1796	24	22	−2	10	32
1801	13	26	+13	1	27
1814	11	15	+4	5	20
1819	27	13	−14	5	18
1823	31	15	−16	4	19
1828	28	6	−22	7	13
1832	25	9	−16	3	12
1860	11	6	−5	1	7
1865	17	2	−15	4	6
1871	9	0	−9	0	0

here. Although there is no reason to assume the population figures for the castle town of Okayama are much more reliable than those of any other domain, the data indicate the general trend, which was one of decline during the eighteenth century. The official figures show a population of around 30,000 in the castle town during the late seventeenth and early decades of the eighteenth century. Then the population dropped from 30,296 in 1721 to 26,349 in 1738, and further to 21,218 in 1798 and to 20,173 in 1838. On an index in which 1680 and 1721 would both be 100, the population by 1838 would be only 67.2.

However, the fall in the castle town population seems to have been due to a drop in the transient population, because the number of home owners rose gradually but steadily during the second half of the eighteenth century, while the number of houses rented dropped steadily from 3,195 in 1753 to 2,137 in 1783. Thus, the total number of houses declined by only 300 during this same period.

From this evidence we can conclude that the number of day-laborers and other marginal members of the town economy who would be expected to constitute the bulk of renters declined because in-migrants in this economic category ceased to come into the town and because some lower-income residents may have left in search of higher wages. It is also possible that the wealth level of some of the renters rose sufficiently to enable them to purchase or construct houses of their own, which would account for the nearly 700 new homeowners created during the period 1753-1783. But in either case, it means that the average income of the people who lived in the castle town must have risen over the course of the period.

However limited it may be, what evidence there is clearly lends support to our view that the intra-domain distribution of population was changing for economic reasons. The absence of data on the possible differentials that might have existed in the natural growth rate of population between the southern and the northern districts prevents us from ascertaining the exact magnitude of economic mobility, but it is most unlikely that the natural growth rate of the population changed at such divergent rates in the two areas of the domain as to invalidate this conclusion.

We must now turn to the question of the relative stability of the total population of the domain. More specifically, if economic growth was continuing and the living standard of the peasants was rising, as we will explicitly argue in the final section of this chapter, why did the population fail to increase? In contrast to our answer that social and individual control exercised over population growth in order to improve the living standard was the main cause of this stability, the traditional answer has been that the increasing impoverishment of the peasants, especially those in the lower income levels, and famine were the major causes of the lack of population growth.

Since we will return to evaluate the changes in the standard of living in Okayama later in this chapter and present evidence for our demographic hypothesis in Chapters Nine and Ten, let us here examine only the effects of the famines on the domain population. As we have seen in Morioka, the readily available descriptions of the famines, if not analyzed with care, can easily lead one to exaggerate their effects. Okayama is no exception in this regard. Since the most severe famine to hit Okayama was the Tempō famine of the mid-1830s—the Temmei famine of the 1780s was much less severe in western provinces than in the northeast—let us first follow the description of the Tempō famines drawn up by Okayama officials of the period.

An outline of the nature and the effects of the famine of the mid-1830s, as compiled in a report of 1888 based on contemporary documents,[43] conveys a grim picture of Kojima:

> Since last winter, the eleventh month, the weather has been inclement, and starting from the New Year, rain has continued to fall. The temperature has been exceedingly irregular, and in the second month no one was wearing padded clothing [because of the unseasonally warm weather]. Flowers and shrubs failed to yield fruit and when they did bear fruit rarely did it mature.

The yield of rice was estimated at about 5 percent of the average yield and that of wheat was equally disastrous. This caused the prices of these crops to rise cxorbitantly, with rice going from 210 *momme* (of silver) per *koku* in the second month to 270 by the fourth month, and to 300 by the eighth month in contrast to the 80-90 *momme* range prevailing before the onset of the famine. The victims of the famine, "sufferers," went to the mountains where they dug out roots of various grasses that they were forced to eat. Some died from starvation while others suffered from "swollen bellies and acute diarrhea" because of the things they ate. Finally, in the beginning of the fourth month of the following year, the domain supplied relief rice to the sufferers, though the total amount is unknown. Earlier in the year some of the local rich made donations of rice and wheat.

Information on conditions in other districts in Bizen is similar. It was reported in the northern district of Tsutaka that there was heavy rain as in Kojima, causing a huge flood on the last day of the fifth month which washed away many dikes and irrigation ditches. The fifth month was so unseasonably cold that the farmers transplanting rice seedlings had to wear garments of double-layered padded cloth and continued to wear heavy winter clothing for weeding. There was more flooding in the sixth month. The temperature was like that of the third month, and it was so cold and wet that the fall mushrooms began to grow. The yield of all crops was below normal; early rice was 70 percent of the normal output, but the late crop was only 30 percent. Summer vegetables, such as cabbages and cucumbers, produced only a fifth of what a usual year brought, and cotton only slightly more than 10 percent. The report from Tsutaka noted that people dug roots, collected nuts of all kinds, and even ate the soft part of the wheat husks. People scattered in all directions in search of food, and vagrants flowed in from other areas to beg for food, often dying on the road, unable to move farther.

In Akasaka, another northern district, the situation was no better. "Most of the people were so weak they were unable even to talk. Their skin swelled in strange colors and they screamed with pain and hunger. Conditions were such that they finally decided to eat their draft animals, despite the consequences. Some were reduced to thievery." The officials in Wake reported that the "yield of rice was most accurate when one says it was nil." Harvests had been poor since 1833 and thus the price of rice continued to rise, reaching 250 *momme* by spring 1837. Because of the continued years of high rice prices, even people with savings could not get by, and many sold "long-possessed meager treasures to prevent starvation."

Even if we do not dispute that a major famine in Okayama did indeed occur and that contemporary perceptions of its effects were expressed genuinely, the danger of accepting these descriptions at face value quickly becomes evident when one examines the evidence more carefully. In reading the report of 1888 more closely we find that in Kojima, of "those who died from diarrhea, seven out of ten were vagrants and not registered people." If they were not registered villagers, they may have been people who fled worse conditions elsewhere and who most likely were transients belonging to the most marginal of the economic groups. The best the head of the Kojima district could do in copying the documents in 1887 was to say that the details on deaths from the famine were unknown. If the conditions in Tsutaka were nearly as bad as described, why was the petition to reduce the *sake* output to one-third ignored? And why was this report, official and supposedly complete, so meager in quantitative evidence, saying only that "eight or nine beggars" are reported to have died, or that "several hundred died from starvation"? And why did the reported yield of rice differ from 70 percent of normal to nil?

In attempting to arrive at a more reliable picture of the effects of the famine, we can take another route. This is to examine the population data themselves. In going to the data (Table 7.2), we discover that the figures for the population of Bizen compiled by the Bakufu dropped by just over 8,000 between the years 1834 and 1846. Though we must be cautious in using the data, a decline of 2.5 percent during the twelve-year period, we believe, reflects the magnitude of the impact of the Tempō famine on the domain population more accurately than the dire descriptions found in the report of 1888. And the Temmei famine reduced the population by only 400 between 1786 and 1798. Our analysis of the impact of the famine on our sample villages in Chapters Nine and Ten supports this assessment.

While we in no way intend to deny that the Tempō famine was severe or that it contributed to the decline in the population during the 1830s and 1840s, the facile use of famine as an explanation for the stability of the population in the domain prompts us to ask: why did population also fail to increase between 1804 and 1822? Or between 1822 and 1828, when all signs indicate that economic growth was accelerating without the interference of famines or any known natural disasters? The major Tokugawa famines may have been responsible for decreases in the population in certain decades and certainly adversely affected the health of thousands, possibly lowering fertility and probably raising mortality in the decades of major crop failures, but certainly famine was not responsible for the continued low or zero rates of population growth in the province of Bizen for the 125 years from 1721 to 1846.

In short, the Tempō and other famines, given their magnitude and frequency in Okayama, provide only a very partial explanation for the stability of the total population. It therefore is evident that to explain the low rate of population growth in Okayama despite its steady economic growth, a hypothesis such as the one we advance on social and individual population control must be pursued. We shall do so in succeeding chapters.

CHANGES IN LANDHOLDING

Important evidence testifying to the continued growth of the Okayama economy, especially in the southern half, is provided in the observed changes in landholding patterns that occurred gradually during the second half of the Tokugawa period. Unlike many Japanese scholars who see in these changes the "disintegration" and the impoverishment of the peasant class, we view them as products of the peasants' economically rational reaction to the effects of economic growth, mainly to the increasing scarcity of labor. We view the changes in the landholding patterns in the Kinai (examined in Chapter Five) and in Okayama as similar, and similar for the same reasons.

Though there were variations due to specific local conditions in factor and product markets and to a variety of other reasons, the changes generally observed in Bizen were a gradual increase in the number of peasants who owned or worked 3-5 *tan* of land, and a rise in the number of persons who owned or worked less than 1 *tan*, dividing his (and his family's) labor between agriculture and by-employments. At the same time, the largest landholders either sold or leased part of their land and thus the number of persons owning more than 5 *tan* declined. Contributing to the increase in the number of less than 5-*tan* farms was the subdivision of land to sons or other relatives (*bekke*), which grew more frequent with time despite the official prohibition of the practice. In short, what took place in Bizen was a visible trend toward a decline both in the mean and the variance of landholding size within villages.

The data presented in Table 7.5 for the village of Fujito in Kojima show perhaps a typical pattern of change that occurred in

Table 7.5
Landholding Distribution by Size (*Kokudaka* Class):
Fujito Village, Bizen 1604-1865 (in household units)

Year	0-1	1-3	3-5	5-10	10-20	20-30	30-50	50-100	Total No. of Landholders
1604	27	11	10	10	8	2			68
1703	16	19	16	16	4	1			72
1721	16	28	13	15	1	2			75
1742	53	42	13	15	1				124
1804	51	38	16	7	10			1	123
1806	56	35	17	9	9	1		1	128
1813	51	43	14	15	4	1			128
1828	46	50	25	18	1			2	142
1841	41	38	37	14	3		1	1	135
1857	35	43	39	19	1	1	1	1	140
1865	38	49	40	18	1	1	1	1	149

Source: Ōta Ken'ichi and Matsuo Keiko, "Bakumatsu-Meiji shoki ni okeru jinushi-sei no tenkai — Okayama-han Kojima-no-kōri Hikasa-ke o chūshin to shite" (The development of the landlord system in the Bakumatsu and early Meiji periods — with a focus on the Hikasa house of the Kojima district in the domain of Okayama), *Okayama Shigaku*, Nos. 7-6 (June 1960), p. 52.

many villages in the more rapidly growing districts in Bizen. A few trends of change in the distribution of landholdings, measured in *koku*, are clearly discernible. Persons holding 1-3 *koku* increased up to the mid-eighteenth century; the number of persons with a holding of 3-5 *koku* rose slowly at first but more rapidly after the early decades of the nineteenth century; these two groups together increased in proportion to the total number of the households from less than one-third to about 60 percent; and the peak number of holders of 0-1 *koku* was reached at the beginning of the nineteenth century and declined thereafter. Though the table does not reveal this, we know that the two largest landholders, the Hoshijima and the Hikasa families, reduced their holdings rapidly during the nineteenth century, preferring to invest their money elsewhere.[44] The former, the largest landholder in the village, had well over 50 *koku* of land from the early nineteenth century until 1841 but, after reaching a peak of approximately 75 *koku* in that year, his holdings fell to 48 *koku* in 1845. The Hikasa, whose holdings rose from less than 20 *koku* in 1810 to 60-70 *koku* in the years 1818-1827, reduced the family's holdings to the 30-40 *koku* level during the period 1828-1838, and they remained at this level to the end of the Tokugawa period.[45]

Similar trends occurred in other villages as well. To cite only a few examples, in Numa village in Kamimichi, the number of peasants holding more than 5 *tan* declined from 11 to 4 during the period 1796-1860, while those holding less than 3 *tan* increased from 35 to 44 during the same period. In this village, the holders of 3-5 *tan* increased by only 1, from 8 to 9, during the same period.[40] In the village of Fujino in Wake district, the number of persons holding less than 1 *koku* and between 1 and 5 *koku* rose during the years 1703-1852 from 32 to 115 and from 56 to 97 respectively, while the two largest landholders with more than 35 *koku* had disappeared by the end of the eighteenth century.[47] The example of changes in the landholding pattern in a section of the village of Tōmi in Mimasaka, a province immediately to the north of Bizen, shows that the less rapidly growing regions to the north also experienced a change similar to that seen in the southern districts of Bizen (Table 7.6). While the number of holders of less than 1 *koku*

Table 7.6
Landholding Distribution by Size (*Kokudaka* Class).
Tōmi Village, Mimasaka 1698-1846 (in household units)

Year	0-1	1-3	3-5	5-10	10+
1698	7	6	3	7	2
1705	2	7	5	7	2
1728	7	8	9	8	0
1741	9	10	6	9	0
1746	9	6	2	10	1
1759	11	4	3	8	2
1779	9	8	3	8	1
1796	4	9	7	10	0
1822	3	4	14	7	0
1840	2	6	11	8	0
1846	1	8	13	7	0

Source: Setonaikai Sōgō Kenkyūkai, ed., *Sanson no seikatsu — Okayama-ken Tomata-gun Tōmi-mura-Ō* (Life in a mountain village — Tōmi-mura-Ō of the district of Tomata in Okayama Prefecture), No. 3, *Sonraku sōgō chōsa hōkoku* series (Okayama: Setonaikai Sōgō Kenkyukai, 1955), p. 46.

of land steadily declined after 1759 in this village where there were fewer opportunities for by-employment, the number of persons holding 3-5 *koku* clearly increased after the mid-eighteenth century. Though not shown in the table, the holdings of the largest landholder in the village declined from 16.69 *koku* in 1698 to less than 8 *koku* in 1846.[48]

The importance of the effect of *bunke* or *bekke* (establishing branch households) on the observed trends of change in the land-holding pattern in Bizen is clearly indicated in the example of Ajino village in Kojima. Though we do not have data on changes in the distribution of landholdings, we know that the number of landholders increased from 103 to 234 between 1681 and 1842 and that most of this increase (105) came after 1785.[19]

We strongly believe that, contrary to the traditional explanation, the increasing number of less than 1-*koku* or 1-*tan* cultivators indicated the increased availability of alternative means of earning and increasing household income in the form of weaving, part-time trading, agricultural day work, or fishing. For example, in Kojima, owning a boat was considered the equivalent of owning paddy. Weaving could be done in the slack seasons or full time, and agricultural day work brought increasingly higher wages, making it an attractive minimum-risk alternative to farming a small plot.

Naitō, who discussed the general trend of the increase in commercial activities in the villages of Bizen, wrote that only *sake*, candies, and footwear were sold during the mid-eighteenth century in Numa and these by passing merchants, but by 1863 there were twenty-four village households trading in ten different commodities on a part- or full-time basis.[50] An even better indication of the relationship between the changing pattern of landholding and the availability of opportunities for alternative employment is the following:

In 1854, in the village of Ajino, 25 of the looms for *kokura*-weave belonged to the poor peasants owning less than 5 *koku*. In 1855, 20 poor villagers of Fujito with landholdings of 3-5 *koku* operated 21 looms for *kokura*-weave and 3 for *sanada*-weave. In the same year, 22 looms for *kokura*-weave were being used by 17 peasants who belonged to the middle level of the peasant class. That is, the holders of looms were the middle to lower levels within the peasant class and each usually operated one or two looms. It is said, however, the total value of the annual output of *kokura*, *sanada* and *unsai* weaves during the 1850s was as much as 74,000 to 75,000 *ryō* in the district of Kojima.[51]

In Naitō's view, this development in Numa and elsewhere in Bizen was the reason why "further land divisions within the peasant class" occurred, in other words, why we find a number of small land-holders coexisting with persons holding larger amounts of land.[52]

Additional evidence indicating increased employment oppor-tunities in general—in agriculture, in weaving, or in part-time commerce—in Bizen villages is the trend toward an increase in the number of persons who came to work in these villages and in the number of villagers who remained in the village rather than seeking employment outside the village. While these trends have already been discussed earlier, let us add another example (Table 7.7), which provides quantitative evidence of increasing employment opportunities within the economically buoyant villages of southern Bizen. As in the three villages in Table 7.5, in this

Table 7.7
The Declining Number of Hōkōnin from Hazama Village,
Kojima, 1754-1806

Year	Male	Female
1754	61	21
1766	37	16
1767	33	18
1771	42	16
1772	44	13
1776	46	22
1778	33	17
1780	30	15
1788	23	8
1791	28	9
1793	23	8
1796	15	7
1797	15	7
1800	14	6
1805	19	6
1806	19	2

Source· Tamano Shiyakusho, Tamano shishi (The history of Tamano City) (Okayama: Tamano Shiyakusho, 1960), pp. 372-373.

village, too, there is a clear downward trend in the number of male and female hōkōnin who went out to seek employment during the half century for which data are available. While the authors of Tamano shishi, in commenting on the data, stated that the mere existence of hōkōnin was an indication of "suffering beyond our imagination,"[53] it would be more accurate to interpret the data as proving the existence of employment opportunities outside the village. The decline, which coincided with the growth of by-employments in rural areas, indicates increasing employment opportunities within the village, which were undoubtedly preferred as it meant people could stay at home.

Despite their adherence to the traditional view of "peasant dis-integration," the authors of *Okayama-ken no rekishi* wrote that "as time went on, commerce and a cash-based economy reached into the villages, and peasants with less than 3 *tan* could now main-tain themselves." Noting also the increasing number of *bekke*, they added that the domain had become more "lenient" in allowing *bekke* and that the households newly created after the mid-eight-eenth century "were able to build, shortly after *bekke*, small houses of their own by supplementing their income from such by-employ-ments as weaving and part-time trading."[54]

If we are correct in attributing the increase in the number of smallest landholders to the increased opportunities for by-employ-ments at a rising wage level, what explains the increases in the number of 3-5 *tan* holders and the tendency for the largest land-holders to reduce their holdings? We believe that the reason for this was because 3-5 *tan* was the amount of land that the labor of a nuclear family could work without using hired labor. Given the increasingly high cost of hired labor, this range of landholding was optimum, that is, the return to labor was highest. According to Naitō's model of an agricultural household in Kojima working 3-5 *tan* of land with the family labor ranging between three and five persons (including one or two male adults), sur-pluses—total yield minus total food requirements and taxes—ranged from 1.162 *koku* for a family of five working 3 *tan* to 7.27 *koku* for a family of three working 5 *tan*. (Naitō infers at least two males or all adults in the family of five, and one male adult plus his wife in the family of three. See Table 7.8.) The total yield was obtained by multiplying the real yield of 2.2 *koku* by the number of *tan*, while the tax was calculated by multiplying the assessed yield of 1.475 *koku* by the nominal tax rate of 78 per-cent. All taxes were calculated according to the laws in effect in 1772, and a consumption of 1 *koku* of rice per head was allowed.[55]

In contrast, Naitō found that a leading family in Numa work-ing 2.5 *chō* (25 *tan*) with eight adults—presumably four were male

Table 7.8
Estimates[a] of Farm Income and Expenditures for Numa, 1772

Size of Holding (tan)	Income (in koku)			No. in Family	Expenditures			Surplus (in koku)
	Rice	Other Grains	Total		Food	Taxes	Total	
3	6.6	3.0	9.6	3	3.0	3.438	6.438	3.162
				4	4.0	3.438	7.438	2.162
				5	5.0	3.438	8.438	1.162
4	8.8	4.0	12.8	3	3.0	4.584	7.584	5.216
				4	4.0	4.584	8.584	4.216
				5	5.0	4.584	9.584	3.216
5	11.0	5.0	16.0	3	3.0	5.73	8.73	7.27
				4	4.0	5.73	9.73	6.27
				5	5.0	5.73	10.73	5.27

[a]This is obviously only a rough approximation. The 2.2 *koku* per *tan* output is the figure Naitō calculated as the average real output for the village. Food is calculated at 1 *koku* per person with no differences allowed for adults or children. Also, surpluses would have to be used for all other expenses.

Source: Naitō Jirō, *Honbyakushō taisei no kenkyū* (A study of the honbyakushō system) (Tokyo. Ochanomizu Shobō, 1968), p. 168.

family members and four were male hired hands—produced an annual gross output in the range of 30-40 *koku*. Given that each of the four hired hands was, on the average, paid 2 *koku* per year plus maintenance and other socially required amenities, the total after-wage yield to the family was considerably less than 28-32 *koku* per year.[56] This means that the per male adult yield for this family was less than 7-8 *koku* per year. If each male had a wife and possibly a child, which is likely, then this per male output must be compared to a total yield of 9.6 *koku* for a family of three with one male adult working 3 *tan*, or to 16 *koku* for a family of five with two male adults working 5 *tan*.

The preceding evidence is admittedly not conclusive, because such studies are rare indeed. However, it does show clearly that in this village the 3-5 *tan* holders must have fared as well or better than the leading family with 2.5 *chō*, if the family size was as hypothesized above. Since this calculation is based on an assumption that only rice and wheat were cultivated, and not a more likely crop, such as cotton—which is known to be more labor intensive than these two grains—any adjustments that we might make to allow for cotton cultivation would make the per

189

labor unit return more favorable to the 3-5 *tan* holders using only family labor than to the larger unit of farming using hired labor. This argument is further strengthened if wages rose (as they did), and if we consider the cost of supervision of hired labor and of the socially required emoluments given to hired labor in addition to wages. In fact, an extant record of 1797 shows a net loss of 255 *momme* "resulting from paddy-upland cultivation," which was made up by a "side income."[57]

We are not, however, suggesting that the very largest landholders in the village became worse off. A family that was engaged in commerce, money lending, and other activities usually retained its position of importance in the village to the end of the Tokugawa period. What is suggested simply is that apparently there were economic reasons for the largest landholders to reduce their holdings over time. One can also envision, under the economic conditions prevailing in southern Bizen during the last century of the Tokugawa period, some farmers who had been working 3-5 *tan* choosing to reduce their holdings if a more profitable alternative was found, or someone engaged in a by-employment deciding to work a little more of another's land or even buy a *tan* or two if that would be more profitable than his current combination of farming and by-employment.

The largest landholders in Okayama tended to sell part of their land rather than leasing it (though tenancy also increased) for several reasons in addition to the apparent diseconomies of scale resulting from high labor costs. One reason was that, in contrast to the Kinai, land converted into capital could be readily and profitably invested in local enterprises because the potential competitors in the castle town of Okayama were much less able to resist the incursion of village entrepreneurs than were the Osaka merchants and the entrepreneurs of the satellite towns of Osaka. Most of the large wholesalers of cotton in this region were originally large landholders who chose to mobilize their capital in commerce. Another reason was that the land converted into capital could be lucratively invested in reclamation which, after a hiatus during the mid-eighteenth century in Bizen, picked up during the nineteenth.

Though the Hikasa's landholdings began to be reduced a few decades later than those of other large landholders in this region, this Fujito family can be considered a typical large landholder that chose to convert its holdings into cash to be invested in *shinden* and in other more profitable activities. During the same period that their landholdings in Fujito were being reduced—the last decades of the Tokugawa period—Hikasa bought nearly 10 *chō* of land in Kōjō-shinden and a similar amount in ten other villages in Kojima. In fact, Hikasa became a "developer" who then leased the land to tenants brought in from all parts of Bizen, Bitchū, Bingo, and even Shikoku, mostly younger sons of peasants. The wholesaling of lime, begun at the beginning of the nineteenth century, was the family's other major enterprise, and this business was expanded during the same period the family's Fujito landholdings declined.

Ōta and Matsuo, the authors of an article on landholding in Fujito, viewed the actions of the Hikasa as evidence of the development of an absentee landlord system in Okayama.[58] We believe, however, the development should be seen for what it was: a large landholder's effort to obtain the highest returns to capital given the changing conditions of the economy, especially the increasing difficulty of obtaining labor.

The policy of the domain was to encourage the easy transfer of capital in search of the highest returns. It was much more oriented toward increasing the total economic activities of the domain than attempting to defend the interests of the urban merchants and industries to the last possible moment, as the Bakufu unsuccessfully attempted on behalf of the merchants and manufacturing enterprises in Osaka and other major urban centers in the Kinai.

As our village samples of changes in the landholding patterns show, these changes rarely exhibit unmistakable trends. Landholding patterns were subject to numerous complex factors, and economic rationality alone should not be overrated in its importance. And, undeniably, some peasants became marginal landowners despite their efforts and others remained on the land for social, psychological, and other reasons. What is argued in this section, however, is that one strong factor motivating many peasants over many decades to change the amount of the land each possessed was self-interest in improving their level of income. We can explain the trend of change in landholding patterns either by emphasizing the rationality of the peasants in their response to changing economic conditions or by following the "peasant disintegration" thesis, which attributes these changes to the intensifying exploitation of the marginal landholders by the *gōnō* (rich peasants with large holdings), by the ruling class, and by the merchants. But if we use the exploitation hypothesis, it is very difficult to explain the rises in the standard of living clearly taking place throughout the rural areas of Okayama, or the rises in the wage level already discussed.

THE RISING STANDARD OF LIVING

In much of our preceding examination of the economic and demographic changes in this domain, we implied that the living standard of the Okayama peasants continued to rise throughout the Tokugawa period, if with minor setbacks caused by occasional poor harvests. The purpose of this section is to present evidence of a rise in the standard of living for the last century and a half of the Tokugawa period.

Both quantitative and descriptive evidence that the real wage level of both skilled and unskilled workers was rising can be found in the standard works on the domain. Indicative of the trend are changes in the officially fixed fare for the services of a porter with a horse. This fare, which is "estimated to have been significantly below the market fare," shows a clearly upward trend.[59] For example, for the journey between the castle town and Amaki (about twelve miles), the officially fixed fare in 1683 was 194 *mon* (in copper coins); in 1684 it was 150 *mon* as the fare was "reduced because of an extremely good harvest"; in 1712, 200 *mon*; in 1814, 229 *mon*; in 1828, 258 *mon*; and in 1829, 277 *mon*.[60] The fares for other destinations from the castle town, of course, changed similarly. Even if it was below the market rate, this fare was good by contemporary standards and it rose ahead of prices. As we have demonstrated in our discussion of daily wages in the Kinai and Morioka, a daily income of around 200 *mon* during the period certainly was "a living wage." If these porters earned, as they must have, market level wages at any time during the month, their average daily wage would, of course, have been higher than 200 *mon*. Also, the distance between Okayama and Amaki was hardly taxing for a day's work, especially for porters with horses. In contrast to the nearly 40 percent increase in the official fare for the period 1683-1829, the price level could not have risen by more than 30 points and the most likely increase was around 25 points.[61] A gain of 10-15 percent in real wages during nearly a century and a half appears small, but the real gain must have easily exceeded 30 percent because of the difference between the official and the market rate.

Also at the unskilled or at best minimally skilled level were the daily wages of the *hamako* (workers in the salt fields), which reached one *momme* of silver and 0.8 to 1.0 *shō* of rice by the early decades of the nineteenth century.[62] Assuming that the *hamako* worked twenty-five days per month, and given the price of rice and the relative value of silver and copper (about 95 *mon* of copper to 1 *momme* of silver during this period), the annual income of these workers could have been as high as 7 *koku* per year.[63] This income, earned mostly by younger sons or brothers of farmers in nearby villages who also worked on the farm as well, is only slightly less attractive than what was earned by porters.

The wage level of skilled workers and agricultural laborers, who undoubtedly worked longer hours under supervision, was even higher than for basically unskilled porters and *hamako*. Though the data is again limited to the official rate paid for the work done for the domain, carpenters by the 1850s were being paid at a daily rate of between 2.4 and 3.4 *momme* of silver. The going rate for agricultural labor, if paid in cash, was within the range of 2.6 to 2.8 *momme*.[64] Since 1 *momme* of silver was worth about 100 *mon* of copper coins during the mid-nineteenth century, these wages were good by most premodern standards. If a carpenter earning 3 *momme* per day worked twenty-five days per month, his annual income at the prevailing price of rice was almost 12 *koku*, an amount which many a lower-ranking samurai in Okayama would have envied.[65]

Descriptive evidence of increasing wages, and how high they were considered, also abounds. Supporting our preceding analysis of the reasons for changes in the landholding pattern, and attesting to high wages, the authors of *Okayama shishi* wrote with regard to Kojima during the early nineteenth century:

> Because the increase in cotton weaving made a large demand on the available labor at high daily wages, [the supply of] agricultural servants was depleted and some tenant cultivators left their land. Landowners could no longer obtain sufficient labor to work their land unless they were willing to pay equally

high wages. Under the circumstances, village officials in Kojima in 1823 requested the domain to either suppress or completely prohibit cotton weaving which was draining off their labor.[66]

There is also indirect, but no less telling, evidence of a competitive labor market. To cite only a few examples, *Okayama-ken no rekishi* notes that the domain had to issue decrees prohibiting "an increasing number of holidays" for peasants and agricultural laborers after the beginning of the nineteenth century. Though the authors explained the decrees as an indication of the domain officials' concern over "increasing poverty seen in the villages," a more logical explanation would be that an increase in holidays was needed to retain workers, and that the peasants began to prefer a little more leisure as life improved.[67]

Another interesting example is the action taken by the *sake* makers in castle towns who, by the beginning of the nineteenth century, must have faced extreme difficulty in finding labor for their needs. The *sake* makers, obviously in secret, agreed in 1805 that no *sake* maker was to bid servants and daily labor away from another *sake* maker and that they would no longer examine prospective employees' legal status, in other words, whether they had come to town legally or illegally. Clearly, some of the *sake* makers had been bidding workers away and violating the domain decree to hire only legal migrants, but wages were so high by this time that they had more to gain by refraining from bidding wages up, and were willing to run the risk of being caught violating the domain's decree regarding employees. By colluding, they reduced the risk of informing on one another.[68]

More evidence for a rising living standard is the stability in the nominal tax rate which, because of increases in productivity, resulted in a decline in the real tax rate. That only one cadastral survey was made for Bizen is undisputed, and this was at the beginning of the Tokugawa period. In addition, "the tax rate remained unchanged" after the mid-seventeenth century, thus "making increases in output an addition to peasant income."[69] To illustrate the amount of real gains to the peasants realized by the decline in the effective tax rate, and also to show the danger in using the nominal tax rate to discuss peasant income, let us return to the data on Numa compiled by Naitō.

The nominal tax rate for Numa, as for the rest of Bizen, was very high: 78 percent—60 percent basic tax plus other dues (*takagari*) —of the assessed yield (*kokumori*). By the 1770s, taxes per *tan* on the assessed yield (1.475 *koku*) amounted to 1.150 *koku* (60 percent of the assessed yield plus 0.265 in additional taxes). However, by this decade, the actual yield was 2.10 *koku* per *tan*, which left 0.625 *koku* of untaxed yield in the hands of the farmer. Thus the farmer retained 0.950 *koku* or 45 percent of the total output per *koku* (0.325 of the assessed yield plus 0.625 that was excluded from taxation). Instead of a 60 percent basic tax, the farmer actually paid only 42 percent in basic taxes.[70] Naitō adds that "the actual increase in total output was even higher than indicated by this calculation based on rice" because wheat, cotton, and rapeseed were taxed at lower rates. In Naitō's mind there was little doubt that "there was an ample possibility of surplus."[71]

The data from other villages tell the same story. In Fujito in Kojima, the assessed yield remained unchanged from 1688 (changes before this year were due to *shinden*) to 1817 (the last year for which we have such data) despite known increases in productivity. The total tax burden was fixed as it was for Numa, save occasional reductions at times of poor harvests.[72] With regard to the peasants in Fujito, *Okayama-ken no rekishi* observed that even the tenant cultivators with less than 3 *tan* of their own land "had no difficulty in paying all the dues [rents and taxes] and enjoy a comfortable living," provided that "they worked assiduously."[73]

This stability in the tax rate, leading to a steady decline in the effective tax rate, is also evident for the village of Korisato in the Akasaka district. Though the relevant data are presented only in graphs, the straight horizontal line drawn for the total assessed yield and the clear negative trend of the real tax rate calculated by Taniguchi, leave no doubt of the steadily increasing surpluses in the hands of the peasants.[74] And the data gathered also by Taniguchi for Ajino village in Kojima and Fujino village in Wake tell essentially the same story.[75]

Furthermore, in discussing the rice tax policy of the domain in general, Taniguchi cites various examples of reductions in taxes for poor harvests, deterioration of land quality, and declines in agricultural labor.[76] Thus, we find that the domain administration not only did not increase tax rates despite certain knowledge of increasing productivity but also reduced taxes when output declined. Higher wages and an increasing agricultural surplus in the hands of the peasants could not but raise their level of consumption, and all attempts of the domain to restrict consumption had little, if any, effect.

During the sixteenth century and until well into the seventeenth, the needs of the rural population were met primarily by peddlers, known as *zarufuri* because of the swaying baskets in which they carried their goods, who went from the castle town into the rural areas, hawking their wares from village to village. As early as 1655 the domain tried to prohibit these activities, feeling that the peasants were spending too much money on articles they did not need. The total prohibition was unsatisfactory, and so within five years peddling was once again allowed, but a license was required and the domain limited the goods that could be sold. A decree of 1666 permitted only eleven items: fishing nets, dried fish, salt, dried seaweed, tea, rapeseed oil, kindling wood, wooden water dippers, oars, basket tops, and some farm tools.[77] As demand—and undoubtedly open violation of the decree—grew, additional goods were added to the list of permitted items. By 1705 there were thirty-one, including pottery, cotton, pans, rice pots, straw mats, paper, fans, and rulers.[78]

Just as the number of goods increased, so did the number of peddlers, "supported by the purchasing power of the villages."[79] A count of peddlers in 1652 totaled less than 1,000; by 1707 the number had more than doubled.[80] Business was so good that during the 1720s it was discovered that many merchants were selling in the villages without licenses, and the domain once more tried to establish control over their activities, again in vain.

By the mid-eighteenth century, as the tempo of increase in peasant demand gathered speed and more and more people in the villages were able to participate in the market, a change took place in rural commerce. Instead of all peddlers originating in the castle town, as they had during the seventeenth century, they were increasingly based in the rural towns. These towns now had wholesalers and jobbers of their own, were becoming capable of meeting the needs of the villages, and were starting to gain a foothold in the markets of the castle town.[81] By the late eighteenth century, daily necessities were supplied not only by *zarufuri*, but increasingly by resident village merchants, either on a part- or a full-time basis. By 1813 one shop in the village of Ōi sold, among other goods: ink, paper, writing brushes, pots, needles, pipes, tobacco and pouches, teapots, various containers and dishes, vinegar, soy sauce, bean paste, salt, noodles, kelp, *sake*, cakes, tea and teacups, *sembei*, grain, oil, candles, hair oil, hair strings and hairpins, cotton cloth, towels, *tabi* (socks), footgear including *zori, geta,* and *waraji,* funeral requisites, and "other everyday necessities." Other shops in the same village sold various kinds of food and farm necessities, such as tools and fertilizers.[82]

Some of the goods sold were imported from other parts of Japan, but by the nineteenth century Bizen was producing an impressive list of goods, which were sold throughout the domain as well as exported to other parts of Japan. A list of over 100 goods produced in Bizen included: *sake*, bean paste, oils, cotton products, a dozen varieties of quality weaves, pottery for daily use and for ornamental purposes, a wide range of agricultural implements, many types of household goods made of iron, tobacco, several kinds of papers, tea, sugar and candies, medicine, dyes, footwear of various kinds, furniture and room dividers, wooden furniture, mats made of straw and of *igusa,* and numerous knickknacks.[83] By the Bakumatsu period villagers in Bizen were not only buying everyday goods but also luxuries such as perfume, cosmetics, and incense; among readily available imported goods were linen from Echigo, medicine from Etchū and Toyama, expensive furniture from Nōtō, and sugar.[84]

The authors of *Okayama-ken no rekishi* did their best to reconcile this evidence of the growth of village market activities with the traditional interpretation of the Tokugawa economy:

The change came with the 1680-1730 period as a divide. Before the early eighteenth century, the pattern of commerce was basically autarkic, with the castle town as the center. This pattern, however, was gradually replaced by the growth of rural commerce and manufacturing undertaken as by-employments everywhere in the villages. The transformation was due to the increased demand for manufactured products by the populace whose living standard was rising, to the growth of transportation and commerce . . . and to the need to supplement income through by-employments on the part of the poor peasants whose number was increasing as the result of the continuing stratification of the peasant class.[85]

Our only disagreement is with the last sentence of the quotation. By-employments transforming the economy did not increase because the poor increased. Rather, the increasing opportunities for by-employments reduced the number of the poor who formerly had depended on land alone. Because the population of the domain was not rising, we can definitely state that the increase in commercial and manufacturing activities must have raised average per capita income, for, if we are to accept the Marxist argument that the *gōnō* were siphoning off all profit from such activities, how would the villagers have been able to buy the increasing quality and variety of goods they obviously were? Our next question is: with a growing economy, why did the population show no basic increase? It is to this problem that we shall turn in the next three chapters.

CHAPTER EIGHT

Fertility, Mortality, and Life Expectancy in Four Villages

In order to examine demographic behavior, to determine what fertility and mortality patterns were, to analyze population trends, and to estimate life expectancy, we must resort to data at the village level that offer the necessary long-term, detailed information. In this chapter, we will examine population growth rates, fertility, mortality, the composition of the population, and life expectancy in four villages in Tokugawa Japan. This small group of villages cannot be considered representative of the thousands of villages in Tokugawa Japan, but they will present some of the trends and patterns that did exist. And trends and patterns that can be found to have existed in most or all of these villages of varied economic, political, and geographical circumstances may be concluded to have been widespread, at least in central Japan.

Three of the four villages were located in Okayama and the last was in Mikawa (the present Aichi prefecture). These villages are:

(1) Fujito, a farming village located in the southernmost district of Okayama on a major route from the castle town to Shimotsui, a thriving port on the Inland Sea. The village economy changed from the mid-eighteenth century because of its growing involvement in the cotton industry in all stages from cultivation to weaving and marketing of the finished goods. Also, through reclamation, the arable land in the village increased by about 20 percent in the early nineteenth century. Demographic records are available for this village for forty-two years during the period 1775-1863, during which the population of the village grew from just under 600 to slightly over 700. Because of the wealth of information on this village, it will be the subject of a study of individual demographic behavior presented in Chapter Ten.

(2) Fukiage, a fishing village on the Inland Sea, which grew rapidly in the eighteenth century as its neighbor, Shimotsui, became a port on the shipping circuit from western Japan to Osaka.

Thirty-one registers, scattered throughout the period 1683-1860, still exist for this village. During this period its population tripled, increasing from 308 in 1685 to 932 in 1860.

(3) Numa, a landlocked farming village, which showed a nearly stable total population of a little over 300 from 1780 to 1871, a century during which data exist for thirty-three years. Although it was located in the plains area on the major road through western Japan, it did not have opportunities for economic expansion to the extent that either Fujito or Fukiage did.

(4) Nishikata, a farming village in the Mikawa Bay area, located next to a post station on the Tokaido, the most traveled road in Japan. Records exist for this village for the crucial famine years of the 1780s and, although they cover only fifteeen years, they are continuous from 1782-1796. Nishikata's population dropped during this period from 271 to 248, a decrease of about 9 percent.

Table 8.1 contains information on the data available for each of these villages, the population and sex ratios for the first and last year for which data are available, and linear regressions of the total population. Figure 8.1 depicts changes in the population of each village. Note that the smooth lines are due to gaps in the data; if yearly data had been available, the chart would all be composed of jagged lines, like Nishikata's.

AN ASSESSMENT OF THE DEMOGRAPHIC RECORDS FOR THE FOUR VILLAGES

The village population records are in the form of *shūmon-aratame-chō* or a variant of them. These registers, compiled by village, enumerate all individuals by household, and within each household by relationship to household head.[1] The registers for the four villages analyzed here contain the age of each person; the names of all men, children, and unmarried women; and information on births, deaths, marriages, migration, and other events of demographic importance, thus forming a vital registration record by year. (See sample entries.) In fact, the information on demographic events is sufficient for the calculation of birth and death rates, statistics on childbearing, age specific death rates, and other statistics pertaining to fertility and mortality.

Although the quality of *shūmon-aratame-chō* in terms of ac-

Table 8.1
Village Data Sources: Coverage and Basic Population Data

Village	Periods Covered (No. of Observations)	Population Base Year (Sex Ratio)	Last Year (Sex Ratio)
Fujito[a]	1775 (1) 1794-1810 (14) 1825-1863 (25)	596 (1.152)	696 (1.128)
Fukiage[a]	1685-1706 (13) 1712-1860 (16)	308 (1.184)	932 (1.062)
Numa[a]	1780-1814 (9) 1819-1832 (13) 1860-1871 (10)	337 (1.106)	315 (1.158)
Nishikata[b]	1782-1796 (15)	271 (1.099)	248 (0.969)

Linear Regressions of Total Population (Y = year)

Fujito	$TP = 532.0 + 1.6Y$	$R^2 = 0.742$
Fukiage	$TP = 420.5 + 3.7Y$	$R^2 = 0.906$
Numa	$TP = 379.5 - 0.6Y$	$R^2 = 0.356$
Nishikata	$TP = 283.0 - 1.8Y$	$R^2 = 0.619$

[a]Okayama prefecture.

[b]Aichi prefecture.

[c]Listed here are only the number of complete registers that could be used for the calculation of vital rates.

curacy of information and amount of information contained varies widely by domain, the data for the four villages analyzed here are reliable to the extent that statistics obtained from them can be considered generally correct without adjustment. In terms of information with regard to demographic events, these registers, particularly those from Okayama, are superior to most of those found in other parts of Japan. This conclusion is based on evidence presented in the following paragraphs.

Although the major omission from most *shūmon-aratame-chō* is children in the year of birth, only 1.9 percent (12 out of 625) of the children who appeared in the extant Fujito registers and whose parents were married and living in the village in the year the children were born were not registered in the first year of life. In Fukiage, 71 percent of the births in the period of 1683-1688

201

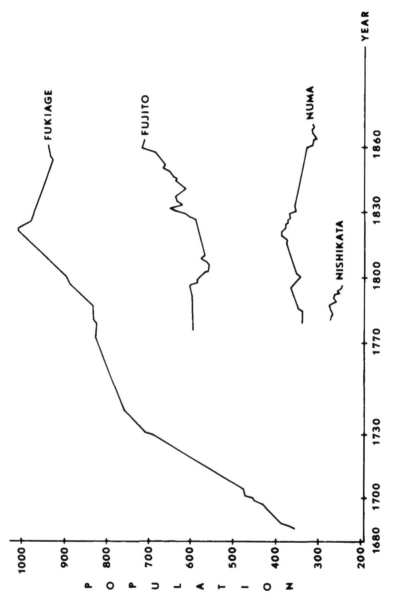

Figure 8.1: Total Population for the Four Sample Villages

Figure 8.2: A Sample of *Shūmon-aratame-chō*
Data from Fujito

1775	*Name*	*Age*
Head	Sabeı	38—[no special status]
Wıfe		29
Younger brother	Yosuke	33
Son	Kıtarō	11
Son	Kakichi	8—went to the vıllage of
Son	Tanijirō	5 Tsubuura to become adopted
Daughter		3 son, on 7th day, 3rd month
Father	Sukenouchı	79
Mother		67
Genın (male)		29—from Okuhazakawa

Totals: 6 males
        3 females
        9 famıly members
        1 *genın*
       10 members in household
       no domestıc anımal

1778	*Name*	*Age*
Head	Sabeı	41
Wıfe		32
Younger brother	Fujızō	36—[changed name]
Son	Kıtarō	14
Son	Heıjırō	8—[changed name]
Daughter		6
Wife of brother		28
Daughter of brother		3
Mother		70
Daughter of brother		1—born 15th day, 9th month
Genın (male)		25—from Hiroe

Totals: 4 males
        6 females
       10 famıly members
        1 *genın*
       11 members ın household
       no domestıc animal

went unrecorded, but from 1693 to 1860 only 1.75 percent were not reported, if 1787 is excluded, a year in which there are no records for 11 out of 19 known births.

These small percentages of unrecorded births indicate that there was a consistent attempt to keep the records updated and, given the methods for recording births and deaths, in actuality these percentages may have been smaller. The reason for this is that the preserved records are copies of documents sent up to the domain government, and as such they were the working copies upon which corrections were made and entries updated for use in the *shūmon-aratame* of the following year. When there was not sufficient space to make notations in ink on the register, a note was made on a small piece of paper which was pasted on the page at the appropriate place (*harigami*) and some of these have become unglued and lost over time.

In comparing one village register with another for the following year, discrepancies other than the omission of births were, of course, found. The most frequent were age discrepancies. These were rarely found in children under the age of about 14, fairly common among persons who were away from the village, and most frequent among older residents. Nearly all were discrepancies of one year, and frequently they were corrected later, particularly for persons returning to the village after some years away. The most amusing discrepancy in age occurred in the entries of a woman from Fujito who left her family at the "age of 27" and married into another family in the same village in the same year and was listed in their records as "age 22." This case was unusual; no bias can be seen in the kind of mistakes made in recording age, and most can be considered to have resulted from the heads of households being responsible for the contents of the registers, and natural forgetfulness due to age rather than any deliberate misrepresentation.

Other discrepancies were also to be found. In a few cases, children were recorded as being of one sex, and later were recorded as another. Discrepancies concerning the relationship of individuals to the household head, particularly for in-laws or distant cousins, appeared a few times, but the only problem in interpreting the records that affected the analysis here concerned to which woman in a household to attribute a birth. In a number of cases infants were classified as sons or daughters of the household head, despite the fact that the wife was past 50. In almost every case this occurred, there was a grown daughter living at home and, since it was presumed that the real relationship of the child was grandchild, he was so classified. These cases were not significant in number, but are interesting in that they indicate how the problem of illegitimacy seems to have been solved within the village.

Another discrepancy occurred in the recording of births that were not nine, or even seven, months apart. Let us take an example from Fujito. In one case, a child was recorded as having been born in the eleventh month, and a second child was recorded born in the first month of the following year. The assumption was made that these children were twins, and that the recording of the second child was delayed to prevent them from being listed as twins in the registers. The reasons are as follows: First, in 1775 there were two sets of children of the same age in two households, but thereafter there was not a single occurrence of twins in the recorded population history of the village. Second, the Japanese have long had an aversion to twins, and even today Japanese parents tend to conceal the fact that twins have been born.[2] If the three examples of known discrepancies can be considered twins, it is also possible that some children whose birthdates are not known but who were merely listed as one year apart were also twins. There is therefore no way to analyze the incidence of twins, and some children throughout the population may have been a year or two younger or older than recorded, but this inaccuracy would in no way affect the basic conclusions to be drawn from analyses of the *shūmon-aratame-chō*.

Still another problem lies in the reporting of brides marrying into a family. Usually a bride was not entered into the family registers until she was pregnant or had borne a child, a custom that makes it impossible to discuss the interval between marriage and first birth, and also makes discussion of the incidence of pregnancy before marriage irrelevant, since presumably a religious ceremony occurred some time prior to the registration, as is still the custom in Japan today. Since fewer than 18 percent of Fujito brides married men from Fujito, and less than 21 percent of Numa brides men from Numa, it is unlikely that most women married because they became pregnant, although the marriage may have been put in the records only after the conception of the first child.[3]

Because of the existence of a few obvious inaccuracies in the records, tests were made to determine whether the information contained in them was sufficiently reliable for calculating birth and death rates and for more detailed statistics. First, individuals and families were traced over time. This created no problem in Nishi-kata where the records are continuous for the fifteen years for which there are data. Yet even in the Okayama villages, which contain numerous gaps, it was possible to trace families over time. For example, in Fujito, of the original 110 households listed in 1775, 63 were identified in the registers for 1794, quite an amazing number considering the nineteen-year time span for most households and the number of changes in household head and members, not to mention the number of persons who changed names. Of the remaining households listed in 1794, 23 were with certainty traced to 1863, the last year for which we have records for this village. In 1825, after a fifteen-year period for which there are no records extant, the 86 households discussed above were identified, plus an additional 25 that continued from 1825 through 1863. The fact that two-thirds or more of all households in this one village, and similar percentages in the other Okayama villages, can be traced over a number of decades or more indicates both the reliability of the data and the continuity of households through time.

A comparison of the age composition of the villages revealed no distortions to be expected from falsified records or underreporting of certain groups within the village. For all the villages, the surviving of age groups over time indicated that any distortions in the age distribution resulted from the small sample size rather than inaccurate registration.

A further test was the compiling of a frequency distribution of births and deaths by day of the month to see whether these events were randomly distributed or not.[4] The example shown for Fujito (Table 8.2) reveals a distinct clustering, particularly of births, on days divisible by five, and an avoidance, again particularly of births, of dates containing four or nine, which have the same pronunciation as "death" and "suffering" respectively. There was also a clustering of births on *misoka* (the last day of the month) and, because of the difficulties involved in determining precisely which day was meant, these have been lumped under the heading *misoka*. Other villages showed a similar pattern.

The months of births and deaths were more evenly distributed

Table 8.2
Frequency of Births and Deaths by Day of Month for 42 Years of
Observation Between 1775 and 1863, Fujito

Day	No. of Births	No. of Deaths
1	21	6
2	31	35
3	24	38
4	9	10
5	47	33
6	18	12
7	25	24
8	28	21
9	16	21
10	25	36
11	25	20
12	25	20
13	26	17
14	12	16
15	81	21
16	18	22
17	8	11
18	31	23
19	10	17
20	24	31
21	11	19
22	7	8
23	11	8
24	11	5
25	16	13
26	7	21
27	8	17
Misoka[a]	51	37
Unknown	22	6
TOTAL	648	568

[a]Misoka (last day) includes every entry marked misoka and any date
from the 28th on.

in the records. (See Table 8.3.) The Okayama data reveal a preference for recording births in the first month of the year, but other
deviations from the mean may well have been the result of actual
peaks and lows in births and deaths rather than faulty recording.
For example, the large number of deaths in the fourth month of
Fujito is due to what seems to have been an epidemic in 1832,
affecting mostly children. A peaking of deaths in the hot months
of the year can reasonably be expected, since in twentieth-century
Japan the death rate follows the same pattern. Given these facts
and the nature of the discrepancies found in the records, it seems

Table 8.3
Frequency of Births and Deaths by Month

Month	Fujito	Fukiage	Numa	Nishikata
		Births		
1	79	70	63	2
2	51	41	32	1
3	54	41	14	2
4	47	29	10	1
5	43	16	7	7
6	37	31	11	5
7	48	24	10	7
8	53	22	31	10
9	58	48	15	2
10	35	35	8	4
11	72	45	16	11
12	49	37	7	8
Intercalary	—	9	1	—
Unknown	22	54	2	8
TOTAL	648	502	227	68
Mean (1-12)	52.2	36.6	18.7	5.0
		Deaths		
1	41	44	18	7
2	50	34	20	7
3	38	44	7	0
4	71	24	8	3
5	34	31	8	8
6	46	31	15	6
7	59	31	16	6
8	67	30	22	15
9	46	34	17	7
10	44	27	14	8
11	36	19	8	9
12	28	20	14	10
Intercalary	2	10	1	—
Unknown	6	21	16	5
TOTAL	568	400	184	91
Mean (1-12)	45.2	30.8	13.9	7.2

208

obvious that failures of memory combined with no compelling need for complete accuracy go a long way in explaining the inaccuracies that appear, rather than deliberate distortion for the purpose of avoiding some obligation assigned on the basis of the information contained in the registers. As far as anyone knows, neither taxes nor any other obligations were allotted on the basis of the *shūmon-aratame-chō*, and thus their compilation was seen as only one more administrative task to be completed each year for the higher authorities.

Before proceeding with an analysis of the data, a word is in order with regard to the definitions of age used here and the definition of total village population. As mentioned in Chapter Three, by the traditional Japanese method of measuring age, everyone was recorded as age 1 in the first year of life, and after each New Year, one year was added to each person's age. Thus, a baby born at the end of one year would be recorded as 2 on New Year's day when according to western calculation he was still age 0. In Japan, however, he was in the second year of life. The advantage to the Japanese system is that all persons of the same age in years are birth cohorts of a particular year.

To obtain approximate western equivalents in age, two methods have been adopted here. In the tables on fertility and marriage, one year has been subtracted from the reported age of women. Thus a woman listed as 24 in the tables was not 24 at last birthday but was between 23.5 and 24.5 at mid-year.[5] In constructing age distributions of the January population, however, two years were subtracted from the Japanese ages. Thus a person aged 1 in our "January" population was at least 1 year and a day but less than 2 years old, or, in other words, age at last birthday plus a day. Age specific death rates and life expectancy estimates were calculated by this second method of reckoning ages.

In determining the total population for a village, any one of several methods can be used since the registers contain information on every permanent resident of the village and anyone who lived in the village for any period during the year.[6] Although the date on most surveys is sometime in the third month, since they are based on the calendar year, the definition of total population used here is the actual population of the village on the first day of the New Year; this population consists of all persons in the census records before any deaths or out-migration took place. All persons who were working outside the village during the year were included, and all persons from outside employed in the village during the year were excluded.[7] Employees were usually permitted to return to their homes over the New Year holidays and thus most can be expected to have been in their home villages then.[8] This definition was selected for calculating birth and death rates for several reasons: (1) fluctuations due to high rates of temporary in- or out-migration were avoided; (2) this was the population to which virtually all births and deaths were attributed; (3) distortions in the age distribution due to employment patterns were avoided; and (4) the accuracy of the population calculated at the beginning of the year is undoubtedly highest as it most closely resembles the figures collected by the survey and would not be affected by omissions in the recording of demographic events during the year.

FERTILITY AND MORTALITY IN FOUR VILLAGES

At first glance the crude birth and death rates for the four villages of Fujito, Fukiage, Numa, and Nishikata prove surprising in two respects: (1) the averages of both rates are lower than one would expect in a premodern society, and (2) in each village the rates tend to parallel each other, rising and falling in seeming unison. (See Table 8.4.) In only a few periods are the rates more than a few percentage points apart, notably in Nishikata from 1787 to 1795, the period just following the Temmei famine. In only two periods did the birth rates exceed 30 per thousand (Fujito in 1830-1834 and Fukiage in 1727-1741) and both of these periods were accompanied by relatively high death rates. If migration is not considered, the net effect of these parallel rates would have been a very slow but steady growth for each village.

The difference between the birth rate means and the means of the death rates in each village are what one would expect from looking at the graph of total population changes. Fukiage, which showed the most growth over the period for which there are data, had the highest birth rate at 26 per thousand, while Fujito was next with 24.2, and both of these were above the average death rates of just under 22 for the two villages. Numa's birth rate of 19.6 was barely under the death rate of 20.1, while Nishikata, which experienced the Temmei famine during the fifteen years for

Table 8.4
Crude Birth and Death Rate Averages (per thousand)

	Crude Birth Rate Averages	Crude Death Rate Averages		Crude Birth Rate Averages	Crude Death Rate Averages
Fujito 1794-1863			*Fukiage 1693-1860*		
1794-1799 (*n* = 4)	20.2	20.5	1693-1700 (*n* = 5)	31.0	15.9
1800-1804 (*n* = 5)	15.4	16.8	1702-1712 (*n* = 5)	26.3	21.1
1805-1810 (*n* = 5)	22.3	17.0	1727-1741 (*n* = 3)	31.9	30.8
1825-1829 (*n* = 5)	25.2	20.5	1773-1781 (*n* = 3)	25.4	24.6
1830-1834 (*n* = 5)	33.1	29.0	1791-1801 (*n* = 3)	26.0	20.3
1835-1841 (*n* = 3)	23.3	25.8	1821-1826 (*n* = 3)	18.4	19.4
1844-1848 (*n* = 5)	28.5	21.6	1854-1860 (*n* = 3)	19.4	22.2
1850-1857 (*n* = 4)	28.6	26.4			
1859-1863 (*n* = 3)	18.3	19.2			
Nishikata 1782-1795			*Numa 1785-1871*		
1782-1786 (*n* = 5)	19.9	14.5	1785-1803 (*n* = 7)	24.9	—
1787-1791 (*n* = 5)	18.6	29.2	1814 (*n* = 1)	23.9	—
1792-1795 (*n* = 4)	16.7	26.9	1819-1832 (*n* = 13)	19.3	22.8
			1860-1871 (*n* = 10)	15.7	16.6

Mean of Means

	Crude Birth Rates	Crude Death Rates
Fujito (*n* = 39)	24.2	21.8
Fukiage (*n* = 25)	26.0	21.5
Numa (*n* = 31)	19.6	20.1
Nishikata (*n* = 14)	18.5	23.3

n = number of years in each period for which data are available.

which data exist, had the highest death rate and the lowest birth rate. Nevertheless, it is interesting in light of the emphasis placed on the effects of the famine in Tokugawa history that Nishikata's birth rate was only 1.1 per thousand lower than Numa's and the death rate just slightly higher than the long-term averages for the three other villages.

Two facts stand out when we examine these rates. First, the crude death rates for Fujito, Fukiage, and Numa, covering varying periods during which the economy in each village underwent a number of changes, are amazingly close to one another, ranging only between 20.1 and 21.8. Second, both the birth and death rates seem extraordinarily low for a premodern society. If we envision preindustrial societies as resembling many of the underdeveloped countries of the mid-twentieth century, then we would expect birth rates nearly double those calculated for these Tokugawa villages, and much higher death rates, particularly since the data for each village cover years of crop failures and famines.

If we examine changes in the birth and death rates in each village, we find that they tend to follow economic changes, which will be discussed further in the following two chapters. Fukiage's birth rates were highest during the period of the rapid development of its neighbor as a major Inland Sea port, but fell in the nineteenth century as this growth leveled off. Numa's birth rate fell steadily, while Nishikata's, low throughout the fifteen-year period, still fell slightly. Fujito's was lowest around the turn of the nineteenth century when out-migration was at a peak, and was highest in the early 1830s just after considerable land had been added to the village's arable through reclamation.

The positive correlation of birth and death rates is unexpected in a premodern population, but it in no way appears to result from faulty data. This correlation may be caused by: (1) a rise in fertility due to fewer abortions and infanticide; more infants lived and were exposed to the risk of death; the death rate is highest in these age groups, hence a rise in the death rate; or (2) permitting more children to live to compensate for a rising death rate among infants and children.

If we go on to analyze the death rates by age group (Table 8.5), we find they vary considerably from sample to sample, particularly at the youngest ages. For example, the highest death rates for the 2-5 age group are 69.43 for Fujito for the years 1825-1835 and 68.93 for Fukiage for 1712-1741, while the lowest are 10.32 for Fujito for 1805-1810 and 12.28 for Numa, 1860-1871. Despite these variations, the pattern of the distribution of deaths by age group within each sample tends to remain the same. Thus, the lowest rate is usually for the 6-15 age group and the highest for the 66-and-over group. Differences result from the smallness of the sample sizes as well as events affecting mortality, such as an epidemic affecting children in Fujito in 1832.

Table 8.5
Age Specific Death Rate Averages

Age Group[a]	1775-1804			1805-1810		
	Male	Female	Total	Male	Female	Total
			Fujito			
0	21.46	0.0	12.99	0.0	0.0	0.0
1	67.53	76.62	71.64	78.57	40.00	53.33
2-5	32.24	11.78	22.42	7.69	12.50	10.32
6-15	5.43	11.40	7.91	10.53	0.0	5.83
16-45	5.22	9.69	7.26	6.36	5.51	6.02
46-65	30.92	12.00	23.23	21.00	15.84	18.80
66+	86.91	81.93	84.56	120.19	91.51	104.13
TOTAL	19.11	18.02	18.63	17.97	15.61	16.96
		1825-1835			1837-1848	
0	0.0	11.36	4.5	0.0	0.0	0.0
1	91.77	58.32	71.25	52.38	60.61	53.14
2-5	70.58	67.40	69.43	50.22	35.84	45.75
6-15	9.87	11.27	10.57	6.92	8.88	8.09
16-45	6.76	12.93	9.74	9.60	13.62	11.61
46-65	27.41	21.19	24.59	33.45	27.15	30.31
66+	75.75	108.69	91.96	69.61	137.06	102.40
TOTAL	22.75	26.32	24.42	22.14	23.50	22.81
		1850-1863				
0	0.0	0.0	0.0			
1	74.29	13.89	47.31			
2-5	39.12	26.19	34.52			
6-15	9.79	5.91	8.01			
16-45	14.79	12.86	13.87			
46-65	26.16	27.62	27.18			
66+	144.93	95.89	120.60			
TOTAL	25.95	19.55	22.86			
			Fukiage			
		1693-1706			1712-1741	
0	11.11	38.89	23.89	0.0	27.78	10.87
1	176.98	55.56	88.92	105.13	167.86	131.53
2-5	19.07	41.78	29.04	104.39	40.75	68.93
6-15	9.61	0.0	4.65	11.60	16.09	13.24
16-45	10.80	9.71	10.32	9.39	15.60	12.42
46-65	25.36	25.12	25.58	20.31	4.10	13.17
66+	103.66	62.57	80.19	98.78	79.47	93.99
TOTAL	21.01	16.34	18.78	31.17	24.61	28.04

Table 8.5 (Continued)

Age Group	1773-1806			1821-1826		
	Male	Female	Total	Male	Female	Total
		Fukiage (Continued)				
0	26.08	42.06	32.75	0.0	47.62	22.22
1	83.36	61.22	73.73	37.04	0.0	20.83
2-5	22.00	34.30	28.21	63.15	47.67	56.22
6-15	5.92	4.27	5.25	0.0	3.47	1.84
16-45	12.83	10.46	11.71	9.67	7.54	8.65
46-65	23.34	14.18	19.52	35.25	29.67	32.63
66+	88.22	71.35	81.43	50.77	74.65	64.77
TOTAL	20.72	18.76	19.85	19.95	18.73	19.37
		1854-1860				
0	55.56	0.0	25.64			
1	30.30	74.07	50.00			
2-5	49.98	40.26	45.26			
6-15	4.12	0.0	2.31			
16-45	10.92	16.36	13.32			
46-65	27.45	20.55	23.93			
66+	74.29	73.19	74.33			
TOTAL	21.92	22.48	22.19			
		Numa				
		1814-1832			1860-1871	
0	0.0	22.22	13.33	0.0	33.33	20.00
1	71.43	20.63	53.53	11.11	75.00	39.90
2-5	22.41	14.06	19.18	23.31	0.0	12.28
6-15	9.74	9.81	9.95	0.0	6.56	3.06
16-45	8.18	17.83	12.68	6.61	7.10	6.82
46-65	22.62	15.51	19.21	30.47	20.88	26.18
66+	105.03	78.56	91.99	126.95	76.36	98.64
TOTAL	20.69	21.51	21.07	16.83	16.36	16.93
		Nishikata[b]				
		1782-1796				
0	0.0	0.0	0.0			
1	13.33	9.52	15.58			
2-5	59.37	25.13	42.29			
6-15	7.14	8.37	7.98			
16-45	9.10	6.95	8.08			
46-65	39.17	9.05	24.16			
66+	86.56	81.46	85.50			
TOTAL	24.91	18.86	22.02			

[a]These age groups are the average age at mid-year. To obtain age as age at last birthday at the beginning of the year, subtract one year from each age. The 0 age group then becomes babies born since the beginning of the new year, while the 1 age group is babies born during the previous year and aged less than 1 year and a day at the new year.

[b]Six persons who died but whose age is unknown have been included in the total death rate but were excluded from the age specific rates.

Infant deaths are underreported, particularly those in the 0 age category. These are deaths of infants in the same calendar year in which they were born and, since infants who died at birth or soon afterwards were usually not registered, they would not appear in either the birth or death rates. We can trace with certainty only the deaths of persons who lived long enough to be registered, and who had therefore passed their first New Year. Thus the death rates presented in Table 8.2 might best be considered crude death rates for the population over age 1.

The problem of estimating the true birth rate and infant mortality is difficult for two reasons: the underreporting of children as just described and widespread birth control in Tokugawa Japan in the forms of abortion and irfanticide. The practice of birth control itself will be discussed in the following chapter, but it will be argued here that, even if the omissions were corrected, the birth and death rates would still have been low, and that the incidence of abortion and infanticide is as irrelevant to ascertaining the birth rate as the births prevented today by the use of modern contraceptives.

There is no evidence that there was widespread knowledge of any effective birth control measures other than infanticide and abortion. These measures were used to prevent unwelcome babies in the same way, and with the same purpose, that contraceptives are used today, and thus infanticide can be thought of as "postpartum birth control." (The major ways that it would differ from contraceptives would be the physical risk to the mother and the fact that while pregnant a woman is not exposed to the risk of becoming pregnant.) While the physical risk to women was higher with Tokugawa birth control measures than those of today, the effect in limiting the number of children to be raised was essentially the same. In any case, babies who were deliberately killed at birth, or "returned" as the Japanese put it, should not be confused with babies who were intended to live but died in the early days or months of life.

Evidence to support our hypothesis that the birth rate would have been low, even if infants who went unrecorded were to be included, will be provided in this section by analyzing the childbearing patterns of women, in a later section by use of the Coale-Demeny regional model life tables, and in the discussion of population control in Chapter Nine.

Age specific birth rates indicate that the modal age group for childbearing in Fujito, Numa, and Nishikata was 25-29, and in Fukiage, 25-34. (See Table 8.6.) Few children were born to women under the age of 20 or over 40. Births were therefore clustered, as one would expect, during the childbearing years considered to be safest for the mothers and to produce the healthiest children.

This clustering of births in the peak childbearing years was partly due to the relatively short span of childbearing in all of these villages. This subject will be analyzed in the following chapter but, in short, the average woman bore children for only about a dozen years. In Fujito the average age at first birth was about 22 in every period. The range of the samples was from 21.1 in Nishikata for the period 1782-1796 to 24.0 for Numa from 1814 to 1832. But, despite this relatively late age at first birth, the average age at last birth was extremely low. In Nishikata, it was only 32 or 33, and thus the average woman had a childbearing span of only a dozen years. In Fukiage and Numa, the averages were 37 and 34 or 35 respectively for women whose marriages lasted until the women were at least 43, and for Fujito the average age at last birth was 34. With an average interval between births of three years, the result was a mean completed family size of just over three children.[9] If we take into consideration the number of miscarriages and stillbirths that must have occurred, plus an infant death rate that, however low, would be far higher than in industrialized nations, then a mean family size of about three produced from a dozen or so childbearing years would be what we would expect.

AN ESTIMATION OF LIFE EXPECTANCY
IN TWO VILLAGES

Due to the small sample sizes of the village populations and the limited periods for which data are available, we cannot construct accurate life tables for the four Tokugawa villages analyzed here. However, an alternative is available: by surviving the village populations for five-year periods where data are available, and then using the information obtained in conjunction with the Coale and Demeny model life tables,[10] we can estimate life expectancy by sex for each five-year period. Records are sufficiently complete to enable the surviving of the population for four five-year periods in

Table 8.6
Age Specific Birth Rate Averages

Age	Births per 1,000 Women			%		
	Male	Female	Total	Male	Female	Total
Fujito, 1775-1863						
0-14	0	0	0	0.0	0.0	0.0
15-19	21	12	33	6.07	3.97	5.09
20-24	67	58	125	19.36	19.21	19.29
25-29	85	78	163	24.57	25.83	25.15
30-34	76	50	126	21.97	16.56	19.44
35-39	43	47	90	12.43	15.56	13.89
40-44	20	15	35	5.78	4.97	5.40
45-49	1	2	3	0.29	0.66	0.46
50+	0	0	0	0.0	0.0	0.0
Unknown	33	40	73	9.54	13.25	11.27
TOTAL	346	302	648	100.00	100.00	100.00
Fukiage, 1683-1860						
0-14	0	1	1	0.0	0.45	0.20
15-19	9	8	17	3.23	3.59	3.39
20-24	49	23	72	17.56	10.31	14.34
25-29	50	68	118	17.92	30.49	23.51
30-34	66	53	119	23.66	23.77	23.71
35-39	50	29	79	17.92	13.00	15.74
40-44	30	25	55	10.75	11.21	10.96
45-49	2	6	8	0.72	2.69	1.59
50+	3	0	3	1.08	0.0	0.60
Unknown	20	10	30	7.17	4.48	5.98
TOTAL	279	223	502	100.00	100.00	100.00
Numa, 1780-1871						
0-14	1	0	1	0.84	0.0	0.44
15-19	5	1	6	4.20	0.93	2.64
20-24	24	19	43	20.17	17.59	18.94
25-29	36	28	64	30.25	25.93	28.19
30-34	24	26	50	20.17	24.07	22.03
35-39	16	20	36	13.45	18.52	15.86
40-44	5	5	10	4.20	4.63	4.41
45-49	0	3	3	0.0	2.78	1.32
50+	0	0	0	0.0	0.0	0.0
Unknown	8	6	14	6.72	5.56	6.17
TOTAL	119	108	227	100.00	100.00	100.00
Nishikata, 1782-1796						
0-14	0	0	0	0.0	0.0	0.0
15-19	4	2	6	11.76	5.88	8.82
20-24	11	7	18	32.35	20.59	26.47
25-29	8	11	19	23.53	32.35	27.94
30-34	6	10	16	17.65	29.41	23.53
35-39	4	4	8	11.76	11.76	11.76
40-44	0	0	0	0.0	0.0	0.0
45-49	0	0	0	0.0	0.0	0.0
50+	1	0	1	2.94	0.0	1.47
Unknown	0	0	0	0.0	0.0	0.0
TOTAL	34	34	68	100.00	100.00	100.00

Fujito and three in Nishikata. All persons who were living in the village at the beginning of the base year were traced through the subsequent five sets of records, and all persons who could be found in the registers five years later were counted as survivors.

Before using this information to estimate life expectancy, death rates were compiled for the survived populations (using the first year of each period as the base year) in order to provide a check on the data used for the crude death rates in Table 8.2, which might fall under criticism for being inaccurate because they are so low. Three death rate estimates were compiled in Table 8.7.

The low and medium estimates in Table 8.7 are in most cases within a percentage point of each other and are very close to the crude death rates for the same periods in Fujito and Nishikata. The actual death rate probably lay somewhere between the low and medium estimates. This opinion is based on the assumption that most of the drop-outs were in fact out-migrations rather than deaths. Most of the drop-outs were in the age groups with the highest migration and lowest death rates, that is, the young adult age groups, and were predominantly male. During this period in Japan, the authorities sought to restrict permanent out-migration from the farming communities in order to maintain an adequate agricultural labor force (since the bulk of taxes was collected on agriculture), and it was often difficult for an able-bodied adult male to obtain official permission to move from his village. As a result, people simply absconded.

To take an example of this phenomenon, let us look at the Fujito records for 1800-1805: During this period, three of the males who were dropped from the registers without explanation were listed as working outside the village in the year that they were last registered, and the other six males who disappeared were all between age 27 and 50. Among the drop-outs were three members of the same family who were all reported as working in the castle town of Okayama in the year they were last registered. Also included in the drop-outs in this period were a 30-year-old mother and her 2-year-old daughter. It is more likely that the woman was divorced and sent home than that both she and her daughter died. Since these records were not known to have been used for tax collection, corvée, or any other purpose that would have directly and adversely affected the villagers, and since no purpose would be served by hiding deaths, the event most likely to go unrecorded

Table 8.7

Estimated Death Rates Based on Survived Sample Populations

Period	Base Year Population[a]	Percentage Lost[b]	Percentage Known to Have Died	Known Deaths	Presumed Deaths	Possible Deaths (i.e., drop-outs)	Annual Average Death Rate (per 1,000)[c]		
							Low Estimate[d]	Medium Estimate[e]	High Estimate[f]
Fujito									
Males									
1800-1805	321	12.1	7.8	25	2	9	16.8	17.5	22.6
1805-1810	316	11.4	7.6	24	3	6	17.1	17.6	21.1
1825-1830	319	10.3	7.8	25	1	3	16.3	16.7	18.4
1830-1835	333	12.9	10.2	34	2	3	21.6	22.1	23.7
Females									
1800-1805	260	18.5	6.5	17	0	9	13.1	14.8	21.8
1805-1810	246	14.6	6.9	16	2	7	14.6	15.8	21.3
1825-1830	269	14.9	9.3	25	0	3	18.6	19.7	21.8
1830-1835	284	18.3	11.6	33	1	4	23.9	25.6	28.1
Nishikata									
Males									
1782-1787	142	11.3	8.5	12	1	2	18.3	18.7	21.3
1787-1792	144	17.4	12.5	18	1	2	26.4	27.5	30.0
1791-1796	137	19.7	10.9	15	1	6	23.4	25.4	33.3
Females									
1782-1787	131	11.5	4.6	6	1	3	10.7	11.4	15.9
1787-1792	133	19.5	14.3	19	0	0	28.6	30.2	30.2
1791-1796	132	16.7	7.6	10	2	4	18.2	19.7	25.4

Table 8.7 (Continued)

[a] Population as of the first of the first year in each sample.

[b] Lost is defined as all persons who were in the base year population who were not in the population exactly five years later. This includes all persons who died, who migrated out, and who dropped out of the records without explanation.

[c] These are death rates for the initial population; that is, deaths during the period to children not alive at the beginning are excluded.

[d] The low estimate was calculated by dividing known plus presumed deaths by the base year population to obtain a five-year cumulative death rate, and then by five for an annual average death rate.

[e] The medium estimate was calculated by the above method except that known migrations and drop-outs (i.e., possible deaths) were subtracted from the base year population.

[f] The high estimate is for known, presumed, and possible deaths divided by the base year population from which known migrations have been subtracted.

would be absconding, particularly since absconders occasionally turned up in the village again after a lapse of several years or even a decade. In addition, if the unrecorded events were deaths, one would expect to find them concentrated at ages of highest mortality instead of being bunched in the age groups with the highest incidence of migration. In any case, the number of drop-outs in most periods was so small that including them in the death rates does not substantially raise the estimated annual average death rates.

Life expectancy estimates were constructed using the information from the samples survived for five years and Coale and Demeny's regional model life tables. The method used was to group into five-year age groups the population in the beginning of the base year and subtract from each group all persons who migrated out or dropped from the records during the subsequent five-year period (thus equivalent to our medium estimates of death rates).[11] Persons over age 65 who dropped out were left in the base year population as they were presumed dead for this analysis. Different sets of five-year survival rates ($5^{Lx+5}/5^{Lx}$) from the Coale-Demeny "West" model life tables were then applied to the base population.[12] The estimate of life expectancy was provided by interpolating between the sets that came closest to reproducing the correct number of survivors in the population after five years. The estimates obtained can be seen in Table 8.8. The calculations were also made omitting the age group 0-4 in order to estimate life expectancy eliminating the group for which the data are most suspect due to the underreporting of infant deaths. This second set of estimates is generally consistent with the first, except that life expectancy is higher with the 0-4 age groups excluded for the decade 1825-1835 in Fujito and the decade of the Temmei mortality crisis in Nishikata. Fujito, during the decade 1825-1835, had higher than its usual birth rates and also a relatively high infant and child death rate, the latter due primarily to an epidemic in 1832.

Life expectancy seems to have varied widely by period within each village. The fall in life expectancy in Nishikata can be readily explained by the Temmei famine of the 1780s. The most surprising of the estimates is that for women in Nishikata for 1782-1787. Even if the age group 0-4 is excluded in making the estimates, life expectancy was over 75 years. This estimate in no way appears to

221

Table 8.8
Life Expectancy Estimates for Fujito and Nishikata
(life expectancy when 0-4 age group is excluded is shown in parentheses)

Period	At Birth		At Age 1	
	Males	Females	Males	Females
	Fujito			
1800-1805	44.1 (41.1)	54.4 (54.5)	50.9 (49.0)	59.1 (59.2)
1805-1810	45.1 (45.4)	52.9 (55.8)	52.1 (52.3)	58.1 (60.3)
1825-1830	40.8 (53.6)	40.3 (49.3)	48.4 (58.7)	47.9 (55.1)
1830-1835	34.3 (38.4)	32.1 (36.5)	43.6 (46.8)	40.9 (44.7)
Mean	41.1 (44.6)	44.9 (49.0)	48.8 (51.7)	51.5 (54.8)
	Nishikata			
1782-1787	43.5 (43.7)	75.3 (75.2)	50.9 (51.0)	75.3 (75.3)
1787-1792	30.6 (37.3)	39.1 (45.0)	40.6 (46.0)	46.3 (51.6)
1791-1796	30.5 (35.1)	50.6 (56.2)	40.5 (44.2)	56.1 (60.6)
Mean	34.9 (38.7)	55.0 (58.8)	44.0 (47.1)	59.2 (62.5)

be the result of faulty data, but instead illustrates the point that wide variations from the regional or national mean can appear in small sample populations; there were only 131 females in the base year sample for 1782.

In Fujito, life expectancy seems to have fallen during the early nineteenth century. The death rate was highest and life expectancy lowest between 1825 and 1835, the decade of most rapid population growth during the period for which data are extant. Conversely, life expectancy was higher earlier, during a period of lower fertility and high out-migration. Part of the explanation for these life expectancies lies in the fact that when fertility rose in Fujito, infant and child mortality also rose, and in periods of lower fertility, fewer children died. This example illustrates the danger of attempting to extrapolate birth and death rates and other patterns of demographic behavior from changes in the total population.

The estimates made in this section on Fujito and Nishikata bear out the general accuracy of death rates for the villages seen in Table 8.4. They also indicate a widely varying life expectancy at birth ranging from the low 30s to as high as 75 for women. Though our sample is very small, the data presented here suggest that life expectancy in rural areas in western Japan during the nineteenth century was somewhere in the 40s.

A NOTE ON THE VALIDITY OF THE BIRTH RATES FOR THE FOUR VILLAGES

Using the Coale and Demeny "West" model life tables and stable populations, birth rates were estimated in order to attempt to determine what the birth rate would have been had the births of all children been recorded, no matter how soon they died after birth. Since it is the recording of births and subsequent mortality in the early years that is suspected of being incomplete, the estimates were made using life expectancy estimates in Table 8.8 with the age groups 0-4 excluded from the calculations. The birth rate estimates in Table 8.9 were made by taking the life expectancy estimates and the mortality levels they represent, and then interpolating the birth rates found in these mortality levels to obtain an estimate of the crude birth rates by sex for five-year periods for Fujito and Nishikata. The means of the male and female birth rate estimates were then obtained and compared to the crude birth rates calculated from the data available for each village.

The comparison shows a very good correspondence between the birth rate averages estimated using the Coale and Demeny tables and the birth rates calculated for Fujito and Nishikata directly from the data. The fit is especially good considering that neither village had a stable population in any period and that the sample for Nishikata is so small. Certainly the birth rate estimates provide strong evidence for considering the calculated birth rates as generally correct. In Fujito the estimates are above the crude birth rates for two periods, but below them for the other two. In Nishikata the estimates range only between 19.6 and 20.5. Given these estimates, it seems difficult to argue that the crude birth rates calculated for our village samples should be adjusted upward.[13]

CONCLUSION

Population data for the eighteenth and nineteenth centuries in scattered Tokugawa villages indicate a relatively low birth rate, a death rate that varied widely at times but tended to fluctuate around the birth rate, and a life expectancy similar to that in western Europe prior to 1850 and not unlike that in Japan in the early twentieth century. Emphasis has traditionally been placed on the

223

Table 8.9

Estimates of Birth Rates for Fujito and Nishikata Using Stable Model Populations

| Period | FEMALE | | MALE | | TOTAL | |
	Growth Rate (per 1,000)	Estimated Birth Rate	Growth Rate (per 1,000)	Estimated Birth Rate	Estimated Birth Rate Average	Calculated Crude Birth Rate
			Fujito			
1800-1805	-12.6	12.6	-1.9	23.0	17.8	15.4
1805-1810	8.1	23.5	-2.5	20.4	21.9	22.3
1825-1830	10.9	28.6	8.6	24.6	26.6	25.2
1830-1835	9.0	35.6	2.4	28.1	31.8	33.1
			Nishikata			
1782-1787	5.9	16.7	1.9	24.4	20.5	19.9
1787-1792	-3.0	20.2	-11.5	19.4	19.8	18.6
1791-1796	-9.4	12.5	-2.3	26.7	19.6	16.7

rapid growth in Japan's population during the early years of industrialization but, even so, the growth rate seems to have been under 1 percent until the late 1890s. If the villages studied here are at all representative of trends in Tokugawa Japan, it would seem unlikely that there was any sharp discontinuity in population patterns between the Tokugawa and Meiji periods, or even between late Tokugawa and the 1920s.

We will now turn to an examination of factors responsible for the low birth and death rates in Tokugawa villages in the late eighteenth and nineteenth centuries.

CHAPTER NINE

Population Control in Tokugawa Japan

Among the Japanese there were fundamental similarities in the cultural conditioning of, and the individual motivations in, the limitation of family size in the Tokugawa and the modern worlds. The pressure of numbers on subsistence and the misery of poverty do not explain the control of fertility in the industrial society; they did not explain the abortion and the infanticide of the agrarian society.[1]

Analysis of fertility, mortality, and life expectancy in Tokugawa villages indicates an average completed family size of about three children, one which cannot be explained by high death rates. Although the traditional explanation for the slow growth of population in the second half of the Tokugawa period has been the recurrent and widespread famines and the resulting practices of abortion and infanticide resorted to by desperate, poverty-stricken peasants, our earlier analysis of the economy and the growing body of evidence that there were improvements in the standard of living in most of the country makes it difficult to explain the slow population growth as resulting from acts of desperation by families struggling for survival.

Why, then, was family size small? According to our analytical framework presented at the end of Chapter Two, at some point in time (probably in the eighteenth century for most of Japan), villagers began to view large families as an economic burden. Shortly thereafter, social controls over marriage and fertility were tightened and, in addition, individuals began to limit their own fertility. We have hypothesized that the major reason for this behavior was that people began to choose to "trade off" additional children for goods and services or for the accumulation of wealth needed to improve or maintain their standard of living and their status within village society.

While it is impossible to uncover the precise motivation of these villagers, we can examine the results of their actions affecting fertility and isolate how behavior differed according to the eco-

226

nomic situation of both families and villages. In this chapter we will (1) examine evidence of efforts to control family size, (2) analyze the methods used to control family size and the village population as a whole, and (3) discuss the pressures for controlling population and the reasons the villagers acted to limit their families.

The major hypotheses presented here are: (1) Parents sought to rear a family of about three to four children. Rather than passively accept as many or as few children as were born to them, families controlled the number of children raised, not only through limiting births, but by adopting children if they could not have as many as they wanted, or by giving their own children out for adoption if they had more than they wanted. Women who suffered the loss in infancy of desired children tried to have more children to attain desired family size and thus often bore more than the average number of children. (2) Birth control, including abortion and infanticide, was practiced within marriage to a considerable degree even in villages that were developing economically. One measure used was sex-selective infanticide. (3) Fertility was regulated not only within marriage but, perhaps more importantly, by varying the age at which persons were permitted to marry and the proportion of the population allowed to marry. Delaying marriage for women shortened their childbearing years. Also, the number of childbearing couples within a household was usually limited to one. In times of poor economic conditions, the number of marriages within a village would drop, and thus the number of children would decline although marital fertility remained fairly constant. In a period of an expanding economy, younger brothers who would normally leave home or remain unmarried were permitted to marry and remain in the village. This response to economic conditions was fairly rapid, within five to ten years at most. (4) Famines had a minimal effect on the social and household structure of all the villages studied here, even those that experienced a rise in the death rate. Any vacuums created by famine, epidemics, or migration were quickly filled through marriages, births, and the adoption of people of all ages, but the need for such adjustments was in most cases minimal.

These hypotheses were posited after a study of the Okayama villages. Here, quantitative data will be provided to demonstrate that they are tenable for the three Okayama villages and for Nishikata in Mikawa. To do so, we will analyze the childbearing patterns in these four villages and then the methods used for fertility control, including adoption, abortion and infanticide, the regulation of marriage, migration, and the possible effect of famines. Finally, we will discuss the social, legal, and economic incentives existing in Tokugawa Japan for controlling family and village size.

EVIDENCE OF EFFORTS TO CONTROL FAMILY SIZE

The low mean birth rates in these four villages—a low of 18.5 for Nishikata and a high of 26 for Fukiage—naturally resulted in a small number of children ever born to couples and a small number of children raised. The number of children ever born averaged from just under three to between three and four for all of the villages. While the average was around three, the modal number of children born was sometimes only two, as was the case of Fukiage between 1773 and 1801, and Fujito for women who married after 1841. (See Tables 9.1 and 9.2.)

The number of children ever born to a woman does not, however, necessarily represent the number of children she raised. Infant and child mortality was frequently high. Due to an epidemic of some disease to which children were particularly susceptible, on the average, women in Fujito who married between 1825 and 1841 bore one more child than the number that survived, or 3.72 instead of 2.76. No one in the village had more than six children survive in any of the three periods shown in Table 9.1.

But, while the size of many families was diminished through death and adoption, other families made up for losses through the birth of additional children or adoption. Thus, in Fukiage in the period 1773-1801, twenty-four families, or nearly one-eighth of the sample, had no children of their own, but only fifteen families raised no children. (See Table 9.2.) The distributions of families by the number of children born to them and the number raised are very similar, but these totals in fact cloak actions on the part of families to ensure that they raised the number of children they desired. Since, for example, as many as 25 percent of the children born to women married between 1825 and 1841 in Fujito died while very young, some of these families adopted children in order to obtain the family size they wanted.

Adoption was a common method of regulating family size in

Table 9.1
Distribution of Completed Family Size in Fujito
for Families with Children

No. of Children	No. Families by No. Children Ever Born	No. Families by No. Children Who Survived
Women Aged 23-44 in 1794 (Cohort Group D)[a]		
0	–	1
1	5	9
2	8	10
3	16	10
4	15	17
5	5	4
6	3	4
7	2	0
8	1	0
Average	3.53	3.11
Women Who Married between 1825-1841 (Cohort Group G)[a]		
0	–	3
1	11	15
2	4	13
3	17	21
4	19	16
5	15	6
6	8	2
7	2	0
8	0	0
Average	3.72	2.76
Women Who Married after 1841 (Cohort Group H)[a]		
0	–	0
1	10	13
2	16	18
3	8	10
4	9	11
5	8	6
6	8	1
Average	3.22	2.69

[a]See the Appendix to Table 9.5 for further explanation of the cohort groups.

premodern Japan and, in fact, was a widespread practice even until World War II. In the four villages studied here persons of all ages were adopted, even some elderly women after the Tempō famine of the 1830s. But the most common adoptions were children above age 2 who became adopted sons and daughters and young men who married daughters of families without male heirs,

229

Table 9.2
Distribution of Family Size in Fukiage and Numa

No of Children	No. Families by No. Children Ever Born	No. Families by Total No. Children at Any One Time
Fukiage 1773-1801		
0	24	15
1	25	27
2	51	50
3	42	51
4	38	38
5	15	13
6	10	12
7	2	3
8	2	0
Average	2.73	2.82
Numa 1814-1832		
0	7	4
1	7	9
2	15	18
3	14	15
4	16	14
5	4	5
6	2	0
Average	2.69	2.63
Numa 1860-1871		
0	3	2
1	3	4
2	5	3
3	13	13
4	3	6
5	0	0
6	0	0
7	1	0
Average	2.89	2.61

took up residence with the family, and became a family member, receiving the family name and usually succeeding the head. Adoptions were so widely practiced that in Numa in the period 1860-1871 there were more adoptions recorded than marriages. The incidence of adoption compared to marriage varied by village and by period (see Table 9.3), but it was never rare and was frequently over 50 percent.

The widespread custom of adoption can be considered one of the major reasons the premodern Japanese were able to limit family

Table 9.3
Incidence of Adoption Compared to Marriage

Period[a]	Be Adopted into a Family	Leave Family to be Adopted Elsewhere	Total No. Adoptions	Marry into a Family	Leave Family to Marry	Total No. Marriages	Adoptions As Percentage of Marriages
Fujito							
1775-1810 (15)	12	8	20	54	58	112	17.9
1825-1841 (13)	24	23	47	54	44	98	48.0
1844-1863 (12)	31	24	55	51	41	92	59.8
Fukiage							
1693-1741 (13)	11	7	18	56	40	96	18.8
1773-1860 (12)	71	45	116	65	54	119	97.5
Numa							
1780-1832 (22)	14	14	28	67	57	124	22.6
1860-1871 (10)	29	25	54	23	24	47	114.9
Nishikata							
1782-1796 (15)	13	10	23	20	16	36	63.9

[a]Figures in parentheses indicate number of years during the period for which there are data.

size in a society in which the continuation of the family line was of utmost importance both economically and socially. This well-known practice by samurai families was even more frequently resorted to by peasant families, at least in the village of Fujito. Of 105 families for whom records exist for at least two or more generations, 56 families, or 53 percent, adopted sons or other relatives—for example making someone an adopted brother—for the purpose of continuing the family line. This is easily twice the rate of adoption found for the *hatamoto* class of samurai.[2] And this percentage may well be an underestimate as there was a tendency in the records to drop the term "adopted" within a few years of the event, particularly after the adopted son succeeded to the headship of the family.

In addition to assuring the continuation of family lines, the system of adoption created an outlet for excess sons in a family that was already assured an heir. The custom of adoption was so widely accepted that at least two families in Fujito permitted their younger sons to leave home or become adopted and, when subsequently their own heir died, the families took in adopted sons to succeed the head rather than have their own children return. The importance of the family name and the continuation of the line in Japan has long been stressed by anthropologists, but what is a crucial difference between Japan and, for example, India is that in Japan any male in the family, whether adopted or not, is eligible to become head, to carry on the family name and business, and to say prayers and care for the memorial tablets of deceased family members.[3]

The practice of adoption ensured continuity to families and thereby gave a certain stability to the village, but it was not a practice with built-in rigidities. Adoption was no more irrevocable than marriage, perhaps less so. Theoretically, an adopted son was to leave his own family behind and become part of the new family just as a bride did—thus the symbolic burning of straw behind a bride to indicate her permanent departure from her old home—but in reality people returned home when the arrangement proved to be unsatisfactory. Thus in Nishikata in the fifteen years under survey, there were 13 adoptions into families and 10 out, for a total of 23, compared to 36 marriages, but during the same period 16 persons who had been adopted out returned home. Adoption seems to have been somewhat more successful in Fujito and it increased over time. In the fifteen years for which there are records before 1810, 12 persons were adopted out and 8 in. In contrast, from 1825 to 1863, in a total of twenty-five years for which there are records, 57 people were adopted in and 47 went out, with the average number of adoptions per year double that of the earlier period. Only 1 person came back from an unsuccessful adoption in the first period and 6 in the second. The largest number of adoptions took place in the 1840s and 1850s, just after the Tempō famine and ensuing epidemics.

BIRTH CONTROL THROUGH ABORTION AND INFANTICIDE

Datai-mabiki (abortion and infanticide) is commonly used as a phrase by Japanese historians, but the older of the two practices is undoubtedly *mabiki*, which means "to thin out" and usually refers to the thinning of seedlings. The infanticide in the Tohoku region during the Temmei famine of the 1780s is legendary; in the domain of Nambu the bodies of scores of dead children wrapped in straw mats were reported seen floating down one river.[4] Fear of the results on the tax revenues of the widespread use of these methods to limit children caused administrators in many areas to issue regulations banning them, and to effect measures to see that the prohibitions were more than exhortatory. Many domains required pregnant women to be registered, and some provided monetary incentives for bearing children.

Various methods of abortion seem to have been well known and, if the numerous regulations and bans against them are any testimony, they were widely used. Many books were published during the Tokugawa period on methods of abortion, the earliest dated 1692.[5] A common method seems to have been to apply continuous pressure to the belly or to vibrate it until abortion was induced. The practice of inserting a stick-like object into the head of the uterus had been perfected by the mid-seventeenth century and was used by professionals—usually midwives—from this time on. Many names exist for the medicines used to induce miscarriages, which were sold as *gekkei yaku* (menstrual medicine). A common medicine was a mercurial compound, and one can imagine what the possibly serious side effects must have been. The most frequently mentioned plant with the reputation of induc-

233

ing menstruation was the *goshitsu*, also known as *inokozuchi*, a member of the burdock family.[6]

Certainly by the nineteenth century, the technique of abortion had advanced far beyond what might be called "folk medicine." During the early nineteenth century, Kagawa Mitsusada published extremely detailed instructions on how to perform an abortion, dealing with various problems that could be encountered and specifying among other things that the procedure was not to be used on women more than three months pregnant.[7]

Attempts by the authorities to stop the widespread practice of abortion began in the seventeenth century and could still be seen in the nineteenth. In 1646 the Shogunate banned the public advertisement of menstrual medicines within the city limits of Edo (Tokyo), and in 1667 it became illegal to perform abortions in the city. Nevertheless, various subterfuges were used and the practice continued.[8] Nearly two centuries later, in 1842, we find an Edo magistrate who ordered that "those who unwarrantedly perform abortions . . . , both men and women, would be driven out of Edo for a distance of 10 *ri* in all directions."[9]

Not all the methods for abortion attempted in Tokugawa Japan had the efficacy of those used by the professionals in Edo. In Okayama there were a number of beliefs about how to terminate pregnancy that were undoubtedly ineffective. To try to induce abortion, Okayama women used to cauterize the navel with moxa, or brew the seeds of the white morning glory and drink the resulting tea. They tried eating carp before they were two months pregnant, and they vigorously massaged the belly. Abortion was considered most likely to be successful if attempted in odd-numbered months. If all of these methods failed, they might try jumping from a "high place" in the seventh or eighth month of pregnancy.[10]

After a child was born or aborted, women often tried to prevent becoming pregnant again. It was thought effective to drink a bowlful of salt water every night before going to bed. Urinating immediately after intercourse was supposed to prevent conception. Women also resorted to religion; many made bottomless sacks out of cloth and dedicated them to nearby shrines to prevent pregnancy. And one might name the last child Sué (the last) if a girl or Tomekichi (*tome* means stop) if a boy. That this last practice was rarely effective is attested to by the number of children in Okayama who bore these names but who had one or more younger brothers and sisters.

While qualitative evidence on abortion and infanticide can be found in numerous sources, it is more difficult to assess to what extent these practices were prevalent and what effect they had on population growth. Takahashi tends simply to attribute declines in population to them and increases in population to the effectiveness of countermeasures.[11] However, a few statistical tests can be carried out to determine whether methods of birth control were being practiced to an extent that affected population patterns.

First, we can examine the average span of childbearing in our four villages (see Tables 9.4 and 9.5). The average age at first birth tended to coincide with the average age at marriage in each village because it was not uncommon for a marriage to be legally registered only after the bride became pregnant or had borne her first child and because, even where such was not the case, women

Table 9.4
Average Age at First and Last Birth in Fukiage, Numa, and Nishikata

Period	Average Age First Birth	Sample Size	s	Average Age Last Birth	Sample Size	s
		Fukiage				
1683-1712	23.1	67	3.4	37.4[a]	82	4.1
				37.3[b]	61	0.4
1773-1801	22.7	80	3.4	37.6[a]	126	4.6
				37.5[b]	107	4.9
		Numa				
1814-1832	24.0	32	2.5	33.0[a]	33	5.9
				35.5[b]	25	4.7
1860-1871	22.7	18	3.4	33.1[a]	14	4.8
				34.0[b]	13	3.4
		Nishikata				
1782-1796	21.1	7	1.7	32.4[c]	26	4.3
				33.3[d]	13	5.3

[a]Women who were married to age 44 or whose marriages ended earlier due to the death of either spouse. The divorced and childless have been omitted.

[b]Based on the same group of women as the first but with all women eliminated whose marriages terminated before the women reached age 43 or whose daughters may have borne the last child listed.

[c]Women between ages 18 and 38 in 1782.

[d]Women who were at least 39 but no more than 55 in 1782.

tended to bear their first child within a year or two of marriage. From this evidence it would be difficult to conclude that women were limiting their family size by delaying the birth of their first child, a practice that is uncommon in Japan even in the twentieth century.

The average age at last birth, however, indicates that women in these four villages stopped having children on the average many years before they would become incapable of bearing them. The highest average age at last birth, 37, is for Fukiage, the village in which the population grew the most rapidly, while the lowest averages, around 33, were for Numa and Nishikata. Even with the elimination of women whose marriages terminated before age 44 due to the death of either spouse, the averages stayed virtually the same. Thus, it is clear that the low average age at last birth was

Table 9.5
Average Age at First and Last Birth in Fujito,
by Cohort Group and *Kokudaka* Class

Average Ages at First and Last Birth by Cohort Group					
First Birth		*s*	*Last Birth*		*s*
			A	36.0	4.9
B	21.5	2.8			
C	23.0	4.4	C	35.9	5.1
D	24.6	4.1	D	34.3	4.5
E	24.4	4.6			
F	26.5	4.2	F	36.6	4.4
G	22.8	3.0	G	33.1	6.0
H	23.1	4.8	H	31.8	6.5
I	22.3	3.6			
TOTAL	23.6	4.3	TOTAL	34.1	5.7

Average Age at First Birth for Women by Kokudaka Class for Cohort Groups G and H					*Average Age at Last Birth of Women Who Bore Five Or More Children*		
	G	*s*	*H*	*s*		*Age*	*s*	*Sample Size*
I	25.3	3.3	25.3	2.9	A	39.5	3.6	8
II	22.4	2.6	25.9	6.5	C	39.4	2.5	13
III	22.0	2.7	24.3	6.0	D	38.8	2.1	12
IV	22.4	2.9	21.2	2.9	E	37.1	3.3	8
V	23.2	2.8	21.5	4.0	F	38.8	3.5	11
					G	38.3	3.1	24
					H	35.8	3.0	17
TOTAL[a]	22.8	3.0	23.0	4.8	TOTAL[a]	38.1	3.3	93

[a]Weighted averages.

Appendix to Table 9.5

---

(1) Cohort Groups for Fujito

Sample Size		
34	A	Those married women who had reached age 39 but no more than 55 by 1775 (or 39 by 1778).
20	B	Women of childbearing age but less than age 39 who appeared in the records only from 1775 to 1778.
34	C	Childbearing women aged 18-38 in 1775 (or 18 by 1778) who could be identified in the 1794 records.
56	D	Married women aged 23-44 in 1794 and who were married prior to 1794 (but who did not appear in the 1775-1778 records).
51	E	Women whose marriages were contracted between 1794 and 1810. This group includes six women whose marriages were terminated prior to 1810.
42	F	Married women aged 31-45 in 1825 who did not appear in records prior to that year.
80	G	Women who were married between 1825 and 1841. This cohort group has been further divided into eight classes by the *kokudaka* size of the household in which each woman lived.
62	H	Women who were married (or who bore children without recorded husbands) after 1841, but who reached age 44 or whose marriage had terminated in or prior to 1863. This cohort group has been further subdivided into eight classes by the *kokudaka* size of the household in which each woman lived.
44	I	Women who were married or bore children without recorded husbands after 1844, but who were still of childbearing age and married in 1863.

(2) Kokudaka Classes

I   Households with no recorded landholdings.

II   Households holding land assessed at 1 *koku* or less.

III   Households holding land assessed at 1-3 *koku*.

IV   Households holding land assessed at 3-6 *koku*.

V   The remaining households, consisting of the following groups:

(1) Households containing ten or more members for the entire period under observation;

(2) Households holding land assessed at from 6-10 *koku*;

(3) Households holding land assessed at more than 10 *koku* (only the Hikasa and Hoshijima lines were in this category from 1825 to 1863, the period for which the classifications were made);

(4) Households that changed *kokudaka* classes from 1851 to 1863, most often switching between the 1-3 and 3-6 *kokudaka* classes.

---

not caused by early widowhood or a high maternal death rate. General malnutrition and poor health can cause early menopause, but a life expectancy in these villages similar to that in Western Europe and the United States in the nineteenth century makes this possibility seem unlikely. If so, one must conclude that women were taking measures of some kind to prevent the births of unwanted children either after the desired family size had been reached or after they had reached an age at which it was no longer considered "proper" to bear children.

If women were using infanticide to control family size, at the margin they may have let only children of a preferred sex live. If this practice was widespread, it is possible that it would create an abnormal sex ratio among children in the village, especially among the last-born children. Boys would most likely be preferred as they would grow up to be economic assets, unlike girls, who married and left home, taking with them part of the family assets in their dowry. We do have contemporary evidence that more victims of infanticide were female than male. For example, Nishikawa Kyūrinsai observed:

> If humble persons living in huts have large numbers of children, they will let the first one or two live, but after that, they often kill the children born. They call this *mabiku* [to thin out]. Female infants by custom are mostly killed.

An examination of the sex ratios of all children born to and living with their mothers in Fukiage, Numa, and Nishikata (Table 9.6) reveals that, despite a sex ratio of 1.21 in Numa during the decade 1860-1871, we fail to reject the null hypothesis that these samples do not come from a normal universe, that is, we

Table 9.6
Sex Ratios of All Children Born to and Living with Their Mothers
During Periods for Which Data Exist

Village	Sex Ratio	Average No. Children	Sample Size Children	Mothers
Fukiage (1683-1730)	1.15	3.69	468	127
Numa (1814-1832)	1.05	3.02	178	59
Numa (1860-1871)	1.21	2.44	117	48
Nishikata (1782-1796)	1.18	2.98	131	44

can say with 95 percent confidence that these samples could have come from a universe in which the sex ratio was 1.04. The sex ratios of children born in Fujito have been divided into nineteen groups: nine cohort groups and five subgroups categorized by landholding size of the mother's household for two of the cohort groups. (See the Appendix to Table 9.5.) Because of the small size of many of the groups, even with sex ratios of 0.56 and 1.42, we fail to reject the same null hypothesis. (See Table 9.7.) In only one group is it statistically probable that families were using *mabiki*

Table 9.7
Sex Ratios of Children Born in Fujito, by Cohort Group
and *Kokudaka* Class of Mother

Group		Sex Ratio (M/F)		Sample Size
A		1.28		139
B		0.96		45
C		1.36		137
D		1.26		203
E		1.23		132
F		1.00		132
G	I	0.56	25	
	II	0.77	39	
	III	1.00	52	
	IV	2.23[a]	100	
	V	1.04	57	
	Total for G	1.21		273
H	I	0.92	23	
	II	0.92	23	
	III	1.07	29	
	IV	1.35	73	
	V	1.42	46	
	Total for H	1.20		194
I		1.38		81
TOTAL FOR ALL GROUPS		*1.24*[a]		*1,336*

[a]Indicates the sex ratio is outside the 95 percent confidence interval.

to weed out undesired girls. This is the sample of 100 mothers who were married between 1825 and 1841 and whose household held land assessed between 3 and 6 *koku*. However, when the groups were aggregated, a sex ratio of 1.24 was obtained for the total of 1,336 children. This sex ratio is outside the 95 percent confidence interval, thus indicating that women were definitely behaving in such a way as to raise more male children than female.[13]

If we test the sex ratios of only last-born children, we find that

239

the sex ratios for Numa show a bias in favor of girls, but the samples are small (Table 9.8). The sex ratios for Nishikata and Fukiage are high, between 1.4 and 1.8, whether samples are used

Table 9.8
Sex Ratios of Last-Born Children

Village	Sex Ratio	Sample Size
Fukiage (1683-1730)		
I[a]	1.41	82
II[b]	1.36	104
Numa (1814-1832)		
I	0.83	22
II	0.90	40
Numa (1860-1871)		
I	0.67	10
II	0.85	24
Nishikata (1782-1796)		
I	1.83	17
II	1.50	30
Fujito		
A	1.20	33
B	2.60	18
C	1.75	33
D	1.45	54
E	1.15	43
F	1.00	38
G	1.30	76
H	1.70[c]	60
TOTAL FOR FUJITO	1.40[c]	355

[a]Mothers who lived with their husbands to age 44.

[b]Mothers married to age 39 or whose marriages ended prior to that age due to the death of either spouse.

[c]Indicates the sex ratio is outside the 95 percent confidence interval.

that include only women who were married up to age 44 or whether women whose marriages ended earlier are included. Again, the small size of the samples (large standard deviations) precludes rejecting the null hypothesis that women were not practicing sex-selective infanticide. However, for Fujito, not only is the sex ratio of 1.70 for last-born children of women in Group H (who married after 1841) outside the 95 percent confidence range, but so is the sex ratio of 1.40 for the total number of last-born children, the 355 for whom we have information. Thus, we can conclude that in Fujito women tended to keep only males when they had reached a point where they felt they had had enough children, and that this behavior influenced the sex ratios of children ever born. It is hypothesized here that such behavior was prevalent in other villages also, given the large number of samples in which the sex ratio is much greater than 1.04, and that this can be shown statistically when larger samples can be obtained.

BIRTH INTERVALS AND FAMILY SIZE

An average age of 23.6 at first birth and of 34 at last birth, as in Fujito, leaves only a decade for childbearing. If a woman has three or perhaps four children during this period, then it means that on the average she has a child every three or four years. And we find that the average intervals between births for both Fujito and Fukiage are always between three and five years. (See Table 9.9.) The interval between births tends to rise with birth order, except for a slight fall in some periods in the intervals after the third birth. This may be because women who have large families do not have long intervals between births or they would not be able to bear five or six children between their early to mid-20s and their early 40s.

The birth intervals shown in Table 9.9 are in units of years rather than in months because of the lack of information on the precise date of births. Therefore, an interval of one year means that the second birth occurred in the next calendar year after the first, which means that the interval could be as long as nearly twenty-four months, or in a few rare cases, less than nine, at least on paper. A few of the one-year intervals may actually be twins. However, the larger the sample the more accurate is the classification of birth intervals as differences in intervals are smoothed out. The difference in the average interval in Fukiage and Fujito may reflect the nature of the data more than a real difference in intervals, as the data for Fujito are more complete. Some of the children in Fukiage who died in infancy or early childhood are undoubtedly missing from the records, as they were born and died in years for which there are no *shūmon-aratame-chō*.

Despite the diversity found in the length of the intervals between births, we find that in Fujito 69 percent of the intervals between births for each order from the first and second through

241

Table 9.9
Intervals between Births in Fujito and Fukiage

No. of Years between Births / Interval	1	2	3	4	5	6	7 or More	Total No.	Average
Fujito, Cohort Group C (Childbearing Age in 1775-1778)									
1st & 2nd	1	10	8	4	0	0	6	29	4.21
2nd & 3rd	0	2	7	5	6	1	6	27	5.04
3rd & 4th	0	4	5	4	3	0	2	18	3.94
4th & 5th	1	4	3	2	0	0	1	11	3.00
5th & 6th	0	1	2	0	1	0	0	4	3.25
TOTAL	2	21	25	15	10	1	15	89	4.21
Fujito, Cohort Group D (Married Prior to 1794)									
1st & 2nd	6	15	10	10	3	2	3	49	3.23
2nd & 3rd	0	5	14	6	5	5	4	39	4.21
3rd & 4th	0	7	6	5	5	1	1	25	3.60
4th & 5th	0	1	5	1	1	0	1	9	3.67
5th & 6th	0	2	1	0	1	0	0	4	3.00
TOTAL	6	30	36	22	15	8	9	126	3.63
Fujito, Cohort Group G (Married 1825-1841									
1st & 2nd	9	18	12	13	7	1	3	63	3.14
2nd & 3rd	5	10	15	14	7	2	8	61	3.97
3rd & 4th	0	3	17	7	8	5	4	44	4.32
4th & 5th	0	4	5	8	1	2	3	23	4.04
5th & 6th	0	3	1	0	1	1	2	8	4.88
TOTAL	14	38	50	42	24	11	20	199	3.83
Fujito, Cohort Group H (Married after 1841)									
1st & 2nd	2	11	15	10	5	2	4	49	3.73
2nd & 3rd	0	6	9	7	5	4	2	33	4.03
3rd & 4th	3	4	9	5	2	2	0	25	3.60
4th & 5th	1	4	6	5	0	1	0	17	3.12
5th & 6th	1	2	1	2	1	0	1	8	3.63
TOTAL	7	27	40	29	13	9	7	132	3.62
Fukiage 1683-1706									
1st & 2nd	1	12	6	11	6	6	7	49	4.67
2nd & 3rd	0	9	10	8	7	0	5	39	4.13
3rd & 4th	1	6	9	2	6	2	1	27	3.59
4th & 5th	0	4	3	3	1	1	1	13	3.62
5th & 6th	0	1	2	2	1	1	0	7	3.86
TOTAL	2	32	30	26	21	10	14	135	4.16

Table 9.9 (Continued)

No. of Years between Births Interval	1	2	3	4	5	6	7 or More	Total No.	Average
				Fukiage 1773-1801					
1st & 2nd	10	33	39	36	17	9	24	168	4.20
2nd & 3rd	5	19	30	15	18	9	14	110	4.09
3rd & 4th	2	10	18	14	7	5	10	66	4.12
4th & 5th	1	7	9	4	1	2	4	28	3.71
5th & 6th	0	3	3	2	0	2	1	11	3.82
TOTAL	18	72	99	71	43	27	53	383	4.11

the fifth and sixth were between two and four years for Cohort Group C (1775-1778), 70 percent were for Cohort Group D (1778-1794), 65 percent were for Cohort Group G (1825-1841), and 73 percent for Group H (1841-1863). Similarly, in Fukiage, 65 percent were between two and four years for women listed in the registers between 1683 and 1706, and 63 percent for women listed between 1773 and 1801. The range for the percentage of births under two years apart is from a low of 1.5 percent for Fukiage between 1683 and 1706 to a high of 7 percent for Cohort Group G in Fujito between 1825 and 1841. A far larger percentage of births had intervals of seven or more years: 17 percent for Group C in Fujito and 14 percent for women listed in 1773-1801 in Fukiage, with a low of 5 percent for Group H in Fujito. In all six samples, between 74 and 83 percent of all birth intervals for births 1-6 were between two and five years.

We hypothesized that infant mortality might influence the length of birth intervals, that is, the intervals between births may have tended to be longer than they are now because of longer nursing periods and the exclusion of stillbirths and early infant mortality from the records. If one child died in infancy, a mother would stop nursing earlier and postpartum amenorrhea would be shortened. She might try to become pregnant sooner, to replace the dead child. This hypothesis was not supported by the evidence. Of children born to women in Fujito in Cohort Groups G and H who had only a one-year interval between the birth of their first and second child or between the birth of their second and third child, 28 percent (4 of a sample of 15) died in infancy or before the age of 5. But the same statistic for a two-year interval was 32 percent, for a three-year interval 18 percent, and for a four-year interval, 23 percent.

However, for Cohort Group G the length of the interval between the births of two children does seem to have had an effect on the health or life expectancy of either child. If there was only one or two years between the birth of the first and second child or the second and third child, in only 38 percent of the cases did both children live to the age of 5. But in 63 percent of the cases in which there were three or four years between them, both children survived infancy and early childhood. For Cohort Group H, however, both children survived in 68 percent of the cases in which there was a one- or two-year interval, and in 63 percent of cases with a three- or four-year interval. Since Cohort Group G consists of women married between 1825 and 1841, their children were subjected to the epidemic of 1832, and women who had their first two children soon after marriage had more children exposed to the epidemic, which suggests that the statistic for Group G may prove to be an exception.

Why were the average interbirth intervals so long in these villages? We can only guess at the reasons, but there are a number of factors that undoubtedly affected the length of time between births. First, the only method at hand for feeding infants would have been nursing and, up to the mid-twentieth century, it was common for rural women in particular to nurse children up to the age of 3 or over. Women who nursed that long would experience the maximum postpartum amenorrhea, which would explain why there were so few children born within one year of each other. The records omit miscarriages and stillborn children, and difficulties in bearing live children may well be the reason why the number with seven or more years between births was relatively large. However, a modal class of birth intervals of two to three years suggests that neither infanticide nor stillbirth was an important factor in determining the length of the birth intervals.

POSSIBLE BIOLOGICAL DETERMINANTS OF TOKUGAWA FAMILY SIZE

The high average age at first birth, the lack of teenage pregnancies, the average interval of over three years between births, and the lack of births attributable to women in their forties in our samples may have been partly due to biological causes. Rose Frisch's research indicates that "a *minimum* level of fatness, about 17 per cent of bodyweight, is associated with the onset of menstrual cycles and their continued maintenance soon after menarche."[14] Menarche is followed by a period of adolescent sterility of about 3.5 years in a well-nourished population, but it is longer in one less well nourished. "One would then expect that a late age of menarche, for example, 16.5 years as found in the middle of the nineteenth century . . . would be associated with a rather late age at birth of the first child, such as 22 or 23 years." According to Frisch's findings on England and Scotland between 1850 and 1870, if menarche occurred at age 15-16, the fitness for procreation was reached at age 22, the ages best suited for procreation were 25 to 29, and the average age at last birth was 41-42.

Furthermore, lactation has "very high energy demands, requiring about 1,000 calories per day" and causes

> much greater nutritional stress than pregnancy. . . . The breast milk of undernourished women does not differ in calories or protein from the breast milk provided by well-nourished women. . . . Thus, the undernourished woman draws on her own energy stores for the provision of adequate food for the growth and development of her infant . . . and would therefore be slower to regain the minimum energy levels required for the restoration of ovulatory cycles.

There is every reason to think that Tokugawa levels of nutrition were closer to nineteenth-century English levels than current levels in the industrialized countries, and certainly the Japanese data from the four villages analyzed here seem to fit perfectly the pattern Frisch found. Adolescent sterility would help explain why there are so very few teenage births in the samples, and a difference in nutrition levels might provide an answer to why the largest landholding families accounted for a disproportionate number of the few teenage marriages and births that did occur. A major reason why Tokugawa mothers did not become pregnant again while nursing can be hypothesized to have been prolonged lactational amenorrhea due to their diet. And, since the highest birth rates were for women aged 25-29, we may assume that these were the peak childbearing years.

In fact, the only data from the village samples that does not fit

Rose Frisch's model for nineteenth-century Europe is the average age at last childbirth. Nineteenth-century Japanese women, on the average, stopped bearing children five or six years earlier than did their contemporary European counterparts. If nutrition was so poor that the menopause occurred in the mid- to late thirties, it seems unlikely that Japanese life expectancy would have been so high—equal to European life expectancy during the same period. But a pattern of birth control whereby women bore all the children they desired as they naturally became pregnant, and then completely stopped bearing children after the desired family size was reached would explain the childbearing patterns found in the sample villages and fit the hypothesized biological model as well.

POPULATION CONTROL THROUGH THE REGULATION OF MARRIAGE

In addition to the control married couples exerted over their own fertility, fertility within the village as a whole and within the household was controlled by customs that restricted marriage to certain individuals and shortened the span of married years for those who did marry. First, the average age at first marriage for women was relatively high for women in a preindustrial society.[15] It consistently exceeded 22, even if women who married for the first time at ages over 30 are excluded. (See Table 9.10.) This high age at marriage explains the average age at first birth discussed earlier in this chapter (Tables 9.4 and 9.5), as women on the average had their first child in their first year of marriage, or rather, their marriages were officially recorded at least before the date of their first birth. This means that though the ceremony and consummation of the marriage often took place some months before the date it was recorded, brides married, became pregnant, and then recorded the marriage in that order, rather than becoming pregnant and subsequently marrying, as is apt to happen today. Thus, the age at marriage does indicate the age at which it was intended for them to start bearing children.

The average age at marriage is remarkably consistent over time and in all four villages, which can be considered an indication that the custom for women to first marry at from 22 to 25 was prevalent at least throughout central and western Japan. Because of gaps in the data, and hence in the records of some of the women,

246

Table 9.10
Average Age at Marriage for Women[a]

Period	Average Age at Marriage	Average No. Marriages per Annum	Sample Size	
			No. Women	No. Years
Fujito				
1775-1778	25.6	9.0	18	2
1794-1802	22.9	6.4	45	7
1803-1810	24.4	6.9	48	7
1825-1830	23.5	7.0	42	6
1831-1837	23.1	8.3	50	6
1841-1850	23.1	7.1	50	7
1852-1863	24.3	7.4	52	7
Entire Period	23.7	7.3	305	42
Average Age if Women over 30 Excluded	22.6	6.7	280	42
Fukiage				
1687-1706	24.5	5.8	64	11
1712-1741	23.9	6.5	26	4
1773-1791	25.1	10.4	52	5
1797-1826	25.8	10.4	56	5
1854-1860	24.6	3.7	11	3
Entire Period	24.9	7.5	209	28
Average Age if Women over 30 Excluded	22.8	6.2	173	28
Numa				
1780-1803	23.0	4.5	36	11
1814-1824	24.6	5.9	41	4
1825-1832	25.1	5.4	43	5
1860-1871	23.2	4.6	46	5
Entire Period	24.0	5.0	166	3
Average Age if Women over 30 Excluded	22.8	4.6	151	28
Ajino				
1689[b]	22.1	16.0	16	1
Nishikata				
1782-1796	24.0	2.5	38	15
Average Age if Women over 30 Excluded	21.9	2.1	32	15

[a]Known second marriages have been excluded from this table.

[b]No women over 30 married in this year.

some second marriages may have slipped into the calculations, but it is likely that many of the women reported marrying for the first time after age 30 actually did so. Thus, the authors believe the average age at first marriage was probably slightly higher than the averages for women who first married under age 30.

A second and very effective means for controlling fertility was for large numbers of women in the childbearing ages to remain unmarried. The 20s are considered the most fertile years for women but, in a sample of twenty-one years from the four villages, the percentage of women in the 20-24 age group who were married was under 40 percent in thirteen of these years. (See Table 9.11.) In fact, the fluctuations in the percentage of women married in this age group are more revealing of the actions affecting fertility taken by the villagers in response to economic conditions than any other statistics compiled. While the total percentage of women married who were aged 15-44 tended to be around 60 percent for the twenty-one samples, the percentage in the 20-24 age group ranged from 14.3 to 81.8. And, while the total was affected by the unintentional disruption of marriage through death, nearly all of the unmarried women aged 20-24 had never been married.

The two extremes of this range come from Numa where nearly 82 percent of the 20-24 group and 73 percent of all women aged 15-44 were married in 1780. The percentage for the total steadily dropped through the following century, reaching 44 percent in 1871 when only 14.3 percent of the 20-24 age group were married. Less than 30 percent of this group were married in 1801 but nearly 56 percent were in 1831. Two factors can be seen at work here. First, the village seems to have been at its maximum population in the late eighteenth century and thereafter the total population in the village ceased to grow. To achieve this "zero population growth," the number of marriages permitted within the village had to be gradually reduced on a long-term basis, and hence the steady but gradual decline in the percentage of women married. But short-run economic conditions also affected marriages. There seems to have been a recession in the villages of Okayama around the turn of the nineteenth century, and persons who would otherwise have married either postponed marriage or remained single. In Fujito and Fukiage the percentages of women in the 20-24 age group were also at a low; all were in the 20-30 percent range around 1800. However, from the 1820s on, conditions improved

Table 9.11
Percentage of Women Married, by Age Group

Age Group	1775	1794	1810	1825	1837	1844	1863
			Fujito				
15-19	7.7	4.5	0.0	0.0	6.1	13.0	2.6
20-24	38.5	20.0	32.0	44.4	53.6	38.2	47.6
25-29	81.3	84.2	66.7	70.6	75.0	70.8	62.1
30-34	92.9	82.6	84.6	96.1	91.7	78.9	64.0
35-39	93.3	100.0	72.7	77.8	94.1	84.2	88.2
40-44	83.3	90.0	73.6	93.3	72.4	73.3	87.5
TOTAL	*56.9*	*59.7*	*49.1*	*63.0*	*57.6*	*56.0*	*52.6*
Sample Size	109	124	112	127	139	134	154

| | | | *Fukiage* | | | | |
Age Group	1683	1702	1730	1773	1801	1821	1860
15-19	26.3	0.0	7.1	3.2	6.3	9.8	5.9
20-24	37.5	21.0	50.0	38.9	21.9	34.1	45.5
25-29	100.0	92.3	72.0	71.4	57.1	70.3	43.8
30-34	71.4	81.8	83.3	75.6	75.6	76.3	53.8
35-39	60.0	76.0	88.5	74.1	86.1	75.0	75.0
40-44	90.0	70.0	84.2	84.6	85.7	79.3	61.5
TOTAL	*57.5*	*56.6*	*62.2*	*56.6*	*55.3*	*55.0*	*47.2*
Sample Size	73	106	148	182	190	225	176

| | | | *Numa* | | | |
Age Group	1780	1801	1831	1861	1871
15-19	9.1	0.0	5.0	7.1	0.0
20-24	81.8	29.4	55.6	40.0	14.3
25-29	66.7	84.6	66.7	37.5	50.0
30-34	100.0	90.0	80.0	80.0	77.8
35-39	100.0	90.9	90.0	83.3	50.0
40-44	83.3	100.0	85.7	83.3	90.0
TOTAL	*72.6*	*61.6*	*56.2*	*51.7*	*43.9*
Sample Size	62	73	73	60	66

| | | *Nishikata* | |
Age Group	1782	1796
15-19	27.3	0.0
20-24	50.0	25.0
25-29	60.0	55.6
30-34	69.2	90.9
35-39	85.7	80.0
40-44	66.7	62.5
TOTAL	*57.6*	*60.4*
Sample Size	59	48

and more marriages were contracted. In the 1830s the percentage of married women aged 20-24 rose to over 50 in Numa and Fujito, probably partly in response to the increase in by-employments, which began to boom at this time.

It should be noted, however, that although the percentage of women never married was higher than it is today, large numbers of Tokugawa women were not forced to remain single for life. For most time periods, over 80 percent of the women aged 30-39 were married, and these percentages should not be misconstrued as representing women ever married; they are for women living with their husbands at the time. Having the highest proportions married in their 30s when fewer children were born—witness the early age at last childbirth—and comparatively few in their early and mid-20s obviously had the effect of reducing births considerably. The high average age at first marriage is well known as one of the most effective means of reducing fertility in Europe; it seems to have been equally effective in Japan. Again, this was not a custom introduced in the late Tokugawa period as a short-term measure for reducing births; in Fukiage in 1683 only 37.5 percent of women aged 20-24 were married, but 100 percent of women aged 25-29 were.

The selection of who was to marry and who was to remain single was not random but clearly can be seen to have had an economic basis. And if not motivated by their own economic considerations, people found constraints to their behavior in government regulations, which will be spelled out later in the chapter. But for whatever reason, there was clearly an effort to limit both the number of households in a village and the number in each household. As can be seen in Table 9.12, the number of childbearing couples in each household tended to be limited to one or none and the number of households grew only slowly over time. On the average, most households contained one woman in the childbearing ages, but nearly a third of these were unmarried. The custom of restricting marriage to the main line of descent is evidenced in Table 9.13. Very few of the women classified as wives were married to men other than a head, his father, his son, or his grandson. The highest percentage was 4, and the years in which these occurred were years of a growing population and expanding economic opportunities in the villages involved. On the other hand, after the Temmei famine no one in Nishikata was married to anyone not in the main line

Table 9.12
Percentage of Households Containing Married Women
in the Childbearing Ages

Year	No. Households	% with Wives 15-44	Average No. Women 15-44 per Household (%)
		Fujito	
1775	110	56.4	0.99
1794	111	66.7	1.12
1810	111	49.5	1.01
1825	112	71.4	1.13
1837	119	67.2	1.17
1844	118	63.6	1.14
1863	132	61.4	1.17
		Fukiage	
1683	65	64.6	1.12
1702	78	76.9	1.36
1730	134	68.7	1.10
1773	190	54.2	0.96
1801	210	50.0	0.90
1821	240	51.7	0.94
1860	255	32.5	0.69
		Numa	
1780	58	77.6	1.07
1801	63	71.4	1.16
1831	70	58.6	1.04
1861	69	44.9	0.87
1871	73	33.7	0.90
		Nishikata	
1782	67	52.2	0.88
1796	68	42.6	0.71

of descent. Thus, only one son could count on inheriting from his father, and the others either had to leave the village to work elsewhere or remain at home, unmarried and subservient to a brother.

Some of the excess males were adopted into other families as sons or sons-in-law, but many chose to leave the village to work elsewhere on contract. More often than not it was the younger son who had to leave, but not always. Both the *shūmon-aratame-chō* and the legal records of the Tokugawa period indicate that quite

Table 9.13
Percentage of Population Comprised of Wives of Persons Other Than
in Main Line of Descent[a]

Fujito		Fukiage		Numa		Nishikata	
Year	%	Year	%	Year	%	Year	%
1775	2.85	1683	0.0	1780	4.15	1782	0.36
1794	2.83	1702	3.77	1801	3.72	1789	0.0
1810	2.47	1730	1.82	1831	3.66	1796	0.0
1825	4.08	1773	0.96	1861	2.22		
1837	4.07	1801	0.88	1871	1.27		
1844	3.28	1821	1.19				
1863	2.28	1860	0.87				

[a]Wives other than those of head, or his father, son, or grandson.

frequently a son other than the eldest inherited the family assets, often because of a quarrel with the head or behavior that would not permit the family to let the eldest succeed to the headship.[16] That only one brother was usually allowed to marry and stay within the family is exemplified by the case in Fujito in which the wife of the oldest brother died and another woman was brought into the family, but this time the younger son married, the eldest remaining a widower.

MIGRATION

Migration, either permanent or temporary, proved to be an extremely important means of adjusting population at the village and regional level in an age when it was more difficult to control births and when death was more unpredictable than today. Also, migration enabled labor to be reallocated effectively in response to changing conditions. Migration within the country was a statistically significant method of shifting population, and political boundaries seem not to have constituted a real obstacle for persons who wished to migrate.

Although we can theoretically distinguish between permanent and temporary migration, in practice it is sometimes difficult to draw a line between the two. Women who migrated for marriage initially left home without intending to return, but divorce was not uncommon and the records show many divorced women who returned to their own families, either by themselves or with a child or two. It is even difficult to classify people who migrated for employment, because many who originally left on a one-year contract never returned. By the eighteenth century at least, migration from the farming villages in Okayama was so prevalent that the domain authorities had adopted a series of restrictive measures designed to prevent the outflow of population from agriculture. Thus, much of the migration for the period of the data presented here was illegal and was not usually recorded in any way in the *shūmon-aratame-chō*; individuals merely dropped out of the records. Occasionally, and usually for the very young, a note was made stating that a certain person had "absconded" on a certain date and that his whereabouts were unknown but, more often than not, an individual on the records one year was simply missing the next.

Since government policy was to restrict migration, moving was made difficult. If a farmer in Okayama wanted to move from one village to another, he had to obtain identification papers signed by the headman of his village, get the permission of his present village, find a guarantor in the village to which he wished to move, and take with him a certificate of his religion signed by his priest. The permanent movement of families tended to be limited to moves to areas being reclaimed or to larger towns and cities, where some families might work in a samurai household and where it was easier for the illegal migrants to escape detection. In addition, regulations prohibited the transfer of houses to anyone but a direct relative, which led to the subterfuge of using adoption to legalize the sale or transfer of property. Theoretically, for a village resident to move to the city, two requirements had to be met: the person had to be poor and without land and he had to be unable to undertake hard farm labor.[17]

Thus, we find that in Fujito in the years 1797 to 1806 large numbers of men were dropped from the registers. During this decade forty-seven persons, or about 8 percent of the population, dropped out. A few of these may have been unrecorded deaths, but more than that is unlikely as forty-five of the drop-outs were men, most of them in their 20s and 30s. Eighteen of these were working outside the village in the year they were last recorded, which is why it is likely that these disappearances were caused by men who illegally left to work elsewhere. Although no economic evidence for Fujito is available for this period, we can assume that economic conditions were hard during this decade. This hypothesis is supported by a low marriage rate, a low birth rate, and a low death rate for the same decade. Thus, the demographic behavior of the villagers in this decade was consistent with poor economic conditions that restricted marrying, having children, or finding employment within the village. Also, some of the men returned a number of years later, and the village economy enjoyed a small boom during the 1820s, thus making it easier to find work at home.

Since the records for the three Okayama villages are not in complete time series, it is difficult to analyze the precise impact of migration over time. When a gap of twenty or more years exists in the records, we do not know whether the families who cannot be linked to a previous family are new or whether family composition and names have changed to the extent that no linking can be made. Nevertheless, we do know that much of Fukiage's early growth was due to in-migration. The village had a population of just over 350 in 1685, but within fifteen years it had grown to over 450, and by 1730 the population was over 700. The number of new families listed in the registers around the turn of the eighteenth century indicates a considerable in-migration of families during this period. Fujito records show that several families moved into the village during the late Tokugawa period, but several families also left. On balance, the migration of families cannot be said to have been a significant factor in Fujito's population growth. Migration of families was insignificant in Numa.

More important than family migration in all of these villages was the temporary migration of individuals, usually to work in another village or a major town or city on a contract of a year or more.[18] This kind of migration not only raised household income, but directly resulted in lowered fertility. Most of the people who left their villages to work in nearby areas were young men and women who had not yet married. The modal age groups of hōkonin of both sexes for most years lay in the 15-30 age group. Scholars studying the Meiji period have stressed the practice of young people, women particularly, working away from home for a period before marriage, but this was not a new custom. While by no means universal, it was common for both young men and women in their late teens or early 20s to work away from home for several years before marrying. It was also not unusual for heads of families to leave home by themselves to work outside the village. This practice not only raised the age of marriage for men and women, thus lowering fertility, but also must have lowered marital fertility in areas in which *dekasegi* (going out to work) was most common. The number of cases in the four villages here is too small to test the impact of this phenomenon statistically, but Hayami found that in Yokouchi village marital fertility fell sharply from the late seventeenth century to the late eighteenth century, a century during which *dekasegi* to Edo became a standard form of employment, even for household heads. Hayami attributes much of the decline in the average number of children to the adoption of "birth control," but it seems likely that some of the reduction was the result of family heads being away from home for much of their married lives.[19]

Migration was thus as important a regulator of population as adoption, if not more so. Migration allowed the efficient allocation of labor, higher wages, the permanent or temporary adjusting of village population, and the regulation of numbers in individual households through marriage, adoption, and migration in or out for employment. It also undoubtedly had an effect on fertility, both by delaying marriage for some and preventing it for others (second sons) and by lowering marital fertility in families in which the husband worked away from home for years at a time.

The importance of migration in village population trends can be seen in the village growth rates of the three Okayama villages. In each of the villages the birth rate nearly equaled the death rate, which meant that if these had been closed societies, the population of each would have been close to stable. Of our samples, Numa best approximates a stable population. Fujito showed a drop in population around the turn of the nineteenth century that was due not to a rise in the death rate, but to out-migration. The out-migrants included both men who went elsewhere to work and women, as reflected in the excess of women who left home as brides over those who married into families in the village. When Fujito's population began a slow rise in the 1820s, migration was again a factor. Men who normally would have migrated out— younger sons, for example—were permitted to marry and establish households, and there was a very slight in-migration in addition to a small excess of births over deaths. Fukiage shows a third pattern: a very rapid growth rate around the turn of the eighteenth century due both to in-migration and to a birth rate averaging around 30 per thousand compared to a death rate with a mean of 15. These three villages all come from areas in the domain of Okayama that showed an increase in population in the second half of the Tokugawa period but, at least for the growing areas of Okayama, it seems safe to conclude that variances in village growth rates were due largely to various forms of migration, as discussed in Chapter Seven, rather than to wide variations and fluctuations in the birth and death rates.

THE EFFECTS OF FAMINES ON FERTILITY

Even if one is to accept the evidence presented thus far that families in Tokugawa villages were following various customs in an effort to limit fertility, it might still be argued that famines and the epidemics that ensued played a crucial role in limiting the growth of population, either in certain periods or in the long run. Thus, one would expect to find famines negating the effects of positive growth rates during normal periods of abundance. Therefore we will here examine changes in fertility and in demographic behavior affecting fertility during and immediately after the years considered to be among the worst famine years in Japanese history.

The dire conditions that the Okayama officials reported the populace faced during the Tempō famine (described in Chapter Seven) were not, however, reflected in the birth and death rates for either Fujito or Fukiage (Chapter Eight). But our most reliable and complete data covering famine years are for Fujito and Nishikata, and so here we will turn to an examination of the effects of the Temmei and Tempō famines in Fujito and the Temmei famine in Nishikita.

Table 9.14 contains the total population figures and the crude birth and death rates for Fujito between 1828 and 1850 and for Nishikata for 1782-1795 inclusive. The highest death rate for either of these villages occurred in Fujito in 1832 when twenty-three people, most of them children under age 10, died in the fourth month. This occurred prior to the Tempō famine, which was considered to be its worst in 1836-1837, although there were several years of bad harvests. The death rate did jump to 30 per thousand in Fujito in 1837 and to 36 and 47 in Nishikata in 1787 and 1788 respectively. But by 1841 the death rate was under 15

Table 9.14
Crude Birth and Death Rates for Nishikata and Fujito
During Nationwide Famine and Epidemic Years

Year	Population First of Year	Birth Rate	Death Rate
		Fujito	
1828	600	28.3	23.3
1829	610	21.3	14.8
1830	617	45.4	22.7
1831	636	29.9	15.7
1832	647	24.7	57.2
1833	620	27.4	22.6
1834	625	35.2	24.0
1835	634	31.5	28.4
1837	638	18.8	39.2
1841	612	29.4	14.7
1844	637	18.8	31.4
1845	628	43.0	20.7
1846	643	14.0	24.9
1847	645	31.0	20.2
1848	649	37.0	12.3
1850	669	32.9	32.9
		Nishikata	
1782	271	18.5	18.5
1783	270	22.2	18.5
1784	269	11.2	7.4
1785	274	11.0	7.3
1786	273	36.6	29.3
1787	278	25.2	36.0
1788	274	11.0	47.4
1789	264	26.5	26.5
1790	264	11.4	15.2
1791	269	14.9	22.3
1792	268	7.4	37.3
1793	251	43.8	19.9
1794	260	11.5	30.8
1795	250	4.0	20.0

in Fujito and in 1790 in Nishikata the death rate was back to 15. It is impossible to tell from the death rates alone how much suffering and illness existed in these two periods, but clearly these so-called famine years resulted in no economic or social dislocation anything like that seen after recurrences of the plague in Europe.

It is more difficult to decipher the results of the famines in the birth rates. The population of Nishikata was so small that there tended to be almost cycles in the birth rate since the average intergenesic interval was three years. Birth rates were low in Fujito during the 1840s compared to the years immediately preceding and following, but this was also a period in which the percentage of women in the childbearing years who were married had begun to fall. It seems likely that the lower birth rates resulted from poor harvests, which caused a period of financial retrenchment after the rapid growth of the 1820s—hence fewer marriages—rather than that women, due to a weakened physical condition, were less capable of bearing children.

There are no registers extant for Fujito between 1778 and 1794 but, using the information obtained from the registers before and after this period (which covers the Temmei famine), we can attempt to determine any changes in fertility during the famine years.

Table 9.15

Estimated Percentage of Women of Childbearing Age in Fujito Who Bore Children, 1775-1800[a]

Year	Percentage
1775	11.6
1776	15.6
1777	15.7
1778	25.9
1779	9.8
1780	6.6
1781	21.9
1782	10.6
1783	14.1
1784	21.7
1785	12.2
1786	5.4
1787	16.0
1788	21.3
1789	21.3
1790	19.4
1791	20.0
1792	22.1
1793	14.3
1794	22.4
1795	18.5
1796	15.4
1797	19.2
1798	13.7
1799	8.3
1800	12.2

[a]Sample was drawn from Cohort Groups C and D.

In Table 9.15 an estimate has been made by year of the percentage of women who are known to have been married and in the child-bearing years who did in fact bear children in any given year. The estimates are only approximations for the years for which there are no registers as it was necessary to calculate backward from the 1794 records, and thus all women and children who dropped out of the records before 1794 have been excluded. Despite these omissions, particularly of children who died in infancy, in the five years from 1788 to 1792 nearly 20 percent of the women in the sample bore children who were still alive in 1794.

There is no discernible trend in the percentage of women bearing children over the 25-year period. Only 5.4 percent of the women gave birth in 1786, at the height of the famine, but 16 percent gave birth the following year, and over 21 percent in both 1788 and 1789. In fact, during this quarter of a century, there were only seven years in which over 21 percent of the women in the childbearing years in this sample gave birth, and three of them occurred between 1784 and 1789. And this sample represents not the percentage of all women who gave birth, but the percentage of women who gave birth and whose children lived at least long enough to be registered in 1794. Certainly, marital fertility does not seem to have been affected by the Temmei famine in Fujito.

Though the data presented here are admittedly less than complete, one conclusion seems obvious: even nationwide famines or mortality crises had widely varying effects on different parts of the country, and certainly on different villages. The effects of the Temmei mortality crisis are obvious in all of the statistics compiled for Nishikata, while the famine seems to have had little impact on Fujito, judging from the births that occurred during what are considered famine years.

This is not to minimize the effects of the two famines, even on these two villages in central Japan. The crude death rates by approximately five-year averages (Chapter Eight, Table 8.4) were higher for Fujito in the 1830s than the mean for the total forty-two years for which there are records. The death rate in Nishikata jumped from 14.5 to 27 during the 1780s. And, even though there was not much apparent effect on fertility, a study of the registers family by family provides evidence of dislocations in some households in the form of increased deaths, the adoption of a variety of people during these years, and a fall in the number of people who migrated to or from the villages to work. Nevertheless, when considering the long-term impact on either fertility or mortality during the last century of the Tokugawa period, we cannot conclude that the Tempō famine had any real long-term impact on the population of at least the three Okayama villages.

PRESSURES TO CONTROL VILLAGE POPULATION

We have now accumulated sufficient evidence to support the hypothesis that villagers, at least in the four villages studied here, were following customs and practices that had the effect of limiting population growth. Our next question is why? In this section we will attempt to identify the reasons people acted—either consciously or unconsciously—to limit family size.

Families in Tokugawa Japan had good economic reasons for preferring small households and a minimum of dependents, as we have seen in preceding chapters. Probably the most eloquent testimony to the desirability of maintaining small households are the estimates Naitō calculated for Numa on the amount of surplus left after taxes had been paid and basic food expenditures made. These were represented in Table 7.11. For every size of holding, the surplus falls as the number of family members rises. If additional family members were adults, they may have added to the family income through by-employments or by working as day-laborers for larger landholders, but children would have had a negative effect on family income until they became old enough to work, and if only one son was to inherit, then additional children would probably add little even when grown, as most left home to marry or work elsewhere.

If we examine the age distribution of people in our four sample villages, we find that the proportion in the working ages (15-64) indicates a society in which a large majority of the members were in the contributing rather than the dependent categories (i.e., the aged and the very young), and that the small family size was due to the small proportion of children in the village as well as to the lack of extended families. In these four villages the proportions in the working ages were always well above 60 (Table 9.16). The major changes in these proportions reflect the general economic changes within the villages. In Fujito, which seems to have experienced an economic boom during the mid-nineteenth century due

Table 9.16
Percentage of the Population in Working and Nonworking Age Groups[a]

Year	14 and Under	15-64	65 and Over	Average Age of the Population
		Fujito		
1775	30.4	61.2	8.4	30.58
1794	32.7	59.2	8.2	28.83
1802	30.7	62.0	7.3	29.71
1810	26.4	66.2	7.4	30.17
1825	31.3	63.3	5.4	28.72
1832	32.8	61.5	5.7	28.45
1833	29.5	64.4	6.1	29.26
1837	29.6	64.9	5.5	28.79
1841	31.4	64.2	4.4	28.17
1848	30.7	64.6	4.8	28.50
1856	33.7	60.4	5.9	27.77
1863	33.8	61.1	5.2	27.40
		Fukiage		
1688	28.0	68.6	3.3	26.85
1697	30.0	65.1	4.9	28.56
1706	29.2	64.6	6.3	29.24
1712	32.2	62.2	5.7	28.79
1727	35.7	59.0	5.3	27.30
1741	31.7	61.8	6.5	28.60
1773	32.9	60.5	6.7	28.66
1780	30.7	63.3	6.1	29.79
1787	28.3	65.4	6.3	29.41
1791	29.6	64.5	5.9	29.29
1801	28.8	63.4	7.8	30.02
1821	28.4	66.1	5.5	29.90
1826	26.5	67.6	6.0	30.84
1854	26.2	67.1	6.7	31.79
1860	24.7	66.5	8.8	33.12
		Numa		
1780	29.7	60.5	9.8	31.39
1786	29.3	65.5	5.2	29.96
1796	29.7	62.4	7.9	30.34
1803	27.7	65.4	6.9	30.59
1814	27.7	65.2	7.2	30.56
1823	28.7	62.1	9.1	30.54
1832	25.3	69.4	5.3	30.69
1860	30.6	64.6	4.9	29.70
1869	26.8	66.9	6.4	29.76
		Nishikata		
1782	22.7	67.3	10.0	32.88
1787	21.9	66.5	11.5	33.95
1791	24.2	66.5	9.3	32.87
1796	23.9	66.0	10.1	33.48

[a]Two years have been subtracted from the age recorded in the *shūmon-aratame-chō* because the population was recorded at the beginning of the year. Therefore, a person aged 1 (less than 2 years old) was aged 3 on the records, and in actuality had passed his first birthday but not his second unless that fell on the first day of the year.

both to land reclamation and expanding by-employments in the cotton industry, the percentage of children age 14 and under rose to nearly 34 percent by the 1850s, which was the highest percentage for any sample except for Fukiage in 1727 when it reached 35.7. In both Fukiage and Numa, the proportion of children fell to under 25 percent in the nineteenth century as these populations stopped growing. Interestingly, the proportions in each of the three groups changed almost not at all in Nishikata during the Temmei famine, so that, for example, in both 1782 and 1796, 10 percent of the population was age sixty-five and over.

Although the proportion in the working ages was always above 60, it was usually much higher. Numa's reached nearly 70 percent in 1832, and Fujito was the only village where the average was not close to 65 percent. Since presumably some of the persons over age 65 were contributing to the family income, the percentage of the gainfully employed in these villages must have been extremely high. The proportions in the working ages were more similar to the proportions found in the industrialized nations of Western Europe both before and after industrialization than to those in the underdeveloped world.[20] These percentages would create a higher per capita income than could be achieved with a larger dependent population. And they also support our findings in Chapter Eight that fertility and mortality were low and life expectancy relatively high.

These consistently high proportions in the working ages, even in periods of economic prosperity, combined with efforts to decrease even further the number of dependents during economic troughs—such as by permitting fewer marriages, as in Fujito at the turn of the nineteenth century—lead us to conclude that people actively sought to achieve an age composition favorable to economic production. Evidence exists showing a strong economic and social incentive for Tokugawa villagers to limit the number of their dependents in order to maintain a standard of living equal to that of other villagers, and to raise it if possible. Part of this incentive came from the desire to maintain one's *kakaku* (the status of the household). According to Kodama:

> The *kakaku* is a combined expression of the position which a household occupied in the village in the past as well as at the present. There existed no rules as to how much weight was as-

signed to the past or present status. But, by the implicit consent of the villagers, the *kakaku* came to be determined and changed.[21]

But although there were no rules for determining *kakaku*, Kodama points out that "the most important factors were economic status and the status accorded by the feudal authority."[22] However, once one was already a member of the peasant class, the primary determinant for status within this class would have been economic status.

Kakaku, of course, was not solely a reflection of economic position. Past status was also important, so that originally, the most influential families in a village, those from which the headman tended to be selected, were more than likely *gōzoku*, powerful families some of whom were classified samurai at the time of Hideyoshi's cadastral survey. In some villages those with the highest status were descended from the people who had been responsible for reclaiming the land belonging to the village, that is, the founders of the village. But almost always status was tied to power, which required that a certain level of wealth be maintained. There was usually a time lag between a change in status and a change in economic resources but, within a few generations if not sooner, adjustments were usually made. Thus, a family whose fortunes were declining would find it difficult to keep the position of village head within the family, and a family that grew increasingly wealthy would gradually be given more responsibility within the village.[23]

Not only did status determine who would be head of the village and who would fill the other official positions, but it even determined who sat where at annual meetings of the village. In a village in Tamba, for example, "the leading peasants sat in the main room which had *tatami* and the middle level peasants were seated in the kitchen on only thin straw mats. Ordinary peasants found their places on the thin straw mats covering the entrance to the kitchen." There were various other levels of seating, with the poorest peasants seated on straw or rice sacks on the ground outside.[24] By the late Tokugawa period, the wealthiest and most influential family in each village had often been granted the right to use a surname or carry swords, though usually this right came with a purchase price.

With status came obligations as well as rights. While the village headman often received a salary or some tax-exempt paddy, he was responsible for paying to the domain the rice tax for the village, and at times must have helped pay the portion of some of the poorest members of the village, widows without other adults in the family, for example.[25] It was the headman's duty to entertain domain officials when they passed through the village. Though many of the wealthiest families set themselves up as moneylenders, such as the Hikasa of Fujito, when the crops failed they were forced to open up their storehouses and provide food. As employers, the well-to-do families not only had to pay the wages of their servants and other employees but had to provide cash, household goods, and often land to former employees at the end of the contract or when they set themselves up as farmers. If an employee was found to be in financial difficulty at some later date, help was expected from the former employer.[26]

Thus, while the families with the highest status in a village could point to illustrious ancestors or some special village position, such as membership in the original shrine association, to legitimate their position, they required wealth to maintain this position. And it was not enough for them merely to maintain the same standard of past wealth; they had to maintain their relative position vis-à-vis other families in the village. It was usually easier for the wealthy to maintain their position than for others to attain wealth, hence the long tradition within many villages for the same lineage to hold the headship. But, particularly with the economic change that accompanied the growth of commerce, family fortunes were made and lost. In the Kinai, for example, conflicts arose over the determination of *kakaku*. Ōtake writes that "as the economy underwent more rapid changes," some who had acquired land "began to threaten the status of the established ranked households." These conflicts began to appear in the mid-eighteenth century.[27]

Not only would the leading families in the village feel the pressure to maintain their social standing but each family down the line would feel similar pressure to keep the present position and, if at all possible, to improve it. Thus, while the leading families would be reluctant to dissipate their wealth through having to provide for numerous children, families at the bottom end of the social scale would feel possibly even more pressure since they had little surplus to rely on. And as more and more goods came into the village and were purchased by a few, the rest of the people would feel a need to own the same items. After the postwar land reform, "farmers replied, when asked whether they were better off now than before the land reform, that fundamentally they were not. There was more money coming in, but on the other hand 'expenditure has gone up too. Altogether it hasn't made much difference.' "[28] Dore reports that "as levels of living have risen, expected standards of living have risen too, at least proportionately and in some cases more than proportionately."[29] If this was the attitude prevalent long after the closed village society and pressures to conform had begun breaking down, one can easily imagine the pressure to add *shōji* or *tatami* or, late in the period, to buy imported furniture. And increasing the number of dependents who not only had to be supported in childhood but then given dowries or land as adults would tend to lower the standard of living and deplete the wealth of the household.

Most scholars who write on life in the Tokugawa period discuss the pressure to limit family size. Sekiyama stated that the idea that a family should be small was widely held throughout Japan, by the samurai and townsmen as well as by farmers.[30] Evidence from Tosa indicates a number of reasons why people resorted to abortion or infanticide: it was not considered proper for a woman to have a child if she had a daughter-in-law bearing children; a child born after a divorce would prove a hindrance to a second marriage; and in some communities families were said to be mocked if they had more than three children.[31] To what extent these attitudes led to smaller families cannot be studied quantitatively, but their existence is proof that large families were not considered desirable in eighteenth- and nineteenth-century Japan and that the prevalence of other customs, such as late marriage, was not coincidental.

CONCLUSION

Based on the statistics on the behavior of families from these four villages in Tokugawa Japan, and if our analyses of the data are correct, we can conclude that families were consciously regulating their size, usually to limit it but sometimes to bring it up to the desired number of members. The methods used included adoption; permitting marriage only when sufficient income was available; regulating the age at first marriage, especially for women; and abortion and infanticide. Through a relatively high age at marriage and hence first birth and a short span of childbearing—about twelve years on the average—marital fertility was reduced to no more than about three children living long enough to be registered. Village fertility was reduced still further through the custom of letting only the successor to a household marry. Thus, a rather large proportion of the village population had to remain single or leave home and, if we add to this group the childless (from 5 to over 10 percent), and reductions due to infant and child mortality (in Fujito around 20 percent from the 1820s on), the nearly zero population growth rate of the second half of the Tokugawa period is not difficult to comprehend.

Why the Japanese in the Tokugawa period were so carefully limiting their numbers and how they were able to achieve these results throughout so much of the country remain more of a puzzle than the methods of their population control. Clearly famines were the cause of neither slow population growth rates nor the practice of abortion and infanticide in these four villages. Even during periods of growth, in Fujito and Fukiage fertility did not vary significantly from that in Numa and other villages during famines or poor harvest years.

Instead we find evidence that the people in these villages followed customs that resulted in maximizing per capita income and thereby in maintaining and improving their standard of living. In short, the evidence supports our explanatory framework on demographic behavior presented in Chapter Two. When the number of children born began to exceed the number desired, the Japanese put tighter controls over who married and at what age and, in addition, seem to have begun controlling fertility within marriage. This kept the dependency rate low and in addition benefited the villagers by maintaining a high marginal productivity of labor.

Although economic growth during the last century and a half of the Tokugawa period was slow by modern standards, the slow increases in productivity and output, combined with a low to zero rate of growth in the population, enabled villagers to increase their standard of living considerably from the eighteenth to the nineteenth century. By forgoing large families, the people of Okayama were able by the mid-nineteenth century to enjoy the luxuries of travel for pleasure and of imitating the life-style of townsmen. And, perhaps most important, a 2-year-old in a Tokugawa village had a life expectancy similar to that enjoyed by his Western contemporary, even though modern industrial technology was not to be introduced in Japan for several decades to come.

CHAPTER TEN

The Village of Fujito: A Case Study

The existence of a variety of sources, in addition to *shūmon-ara-tame-chō* in time series sufficient for tracing families and individuals over time, permits a study in greater depth and a closer analysis of economic, social, and demographic variables for the village of Fujito than are possible for the other three villages included in this study. The study of individual families brings to life population patterns, which are after all the result of individual behavior, and it makes it easier to understand possible motivations for demographic behavior when we can see the results of each action and when we know the environment in which the decisions are made.

In this chapter we will provide further evidence to support the hypotheses presented in the preceding chapter and also add two more, which we will test with information available for Fujito. Summarized briefly, the first four hypotheses are: (1) that families actively sought to rear what they considered an optimum number of children; (2) that birth control was practiced within marriage even in growing economies; (3) that fertility was also regulated by social customs that controlled who married and when; and (4) that famines and other disasters had a minimal effect on the social and household structure. The two additional hypotheses are: (1) household size tended to remain constant, that is, tended to fluctuate very closely around the mean of its size over time, despite changes in the life cycle of the head of the family and changes in who was head; and (2) size of landholding had very little visible influence on the demographic behavior of a family. If anything, there was an inverse relationship between size of holding and size of family, as families with large holdings tended to limit their heirs in order to prevent the dispersion of their wealth, while families with little or no land were often not dependent on the land for their livelihood or had few family assets to protect.

We test these hypotheses here to provide support for our larger framework, that is, to demonstrate that controlling family size was not limited to the poor but was practiced throughout village soci-

267

ety. We will attempt to show that optimum family size differed by household but was not determined strictly by the amount of land held. In addition, with the quantitative evidence from Fujito, we will attempt to support the argument introduced in the last chapter that all households within the village, regardless of income level, were under strong pressure to maintain and improve their relative status within the village society, and that the maintenance of status depended primarily on wealth.

THE VILLAGE OF FUJITO

Fujito can be considered representative of a number of villages in the Kojima district in terms of its development, but it was chosen for an intensive study because of the availability of an unusual amount of information, including good time series data on population.[1] During the period that the Hikasa family[2] dominated the administrative and economic life of the village, it maintained the village records and carefully preserved these in its storehouses.[3] Because of the official positions held by this family, it stored copies of records sent to the domain government, such as tax registers and the *shūmon-aratame-chō*, in addition to the bookkeeping records of the family itself. The Hikasa records, analyzed in conjunction with additional information on activities of the villagers, are extremely revealing as to village life.

Shūmon-aratame-chō are extant for Fujito for forty-two years between 1775 and 1863. Forty of these documents are complete, and two are partial. Major gaps exist between 1778 and 1794 and between 1810 and 1825, but otherwise the registers have been preserved for nearly every year until 1835 and for approximately every other year after that. While an early cadastral survey had placed the number of households in Fujito at 58 in 1604,[4] by 1775 the village had grown to 100 households and approximately 550 registered inhabitants. A gradual but unsteady increase in both the number of households and the population occurred over the course of the following ninety years, so that by 1861 the totals stood at 127 households and just over 690 registered inhabitants, again an average of 5.5 per house. A demographic analysis of these records has been presented in Chapters Eight and Nine.

In addition to the *shūmon-aratame-chō*, documents exist for Fujito that reveal changes in the size of holdings over time and in the taxes assessed on the village.[5] In 1645 the rice yield of Fujito was officially assessed at 377 *koku*, or approximately 1,870 bushels, a yield that placed the village higher than average in terms of *kokudaka* in a region in which assessed yields ranged from slightly under 100 to over 700 *koku*. In 1789 the village still had the same officially assessed *kokudaka*, but it had gained an additional 239 *koku* in yield, an increase obtained primarily from land reclamation and increases in productivity.[6] Land reclamation projects were actively carried out throughout the mid-seventeenth century and then, after a hiatus of 160 to 170 years, they were begun once again in the 1830s, this time on a larger scale. Three projects, completed in 1837, 1854, and 1865, may have added as much as 20 percent to the arable land in the village.[7]

The changes in landholding size over time in Fujito have already been discussed in Chapter Seven (see Table 7.8), so let us merely summarize here what the major ones were. Throughout the period 1604-1828, the two largest landholding groups were holdings of less than 1 *koku* and of between 1 and 3 *koku*. By the Bakumatsu period, however, the largest groups were the 1-3 *koku* holdings and those of 3-5 *koku*. A trend is evident toward slightly larger holdings, which probably resulted from the reductions in holdings made by the two largest owners in the village during the late Tokugawa years. The largest holder, the Hoshijima, after reaching a peak of 75 *koku* in 1841, began to sell off its land, reducing the amount to 48 *koku* within four years. The other major landholder, the Hikasa, increased the family's holdings from less than 20 *koku* in 1810 to 60-70 *koku* in the 1820s, but then reduced them to the 30-40 *koku* level where they remained from 1838 through the end of the Tokugawa period. This decline in the largest holdings during the last decades of the Tokugawa period reflects the greater profits to be had from commercial activities and investments in the creation of *shinden* for the wealthiest, and the gradual rationalization of the smaller holders' farm unit to one that could be farmed with family labor.

These changes in the landholdings of the major holders occurred during the period when commerce was rapidly developing in this part of Okayama. By 1814 one Gohei from Fujito had been authorized to form a cotton *tonya* along with two men from neighboring Amaki.[8] By the early 1840s Fujito villagers were engaged in the cotton-processing industry to such an extent that a poll taken of the number of looms in the village revealed an average of one per household, and some had as many as three.[9] By mid-century, Hikasa Yūtarō was authorized by the domain to sell Kokura-ori, the weave for which this area was famous, to "distant places."[10] It is during the last half century of the Tokugawa period that we find a sharp reduction in the amount of migration both to and from the village, as the economy grew and all villages in the area found themselves with a demand for their own labor. During these years the large landowners in Okayama complained that they could not obtain sufficient agricultural labor, and the Hikasa family began to sell its land within the village and invest instead in Kōjō-shinden.

With the background provided here and in the preceding three chapters, let us now turn to what happened to various families in Fujito during the Tokugawa years.

A SAMPLE OF FAMILY HISTORIES FROM FUJITO-MURA

To breathe life into the quantitative picture of Fujito, examples will be drawn here from family histories compiled from the *shū-mon-aratame-chō*. The samples have been chosen both for the extent to which they represent various patterns of family composition and change, and as examples of unusual demographic and social behavior or of problems to be encountered in using such documents.

(1) The Hikasa family can be identified in all forty-two registers still existing. Being one of the two largest landholders in the village, the family was not at all typical. Also, the household contained a number of servants in all the years for which we have records except for one, the exception being 1837, the worst year of the Tempō famine. Furthermore, the position of *nanushi* (village head) had passed from one generation to the next through the household head and continued to do so through the remainder of the Tokugawa period. In 1775 Sukeuemon was *nanushi*, but this post had passed to his son Kotarō by 1800, and his grandson Yūtarō sometime before 1825. In 1846 Yūtarō was promoted to the position of *ōjōya* (the head of a group of village heads) whose primary responsibilities were as a coordinator. At the time he took this post, Yūtarō was the *nanushi* of Hiroe, and his son, Takei-

chirō, was *nanushi* of Fujito itself. Thus, the Hikasa managed to remain almost continually in village office and to advance in office over the course of generations.

The number of *genin* (employees) in the Hikasa household was equal to or greater than the number of family members through 1810. There were 7 in 1775, 8 in 1778, and usually 6 or 7 during the period 1794-1810, though there were four years with only 4. From 1825 on, the number of *genin* fluctuated between 1 and 5, with an average of about 3, but no trend was discernible. An occasional *genin* came from Fujito itself, but usually they were drawn from neighboring villages and other areas within Kojima, such as Hayashi, Kimi, Fukue, Kushida, Ohara, and Kōjō-shinden.

Most of the *genin* were male. They were usually in their late teens and early to mid-20s, and most worked for the Hikasa family on a one-year contract, arriving just after the New Year holidays on the fifth day of the first month and returning home on the twentieth day of the twelfth month. This was the usual pattern of employment in the village, both for the *genin* who came from other villages and for the *hōkōnin*, or those persons who left Fujito to work elsewhere. Occasionally, a man in his 40s worked for several years running, and between 1800 and 1803 a boy from Fujito itself, who was only 11 when he started to work, served the Hikasa.

In terms of demographic behavior the family was much like any other family, despite the official position it held, the amount of its landholdings, and the continual employment of a number of *genin*, which placed the Hikasa family both politically and economically at the top of the village society. The Hikasa family itself was never at any time large, which is partly explained by the fact that at no time did any relative outside the nuclear family other than grandchild or grandparent live within the household. As did half of the other households in the village, the Hikasa took a *yōshi* (adopted son), but he became the head of a new branch household rather than a member of the main line of the family.[11]

There were several divorces in the family during the period for which there are records, but divorce was not uncommon in the village, especially when the bride married under the age of 20. When in his early 20s, Kotarō married a teenager from the Kuboya district in Bitchū, but the marriage was dissolved and the girl returned home at the age of 18 in 1797. In 1798, Kotarō married a 24-year-old woman by whom he had two sons and a daughter. Their eldest son, Yūtarō, married the daughter of a *shōya* (headman) in Kuboya in 1825, and she bore him five children.[12] The younger son was adopted into a family in the castle town of Okayama in 1830 at the age of 26.

In the Hikasa family, the eldest son always succeeded his father during the ninety-year period for which there are records. The sons married in their early 20s, usually to girls in their late teens from families outside the district with the same social standing. This meant that the brides' families would have come from the same level of wealth and presumably also held similar official positions. Since the number of families of this wealth were limited, it meant that the Hikasa and Hoshijima had to look outside the village, and even outside the district, for brides. The Hikasa family seems to have had fairly close ties with the district of Kuboya. In addition to several brides coming from Kuboya, the daughter of Yūtarō went to this district as a bride of 18, but she was divorced and returned home nine years later.

(2) The family of Hisauchi and his descendants might be termed unusual for just the opposite reasons that the Hikasa family was. At no time did the family have fewer than fourteen members, and it had more than twenty for a time during the late 1820s. Yet, despite its size, the family had almost no land and never owned a draft animal. In 1804 three male members of the family shared land totaling about one-fifth of 1 *koku*. The land was jointly held by the household head, who had married into the family and who had an official listing of 5.3 *shō*, the younger brother of his wife, who held 8.2 *shō*, and by Kiyogorō, the younger brother of the former head, who held just 8 *shō*.

The size of this family cannot be attributed to the presence of *genin*. And, with the exception of Kiyogorō who had seven children, the size of the completed families within the household was three or four children, no larger than average for this village. However, all male members of the family were permitted to marry and remain in the household, and in addition the family took in a *yōshi-muko*, an adopted husband, for at least one daughter. There were, in fact, so many nuclear families within the household and such a profusion of births that it was virtually impossible to code this household with any degree of reliability. Within the nine-year period from 1824 to 1832, eight babies were born to five nuclear families, but this was not unusual for this family; between 1794 and 1805, eight births occurred, and in this household nearly all children survived infancy and childhood.

It is obvious that this family relied on a very different livelihood than did the Hikasa. They did not depend on land, they neither employed nor were employed, and yet the family was able to support all the members it could possibly have and still feel the need to bring in a husband for a daughter. One can be reasonably certain that the family was in some sort of business within the village and relied upon family members for its labor.

(3) Much more representative of the families in Fujito was that of Sen'uemon. In 1775 when he was 32, he was the head of a household consisting of himself, his 73-year-old father, and his 63-year-old mother. By 1794 his father had died, but Sen'uemon now had a wife and two young daughters. In 1802 his mother died at the age of 90, and in the following year he took in a *yōshi* from Fujito to be the husband for his now 19-year-old daughter. By 1825 the pattern of 1794 was repeated; the adopted son was household head and living with his wife, his three children, and his wife's mother. A fourth child was born in 1827 when his wife was 43, but it died the following year at just over 16 months. The mother-in-law died in 1833 at the age of 84.

Seemingly unaffected by the Tempō famine, the family not only retained all its members but gained a daughter-in-law and two grandchildren in 1836-1837. Chōjūrō, the once adopted son-in-law, retired as household head sometime between 1837 and 1841, before reaching age 65, leaving affairs to his son, Hyōkichi. The parents appeared in no records after 1848 and, since the father was 72 and the mother 64 in that year, it is likely that they died. Hyōkichi and his wife had a total of four children, and the oldest son, the second child, married during 1862 and produced a grandson.

The only event of note in the family genealogy was the establishment of a branch line sometime between 1841 and 1844. Hyōkichi's younger brother, Katsusaburō, established his own household, married, and had five children, all of whom were still living with their parents in 1863. Despite the establishment of a branch family, the family did not have a large landholding. Sen'uemon's *kokudaka* in 1804 was only 2.92 *to*. However, by 1851 the main line held 2.895 *koku* while the branch line had 2.9 *koku*. What happened to the branch family economically is not known but, during the late Tokugawa years, their land was reduced so that by

1857 Katsusaburō held just over 2 *koku*, and by 1863 his holdings were reduced to 2.5 *to*.

(4) In some cases the family records show the continuity of a house and a tract of land rather than of a blood line. Several households were identified from 1775 to 1863 in which persons living in the household in the last year were of no blood relation to those in it in the eighteenth century. Such was the case for the house of Kamejirō. In 1775 at age 25, he formed—on paper at least—a household with his three younger brothers and his mother. However, only his mother and youngest brother lived in the village that year. Kamejirō spent from the second month through the twelfth in Osaka on short-term contract employment. The middle brothers were in Osaka in both 1775 and 1778, and by 1794 the three oldest brothers had all disappeared from the registers. The youngest, who had changed his name from Ishijirō to Kiyogorō, was head of the family and living with his mother, who subsequently died at age 69 in 1797. Kiyogorō was now alone, and he spent from 1799 to 1802, his 36th-39th years, working in Osaka. Returning to the village and his land, which had an assessed output of 6 *to*, he finally married in 1806 at age 43, taking a 34-year-old bride. One son was born the same year. By 1825 the pattern of 1794 had reoccurred, and the son, Ichizō, was living alone with his mother.

It was at this point that the household and land changed hands. The mother died at age 54 in 1826, and Ichizō himself died at age 28 in 1828. However, just before he died, he adopted an "older brother" from the same village—the oldest son of Bunjirō—who came into the household with his wife and three children. Yet even then the line had to rely on continued adoption to survive. The wife died after bearing a fourth child, the second son disappeared from the records between 1841 and 1844, and the oldest son died in 1848 at age 29. After marrying off his eldest daughter, the head took in a *yōshi-muko* for his youngest daughter, and this man subsequently became the head of the family. By 1863 the father and the daughter had both died, and the adopted son lived with his daughter and two sons on the 4.389 *koku* of land he had inherited.

Thus, the head of this family in 1863 was not a direct descendant of the Kamejirō who headed it in 1775 and, more likely than not, was not a blood relation at all, since he was adopted in to marry a daughter of the house. In less than a century the family had had to resort to adoption twice to preserve the household identity. But this practice of maintaining family lines and, as we shall see in the next section, a desired number of family members, gave a certain stability to village society because it tended to keep constant the number of households, to prevent the social upheaval that would have resulted from the creation of family units without adult members capable of supporting them, and to perpetuate households most of whose members lived most of their lives within the village. Adoption could be a form of social welfare by which persons incapable of supporting themselves were adopted, or it could mean the redistribution of wealth and resources when an able young man unable himself to inherit was brought in to succeed the head.

(5) While adoption for the purposes of succession was common in Fujito, a few houses were allowed to die out during the period under observation. One such example was the line of En'uemon, which underwent *zekke* (discontinuation) during the 1850s. In 1775 En'uemon lived with his wife, two sons, daughter-in-law, and two grandsons. He owned one draft animal and employed three male and two female servants, three of whom came from Fujito. By 1794 the oldest son, Risuke, had taken over the duties of head of household and was also one of the *hangashira*[13] (village secretary), which meant that he was one of the village leaders. He lived with his wife, three sons, and parents. The employees numbered five in 1794 and 1797, but gradually the number declined to two by 1808-1810. In 1804 Risuke's *kokudaka* was listed at 2.985 *koku*, which meant that he held an amount of land that by itself would scarcely justify employing so much hired labor. Presumably the family also had some by-employment or perhaps a main source of income that required labor.

Risuke's oldest son was adopted out in 1808, and by 1825 the third son was head of the family, living with his wife, older brother, and mother. Though the second son had been employed in the castle town and hence was presumably neither physically nor mentally incompetent, he was passed over for the headship of the family and the position of *hangashira*, a phenomenon not uncommon in this village. While the family maintained its position in the village administration during the 1820s, it no longer had any employees.

It was at this time that the family began to die off without replacements being made. Ryūzō, the head in the 1820s, had only one son, born in 1827, and when his mother died in 1830 and his older brother in 1831, the family was reduced to three. Ryūzō died sometime between 1837 and 1841 while in his 60s, and his widow died between 1841 and 1844, leaving in 1844 a son of 18. The son lived alone and did not receive his father's official position. He went to work for a samurai in 1848, was subsequently recorded as being in the village in 1850 and 1852, and then disappeared from the records. No *kokudaka* was recorded for the family in 1851, and no one was adopted to take over the family, so that we can presume there was nothing worth taking over. It is probable that the son either died or permanently left the village.

As in any human society, variations on patterns of household composition and demographic behavior are numerous; these examples are meant to give glimpses of life in Fujito at the individual level, but they were also selected as typical cases of behavior or events seen again and again throughout Fujito and the other villages studied.

CHANGES IN HOUSEHOLD SIZE

While individual families changed in size from year to year, time series and cross-sectional analyses of household size in Fujito suggest two hypotheses. The first is that the average size family was not the optimum size for many families. The second is that, whatever the fluctuations in fortune for the village as a whole, the relative position of each family within the village seems to have changed little, which is supported by an analysis of the size of individual households over time.

The average household size in Fujito, obtained by dividing the total population by the number of households, was 5.5 for the entire ninety-year period for which data exist. The mean and mode were close in value; in 1775, 43 percent of the families had either five or six members (exclusive of servants) and, while there was a greater spread of household in terms of family size in the later years, the modal class was either five or six for most years until 1856, when it changed to four. (See Table 10.1.) In all years there were more families of four or fewer persons than of seven or more.

Large families were not common. There were usually no more

Table 10.1
Frequency Table of Households Headed by Males (Females),
by Size of Family

No. in Family	1775	1794	1808	1825	1833	1841	1847
1	5 (1)	4 (2)	10 (1)	4 (0)	4 (4)	5 (5)	1 (3)
2	3 (1)	8 (0)	5 (0)	12 (1)	8 (1)	9 (2)	4 (3)
3	9 (0)	12 (0)	10 (1)	14 (0)	13 (0)	15 (0)	14 (1)
4	9 (1)	11 (0)	16 (0)	14 (0)	17 (0)	10 (1)	14 (1)
5	23 (0)	18 (0)	14 (0)	20 (0)	15 (0)	23 (0)	23 (0)
6	22 (0)	13 (0)	18 (0)	11 (0)	21 (0)	17 (0)	19 (1)
7	10 (0)	15 (0)	13 (0)	10 (0)	7 (0)	9 (0)	11 (0)
8	7[a]	8	6	9	5	6	5
9	5	3	4	4	9	4	5
10	3	6	4	6	6	3	3
11	5	1	3	1	1	1	5
12	2	4	2	2	2	3	4
13	1	1	0	0	0	2 (1)	1
14	0	1	0	0	1	0	1
15	0	0	1	0	0	0	0
16	2	1	0	1	0	1	0
17	0	0	0	1	1	1	0
18	0	0	1	0	1	0	0
19	0	1	0	1	0	0	0

[a]Only 1 female headed a household with more than 7 members.

than fifteen households in the village in any one year with more than eight members, though the inclusion of *genin* would make a few additional households exceed this size. On the other hand, there was a surprising number of one- and two-person households. It is not known whether the individuals so listed were living alone with a house to themselves, but they were considered to constitute separate households—on paper at least. The peak in the number of one-person households came in the period 1800-1810, when there was an average of twelve such households per year. From 1845 on, the number of very small households declined, so that by the late 1850s there were only two one-person households. Thus in the late Tokugawa years when the average number of persons per household was falling, there was also a decrease in very small households, creating a more leptokurtic distribution of households.

As is to be expected in a population in which the average family size is in the five- to six-person range, the modal number of married couples per household was one. If all families in the village are classified both by the number in the family and the number of married couples in the family, the modal groups distinctly fall into the one married couple and four- to six-family member classes. Until the late 1820s there were more families that contained no married couples than there were families with more than one married couple.

The most prevalent form of family composition in Fujito-mura was the nuclear family, with one married couple and its children. This is readily seen in Table 10.2, which lists the percentage of

Table 10.2
The Composition of the Population

Year	Percentage	Year	Percentage
A. Percentage of Persons Classified as Nuclear Family Members[a] in the Total Population (Minus Genin)			
1775	63.4	1837	58.6
1794	64.4	1841	61.5
1802	67.9	1844	60.5
1810	65.0	1848	63.9
1825	63.8	1856	65.4
1833	64.9	1863	63.0
B. Percentage of Persons Classified as Nuclear Family Members plus Direct Descendants and Successors[b] in the Total Population (Minus Genin)			
1775	77.1	1837	71.9
1794	75.8	1841	76.9
1802	77.1	1844	75.0
1810	77.2	1848	75.6
1825	73.4	1856	78.8
1833	74.5	1863	77.6

[a]Nuclear family members are here defined as household head (male or female), wife, son, and daughter.

[b]This category includes those persons in Group A plus parents (of head), grandparents, grandchildren, son-in-law, daughter-in-law, and great-grandchildren.

persons in the village classified as nuclear family members. Category A includes only those persons who were registered as head of a household (either male or female), wife, son, or daughter. In eleven of the twelve years listed, over 60 percent of the persons registered in the village (exclusive of the *genin*) were in these categories. When persons in the direct line of succession are added to the first group, the percentage rises to over 75 in every year but two. Thus, more than three-quarters of the persons registered in the village were immediate members of the nuclear family of the household head. A large proportion of the remaining quarter would also come under the category of nuclear family if the categorization were slightly changed. Young household heads frequently had younger brothers and sisters living at home, but under this categorization they are not considered nuclear family members.

The data on household composition combined with those on average family size make it apparent that the extended family did not form the usual household unit in Fujito-mura. While several extended families did exist, they were the exception rather than the rule. It can be safely concluded that in Fujito, as elsewhere in Japan, the nuclear family formed the basic social and economic unit in at least the last century of the Tokugawa period.

The relatively constant mean in household size for the village as a whole over the period was in large part due to the small fluctuation in the number of family members around the mean in each household. In short, a family in which the mean number over time was five tended to return to this number whenever the number of members either exceeded or fell below five. This was true for families of whatever size. This tendency has been statistically tested by calculating the coefficient of variation for each household over time.[11] Only those households that could be identified over a span of time were used in the sample, which included 87 families identified from at least as early as 1825 and found in the registers until the end of the period under observation.

Of the 87 households, 24 had a coefficient of variation of less than 0.25, 50 had a coefficient of variation of less than 0.33, and 80 had a coefficient less than 0.50. These findings lead to the conclusion that the variation in the annual population of each household was small. It is suggested here that the reason for this was that the economic base of each household tended to change relatively slowly over time and that any changes were shared by other households, thus necessitating each household to maintain the same number of members—the optimum economically—in order for the household to maintain its position within the village. That the fixed wealth base in terms of land tended to remain constant

279

is evidenced in the fact that of the 142 women in two nineteenth-
century cohort groups only 8, from seven households, came from
families who changed landholding class from 1851 to 1863.

THE EFFECTS OF THE TEMPŌ MORTALITY CRISIS
ON FUJITO FAMILIES

In Chapter Seven we described the conditions in Okayama during the Tempō famine as reported by contemporary officials of
the domain. Our analysis of the demographic data in Chapter
Nine, however, indicates that the suffering and misery depicted in
the official records were not borne out by changes in fertility and
mortality in Fujito. The death rate in 1837 was higher than usual
at 39.2 per thousand, but nowhere near the peak of 57.2 for the
epidemic year of 1832. The birth rate was low at 18.8, but it was
lower for seven other years scattered throughout the forty years
for which we have data. But, though the Tempō famine neither
decimated the population of this village nor even had any significant effect on long-term growth, can we conclude on the basis of
the statistics alone that the village was virtually unaffected by the
crop failures of the 1830s? Here, in order to assess the impact of
the famine on Fujito, we will examine what happened to sample
families in terms of family composition and demographic behavior during the period covering this famine.

The effects of the Tempō famine are more apparent in the gene-
alogies of Fujito families compiled from the *shūmon-aratame-chō*
than in the village statistics. A sample of twelve families, about 10
percent of the total, was arbitrarily selected from Fujito households for which records were available for a period of at least
several decades, starting with the boom years of the 1820s and
early 1830s. Of these twelve, only four can be considered to have
undergone no changes that might have resulted from the famine
and its aftereffects.

The first family in the sample that suffered from no ill effects
and appeared in the *shūmon-aratame-chō* was composed of the
head, Kajūrō, aged 34 in 1827, and his wife and children. His oldest daughter was born in 1827, a second came in 1834, still a third
in 1837, and subsequently two sons were born, in 1841 and 1848.
No deaths occurred during this period. A second family seemingly
unaffected was composed of the head, Sōuemon, his wife, their

three children, and the unmarried sister of the head. The family remained unchanged from 1833 through 1844, when one of the children went as a *hōkōnin* to Tsubuura and the oldest son became head of the house. A third family consisted of the head, Kichigorō, his son, and an adopted daughter. The daughter married out in 1832, and father and son lived together until 1837, when a granddaughter was registered. A bride appeared on the registers in 1841, along with another grandchild. Still a fourth family was headed by a 20-year-old man, Hikojirō, who lived with his two younger sisters, a younger brother, and his mother. The family remained the same from 1833 through 1841. By 1844 the oldest of the sisters was no longer on the registers and the head had acquired a family of his own.

Other families did not fare so well. One family was plagued by frequent deaths throughout the 1830s and was finally discontinued at the end of the 1840s. This family numbered seven in 1825, the year the daughter of the head married out of the family. Then, well before the famine years, the family members began to die, one by one. In 1831 the 62-year-old younger brother of the head died, and in the following year, the wife of the head. In 1833, the 44-year-old new head, Genkichi, the son of the former, briefly absconded but returned to Fujito. He was also married in 1833, but in the following year his wife died in the seventh month, having given birth to a son in the first month. Thus, by 1835 the family was reduced to four members, two of whom died between 1837 and 1841 (the uncle and the father of the head, both in their 70s). In 1848 the son of the head died at age 15, and the father, aged 59 in 1848, appeared on no subsequent records. The problems of this family may not have been linked to the famine at all, and the deaths between 1837 and 1841 of the two elderly men in the family might have occurred even in times of prosperity. However, it was the larger than usual number of deaths like these that caused the higher death rates for the years for which we have data during and after the famine.

A second family also suffered *zekke* during the same period. The head, Katsunojō, died in 1832, leaving a wife and three children. This death would have made survival of the famine years even more difficult than for most families. In 1835 the youngest child, an 8-year-old boy, was given for adoption to a family in the village of Kimi. The mother dropped out of the records in

281

1836 and may be presumed to have died. Between 1841 and 1844 the young head of the family dropped out of the records, and when his younger sister married into a family in Kimi in 1848, the family permanently disappeared from Fujito records.

Several other families experienced significant and unusual changes in composition, which may have been due to upheaval resulting from the Tempō famine. One such household contained only an elderly head, Otonosuke, and his daughter during the 1830s. In 1837 the head died at age 78 leaving his 26-year-old daughter to live alone until 1844, when the oldest son from another household in the village was adopted into the family with his 12-year-old daughter. But, instead of marrying the surviving daughter, he brought in another woman as his wife and a child was born to her in the same year. Possibly the man bought out the family property, but appeared as an adopted relative on the books because of *han* regulations forbidding the sale of property.[15]

Although adoptions were common in Fujito throughout the period, there seems to have been an unusual number during the Tempō period, and particularly of the kind in which members other than a son or a son-in-law were adopted into a family. One rather unusual case concerned a *hangashira* of Fujito, Kōhachirō. This man headed a family composed of his wife, two sons, and his own two younger brothers. In 1835 the *hangashira* moved with his wife to Kōjō-shinden to work for a *nanushi* in one of the villages there. The second brother became both the head of the family and the new *hangashira*, and was also left with the care of his two young nephews, aged 4 and 7, in 1835. By 1841 the new head had taken a wife and subsequently had a son. This family continued to live together until 1850 when the two nephews, aged 22 and 19, went to Kōjō-shinden as *yōshi*.

Among the four remaining families, the records for 1837 are missing for Eikichi's household, and the fate of this family during the famine years is not known. In a second family, that of Shō-kichi, two young children died between 1835 and 1844. In a third household the head, Sawashirō, and his wife both died between 1837 and 1844, and the new head subsequently died in 1846. In the last family, Jirōzaemon's, two children died within three weeks of each other in the ninth month of 1844, and early the next year both Jirōzaemon's older brother and his mother died, again within three weeks of each other. In this last family the 23-year-old son was adopted in 1837 by an elderly widow who lived alone. And it is likely that the four members of Jirōzaemon's younger brother's family also were adopted into some household between 1835 and 1837, when they dropped out of Fujito records.

While it was possible to trace nearly all families in Fujito throughout the Tempō period, the number and kind of changes that occurred within families lead to the conclusion that these were not ordinary years. A major reason that so many family lines continued during the Tempō period was the number of adoptions that took place. Adoptions both into and out of families were more common during the 1830s and 1840s than at any other period. Also, we find a number of households with a composition that deviated from the norm for these villages, the nuclear family. For example, one household consisted of an elderly man, an adopted daughter in her 20s, and an increasing succession of grandchildren. A second girl was adopted into the family and she, too, began bearing children. There is no example like this for any other period.

During the late Tempō period there was an increase in the number of children who had only one parent registered in a household. Brides were often registered several years after the first child had been born, and it was not uncommon to find that a younger son or brother started to have children registered to him and either remain single or years later take a bride who was in her 30s. Presumably such a bride was the mother of his children. The number of women who had children but no registered husband also increased. All children were still registered from birth, but it was impossible to code many of the children for parentage during the late Tokugawa years. For the same reason, it was impossible to attempt to calculate proportions married or the rate of illegitimacy, since it is not known whether these single persons listed as having children were in fact considered married by Fujito residents or not.

Table 10.2 shows a distinct dip in the percentage of persons classified as nuclear family members or their successors in 1837. This was the only year in which fewer than 60 percent of persons registered (minus *genin*) were classified as nuclear family members. This dip was clearly due to the number of adoptions taking place at this time and to an increase in peripheral relatives living in the household. The percentage of nuclear family members, including only father, mother, and children, did not reach its pre-famine proportions until 1848, but the category that included descendants and successors was even higher by 1841 than it was before the famine. Reasons for this quick adjustment in the second category are the relatively high birth rate during the period 1835-1841, the tendency for *yōshi* to be listed as son or grandson soon after the year of adoption, and demographic behavior, which acted to replace through birth or adoption or marriage those family members who had died. Many family heads who were in their 50s and 60s either died or retired between 1837 and 1841, leaving the headship to sons. Thus, there was an increase in the proportion of persons who were in the generation above the head and his wife.

While it is difficult to assess the effects of the Temmei famine other than to state that population did not grow during the twenty-year period surrounding it, the effects of the Tempō famine are more evident. In addition to a higher death rate, at least in 1837, there was a considerable amount of social change, much of which may have been the result of the number of deaths and illnesses that must have occurred during these years. Interestingly, the highest sex ratio for the 1-5 age group for the twelve years listed in the age structure table (Table 9.16), occurred in 1841 when the ratio reached a height of 1.72. While there is no statistical evidence to show that this ratio may not have been accidental, if the people were going to commit infanticide, a period of mortality crises would have been the most likely time for it.

The highest death rate for the Tempō period, however, and in fact the highest for all the years observed, occurred in 1832, when thirty-nine persons died, twenty-three of them in the fourth month. Of the deaths in that year, 69 percent were among children under age 10, but in all other years with the exception of 1844, far more persons over age 36 died than did children.

These deaths in 1832 must be attributed to disease. While there was nothing as devastating as the plague, a number of epidemic diseases were endemic in Japan, and 1832 was listed as a particularly bad year. Cholera was the largest killer in this year in the nation as a whole. The epidemic began in Ise and spread throughout southern and western Japan. It was characterized by vomiting and sudden death. This disease may have been what struck Fujito, but the prevalence of child deaths may have been due rather to one of the diseases that particularly struck the young, among which were measles, smallpox, and *ekiri* or children's diarrhea. Other diseases causing high death rates in Tokugawa Japan were influenza, tuberculosis, and syphilis, plus a variety of others that are known only by vague symptoms, thus making it difficult to determine which particular disease they were.[16]

For Fujito at least, we can conclude that the population was not unaffected by the series of crop failures in the 1830s and the ensuing epidemics. We find evidence of higher death rates than usual, slightly lower birth rates but, more important, evidence of disruptions within families in terms of their composition. Most persons in Fujito did survive the period, but nearly all lived within the village during the famine years. In both 1837 and 1841 there was a drop in migration for employment both to and from the village to almost zero, and thus we might conclude that families fed only their own, waiting for better years to rehire contract labor. But, despite a drop in the population from 639 in 1837 to 614 in 1841, and then another drop from 637 to 628 between 1844 and 1845, the village not only recovered but began to grow immediately after this period, rising to over 700 by the late 1850s.

THE INTERRELATIONSHIP BETWEEN ECONOMIC ACTIVITIES AND POPULATION

We seem to find then in Fujito a pattern of families controlling the size of their household to maintain as far as possible a constant, optimum size given their individual labor requirements, income, and desire to perpetuate the family line. If land was the primary fixed asset in Fujito, we should then expect to find differences in the number of children born and raised according to the size of landholding. For Fujito it is possible to examine fertility among women who have been divided into groups according to the size of landholding of the households in which they lived. *Nengumai toritate sanyō-chō* (Records for the collection of the rice tax) are available for six scattered years during the nineteenth century. These records provide a breakdown in units of *koku* of the landholdings of individuals within the village. Because the population records exist for every year from 1825 to 1835 and nearly every other year after that until 1863, women from these registers were divided into two cohort groups and then further subdivided into five *kokudaka* classes. (See the Appendix to Table 9.5 for a

285

complete description of these.) Cohort Group *G* consists of women who were married between 1825 and 1841 while Group *H* is comprised of women who were married or who, without recorded husbands, bore children after 1841 but who reached age 44 or whose marriages had terminated prior to 1863. The *kokudaka* classes range from no landholdings (Class I) to 3-6 *koku* (Class IV) and a miscellaneous category of the large holders, those who switched classes, etc. (Class V).

In Table 10.3, we find for Cohort Group *G* that the average number of children in the completed family size for each *kokudaka* class is within two-tenths of a percent of the mean for the entire

Table 10.3
Average Number of Children in the Completed Family in Fujito,
by Cohort Group and *Kokudaka* Class

Cohort Group	No. Children	Class	No. Children G	No. Children H
A	3.5	I	3.6	3.3
C	4.0	II	3.5	2.9
D	3.6	III	3.5	2.6
E	2.9	IV	3.7	3.5
F	3.5	V	3.4	4.2
G	3.5	Total[a]	3.5	3.4
H	3.4			

[a]The total averages are weighted averages. See the Appendix to Table 9.5 to identify the cohort groups and *kokudaka* classes.

cohort group, which was 3.5. For Cohort Group *H*, however, Class III, comprised of women from households holding land assessed from 1-3 *koku*, had an average of only 2.6 children while Class V, including women from the largest landholdings and households containing ten or more members, had an average of 4.2 children. Nevertheless, the mean for the entire cohort group was 3.4. Returning to Table 9.5, we see that the average age at first birth was just over 22 for Cohort Group *G* as a whole and close to it for most of the classes within this group, with the exception of women who came from families holding no land at all and married on the average at age 25. For Cohort Group *H*, though, the average age at marriage tended to fall as the amount of land held by the brides' families rose. Thus, women from families with larger fixed assets married at just over 21 while families with extremely little or no land married at over 25.

If we turn to sex ratios of children born to these two cohort groups (Table 9.7), we find that only for women married between 1825 and 1841 into families with from 1-3 *koku* of land (*G*, IV) is the sex ratio of all children so distorted at 2.23 (sample of 100) that we can conclude that sex selective infanticide was being carried out. But, if we look at the sex ratios of last-born children (Table 9.8), we can say with 95 percent confidence that the sex ratio of 1.7 for Cohort Group *H* does not come from a universe in which the sex ratio is unity. The sex ratio of last-borns for Group *G* is 1.3, though we cannot statistically reject this group as having come from a normal universe. Thus, it seems highly likely that these two cohort groups and others were practicing "post-partum birth control" to some extent.

Families may have used still a third method for reducing family size in addition to abortion and infanticide: careless attention to a child's physical safety, which might show up in higher infant and child mortality figures for some groups. (See Table 10.4.) For Cohort Group *G*, fully 25 percent of the children registered died before age 10, in part due to the epidemic of 1832. The percentages of children dying before 10 vary by *kokudaka* class, reaching as high as 40, but even this 40 percent, who came from landless families,

Table 10.4
Incidence of Infant and Child Mortality in Fujito, by *Kokudaka* Class

Class	No. Children	No. Died Age 10 or Less	% Died
For Children Born to Women Married 1825-1841 (Cohort Group G)			
I	25	10	40
II	39	7	18
III	52	18	35
IV	8	3	38
V (1)	110	23	21
(2)	26	5	19
(3)	10	1	10
(4)	13	3	23
TOTAL	*283*	*70*	*25*
For Children Born to Women Married after 1841 (Cohort Group H)			
I	23	2	9
II	23	2	9
III	29	4	14
IV	17	3	18
V	101	21	21
TOTAL	*193*	*32*	*17*

can be assumed to be within the same universe as the total, using a 95 percent confidence interval. The percentages are lower for Cohort Group H (a total of 17 percent) but, if anything, the death rates rose in direct relation to size of landholding. But we cannot say from these percentages that any one group faced statistically higher infant and child mortality rates than did any other.

Two conclusions can be drawn from the above comparison of fertility by landholding class: First, despite slight variations such as the age at marriage for women married after 1841, it is difficult to discern major differences in fertility among women from various landholding classes in Fujito, ranging from the poorest to the few wealthy families. This lends credence to the idea that the Japanese limited their families across the board and that they raised only wanted families. Making the decision whether to raise a child before or immediately upon birth is less economically and socially wasteful than limiting families through careless attention to children already being raised.

Second, the behavior of families to maintain optimum family size over time, no matter whether the family was large or small, combined with the fact that fertility control did not vary significantly by landholding class, leads to the conclusion that the fixed capital base of land was possibly not the determining economic factor in optimum family size in many cases. This one would only expect to find true in a society in which land was not the only or the most important asset. Thus, families with no land but thriving businesses would find it most profitable to maintain large families in order to have available a ready supply of labor in a labor-short economy, whereas a family with holdings in the modal class who depended on agriculture might have found it necessary to limit children to two to maintain or improve their standard of living.

CONCLUSION

Although our information on the history of individual families in Fujito and their demographic behavior is limited almost entirely to lists of names, ages, and landholdings in the *shūmon-aratame-chō* and the tax records, tracing families over time creates a rather vivid picture of what life must have been like in Fujito from the turn of the nineteenth century through to the years just prior to the Meiji Restoration. Household size and composition, age at marriage, the spacing, number, and sex of children, and various activities such as migration and employment, varied so much from family to family and individual to individual that to speak of the "average" villager would create distortions. But, from the collective activities of the population of the village, we can see changes in village life and the response of the inhabitants to these changing conditions.

During the first period for which we have nearly continuous records, 1794-1810, we have a picture of a village in which economic conditions do not seem to have been good, judging from the behavior of the villagers. The cause of these conditions was clearly not famine and disease, as the death rate was lower than during many other periods. But the birth rate was also kept low, not by reducing the number of children born to each married woman, but by reducing the number of women married within the village. In addition to postponing marriage for many, the village managed to create a negative balance of brides, sending out more than it brought in. Migration was high, particularly among men in the peak working ages. Most who left did so illegally, and thus just dropped from the records, but some returned to their families years later. The population of the village fell by some 10 percent during these years, due to out-migration rather than to a negative natural increase in population.

In contrast, by the next period for which we have population records, the 1820s, the economy was on the upswing. Land belonging to the village was being reclaimed and, in addition, commerce was developing at an accelerated rate. Not only were more young women permitted to marry but younger brothers who formerly left the village now remained at home and married as well. As a result the number of births rose, but in 1832 an epidemic, which primarily struck children, negated this increase in births. And five years later the Tempō famine began to take a visible toll on the population of Fujito. It must have been especially hard to live through, as the village seems to have escaped the Temmei famine and thus no one alive in the 1830s had the experience of knowing how to survive a major famine. But, although the death rate rose in the famine years, at no time did it reach the high levels of other parts of the country; Fujito lost more population at the turn of the century than in the late 1830s and early 1840s. The village quickly recovered, increasing its population and restoring

289

its family social structure, the latter accomplished through adoption and marriage.

But it is in the 1830s and 1840s that we begin to perceive social changes occurring in the village society. For the first time there was a significant number of both men and women who had children registered to them but no spouse. For the first time children were entered on the records as illegitimate, that is, children were attributed to unmarried women whereas earlier they were recorded as being children of the head of the household, even when his wife was clearly past childbearing age. We also see an increase in households composed of people other than the head, his wife, his parents, his children, and other close relatives. There were adoptions of "brothers" who brought with them wives and children. Several men had more than one child before a wife was recorded. These examples may represent changes in the recording methods but, even if that is true, some social change had occurred so that it was no longer considered necessary to disguise the parentage of an illegitimate child. But, again, we should not make too much of these changes as they are more noticeable in the recording than in actual shifts in demographic behavior within the village.

We know that the village economy was prospering during the 1840s. This was the decade in which the number of looms within the village averaged one per household and in which a few villagers were doing large-scale business in the cotton industry outside the village and outside the domain. And after the Tempō mortality crisis—which lasted until the mid-1840s—was over, the population of the village began to grow, although slowly by modern standards.

Evidence suggests that the population of Fujito was consciously limiting its numbers. Not only do we see a fluctuation of the proportion of women in their early to mid-20s who were married and few marriages and births in the teens, but on the average a woman in Fujito bore between three and four children, and only two women are reported giving birth to more than six children after the turn of the nineteenth century. A sex ratio that was as high as 2.23 for all children born to women who were married between 1825 and 1841 and whose families held from 1-3 *koku* of land, clearly suggests that infanticide was one of the means used to limit family size.

Birth control and other methods to restrict population growth were not limited to any one group within the village, however. With small variations of no statistical significance, demographic behavior was similar in all economic groups as measured by landholding size, and across social class as determined by the holding of village office. Everyone seems to have felt equal pressure to maintain his social standing and relative standard of living, and some managed to improve theirs, as is attested to by the successful entrepreneurs in the village.

Thus, while the people of Fujito were responsive to changing economic conditions within the village and the domain, and varied their demographic behavior accordingly, at no time did they release controls over population growth and permit their birth rate to soar. All evidence points to a noticeable rise in the standard of living, especially during the nineteenth century, made possible by accelerated economic growth and the continued control over family size and over the formation of new families. The changes in life-style created by this rise in per capita income were sufficiently great to make every villager aware of the change and, we hypothesize, to prepare him for the even more rapid changes that were to occur after the Meiji Restoration.

CHAPTER ELEVEN

A Comparison of Population Trends

In our study of four villages we analyzed fertility and mortality, and patterns of demographic behavior, especially methods of population control, but our sample included only a small fraction of the tens of thousands of Tokugawa villages, and three of these were located in the same domain, Okayama. Consequently, the question arises as to how applicable the findings for these four villages are to the entire rural population of Tokugawa Japan. And how similar or different were population trends in Tokugawa Japan from trends in other preindustrial societies? In this chapter we will briefly look at population trends in other villages and areas in eighteenth and nineteenth-century Japan and compare them with Fujito, Fukiage, Numa, and Nishikata. And then we will compare population trends and population control in Tokugawa Japan with those in other countries in similar stages of development or in the same centuries.

Because the *shūmon-aratame* was carried out on a nationwide basis, thousands of copies of the registers are in existence, sometimes for only one or two years for a village, and sometimes in relatively good time series, even covering several centuries. However, most of the records are so scattered both in time and location that an analysis of the data contained in them will not yield answers to the kinds of questions we have been asking in Chapters Eight to Ten. And, since there were thousands of villages in Tokugawa Japan, we can expect to find dozens of patterns of growth, so that an analysis of changes in total population in the absence of other information will not be revealing.

Fortunately, however, demographic changes in a number of villages have been studied, using relatively good data, and the central purpose of this chapter is to present the results of these studies on a comparative basis with our findings. One *caveat* is that the information we are given in these village studies may not be directly comparable either with the statistics presented in this book or with one another because the methods used to calculate fertility and life expectancy often varied, as did the definition of the specific statistical universe, such as who was and was not a member of the village, whether all married women were used in calculating fertility or only those with children, and so on. The source of the data is the same, however, and thus the information obtained can be considered roughly comparable, certainly for our purposes.

The samples of village population patterns range from Shimoyuda in northern Honshu, which was severely affected by famine, to a village in central Japan that was settled on reclaimed land early in the eighteenth century, and therefore had resources for unusual growth. In terms of geographic location, our samples come from as far north as Tohoku to as far west as the island of Tsushima off the coast of Kyushu, but most are from central Honshu. Most of the village samples are very small, some, such as Yokouchi and Asakusanaka, with early populations of less than 200. However, while earlier research tended to be on the village level, two recent studies cover much larger populations: Hayami's on the Suwa region of the present Nagano Prefecture with a sample population of well over 10,000 and Sasaki Yōichirō's on the Ni-no-machi section of the city of Takayama (Gifu Prefecture) with a population of over 2,600 (out of a city total of 9,237) in 1842.

Since the method of compiling data and the forms used to present them vary by study, we will concentrate here on measurements that can be obtained for the maximum number of areas and are most comparable to those compiled for the four villages analyzed in Chapters Eight and Nine. These are life expectancy, crude birth and death rates, and the percentages of the population in the working and dependent age groups. We present these to test our hypotheses that birth and death rates were both low in Tokugawa Japan, that life expectancy was in the 40s for the second half of the Tokugawa period, and that the percentage of the population in the working ages was high, creating an age structure conducive to a high per capita output.

Table 11.1 presents the life expectancy in sample areas in Tokugawa Japan. Most of these are estimates of life expectancy in the second year of life and therefore at approximately age 1 by Western (and modern Japanese) calculation, and were calculated by age at death for birth cohort groups. The disadvantages are the small sample sizes for most of the areas and the biases introduced by relatively high mobility, which makes it impossible to trace

Table 11.1
Life Expectancy for Sample Areas in Tokugawa Japan
(Deaths in parentheses)

Village (Present Prefecture)	Period	At age[a]	LIFE EXPECTANCY			
			Males	Sample Size	Females	Sample Size
Yokouchi (Nagano)	1671-1725	2	36.8	(226)	29.0	(144)
	1726-1775		42.7	(253)	44.0	(97)
Iinuma (Gifu)	1712-1867	2	41.8		39.7	Village of 250-375
14 villages in (Wakayama) Kii Province	1780s and 1790s	8	44.6		42.2	Total about 4,000
Asakusanaka (Gifu) (also referred to as Nakahara)	1717-1830	1	46.9		50.7	Total grew from 120 to 284
Toraiwa (Nagano)	1812-1815	Birth	36.8[b]	(105)	36.5	(95)
Shimoyuda	1773-1778	Birth	35.1		30.3	Village of 664 in 1773
	1773-1778	1	44.2		39.5	
	1808-1813		26.7		30.1	Village of 561 in 1808
	1808-1813		37.3		39.3	
Kando-shinden (Aichi)	1839-1869	2	33.2	(137)	31.6	(138)
Takayama City (Gifu)	1806-1810	Average Age at Death	39.2		39.6	Section of city, 2,681 in 1842
	1811-1815		49.5		42.8	
	1831-1835		43.1		41.7	
	1836-1840		38.8		39.8	
	1841-1845		37.1		32.9	

many members of birth cohort groups to their death. The omission of these members would tend to lower life expectancy, as most deaths at the lower ages would be included in the figures while many at higher ages would be omitted. On the other hand, life expectancy would be biased upward in areas experiencing net in-migration as the immigrants have already survived childhood, and thus they represent the survivors of a cohort group rather than comprise a birth cohort group themselves. Sasaki readily admits the difficulties in using average age at death, but was forced to do so because of the high mobility in Takayama.[1] The second method used to calculate life expectancy was to use life tables, and the estimates for Asakusanaka, Toraiwa, and Shimoyuda were all calculated in this way.

If we consider life expectancies calculated for age 2 by Tokugawa reckoning equivalent to those for age 1 by Western calculation, then we find that life expectancy did tend to be around 40 for both men and women. The lowest estimates are for Yokouchi in the half century prior to 1725 and for Kando-shinden between 1839 and 1869. Both of these villages had relatively high birth rates (see Tables 11.2 and 11.3) and thus there were more children in the high-risk years compared to other villages, and we must remember that these life expectancies were calculated from average age at death. Toraiwa's looks low, but the male life expectancy at birth of 36.8 is comparable to Shimoyuda's, and this would put life expectancy at age 1 in the mid-40s. Also, we must remember that Kobayashi doubled the number of deaths for children under 5, simply because he thought the number recorded looked too low.

---

[a]Ages are given as in each source, which usually means ages by Japanese reckoning. The life expectancies for Shimoyuda have been adjusted for this difference, and presumably those for Asakusanaka as well.

[b]Kobayashi believed that young children were undercounted, and doubled the number of recorded deaths for children under 5.

Sources: Yokouchi. Hayami Akira, Kinsei nōson no rekishi jinkō-gakuteki kenkyū, p. 204; Iinuma: Hayami Akira, "Tōnō ichi sanson no jinkō tōkei," p. 278; Kii: Hayami Akira, "Kishū Owashi-gumi no jinkō sūsei," p. 347. Asakusanaka: Robert Y. Eng and Thomas C. Smith, "Peasant Families and Population Control in Eighteenth-Century Japan," p. 418; Toraiwa: Kobayashi Kazumasa, "Edo jidai nōson jūmin no seimei-hyō," p. 21; Shimoyuda: Calculated by the method used in Chapter Eight using the shūmon-aratame-chō for the village of Shimoyuda; Kando-shinden: Hayami Akira, "The Demographic Analysis of a Village in Tokugawa Japan: Kando-shinden of Owari Province, 1778-1871," p. 68; Takayama: Sasaki Yōichirō, "Hida-no-kuni Takayama no jinkō kenkyū," p. 112. For full references, see the Bibliography.

The highest in the sample is for the small village of Asakusanaka, but even this is nowhere near as high as the life expectancy for women found in the small village of Nishikata just prior to the Temmei famine. The sample that offers the most support for our hypothesis that life expectancy was 40 or over at age 1 is the sample from Takayama which, with the exception of life expectancy for women in the period 1814-1869, ranged from the high 30s to the low 40s, and even 49.5 for men from 1811 to 1815. Sasaki notes that when the small sample available for the years 1773-1775 is used, life expectancy for both men and women climbs to over 60, but since he does not think this can be accurate, he has omitted these estimates from his tables.[2]

Probably more reliable than life expectancies that have been calculated by differing methods and often for small samples are the crude birth and death rates for a number of villages in Tokugawa Japan. These we will analyze here by village or area, including a discussion of the place from which they come and possible reasons for the rates that occur.

Let us begin with the first village analyzed by Hayami using the family reconstitution method: Yokouchi in the district of Suwa in Shinano Province, the present Nagano Prefecture.[3] *Shūmon-aratame-chō* are extant for this village for 144 of the 201 years from 1671 to 1871. The population of the village grew from 184 to 524 in 1771 and then fluctuated around 500 for most of the next century but, during the last decade for which we have records, the population suddenly jumped from 444 to 534. For all of the eight 25-year periods the average birth rate was well above the average death rate. (See Table 11.2.) However, both birth and death rates fell over the course of the two centuries, the death rates dropping from 25.5 per thousand during the first half century to under 20 for the last 125 years and the birth rate falling from the high 30s to the low 20s per thousand.

Hayami attributes the decline in the birth rate to birth control:

In the first place, they came to delay the age of marriage, and then to check the number of births. . . . The age of marriage rose, especially for females: from age 17 in 1701-1725, to 19 in 1751-1775, 20 in 1801-1825, and 22 in 1851-1871. The evidence of birth control can be seen in the relationship between the age of marriage and the number of births. From 1671 to

Table 11.2
Birth and Death Rates for Yokouchi
(per thousand)

| Period | BIRTHS | | | DEATHS | | Natural Rate of Increase |
	Total No.	Birth Rate	Sex Ratio	Total No.	Death Rate	
1671-1700	235	35.3	113.6	170	25.5	9.8
1701-1725	316	39.8	109.3	202	25.5	14.4
1726-1750	287	28.8	127.8	209	21.0	7.8
1751-1775	318	26.3	106.5	198	16.4	9.9
1776-1800	243	20.1	100.8	234	19.4	0.7
1801-1825	283	23.5	100.7	236	19.6	3.9
1826-1850	253	21.4	120.0	216	18.3	3.1
1851-1871	224	23.7	113.3	174	18.4	5.3
TOTAL	2,159	26.3	110.8	1,639	20.0	6.3

Source: Hayami, Kinsei nōson no rekishi jinkōgakuteki kenkyū, p. 160.

1725 married women who survived until age 45 with their husbands had 6.5 births if the women married between 15 and 20, 5.9 if married at 21-25, and 1.5 if at over 26. From 1726 to 1775 they averaged 4.2 births if married between 15 and 20, 3.4 if at 21-25, and 3.0 if at over 26. And after 1776, women averaged 3.6-3.8 births whenever they married. I think this was due to the practice of birth control.[4]

The example of Yokouchi would seem a perfect piece of evidence to support the hypothesis proposed in Figure 2.3 that fertility was high during the seventeenth century, but that during the early eighteenth an additional increase in children was seen as an economic burden, and that at this point villagers began to limit their own fertility.

In the village of Kando-shinden, also analyzed by Hayami, we find birth and death rates for the last century of the Tokugawa period that are similar to those for Yokouchi for the late seventeenth and early eighteenth century.[5] (See Table 11.3.) However, Kando-shinden differed from Yokouchi in terms of its history and economy: whereas Yokouchi was a settled village by the seventeenth century, it did not have the easy access to land that Kando-shinden did, although Yokouchi did substantially increase its tax base from 350 koku at the beginning of the Tokugawa period to 535 by the 1830s. In contrast, Kando-shinden was settled only in

Table 11.3
Birth and Death Rates for Kando-shinden
(per thousand)

Period	No. Births	No. Deaths	Birth Rate	Death Rate	Natural Rate of Increase
1778-1782	24		29.7		
1783-1787	24		27.6		
1788-1792	36		38.5		
1793-1797	22		22.5		
1798-1802	29		28.4		
1803-1807	33		36.2		
1808-1812	37		30.4		
1813-1817	51		39.6		
1818-1822	58		40.0		
1823-1827	59		38.5		
1828-1832	62		37.9		
1833-1837	51		30.2		
1838-1842	60	46	34.4	26.2	8.2
1843-1847	54	30	30.6	17.0	13.6
1848-1852	61	42	32.5	22.4	10.1
1853-1857	74	48	37.5	24.6	12.9
1858-1862	49	46	24.2	22.8	1.4
1863-1867	55	43	31.1	20.6	10.5
1868-1870	36	39	28.7	31.2	2.5
1778-1812 average			30.5		
1813-1837 average			37.0		
1838-1870 average			31.2	22.9	8.3
1778-1870 average			32.6		

Source: Hayami, "The Demographic Analysis of a Village in Tokugawa Japan: Kando-shinden of Owari Province, 1778-1871," Keio Economic Studies, Vol. 5 (1968), p. 67.

the early eighteenth century by a timber dealer from Nagoya. Hayami considers this village "a good example of how a population shift occurred . . . where the amount of arable land could be easily expanded."[6]

During the ninety-four years from 1778 to 1871 the population of Kando-shinden increased from 162 to 410, an average annual increase of about 1 percent, but prior to 1833 the growth rate was 1.4 percent, while it slowed to 0.5 percent after this year. The increase was due to a surplus of births over deaths and not to inmigration; in fact, an exodus of women who married outside the village kept the growth rate from being even higher.

We do not find in Kando-shinden, however, demographic behavior on the individual level that differed substantially from other villages. While the average age at marriage tended to be about 22 (21 in Western terms) and lower than the average age in Okayama by a year or two, the average completed family size was 3.45 births for women born before 1800 and 3.38 for women born after that year. The demographic indices are similar to those in Fujito during the mid-nineteenth century when the population of that village was also rising. The proportions of women aged 20-24 who were married ranged in Kando-shinden from 34 to 47 percent, and we found proportions over 40 percent for this age group for our four sample villages (Table 9.11) when economic conditions tended to be good. Kando-shinden's were over 40 both for the period 1801-1825 and 1851-1871; and the intervening period covered the Tempō famine. In summary, Kando-shinden had a positive natural growth rate for the entire century for which there are records, though it slowed in the second half and, unlike in other villages, this balance of births over deaths was not counterbalanced by significant out-migration.

A third village studied by Hayami is Nishijō located on the Nōbi Plain in the province of Mino (present Gifu Prefecture).[7] Despite birth and death rates (Table 11.4) that look similar to those in both the Okayama villages and the others presented here, the population rose only from 366 in 1772 to 381 in 1869, nearly

Table 11.4
Birth and Death Rates for Nishijō
(per thousand)

Period	No. Births	No. Deaths	Birth Rate	Death Rate	Natural Rate of Increase
1773-1780	72	61	24.5	20.8	3.7
1781-1790	87	101	26.1	30.3	−4.2
1791-1800	122	73	38.4	23.0	15.4
1801-1810	106	76	32.6	23.4	9.2
1811-1820	92	70	29.6	22.5	7.1
1821-1830	107	63	34.7	20.5	14.2
1831-1840	102	110	34.5	37.2	−2.7
1841-1850	102	59	33.8	19.6	14.2
1851-1860	108	59	32.4	17.7	15.7
1861-1868	95	50	32.7	17.2	15.5
TOTAL	993	722	31.9	23.2	8.6

Source: Hayami Akira, "Kinsei nōmin no kōdō tsuiseki chōsa," Kenkyū Kiyō (Tokyo: Tokugawa Rinseishi Kenkyūjo, 1971), p. 230.

a century later. There was an excess of 271 births during this period, but the village showed no significant increase in population, due to out-migration.

In his study of Nishijō, Hayami undertook a new form of analysis of the *shūmon-aratame-chō*: the tracing of all significant demographic behavior of each individual in the population from his birth to his death, or until he was lost sight of in the records. Through his analysis Hayami has shown that—for this village at least—migration, even temporary migration for the purpose of working elsewhere and eventually returning home, had a significant effect on the population of the village. First, of the people who left the village on *dekasegi* with contracts usually under five years in length, only 27 percent returned home to Nishijō. Thirty-eight percent died while working outside the village, and the rest either continued to work elsewhere or went to some other village to marry. And in this village 48 percent of the males who survived to age 10 and 62 percent of the females went out to work sometime in their lives.

Even the demographic histories of the 15 percent of women who eventually returned to Nishijō differed from those of women who never left home. The average age of marriage for women who had *dekasegi* experience was 26.3, while it was 20.7 for those who had not. And in this village women who married at age 20 had on the average 6.16 children, while those who married at 26 had only 4.31, or two less. Furthermore, while men who worked outside the village tended to have a higher death rate than those who remained at home, the reverse was true for women, believed by Hayami to be the result of their having less risk of dying in childbirth.

While analysis of this kind is so far limited to this one village, the findings suggest that migration to cities and larger towns, both temporary and permanent, had a significant impact on population trends in at least the second half of the Tokugawa period. Since migration was a widespread phenomenon in the eighteenth and nineteenth centuries, Hayami hypothesizes that *dekasegi*, in raising the death rate for men, lowering the fertility of women, and taking a large number of people from the village permanently, kept the population in numerous villages from growing even when birth and death rates were similar to those in villages in which the population was growing at nearly 1 percent per year.

Thus far our village samples have all come from central Honshu because of the existence of good series of *shūmon-aratame-chō* for this part of Japan, but records do exist for some villages in other parts of the country. One such example is Shimoyuda in the present Iwate Prefecture.[8] (See Table 11.5.) This was the area hardest hit by famine and natural disaster during the second

Table 11.5
Birth and Death Rates for Shimoyuda
(per thousand)

Period	No. Births	No. Deaths	Birth Rate	Death Rate	Natural Rate of Increase
1773-1777	61	95	18.4	28.6	−10.2
1808-1812	81	78	28.2	27.2	1.0
1832-1836	43	107	19.1	37.3	−18.2

Source· Calculated from the *shūmon-aratame-chō* for Shimoyuda.

half of the Tokugawa period, and the sample birth and death rates reflect this fact, with high negative growth rates for two of the three sample five-year periods. However, that these rates were not continuous throughout the period is attested to by the fact that life expectancy at age 1 in both of the first two periods was around 40, or about the same as most of the other samples we have. (Refer to Table 11.1.) For the Tempō sample, however, life expectancy could not be calculated by the Coale and Demeny method because it fell below Level 1, and thus was less than 20 for this sample period.

We also know that negative rates were not continuous because the population of the village fluctuated around 600 from 1670 through the mid-nineteenth century. It rose to over 700 in the late 1730s, but after 1754 it did not reach this figure again until 1869. The population dropped by 100 persons in the Temmei famine years and reached its lowest point of 496 in 1839, at the end of the Tempō famine, but had the death rate usually been higher than the birth rate, the population would not have been maintained at the level it was, nor would it have recovered from the famines. Thus, we have in Shimoyuda an example of the negative growth rates that many villages experienced at various times, but what is significant is that the rates occurred not because the death rate rose so terribly high, but because at the same time that death rates rose, *the birth rate fell drastically.*

301

In addition to various village studies, Hayami has undertaken the analysis of *shūmon-aratame-chō* of the Suwa region in what is now Nagano Prefecture in the inland mountainous area of central Honshu.[9] While the extant records are in most cases not of sufficient time series to permit family reconstitution, birth and death rates could be calculated. (See Table 11.6.) These are of

Table 11.6
Birth and Death Rates for the Suwa Region
(per thousand)[a]

Decade	No. Births	No. Deaths	Birth Rate	Death Rate	Natural Rate of Increase
1671	232	148	26.0	21.8	4.2
1681	956	561	37.4	24.4	13.0
1691	913	703	32.6	25.3	7.3
Subtotal	2,101	1,412	33.1	24.5	8.6
1701	769	689	29.4	24.2	5.2
1711	745	612	32.2	26.0	6.2
1721	739	654	28.6	23.6	4.9
1731	345	319	22.5	22.2	0.3
1741	554	679	20.9	22.5	−1.6
Subtotal	3,152	2,953	26.9	23.8	3.2
1751	741	573	25.0	21.0	4.0
1761	801	645	24.3	20.9	3.5
1771	434	443	22.3	20.8	1.5
1781	474	465	20.1	20.7	−0.6
1791	752	618	23.7	19.7	4.0
Subtotal	3,202	2,744	23.3	20.6	2.7
1801	416	291	25.2	19.7	5.5
1811	430	379	22.0	19.9	2.1
1821	178	211	22.7	23.4	−0.7
1831	345	406	21.9	25.4	−3.5
1841	238	174	23.9	16.9	6.9
Subtotal	1,607	1,461	23.1	21.2	1.9
1851	498	447	21.8	20.1	1.7
1861	449	330	22.2	16.5	5.7
Subtotal	947	777	22.0	18.4	3.6
TOTAL	*11,009*	*9,347*	*25.5*	*21.8*	*3.7*

[a]These rates were compiled using the ten-year averages for the population of each village and the birth and death rates. The ten-year period starts with the year listed, and thus 1671 refers to the decade 1671-1680. Hayami also calculated birth and death rates using villages for which he had births, deaths, and population for the same year, but the results from the smaller sample were almost identical. a birth rate for the entire period of 24.9 and the same death rate, 21.8.

Source: Hayami, *Kinsei nōson no rekishi jinkōgakuteki kenkyū* (Tokyo: Tōyō Keizai Shimpōsha, 1973), p. 46.

302

particular importance because the sample size ranges from 10,000 to over 17,500, varying by period and by availability of the documents. The average birth rate for all sample villages for the entire period is about 25 per thousand, whichever of two methods is used to calculate them. This is a lower birth rate than in Nishijō and Kando-shinden, but the same as Yokouchi's and the Okayama villages of Fujito and Fukiage, all of which are between 24 and 26 per thousand. The death rate of 21.8 for the Suwa region is approximately the same as all three Okayama villages, Kando-shinden, Yokouchi, and Nishijō, all of which are in the low 20s.

These birth and death rates create for the Suwa region a rate of natural increase of about 3 per thousand per year, or 0.3 percent, which is similar to the rate of increase of the population for the period 1721-1846 for the "fastest" growing provinces of Aki, Suō, Oki, and Satsuma, in other words, domains such as Satsuma and Chōshū. And we find the pattern of growth for the Suwa region in many ways paralleling what is considered to have occurred in the national population, even in the more rapidly growing regions. The growth was most rapid during the period 1671-1681, the first years for which there are data, and the 1720s. During this half century the population in this area increased by 50 percent. Then for more than a century the population fluctuated around the level of the 1720s and only began to grow significantly again after the Tempō famines. By the 1860s the population was 70 percent above the level of 1671-1681.

We believe the greatest significance of Hayami's study of Suwa lies in the broad support it provides for relatively low birth and death rates for the rural areas in Tokugawa Japan from the early eighteenth century on and for a significant decrease in birth rates and a smaller decrease in death rates over the course of the Tokugawa period. Thus, while Suwa's birth rates for the seventeenth century were 33 per thousand, these had fallen to the low 20s by 1750 and remained there throughout the remainder of the Tokugawa period, supporting our hypothesis presented in Chapter Three that the population began to tighten control over family size in the early eighteenth century.

The fall in the death rates in Suwa was more gradual and cannot be seen to be as distinct a trend as the fall in the birth rates. Because of periodic crop failures and epidemics in the latter half of the Tokugawa period, the death rate could not be controlled so easily, if at all, or even predicted. But because of the fall in

303

the birth rates by almost 10 per thousand over the course of these two centuries, the rate of natural increase of the population was cut nearly in half, despite a modest decline in the death rates over time. Although there were wider fluctuations in the death than in the birth rates, at no time did the decade averages reach crisis proportions and thus, had the Tokugawa villagers wished to increase their population, all they had to do was increase their birth rate to the late seventeenth-century level, which at 33 was far below maximum fertility for any population.

Hayami's hypothesis—that the decline in the population of central Japan was due to the flow of people into cities where there was a higher death rate rather than to a negative growth rate in the rural villages—rests on a higher death rate found in the cities and the need for "feeding" the city population even to maintain a constant total.[10] Thanks to Sasaki's work,[11] we at last have birth and death rates for a city: Takayama in the present Gifu Prefecture. His study of this population for the century from 1773 to 1871 confirms the hypothesis that here, at least, there was a negative rate of natural increase. (See Table 11.7.) The crude birth rate for this period was 25.5, while the death rate was higher at 26.2, creating a negative rate of natural increase of −0.7 per thousand. But in spite of this negative natural growth rate the population of the city rose from 2,614 in 1773 to 3,333 in 1871. The increase was due to in-migration and, in fact, mobility was so high in this city that Sasaki, in calculating life expectancy (Table 11.1), was forced to use average age at death rather than trace birth cohorts to the end of their lives as Hayami did in his studies.

Takayama was a small city by Tokugawa standards, certainly compared to Kyoto and Osaka and the more than 1 million residents of Edo. One might reasonably expect the death rate to have been even higher in these metropolises than in Takayama, due to crowded conditions among the poor and among daily laborers, which created unsanitary conditions conducive to the rapid spread of epidemic diseases. Thus, while the evidence is only starting to come in, what little we do have confirms Hayami's hypothesis— and E. A. Wrigley's with regard to premodern Europe—that the cities drained the surrounding countryside of population, thus creating negative growth rates in the areas immediately surrounding cities despite a positive balance of births over deaths in these same rural areas.

304

Table 11.7
Birth, Death, and Growth Rates for the City of Takayama

Period	Birth Rates (per thousand)	Death Rates (per thousand)	Balance of Births and Deaths (per thousand)	Actual Growth Rate (including migration) %
1773-1775	21.59	21.59	0.00	3.18
1776-1780	20.41	27.94	−7.53	−2.61
1781-1785	22.16	26.55	−4.49	−0.61
1786-1790	22.39	25.73	−3.34	−7.49
1791-1795	29.83	18.93	10.90	15.93
1796-1800	28.46	24.69	3.50	3.42
1801-1805	23.58	30.55	−6.97	−4.02
1806-1810	23.91	25.23	−1.32	2.53
1811-1815	24.58	18.74	5.83	2.26
1816-1820	25.87	25.37	0.50	−1.55
1821-1825	27.71	28.33	−0.62	3.53
1826-1830	28.75	23.45	5.30	4.59
1831-1835	24.41	25.83	−1.42	−0.51
1836-1840	26.47	44.57	−18.10	−11.32
1841-1845	31.52	22.13	9.39	8.69
1846-1850	31.44	22.98	8.48	7.63
1851-1855	30.70	21.01	9.69	6.59
1856-1860	28.92	24.12	4.80	7.25
1861-1865	26.11	26.23	−0.12	4.92
1866-1871	20.48	28.85	−8.40	−7.03

Source: Sasaki Yōichirō, "Hida-no-kuni Takayama no jinkō kenkyū," Keizai-shi ni okeru jinkō, Report of the 37th meeting of the Shakai Keizai-shi Gakkai (Tokyo: Keiō Tsūshin Kabushiki Kaisha, 1969), p. 106.

Although we have yet only a small number of studies giving us fairly complete knowledge of fertility, mortality, and other demographic measurements, we do have partial information on other areas that can be compared with the samples presented earlier in this book as well as with Hayami's and Sasaki's. For example, we have birth and death rates for three additional areas, which for comparison have been listed with those for Yokouchi in Table 11.8. There is a significant difference in the mode of birth and death rates in these four samples. The mode for both rates was the same for Kōmi village of Mino Province, where the population showed no definite trend, and for the island of Tsushima taken as a whole, where differences in the birth and death rates for the decreasing and increasing areas (rural-urban differences) would be balanced out.

The average birth rate in Kōmi was 17.9 for the period 1674-1866, while the average death rate was higher at 22.4, giving

Table 11.8
Frequency Distribution of Birth and Death Rates for Four Samples
(per thousand)

Range	BIRTHS No. Years in Which the Rate Was within the Range	DEATHS No. Years in Which the Rate Was within the Range
%		
(a) Imafuku Village (Kai Province) 1816-1875 (n = 40)		
0-10	1	3
11-20	5	11
21-30	13	14
31-40	16	7
41-50	4	3
51-60	1	1
Over 60	0	2
(b) The Three Areas of Tsushima 1701-1712 (n = 36)		
0-10	4	0
11-20	14	5
21-30	18	17
31-40	0	11
41-50	0	3
(c) Kōmi Village (Mino Province) 1674-1819 (n = 67D, 68B)		
0-10	7	9
11-20	34	26
21-30	20	23
31-40	4	3
41-50	2	3
51-60	1	0
Over 60	0	3
(d) Yokouchi Village (Shinano Province) 1671-1867 (n = 140D, 141B)		
0-10	6	10
11-20	32	60
21-30	46	45
31-40	28	15
41-50	23	9
51-60	4	1

Sources: Imafuku: Takahashi Bonsen, Nihon jinkō-shi no kenkyū,
Vol. 1 (1941), pp. 187-190; Tsushima: Ibid., pp. 149-153, Kōmi: Nomura
Kenkyūkai, Kōmi Mura Kyōdō Kenkyū Han, "Ogaki hanryō Mino no kuni
Motosu no kori Kōmi mura no kokō tōkei" (Population statistics on
Kōmi villages, Motosu district, Mino province in the domain of Ogaki),
Mita Gakkai Zasshi, Vol. 53, Nos. 10-11 (1960), pp. 202-203, Yokouchi:
Hayami Akira, "Shumon-aratame-chō o tsūjite mita Shinshū Yokouchi
mura no chōki jinkō tōkei," p. 81. For full references, see the Bibli-
ography.

this village a negative rate of natural increase. These rates are similar to Nishikata's during the fifteen-year period covering the Temmei famine, but for Kōmi they cover nearly two centuries, resulting in a population that fluctuated around 400 during this period, starting at 361 in 1674, reaching a peak of 443 in 1759, and ending at 422 in 1872. The mode for birth rates was slightly higher than that for death rates in Yokouchi village of Shinano Province, and it was slightly higher for Imafuku village of Kai Province. Partly because of the small sample sizes, yearly birth and death rates fluctuated widely, which is why decade or even longer averages have been used for most sample areas.

In addition to these villages for which we can obtain fairly accurate information on fertility and mortality, there are villages for which such data cannot be accurately compiled but which yield other demographic information that can be compared to the samples already presented. The data we have chosen to present here (Table 11.9) are proportions of the population in the working and dependent age groups. Our major hypothesis has been that Tokugawa villagers had relatively low birth and death rates, which resulted in a composition of the population favorable to maintaining a high average output per person, thus a relatively high per capita income; that is, the proportions in the working age groups were high, which meant that a very large percentage of the population was contributing to the economy and supporting a much smaller proportion of the population composed of children and the elderly who contributed much less, many nothing at all.

In Table 9.16 we presented the percentage of the population in the working and nonworking age groups in Fujito, Fukiage, Numa, and Nishikata. In all of these villages the percentage of the population aged 15-64 was always above 59, and in the villages and periods in which the population was not growing it was in the mid-60s. We find similarly high ratios in the villages of Shimoyuda in the present Iwate Prefecture, Nagayama and Akasaka-shuku in Aichi Prefecture, and Imai in Nagano (in the Suwa region). (See Table 11.9.) Again, all proportions in the age group 15-64 are above 59 percent, with a few exceeding 70 percent. While there seems to have been no distinct trend of change in the proportion of the population in this working age group, the percentages in the 14-and-under and the 65-and-over categories seem to vary over time. We also find that in Shimoyuda, Nagayama, Akasaka-shuku,

Table 11.9
Age Composition of Sample Village Populations
(percent)

| Year | Percentage of Population in Working and Nonworking Age Groups | | | Average Age of the Population |
	14 and Under[a]	15-64	65 and Over	
	Shimoyuda			
1687	33.1	65.5	1.4	24.89
1738	18.2	68.4	13.5	37.77
1742	20.4	67.0	12.7	37.00
1773	23.8	66.0	10.2	33.39
1799	20.9	71.3	7.8	32.86
1808	22.3	70.8	7.0	33.40
1832	24.3	71.3	4.4	30.23
	Nagayama			
1779	32.5	59.5	8.1	29.88
1795	26.6	63.5	10.0	32.02
1801	24.2	65.9	9.9	32.55
1811	29.7	61.2	9.1	31.19
1821	25.7	66.0	8.3	31.75
1831	24.8	66.5	8.7	32.36
1845	23.5	68.0	8.5	32.13
1855	30.2	62.6	7.2	30.50
1867	33.0	60.3	6.8	29.50
	Akasaka-shuku			
1770	19.9	71.4	8.7	35.29
	Imai			
1671	32.8	63.4	3.8	27.21
1689	39.6	55.8	4.6	24.27
1713	33.4	63.2	3.3	25.72
1733	28.9	66.5	4.6	28.99
1760	23.8	68.3	7.9	32.28
1781	30.3	61.1	8.6	30.31
1799	25.9	66.8	7.3	30.02
1819	28.0	65.7	6.3	31.13
1848	26.9	67.8	5.4	29.04
1865	31.3	62.3	6.4	29.12

Year	15 and Under	16-60[b]	61 and Over
	Kōmi		
1674	38.2	51.8	10.0
1688	29.4	60.1	10.5
1751	25.2	64.5	10.4
1781	28.3	63.3	8.4
1788	22.3	65.6	12.1
1821	32.5	55.7	11.8
1831	29.1	61.0	9.9
1841	28.1	64.3	7.6
1856	31.4	60.4	8.2
1872	28.9	62.3	9.8

Table 11.9 (Continued)

Year	15 and Under	16-60[b]	16 and Over
Iinuma			
1710	27.2	64.0	8.8
1740	24.7	64.4	10.9
1770	23.2	60.8	16.0
1800	29.7	57.1	13.2
1830	26.8	59.9	13.3
1860	30.8	59.7	9.5
Yokouchi			
1690 Male	34.3	58.3	7.2
Female	34.4	57.6	7.9
1830 Male	28.2	59.3	12.6
Female	25.4	57.6	16.7

Year	15 and Under	16-60	61 and Over
Suwa Region			
1671-1690 Male	34.2	59.1	6.7
Female	34.3	58.9	6.8
1711-1740 Male	31.2	59.8	9.1
Female	29.4	62.1	8.4
1761-1790 Male	28.0	60.4	11.6
Female	26.5	61.7	11.8
1811-1840 Male	27.8	58.9	13.3
Female	28.1	57.3	14.6
1851-1870 Male	29.8	60.7	9.5
Female	28.1	59.8	12.1

[a]Two years have been subtracted from the ages listed in the records to obtain ages in Western equivalents for the beginning of the year.

[b]16-60 Japanese reckoning.

Sources: The percentages and average ages for Shimoyuda, Nagayama, Akasaka-shuku, and Imai were calculated by the authors from the *shūmon-aratame-chō* of these villages. The percentages for the other four villages were taken from the studies on them previously cited.

and many of the samples for Imai, the average age of the population was well above 30, an average higher than for the United States today.

We have also included in Table 11.9 the age distribution of the population in three villages analyzed by Hayami. He defined the working ages as 16-60 by Tokugawa reckoning, which means that this age group contains a smaller proportion of the population than our definition, the 15-64 group usually used in international comparisons. However, even with this smaller group, the percentage in the working ages was always around 60 percent and, if the 61-65 age group were to be included to make the sample comparable to ours, the same very high proportions would be found.

Finally, we find in our largest sample, the Suwa region, averages for the age group 16-60 close to 60 percent for every period for both males and females. If we were to include the 61-65 age group, the proportions would certainly rise above 60 in every case. Since there is not a single exception to a high proportion of the population in the working age groups in our samples, we can conclude with reasonable certainty that for the last two centuries of the Tokugawa period 60 percent, often 70 percent, of the rural population was in the age group that contributed most to the economy but, given the nature of employment in the countryside—predominantly agriculture plus by-employments commonly carried out at home—it is likely that many children and some of the 65-and-over group were also actively employed at least some of the time.

We shall deal only briefly with the subject of population control. Hayami believes that the population of Yokouchi was limiting births, and Eng and Smith are convinced that the residents of Asakusanaka were also practicing birth control.[12] But it is not necessary for us to make the case that population control was being carried out; scholars—both of the Marxist persuasion and those who clearly are not—are agreed that population control took place in Tokugawa Japan. What we wish to emphasize are the results of that control: the fact that close to two-thirds of the population had to support a dependent population only half its size.

In comparing studies made by other scholars with our analysis of the four villages presented earlier, the difference in the impact of famine on many of the villages in central Japan compared to Okayama is striking. During the 200 years for which there are data on Yokouchi, the only two quarter-century periods for which there were negative growth rates were those covering the Temmei and Tempō famines. Nishijō had negative natural growth rates only during 1781-1790 and 1831-1840. During the two centuries for which we have data Kōmi's population reached its low when it fell to 349 in 1788. It grew back to 430 by 1836, but then dropped to 404 in 1837 and had plunged to 351 by 1840. Between 1832 and 1837 Shimoyuda lost 18.7 percent of its 1832 population of 572 due to known deaths, and if we add 12 who dropped out of the records for unknown reasons, the percentage would rise to 20.8.

On a larger scale we have Hayami's study of fourteen villages in the province of Kii (present Mie Prefecture) from 1775 to 1871.[13] The population of these villages remained stable at about 5,800 during the Temmei years, except for a drop of less than 100 between 1784 and 1785, but it was severely affected by the Tempō mortality crisis. By 1833 the population was over 7,400 where it remained through 1837, but then in 1838 it dropped to 6,366, and still further to 6,144 by 1840. The death rate of persons over age 8 between 1837 and 1838 was 162.0 for the area as a whole, but in some villages it rose well above 200. But, if we look at the causes of death listed for 1837, we find most numerous the vague categories of "pestilence," "sudden illness," and the like, which accounted for 707 of the 1,210 deaths recorded that year. Thus, the deaths resulted not from starvation but from epidemic disease, which may have struck particularly hard a population suffering from a poor diet after a series of poor harvests.

On the other hand, population in the largest sample we have, the Suwa region, declined only slightly during the 1780s, from 151.7 percent of the 1671-1680 level in the 1770s to 149 percent, and it actually rose from 151.8 percent of the base level in the 1820s to 154.1 percent in the 1830s, the decade of the Tempō famine. Neither did famine significantly affect the population of Kando-shinden in terms of its total numbers: it dropped from 186 to 177 between 1787 and 1788, but was back to 183 in 1789, and the population was around 335 for the decade of the 1830s.

While we have presented evidence to demonstrate the effect of the periods of harvest failure and ensuing epidemics on the population, these data taken in context with the other demographic information on the same areas lead us to the following conclusion: Though population growth rates slowed, if they were not negative, during the 1780s and 1830s, famines were not responsible for the slow rates of growth—the low birth and death rates—during the other eight decades of the last century of the Tokugawa period. Thus, while we do not want to underestimate the impact of famine on the history of the Tokugawa period, we do not believe that famines can be used as the major explanation for slow population growth in the late eighteenth and nineteenth centuries. Rather we must look to what was happening during periods of normal harvests for an explanation of why growth was slow and why people did not try to raise their birth rates after the famine years to make up for lost population.

Throughout this book we have been referring to population growth rates as slow and birth rates as low without specifying with what we are comparing them. The implication has been that they are low compared to other populations, and here we wish to put the demographic data we have for Tokugawa Japan in perspective with other populations, both premodern and modern. Japan has long been singled out as the only Asian nation that has succeeded in modernizing and industrializing as successfully as the Western nations, and here we wish to point out that one factor among many others in common with Western nations, was a similar population growth pattern just prior to the beginnings of industrialization.

Japan's late Tokugawa population was in no way like any country in the twentieth century for which statistics have been compiled. If we compare Tokugawa estimates with those made by the U.S. government in 1973 for the countries and regions of the world,[14] we find the only country with similar birth and death rates and life expectancy is North Vietnam, with a birth rate of 31, a death rate of 25, and a life expectancy at birth of 45. The rate of natural increase in 1972 was 0.6 percent. However, with 41 percent of this country's population under the age of 15, North Vietnam's population has considerably more children than did eighteenth- and nineteenth-century Japan, which means that it should grow more rapidly in the future and has a larger dependent population than did Japan. All other countries with a birth rate as low as Tokugawa Japan's have a death rate far below it, and the countries with a similar death rate have birth rates in the 40s or 50s, both of which signify rapid rates of natural increase.

If we compare age composition in Tokugawa Japan with that in twentieth-century nations as well as Europe prior to the Industrial Revolution, again we find that preindustrial Japan differed from the underdeveloped nations of today but was similar to the preindustrial European populations. To quote Spengler:

Persons aged fifteen to sixty-four constituted 60.5 and 62 per cent, respectively, of Sweden's population in 1750 and 1800;

62.2 and 61.4 per cent of France's population in 1775 and 1801; and 58.4 and 60.8 per cent of Japan's population in the eighth century and 1888. The proportion of the Danish population aged fifteen to sixty-four in 1787 was similar to that in Sweden in 1750. Iceland's population in 1703 included a larger proportion aged fifteen to sixty-four. Data on the age composition of eighteenth-century Europe suggest . . . that this age composition was more favorable to economic production than that now found in much of the underdeveloped world with its high fertility and relatively low mortality.[15]

In contrast, countries with high growth rates and life expectancies between 40 and 55 never have as much as 60 percent of the population in the working ages, and the average is closer to 50 percent. Thus, as of 1965, only 52.5 percent of the population of East Asia (Japan excluded) was aged 15 to 64.[16]

The similarities between Tokugawa Japan and preindustrial and early industrial Europe become even more striking when we compare life expectancies. Again let us quote Spengler:

> Around 1800, expectation of life at birth may have been as high as thirty-five to forty years in some Western European countries; if so, it was higher than it was during the sixteenth and seventeenth centuries. Life expectancy at birth rose in Sweden between the period 1755-76 and the period 1816-40, increasing from 33.2 to 39.5 for males and from 35.7 to 43.5 for females. Female life expectancy at birth . . . was 44.7 years in Denmark in 1835-44; 42.18 in England and Wales in 1841; 40.83 in France in 1817-31; 37.91 in Iceland in 1850-60; and 35.12 in the Netherlands in 1816-25.[17]

A composite figure for life expectancy for males in Western Europe in the nineteenth century, as calculated by the United Nations, is 39.6 in 1840, 41.1 in 1860, and 48.9 in 1900. Female life expectancy is estimated to have risen from 42.5 in 1840 to 52.1 by 1900.[18] These estimates look similar to those we have on Tokugawa Japan. And scholars seem agreed that the nineteenth-century estimates for Europe are higher than the estimates for the seventeenth and late eighteenth centuries because famines and epidemics caused substantially higher mortality then. Thus we have for Japan in the century and a half prior to the Meiji Restoration, which had long been characterized by periodic famine on a nationwide level, estimates of life expectancy similar to those in Europe after the onset of industrialization and after major mortality crises had ceased.

In fact, in the light of the birth and death rates and the estimates of life expectancy we have for the latter half of the Tokugawa period, we believe that the concept of a "demographic transition" in the sense of a transition from high fertility and mortality to low, should be rejected as inapplicable to Japan. In the century and a half prior to the onset of industrialization in Japan there is no indication of a population characterized by high birth and death rates. On the contrary, all of the Tokugawa samples we have for the eighteenth century onward suggest that the birth and death rates of preindustrial Japan were similar to those of the early Meiji period, if we treat infanticide as postpartum birth control. And the highest average birth rate for Japan in the first half century after the Restoration was 33.6 for 1910-1914. (See Table 11.10.) What seems to have produced population growth during

Table 11.10
The Vital Rates of the Japanese, 1875-1919

Year (Dec. 31)	Honseki Population ('000)	Birth Rate	Death Rate	Natural Rate of Increase
1875-1879	35,111	25.2	18.0	7.2
1880-1884	37,079	26.3	19.5	6.7
1885-1889	39,081	28.3	21.5	6.8
1890-1894	41,093	28.4	21.1	7.2
1895-1899	43,248	30.6	20.7	9.9
1900-1904	45,984	32.0	20.4	11.7
1905-1909	48,759	32.0	20.9	11.1
1910-1914	52,140	33.6	20.2	13.4
1915-1919	55,527	32.4	22.5	9.9

Source: Nihon Naikaku Tōkei-kyoku, Jinkō dōtai tōkei, 1942. Ratios of children to women computed from age distribution in: Idem, Nihon teikoku tōkei nenkan, 1886-1902, Nihon teikoku jinkō seitai tōkei, 1903, 1908, 1913, and 1918. The above are cited in Irene B. Taeuber, The Population of Japan (Princeton: Princeton University Press, 1958), p. 50.

this half century was that birth rates were consistently at the maximum and death rates consistently at the minimum found in the second half of the Tokugawa period. However, at no time did the rate of natural increase for any one year exceed 1.37 per cent (1911), which is a rate well under half of what many countries in the world face today.

If fertility in both Tokugawa Japan and preindustrial Europe was well below maximum, were the methods used to achieve low birth rates similar? The answer seems to be both yes and no. Northern Europe controlled fertility of women through late marriage, sometimes in the late 20s, and by the high proportion of women who never married at all, sometimes between two- and three-fifths of all women between the ages of 15 and 44. Japan seems to have been midway between this northern European pattern and Wrigley's characterization of marriage in preindustrial populations outside Europe: "almost universal and . . . at a very young age."[19] Usually no more than one-fifth of Tokugawa village women seem to have remained unmarried and the average age at marriage never rose above the mid-20s, but it was far from "universal" and came at an age that made possible one or two less children than had women married in their mid- or late teens.

In both societies, population control seems to have been practiced within marriage. We have found no mention of coitus interruptus in Japan though it was a common practice in Europe, where there had been knowledge of this method of contraception for centuries. Europeans could resort to abortion as could the Tokugawa Japanese. And, while no one has wanted to discuss it until recently, there is a growing body of evidence that Europeans also resorted to infanticide.[20] Because of the strength of the Church in Europe, this subject and the practice of it was even more of a taboo in this part of the world than in Japan, where it was considered an undesirable practice but never a sin.

The European method of infanticide seems to have varied in method from the Japanese, and could be considered by some to have been more inhumane, that is, there was far more suffering involved for the child who was to die. The Japanese usually let the child die at birth, preventing its first cries or smothering it as soon after as possible. Thus, it would be difficult if not impossible in many cases for anyone but the mother and the midwife to know if the birth had been a stillbirth or not. But in Europe, death seems to have come later, in infancy or early childhood. The child was put out to a wet nurse who, either because she was not paid or

315

because of other reasons, might stop nursing it; or the child was killed by "overlaying," that is, smothered in bed; or the baby was customarily left where it could easily come to bodily harm, such as unattended by the fire or a pond or well. Many of the infant deaths therefore could be considered by the parents to have been "accidental," but the number of such deaths was so high that the authorities recognized the true cause and tried to seek out and punish parents who willfully caused their children's deaths. In many periods, children were given gin or laudanum to quiet them, but too much of these drugs must have been the cause or contributing factor to many an infant death. We emphasize these facts with regard to Europe only because they are not generally known, whereas the inhumane practices of the Japanese have been written about for decades in the West.

While the motive for infanticide was almost certainly the same in Japan and in the West—unwanted children—the methods can be considered to have differed because of fundamental differences in society. Whereas in the West the child was considered to have a soul at birth and killing it was therefore murder, the Japanese child has traditionally not been a true member of society at birth, and hence letting it die—or killing it—before it became a member of village society was not the offense that murder was. For example, even in the 1930s John Embree wrote of a small, relatively isolated village:

> This naming ceremony and party is the first introduction into society. The local group now recognizes the child as a new member, with a name and a real, if limited, personality. . . . During the first thirty days or so of a child's life his soul is not very well fixed in his body—it is a period of danger and uncertainty. *Hiaki* [event that takes place about a month after birth], therefore, represents the end of the birth period and is, significantly, the same term as that used for the end of the forty-nine-day period of mourning for the dead. The child has now passed another stage. From now on he may be carried on the back and may cross water safely, for he is now recognized by the gods as well as by the people of his world.[21]

We thus find that in premodern societies that wished to limit their fertility, method was a major problem. Births being difficult to prevent within marriage, both the Japanese and the Europeans resorted to the only methods at hand and, because both societies were ashamed that they had to use these methods, it makes our analysis of them extraordinarily difficult.

CONCLUSION

Our comparison of the data compiled for our four sample villages with data from other villages and larger samples—a city and a region—also from Tokugawa Japan, and with data compiled for Western Europe, leads us to the following conclusions:

(1) In Japan the eighteenth- and nineteenth-century birth rates were low, usually between 20 and 30 per thousand, and similar at the upper end to birth rates during the Meiji period and later, suggesting that the concept of a "demographic transition" may not be applicable to Japan at this period.

(2) Death rates were usually just below the birth rates, though sometimes just above, but the difference between the two was not large. This led to a stable or very slowly growing population in most of the country. These rates are very different from the high birth and low death rates prevalent today in countries that have not yet industrialized.

(3) Life expectancy for the last century of the Tokugawa period seems to have been in the low 40s, although estimates vary more widely than the crude birth and death rates. In any case, they seem comparable with Western Europe's for the first half of the nineteenth century and are high for a premodern nation in which famine is supposed to have taken a heavy toll. These estimates, added to our earlier findings that the number of deaths attributable to the Temmei and Tempō famines are grossly exaggerated, make us feel even more certain that the role of famine in the late Tokugawa period has been overemphasized.

(4) In all samples from the Tokugawa period there were relatively small proportions of children under age 15 and usually two-thirds of the population was in the working ages, always over 60 percent. This is high even compared to Europe, and must have been conducive to a high average productivity, and a larger total output than would have resulted if the same total population had contained a smaller proportion of people in the working age group.

(5) Famines did affect Japan's premodern population, at times killing 10 to 20 percent of a village's population, and can be considered to have slowed Japan's naturally slow population growth rate even further. But famines were not the basic cause of the slow growth rates, which continued even in periods of economic prosperity, and we see little evidence of efforts to boost the population back to its former levels through high birth rates after famine periods.

(6) There are some limited indications of a change in population patterns that support our hypothesis advanced in Chapter 3: that higher birth rates in the seventeenth century were reduced when the population began to "trade off" extra children for a higher standard of living.

(7) We see a slight rise in many places in the rate of natural population increase after the Tempō mortality crises, which may indicate the onset of faster population growth. This continued through the Meiji period but did not start with it. These higher growth rates from the mid-nineteenth century would also help account for some of the gap between the last Tokugawa and the first Meiji figures.

Finally, all evidence points to a remarkable similarity with pre- and early industrial population trends in Europe and no similarity at all between Tokugawa Japan and the other nations of Asia today. Since we are increasingly recognizing the importance that population has in industrialization, this similarity with the other industrialized nations prior to industrialization may well provide one of the keys to Japan's success after the Meiji Restoration. In a study of Meiji Japan, Kelley and Williamson hypothesize that *"the unusual rapidity of Japanese development was the result of low population growth rates."*[22]

Even though the *structure* of Japanese growth is fairly consistent with our modelled contemporary Southeast Asian economy, to what extent can the "Japanese miracle" in terms of the *pace* of development be explained by unusually low rates of population and labor force expansion? The tentative evidence presented in a previous section and elsewhere suggests that much of Meiji Japan's impressive performance can be explained by unique demographic features. In most key aspects, the modelled Southeast Asian economy generates a development trajectory and structural change very similar to Japan. Much work remains to be done on this issue, especially given the pressing contemporary problems in Asia with the current labor force explosion. However, if our tentative findings are supported by further quantitative research, then the relevance of Japanese experience as a contemporary lesson must be carefully qualified. Contemporary Asian nations may mistakenly look to Meiji Japanese history as a model of what is feasible. Given their limited control over demographic variables to date, the lesson of history may not only be irrelevant, but cruel.[23]

CHAPTER TWELVE

Conclusion

There is little doubt that the Japanese economy grew between the early sixteenth and the mid-nineteenth century, but what we set out to demonstrate in this book is that the economy grew throughout these two and a half centuries, though at differing rates, rather than stagnating during the latter half of the period as traditional Japanese economic historians would have us believe. However, while the economy continued to grow during the eighteenth and nineteenth centuries, the rate of population growth slowed, thus creating throughout the country a rise in the standard of living of most Japanese and the accumulation of a considerable surplus in the hands of many. The low rate of population growth was not due primarily to famines and the economic misery that led people to limit their numbers through infanticide, but rather to the desire to maintain and improve their standard of living, and thereby their relative status in the village.

During the seventeenth century the economy grew steadily, due to: increases in the cultivated area through reclamation; an increase in population, which provided the labor to work the new fields; a rise in agricultural productivity brought about by improved agricultural implements and techniques, by an increase in the variety of rice seeds, and by other factors; and the gains resulting from the expanding trade made possible by peace regained after a century of civil wars and by investments made by the domains and the Bakufu in improving transportation and communication.

The center of commerce was the Kinai region surrounding Osaka. The Kinai enjoyed a significant comparative advantage from the beginning of the Tokugawa period because of its centuries-old head start in skills and institutional development, its exceptional ports, a rich plain suitable for commercial agriculture, and considerable special privileges accorded by the Bakufu to the *tenryō* scattered throughout the Kinai. The growth of commerce and manufacturing (mostly the processing of agricultural products), however, was not limited to the Kinai. Quickly following the Kinai were Edo and the domains around it, the western domains, and some eastern domains located between Osaka and Edo—generally those domains located on or near the routes most used by the daimyo going to and returning from Edo on *sankin kōtai*. Commerce and manufacturing in these regions, too, had to grow to meet the demand of their rapidly expanding urban centers. While the economy grew more slowly in domains located further from the center of administration and commerce, even in Kyushu, the Tohoku region, and along the Sea of Japan there were noticeable gains in commerce and manufacturing and a growing agricultural output.

Stimulated by the growing economy, the population seems to have increased fairly rapidly in most areas during the seventeenth century, though we have almost no data, and estimates of growth vary widely. No one denies that a population increase took place, however. Because of a change in farming to a landholding unit that could be worked by family labor, family members who formerly had remained within their households and indentured farm labor were set up as tenants or given land. These people then married, whereas formerly they would have remained single. The seventeenth century was also blessed with favorable weather conditions, and no major famine is on record.

However, by sometime in the first half of the eighteenth century, the rate of population growth began to slow, although economic growth did not stop. And it is here that we depart from the traditional view of what took place in the last half of the Tokugawa period. In contrast to the traditional and Marxist interpretation, which emphasizes stagnation in both the economic and population growth rates, we believe that the economy continued to grow throughout the next century and a half. Occasional major famines reduced output considerably, but we see their effects as neither so severe nor so lasting as to reverse the trend of economic growth. This growth continued for reasons basically similar to those of the seventeenth century: a rising productivity in agriculture resulting from improved implements, more varieties of rice, better techniques and methods of farm management, the increased use of fertilizers, and, most important, the growth of commerce and manufacturing. These changes promoting the productivity of agriculture came mainly in response to the growing market demands for cash crops and to the rising cost of labor.

Productivity and output continued to increase in commerce and manufacturing more than in agriculture, not only in more developed regions but also even in the "backward" areas of Japan, such as the Tohoku region. Contributing to the growth of these economic activities were the increasingly efficient network of trade across domain boundaries and the growing demand for the products and services of these industries by the peasants whose real income continued to rise. In the more developed regions, the leadership in these economic activities shifted to the rural towns and villages, which continued to increase their institutional capacities to engage in wholesale and long-distance trade and to realize economies of scale by adding larger-scale manufacturing establishments. The rising income of peasants, rural entrepreneurs' advantages in obtaining labor relative to their urban counterparts, monopolistic and monopsonistic restrictions practiced by the city guilds, and the changing Bakufu policies towards commerce and manufacturing— all contributed to the growth of the rural economy. Even in less developed regions, the peasants continuously pressed for the freedom to trade without restrictions and, by the beginning of the nineteenth century, the base of nonagricultural activities had expanded far beyond what existed in the mid-eighteenth century.

Because commerce and manufacturing were expanding more rapidly than agriculture, and because productivity (thus wages) tended to be higher in these sectors than in agriculture, one consequence of the growth of nonagricultural economic activities was to encourage the migration of peasants in search of higher returns to their labor. In the Kinai, Okayama, and other domains that were economically advanced, we saw migration, first to the urban centers of commerce and manufacturing and then, during the last century of the Tokugawa period, shifting gradually to the rural towns and villages, where better-paying opportunities were increasing and where many peasants could work on a part-time or seasonal basis. In less-developed regions, represented by Morioka in this study, the same pattern of migration was observed, though smaller in magnitude and later in the Tokugawa period than in the more developed areas. The magnitude, direction, and timing of migration varied widely from domain to domain and even from village to village, as our study of the Okayama villages shows. The important fact, however, is that the Tokugawa peasants were mobile, and their mobility contributed to increasing their income and to raising the marginal productivity of labor in all economic pursuits in cities, towns, and villages.

The movement of labor to nonagricultural activities resulted in a shortage of labor in agriculture, which had the consequences of raising the wages of agricultural laborers and servants and of improving the terms of contract for tenant farmers. Under these circumstances, some arable land remained unworked, and the efforts of the ruling class to stabilize wages in defiance of the dictates of the labor market usually proved unsuccessful. The increasing returns to labor, imputed for tenants or paid to wage earners, necessitated the more efficient use of labor. In the manufacturing industries this often took the form of an increased scale of production. In agriculture, the result was for many to change the size of their unit to make it as close as possible to what would be optimum, given the prevailing level of wages, relative advantages in the types of crops that could be grown, climatic and topographical conditions, and the market conditions (relative prices of crops and the volume of demand) at the time.

For holdings to approach optimum size, some owner cultivators had to increase their holdings, while some of the largest landholders began to lease part of their land to tenant cultivators, even though it meant they had to offer tenants terms of contract promising them a return for their labor equivalent to what they could earn by migrating to towns, by engaging in rural commerce on a part- or full-time basis, or by becoming agricultural wage laborers.

While farmers sought to optimize the size of their holdings, they also acted in such a way as to create a family size that would maximize income and at the same time ensure the continuation of the family line. Thus, in the rural villages whose population records have been analyzed, the average number of children in the completed family tended to be only three and a half. An average of three or four children would have ensured an heir for most families, but low fertility prevented numerous children who would have been a drain on the family income when young and required dowries or land when grown. It also meant that the proportions in the working age were high, above 60 percent in the four sample villages in our study, and this maximized per capita income both within the household and the village.

Families used a number of means to regulate family size, some of which were in the form of generalized social customs enforced through social pressure. One of the most common was for women to marry in the mid-20s, which delayed childbearing and thus helped limit family size by reducing the numbers of years during which women were exposed to the risk of becoming pregnant. A second was the custom for only one son within each household to marry and have a family. His brothers usually left the village to work elsewhere if there were no economic opportunities within the village. In periods of economic hardship, marriage was delayed in order not to add dependents, and this is reflected in the high proportion of women in their 20s whose marriages were deferred in certain periods. And, if families failed to have an heir or produced only girls, they could adopt a younger son from a family with too many boys. Our evidence indicates that, in Okayama at least, more than 50 percent of village families within the last century of the Tokugawa period resorted to adoption to continue the family line.

Within marriage, one of the methods used to limit children seems to have been sex-selective infanticide, usually discriminating against girls. However, descriptions of abortion, abortionists, and the effects of this practice are abundant in the contemporary literature, and abortion is known to have been widely practiced throughout the country, especially in the more advanced areas near urban centers. Given that women in our sample villages on the average bore their last child at 36 or 37, even while living with their husbands at least through age 43, it is likely that abortion was used in these villages, at least by the last century of the Tokugawa period. Except during famines and in extremely impoverished isolated villages, these practices were not followed out of desperation, but rather should be considered methods of birth control. Since infanticide was "to return" an infant at birth before it had become an individual, a part of society, it was thought of more as a form of postpartum birth control than as murder. Though it was considered an undesirable practice by contemporaries who wrote about it, it was possibly less cruel than the premodern European custom of doing away with unwanted children through carelessness in the form of "accidents," gin and laudanum, or lack of food.

Tokugawa fertility was low, but so was mortality, which as a trend tended to parallel fertility in our four villages. If all children allowed to live at birth were wanted children, then infant and child mortality would undoubtedly be lowered because more care would be given to each child. But mortality was low for a premodern society in all age groups, and frequently 5 to 8 percent of the population consisted of persons aged 65 and above. There were no epidemic diseases in Tokugawa Japan with the devastating effects the plague had on premodern Europe and, given Meiji hygiene and glimpses we have of Tokugawa life—the popularity of the hot bath, the custom of drinking boiled water in the form of tea—we are led to assume that the population was probably fairly healthy. The crude death rates in the villages ranged in our samples from about 25 per thousand to 18 or 19, and these averages included famine years. Estimated life expectancies in the 40s gave late Tokugawa 2-year-olds a life expectancy similar to Western Europe's in the mid-nineteenth century and one not much different from Japan's in the early twentieth century.

The effect of the low birth rates combined with low death rates for the eighteenth to the mid-nineteenth century was to create a very slow rate of population growth for most of the country. Since the economy was growing, even if at a rate considered slow by twentieth-century standards, per capita income slowly rose and with it the standard of living in the villages. By the end of the Tokugawa period the farm village was far from a self-sufficient society; commercial crops dominated in many areas, farmers relied on commercial fertilizers and other inputs, village shops sold everything from daily necessities to luxuries imported from other parts of Japan, and by-employments in the processing and manufacturing of local specialties and the employment of villagers in towns and cities were an integral part of life.

While we must be fully aware that the growth rate of the economy differed from domain to domain and even from village to village and that the famines caused reductions in output, starvation, and even infanticide in some instances, we do maintain that many of the changes observed in the economy during the last century and a half of the Tokugawa period cannot be satisfactorily

325

explained unless we accept as fact the continued growth of the economy and the improvement of the peasants' living standard over time.

The above summary of our view of economic and demographic change in Tokugawa Japan is based on our examination of hypotheses and propositions that were derived or resulted from our general framework of analysis. And, given the evidence presented on the nation as a whole, the Kinai region, and the domains of Morioka and Okayama, we believe that the patterns and directions of economic changes as hypothesized in our analytical framework provide a consistent explanation of Tokugawa economic change. It is important to note that much of the evidence presented on economic change comes from the works of Japanese scholars, many of whom adhere to the traditional Marxist interpretation of Tokugawa economic change.

We also believe that our intensive examination of the religious investigation records of four sample villages, along with the results of the village studies made by Hayami and others, supports our view of demographic change. Indeed, when the quantitative evidence on a variety of demographic changes is evaluated and some of the village records are examined by household over several generations, our non-Malthusian propositions concerning the peasant motivation to reduce fertility in order to improve the living standard appear difficult to reject.

We do not wish, however, to claim more than is justified by our evidence. Our economic evidence is limited to general observations at the nationwide level and to three case studies. Quantitative evidence on some crucial economic variables are either fragmentary or next to nonexistent. Our demographic examination is limited to a small fraction of Tokugawa villages and to some aggregate data that must be used with caution. Thus, our only claim is that all our evidence can be accommodated as internally consistent historical facts within our analytical framework and is supportive of the hypotheses and propositions originating in our framework of analysis.

We fully expect that our view will be received at best skeptically by many Japanese scholars and some Western students of Tokugawa Japan because it advances hypotheses that are fundamentally at odds with theirs, and because it questions the traditional interpretations and evidence on the tax burden, famines, peasant re-

326

volts, the consequences of the growth of commerce, and many other significant economic and demographic changes. To the proponents and supporters of the traditional view of economic and demographic change in Tokugawa Japan, we only ask that their initial reactions to our study be replaced by an open-minded willingness to consider and evaluate the findings of this study. We remind our critics that the earlier dark view of the Webbs and many others of the effects of the English Industrial Revolution on wage earners was later questioned by "optimists" such as Clapham, Ashton, and others. Then, in time, the work of Deane and Cole, supported by quantitative evidence and modern economic analysis, replaced the works of the "pessimists" whose image of nineteenth-century England was symbolized by the Poor Laws, the Sadler reports, and Oliver Twist. The reformist ideology had a strong grip on the "pessimist" scholars and long colored their interpretation of the lot of industrial workers in Britain. The pessimists' interpretation, once established and grown respectable over time, held sway for more than two generations before yielding to the new one.

We should add that we came to question the traditional view of economic and demographic change in Tokugawa Japan only gradually. Analytical internal inconsistencies of economic evidence found in the works of more recent writers at first were puzzling, and our assessment of such evidence and the data on demographic changes suggested that the traditional view of the relationship between economic and demographic change required a thorough reexamination. To carry out our reexamination, we adopted a new framework of analysis based on economic theory and on a behavioral assumption concerning the trade-off decisions that the Tokugawa peasants tended to make between a higher living standard and a larger family. Once we began to reexamine the Japanese literature and our own evidence within our framework of analysis, much of what puzzled us began to disappear and what was suggested by our demographic data could be analyzed more satisfactorily.

Our research, however, proceeded slowly, given the knowledge that a generation of earlier scholars firmly held a view so diametrically at variance with many crucial aspects of our interpretation of evidence and of the whole interrelationship existing between economic and demographic changes. For example, the task of reevaluating the economic and demographic history of Morioka re-

327

quired us to cull historical evidence from within the Marxist framework of the works of Mori, lifelong scholar of the domain. Repeated descriptions of the severity of famines, infanticide, peasant uprisings, and an increasingly harsh tax burden on the peasants create a vivid picture of misery and desperation. Only after reexamining the evidence of economic growth and the demographic data and realizing that the evidence for this picture of stagnation and impoverishment to a large extent relied on decrees issued by the domain, on contemporary hearsay, and on questionable quantitative evidence, could we place some of Mori's descriptions in perspective and become aware how effective the images of desperate peasants, perceived through the mind's eye, have been in persuading readers of the truth of the Marxist view.

But in the West where Marxism does not dominate scholarship, why has the negative image of the Tokugawa period persisted if economic growth continued throughout the period, if the standard of living continued to rise for an undoubtedly large majority, and if the basis was established for the rapid industrialization of the country after the importation of technology from the West during the Meiji period? One reason, of course, is the Marxist domination of the Japanese secondary literature which Western scholars read. A second is the mood permeating Meiji writings used as sources by both Japanese and Westerners. There was a pervasive feeling during the Meiji period that Japan should modernize, become enlightened and cast off all that had gone before and, because what was past was not wanted, it perforce became "old," "feudal," and "bad."

But this view is not merely the creation of historians and Meiji writers; all things were not rosy during the second half of the Tokugawa period. The control of the government over the country clearly declined; how else can we explain the failure of the government to tax increases in productivity of traditionally taxed goods or to cash in on the growing commerce? How else can we explain the failure of samurai incomes to keep pace with incomes of other groups within society? How else can we explain the growing indebtedness and financial chaos in many, if not nearly all, domains? And famines did occur, killing off as much as 10 percent of the population in the worst-hit areas and perhaps debilitating the survivors for years to come, leaving them prey to endemic diseases. No disasters of the magnitude of the Kyōhō,

Temmei, and Tempō famines are recorded for the first century of the Tokugawa regime. But the decline of a political regime or the occurrence of famines in parts of the country every half century does not mean that life for the majority worsened any more than it signals general economic decline.

Before turning to assess the implications of our findings, we should note explicitly that, in arguing that the traditional image of the increasingly impoverished peasants is incorrect, we in no way assume that the Tokugawa peasants became more content or happier with their life. Since one's contentment is a function of a variety of social, political, economic and other factors affecting one's life, we argue only that the living standard rose and not the degree of contentment. The experience of the black population in the United States and that of other groups elsewhere in history serve as examples that one can be more discontented, politically and economically, because of, rather than despite, improvements in the economic standard of life. In Tokugawa Japan, too, economic change, however important, was only one among many factors determining the totality of the peasants' lives. Ironically, the point being made here is the same as that made in E. P. Thompson's critique of the optimist literature in the English Industrial Revolution:

> It is quite possible for statistical averages and human experiences to run in opposite directions. A per capita increase in quantitative factors may take place at the same time as a great qualitative disturbance in people's way of life, traditional relationships, and sanctions. People may consume more and become less happy or less free at the same time.[1]

If the economic and demographic changes in Tokugawa Japan followed the course we put forth in this study, then we believe that the reasons often advanced to explain the rapid industrialization of Japan after the Meiji Restoration should either be changed in their order of relative importance or revised. Certainly, it is no longer justifiable to stress, as was frequently done before 1945 and during the 1950s, the discontinuity existing between the economy of the second half of the Tokugawa period and that of the Meiji years. The explanation, encouraged by the works of many Japanese scholars, was that the economy transformed itself from feudal agrarian to modern industrial in a brief period, rapidly reacting to the stimuli coming from the West and led by the vigorous leadership provided by the new government.

During the past fifteen years, this explanation stressing discontinuity has been revised gradually, and we have come to place more emphasis on the already high level of agricultural productivity attained by the end of the Tokugawa period, on the existence of pools of potential capital and easily trainable industrial labor that could be tapped by emerging industries, on the already developed economic institutions, and on the importance of traditional manufacturing and commercial activities throughout the early phases of industrialization. Except in a few textbooks and occasional writings by nonspecialists, the emphasis placed in the 1950s on the importance of the rapid transformation has been yielding to suggestions to reexamine the importance of the Tokugawa experience to help explain the rapid industrialization of Japan.

In the light of what we have argued in this study, we urge that this reexamination be carried a step further to place even greater importance on the Tokugawa economic and demographic changes in order to explain why Japan alone in Asia succeeded in industrializing so rapidly. If we are correct, Tokugawa Japan, unlike other societies in Asia, succeeded in making increasingly efficient use of its resources. The restrictions imposed by government on economic institutions and arrangements and on the economic activities each social class could engage in became ineffectual or were eliminated in the face of the commoners' desire to raise incomes. Once the trend toward a rising living standard was initiated, these commoners—now able to accumulate capital needed for improving the efficiency of land and labor and to support the market activities expanding by their increasing demand for goods —were even more motivated to improve their level of life.

A part of this motivation was manifested in the control of fertility by most in Tokugawa Japan. And this became, in our view, a crucial difference between Japan and other Asian nations in the nineteenth century as well as many of today's underdeveloped nations, which are still trapped by high fertility. The decision to limit population for the sake of an improved standard of living not only helped to accumulate the all-important capital in the society and to increase the level of demand required in maintaining expanding market activities but also was undoubtedly left as one of the most important legacies for Japan in years to come while she

330

continued to industrialize. Had it not been for the slow growth of population during the first years of industrialization—averaging less than 1 percent per year between the 1870s and the turn of the century—the rate of industrialization in Japan would have been much slower. And such a slow population growth would not have come about were it not for the deeply ingrained and long-practiced (to the point of becoming socially well institutionalized and sanctioned) experience of fertility control in Tokugawa Japan. When Kelley and Williamson, in their study of industrialization in Meiji Japan, reached the conclusion that the slow rate of population growth was the most important explanatory factor for Japan's successful start, they in fact were singling out the importance of the Tokugawa legacy.[2]

In attempting to explain why Meiji Japan was able to industrialize so rapidly, we must of course allow for the good fortune Japan had in beginning to industrialize during the second half of the last century, when entry to the industrial world was in many ways easier than the period following the Second World War. But Japan also possessed a set of political, cultural, and social endowments highly conducive to achieving rapid industrialization. No less fundamental ingredients for Japan's success were the economic and demographic legacies left by the generations who lived before the arrival of Commodore Perry and the Meiji Restoration. Thus, we believe that to better understand the Tokugawa economy and its demographic characteristics and the reasons for the remarkable economic achievement of post-Restoration Japan, we must continue to increase our knowledge of the economic and demographic aspects of Tokugawa Japan based on quantitative and qualitative evidence analyzed within an analytical framework more refined and better constructed than that we were able to enlist in this study.

The findings of our study also suggest that some of our current knowledge concerning the reasons for the changes in political, social and other aspects of Tokugawa Japan should perhaps be reappraised. In analyzing the decline and eventual demise of the political power of the Bakuhan structure, the answer to whether the samurai class was able to intensify the tax burden on the peasants or whether the peasants were able to press their demands to better their lot could not but have profound significance. In evaluating the political and social consequences of the changing landholding patterns, it is important for our evaluation to know whether the change came about as the result of intraclass economic polarization or as the result of the peasants' desire to exploit all possible avenues for increasing their income under the given conditions in factor and product markets. In searching for reasons for the development of urban centers and in examining the enormous impact these centers had on life-style and culture in Tokugawa Japan, the answer to the question of whether new arrivals to these centers came from the villages out of desperation or in search for a better life will affect our findings.

And the reasons we advanced for the slow rate of population growth, in contrast to those given by many Marxists, must lead to fresh assessments and analyses of the sociologically relevant aspects of life in households and in villages. For example, can we really call the people living in agricultural villages in the late Tokugawa period "peasants"? Even the Marxist scholars in Japan use the term *nōmin*, which applies equally to the premodern as well as to the twentieth-century farmer. But the term peasant in English connotes a rustic, a "rude clod" who tills the soil in the same manner his ancestors did for no other reason than that was the way it had always been done. Can we use this term for men who continually changed their crop mix to take advantage of market conditions and maximize their incomes? Or who used the latest methods of cultivation and irrigation techniques, the best seed varieties available according to local soil and weather conditions, who purchased improved fertilizers and tools as soon as they were proven effective and became available, and who were constantly working to improve productivity? We have used the term peasant in this study with many misgivings, and in the end used it interchangeably with farmer and villager. But a better understanding of the economic behavior of the classes may change our perception of what the Tokugawa commoners were like and give us a new sense of continuity between pre-Restoration and post-Restoration Japanese.

A continued reassessment of the implications of economic and demographic change on other aspects of Tokugawa life may help clarify our understanding of political change as well. Many scholars find puzzling the continued domination of the Bakuhan system through the nineteenth century, by which time it seemed to have lost its ability either to effectively collect sufficient revenue or to enforce many of its regulations, particularly regarding the actions of broad classes and their economic activities. Might not the slow rate of population growth have had much to do with the stability of the political regime? The government was at least spared the pressure of finding employment or land to feed vast numbers of additional people within a few decades.[3]

Equally important, is it not possible that a change in the economic and demographic balance was a significant factor behind the Meiji Restoration and in determining who the important actors would be in this political change? While the population of the country as a whole increased by only 3 percent from 1721 to 1846 according to the official figures, the population of the areas comprising the four domains of Satsuma, Chōshū, Tosa, and Hizen, long considered the most important in the Restoration, increased by 30 percent.[4] The increase in the population of Satsuma alone was 62 percent and of Suō (in Chōshū) 65 percent, making these two regions the areas of greatest population increase in the three major islands. Yet studies of the Restoration tend either to deal with the Restoration as a class struggle within the Marxist framework or, within Western tradition, as a movement carried out by a remarkably small number of political leaders whose relationships to domain developments are at best imperfectly understood. We believe that studies of political events in the light of economic and social change within domains that did and did not participate in the Restoration would yield fruitful results in enhancing our understanding of this critical juncture in Japanese history.

Finally, the last of what we believe to be the major implications of our study concerns the long-standing search by economic and demographic historians for a better understanding of the possible relationships between economic and industrial change in preindustrial societies and in the early stages of industrialization. Though we are far from having established the precise relationships linking these two factors, we believe we have demonstrated the importance of cultural factors in determining the course of economic and demographic change. We cannot ignore the motivations of the many individuals whose actions, taken in concert, do much to determine how a population and an economy grow. We also believe that our study, combined with the work done on preindustrial England, demonstrates that population control prior to industrialization may be a crucial element in the ability to industrialize at all, rather than something that happens after industrialization has taken place.

333

CONCLUSION

Through the efforts of a small but an increasing number of Japanese scholars and Westerners such as Crawcour, Hall, Reischauer, Smith and others, considerable progress has been made in questioning and reevaluating the generations-old view of the Tokugawa economy and population. And we hope our own effort is but another step toward the goal of increasing knowledge of the important two and a half centuries which, in many ways, shaped the course of Japan following the Meiji Restoration.

GLOSSARY OF JAPANESE TERMS

aburakasu	rapeseed from which the oil has been extracted; used as fertilizer
Bakufu	the Tokugawa Shogunate or government
Bakuhan	an abbreviation of Bakufu and *han*; an adjective denoting the Tokugawa political system
bekke	to leave one household to set up a separate household unit
Bitchū-*guwa*	3- or 4-pronged hoe developed in the seventeenth century in Bitchū province (present Okayama)
bu	unit of money in silver equal to ¼ *ryō*
bunke	branch household
chō	measure of land, 2.45 acres or 0.992 hectares
Chūgoku region	12 *kuni* in western Honshu. It included the domains of Okayama and Chōshū
daikan	local magistrates
daimyō	those samurai possessing domains officially assessed at a minimum of 10,000 *koku* of rice yield; rulers of the 270-odd *han* in Tokugawa Japan
datai	induced abortion
dekasegi	temporarily working away from home
Edo period	1600-1868, same as Tokugawa period; refers to the period when Edo (present Tōkyō) was the seat of government
gejo	female servants
genan	male servants
genin	servants or employees. In the Okayama records this term usually refers to people who migrate or come into a village or household to work, while *hōkōnin* refers to persons who have migrated out to work
Genroku period	1668-1703
gō	0.317 U.S. pint or 1/1000 *koku* (10 *gō* = 1 *shō*)
gōnō	wealthy peasants

han	a domain or fief; a political and economic unit ruled by a daimyō under the hegemony of the Tokugawa Shogunate
hangashira	an official position in village administration. The principal duties were to verify the accuracy of village reports and be responsible for their contents
hatamoto	the samurai directly retained by the Shogunate, who received stipends or fiefs yielding at least 100 *koku* but not more than 10,000 *koku*
hōkōnin	servant, hired worker, or apprentice. This is a very broad term specifying persons who go to work for employers other than their own families
honbyakushō	"independent peasants" who cultivated an amount of land at least sufficient in size to enable them to perpetuate their economic existence
hyō	denotes straw rice bag containing 4 *to* or 0.4 *koku* (2.5 *hyō* = 1 *koku*)
igusa	rush used for matting (*tatami*) and other household items
jōmen system	fixed rate tax that dispensed with annual assessments of yields and was used widely beginning in the 1720s, first in the *tenryō* and then in various *han*
kan	unit of money as well as weight; equal to 1,000 *momme*; 8.27 lbs. or 3.76 kilograms
Kantō region	8 *kuni* located on the Kantō Plain, and which included the city of Edo (Tōkyō)
kazoedoshi	premodern Japanese method of calculating age; a person was considered in his "first year" of life at birth and added a year at each succeeding New Year
kin	1.32 lbs. or 0.6 kilograms
Kinai region	5 *kuni* surrounding the cities of Kyōto and Ōsaka
koku	the traditional measure for rice and other grains; equal to 4.96 U.S. bushels

kokudaka	literally "amount in rice"; used vis-à-vis yield or stipends
Kokura-*ori*	the best-known weave produced in Okayama during the latter half of the Tokugawa period
kōri	district(s)
kuni	province(s); geographic units originating in prehistoric times. In the Tokugawa period *kuni* boundaries often coincided with *han* boundaries, but often *han* were larger or smaller than *kuni*
Kyōhō period	1716-1735
mabiki	infanticide; literally "thinning," a term usually applied to the thinning out of young rice plants
machi	a town and/or administrative part of a city, e.g., Edo, Ōsaka, and the castle towns of domains were made up of *machi*
Meiji period	1868-1912
miso	soybean paste
momme	unit of money in silver as well as measure of weight; 1.325 oz. or 3.76 grams; 60 *momme* usually equalled 1 *ryō*
mon	unit of money in copper; usually 60-70 equaled 1 *momme* of silver and 4,000 equaled 1 *ryō*
mura	village, usually averaging about 300-500 inhabitants and nearly autonomously governed under a headman appointed by villagers
myōga-kin	"thank-money" remitted for official permission to conduct business, frequently on a monopoly basis
nago	marginal tenant farmers or agricultural laborers on long-term contracts
nanushi	village headman
nengu	tax or rent paid in kind, often rice
ninbetsu-aratame	census investigations. These originated before the *shūmon-aratame*, but later the function and form of the two were often the same and only the term used varied by location
ōjōya	the head of a group of village heads. His primary responsibilities were as a coordinator

omotedaka	the official rice yield of a domain as stipulated by the Bakufu; not necessarily equal to real yield
ri	2.44 miles or 3.93 kilometers
ryō	monetary unit in gold; 1 *ryō* usually equaled 60 *momme* of silver or 4,000 *mon* in copper coins
sankin kōtai	residence in Edo in alternate years; required of the daimyō to ensure their continued loyalty to the Bakufu
shinden	new field(s), usually referring to land newly reclaimed for cultivation within the Tokugawa period. The term was often used instead of *mura* with references to villages settled on *shinden*
shō	1.587 quarts or 1/100 *koku* (10 *shō* = 1 *to*)
shōya	village headman (alternate term for *nanushi*)
shūmon-aratame-chō	religious investigation registers. The surveys were first undertaken in the seventeenth century to control and eliminate the practice of Christianity, but by the eighteenth century had become sources of data on the population
tan	a measure of land; 0.245 acres or 993 sq. meters (10 *tan* = 1 *chō*)
tawara	straw bags; *tawaramono* refers to goods in straw bags
teitai	stagnation
Temmei period	1781-1788
Tempō period	1830-1843
tenryō	land administered directly by the Bakufu
to	0.496 U.S. bushels (approximately 2 pecks) or 1/10 *koku* (10 *to* = 1 *koku*)
Tōhoku region	7 *kuni* located in the northeastern part of Honshū
Tokugawa period	1600-1868, referring to the period when the Tokugawa family headed the Bakufu
tonya	(or *toiya*; pronounced *donya* when used as a suffix) wholesalers who specialized by commodity

tozama	"allied" or "outside" daimyō; those who pledged allegiance to the Tokugawa Shogun as peers and whose domains therefore tended to be among the largest
yōshi	adopted son
yōshi-muko	adopted son-in-law
zekke	discontinuation of a family line

NOTES

CHAPTER ONE

1. Nomura Kanetarō, *Nihon keizai-shi* (An economic history of Japan) (Tokyo: Yūhikaku, 1953), p. 308.

2. Kodama Kōta, *Kinsei nōmin no seikatsu-shi* (A history of the life of peasants in the Tokugawa period) (Tokyo: Yoshikawa Kōbunkan, 1957), p. 287.

3. Endō Moto'o *et al.*, *Nihon-shi tsūron* (An introductory history of Japan) (Tokyo: Asakura Shoten, 1959), p. 169.

4. Hatanaka Seiji, "Kiki no shinka to shokaisō no taiō" (The deepening of the crisis and the countermeasures [taken] by various classes), in Rekishigaku Kenkyūkai and Nihon-shi Kenkyūkai, eds., *Kōza Nihon-shi 4: Bakuhan-sei shakai* (Lectures in Japanese history, Vol. 4: The Bakuhan Society) (Tokyo: Tokyo University Press, 1971), p. 220.

5. George Sansom, *A History of Japan, 1615-1867* (Stanford: Stanford University Press, 1963), pp. 183, 186.

6. Mikiso Hane, *Japan: A Historical Survey* (New York: Charles Scribner's Sons, 1972), p. 227.

7. Andō Seiichi, *Edo jidai no nōmin* (Farmers in the Edo period) (Tokyo: Shibundō, 1966), pp. 194-195.

8. Ito Kōichi and Kawana Noboru, "Kawari hajimeru shōgyō to kōtsū" (The beginning of changes in commerce and transportation), in Morimatsu Yoshiaki *et al.*, eds., *Seikatsu-shi* (A history of lifestyles), Vol. 2 (Tokyo: Yamakawa Shuppansha, 1969), pp. 358-359.

9. Hayami Akira, *Nihon keizai-shi e no shikaku* (A [new] perspective on Japan's economic history) (Tokyo: Tōyō Keizai Shimpōsha, 1968), pp. 39, 41.

10. Thomas C. Smith, "The Land Tax in the Tokugawa Period," in John W. Hall and Marius B. Jansen, eds., *Studies in the Institutional History of Early Modern Japan* (Princeton: Princeton University Press, 1968), p. 284.

11. E. S. Crawcour, "Changes in Japanese Commerce in the Tokugawa Period," in Hall and Jansen, *Studies in the Institutional History of Early Modern Japan*, p. 198.

12. See Susan B. Hanley and Kozo Yamamura, "A Quiet Transformation in Tokugawa Economic History," *Journal of Asian Studies*, Vol. 30, No. 2 (February 1971).
Though we were unaware of the movement when this article was written, in May 1971 several Japanese economists and historians or-

ganized a study group for the purpose of promoting quantitative economic history (Sūryō Keizaishi Kenkyūkai) in Japan. Since then this group has had numerous discussion sessions and three major conference meetings (the third, in 1976, attended by the authors). By mid-August 1976, the members of the study group, either as a group or individually, had published: Shimbō Hiroshi, Hayami Akira, and Nishikawa Shunsaku, eds., *Sūryō keizaishi nyūmon* (An introduction to quantitative economic history) (Tokyo: Nihon Hyōronsha, 1975); Umemura Mataji *et al.*, eds., *Nihon keizai no hatten* (The development of the Japanese economy), Vol. 1 of the Sūryō Keizaishi Ronshū (Quantitative economic history series) (Tokyo: Nihon Keizai Shinbunsha, 1976), and nearly a dozen articles. Several of these articles relevant to this study will be fully cited in Chapter Four, note 27.

As Nishikawa's introductory chapter of *Sūryō keizaishi nyūmon*, pp. 1-20, makes clear, the study group sees itself as following in the footsteps of the "new economic historians" in the United States and using a "Kuznetsian approach." Its basic stance is to question the dominant Marxist interpretation of Japanese economic history, especially of the Tokugawa and Meiji periods. For example, after stressing the importance of having an explicit model and using quantitative evidence in economic history studies, Nishikawa noted that "it is not an error in itself to direct our attention to the rigorous collection of taxes from the peasants. However, before going on to describe the escalating hardships suffered by the peasants resulting from the tax rates, which are said to have risen from 40 to 50 and then even to 60 percent . . . attention must be paid to the fact that a nominal rate of under 40 percent and an effective rate of under 30 percent prevailed in the land held directly by the Bakufu. This is the basic stance in our research." (*Ibid.*, p. 16.)

The transformation in the study of Tokugawa economic and demographic history is no longer "quiet" as we characterized it in 1971. We welcome this development. Our only regret is that we are as yet unable to assess the impact of the works of this group on the wider circle of specialists on Tokugawa economic and demographic history in Japan.

13. John K. Fairbank, Edwin O. Reischauer, and Albert M. Craig, *East Asia: Tradition and Transformation* (Boston: Houghton Mifflin Co., 1973), p. 417.

14. *Ibid.*

15. John W. Hall, *Japan: From Prehistory to Modern Times* (New York: Dell Publishing Co., Inc., 1970), pp. 203-205.

16. *Ibid.*, pp. 203-204.

17. *Ibid.*, p. 204.

18. *Ibid.*, p. 202.

CHAPTER TWO

1. Among the many sources consulted in writing this section, the following are perhaps the most useful in conveying the dominant Japanese view of the Tokugawa economy: Nakamura Kichiji, *Kinsei-shoki nōsei-shi kenkyū* (A study of the history of agricultural policy during the early Tokugawa period) (Tokyo: Iwanami Shoten, 1938); Oishi Shinzaburō, *Kyōhō kaikaku no keizai seisaku* (Economic policies of the Kyōhō Reform) (Tokyo: Ochanomizu Shobō, 1961); Tsuda Hideo, *Hōken keizai seisaku no tenkai to shijō kōzō* (The development of feudal economic policies and the market structure) (Tokyo: Ochanomizu Shobō, 1961); Sasaki Jun'nosuke, *Bakuhan kenryoku no kiso kōzō* (The basic structure of the Bakuhan authority) (Tokyo: Ochanomizu Shobō, 1964); Shiozawa Kimio and Kawaura Kōji, *Kisei jinushi-sei ron* (A theory of the parasitic landlord system) (Tokyo: Ochanomizu Shobō, 1957); Araki Moriaki, *Bakuhan taisei shakai no seiritsu to kōzō* (The formation and structure of society within the Bakuhan system) (Tokyo: Ochanomizu Shobō, 1969); Kimura Motoi, *Bakuhan taisei-shi josetsu* (An introduction to the history of the Bakuhan system) (Tokyo: Bungadō Shoten, 1961); Furushima Toshio, *Kisei jinushi-sei no seisei to tenkai* (The emergence and development of parasitic landlordism) (Tokyo: Iwanami Shoten, 1952); and Ueda Tōjirō, *Kinsei no kōsei* (The harsh policies of the Tokugawa period) (Tokyo: Daigadō, 1947).

2. An example that succinctly spells out the gist of the Marxist view of Tokugawa economic history and the role of the zero-sum assumption is Oishi Shinzaburō et al., *Nihon keizaishi-ron* (A study of Japanese economic history) (Tokyo: Ochanomizu Shobō, 1967), pp. 94-98, the section entitled "The Characteristics of the Disintegration of the Peasant Class." For an example of a work that does not explicitly make use of this assumption, but in which the increased use of money by peasants is seen as the cause of their impoverishment and the collapse of Tokugawa feudalism, see Endō Moto'o et al., *Nihon-shi tsūron* (An introductory history of Japan) (Tokyo: Asakura Shoten, 1959), pp. 164-167. So generally held is the zero-sum assumption that Miyamoto Mataji, who has contributed significant empirical studies on Tokugawa economic history outside of the Marxist camp, was driven to say that: "As commerce develops, the merchants perform the role of risk bearers. I believe that [Japanese economic] historians place unwarranted emphasis on the merchant exploitation of peasants. I doubt the validity of arguments based on the belief that in feudal society the principle of trading two equal values is violated." Miyamoto Mataji,

ed., *Kinai nōson no chitsujo to henbō* (The [social] order and transformation of the villages in the Kinai) (Tokyo: Yūhikaku, 1957), p. 8.

3. The term *honbyakushō* can be translated either as "principal peasants" or "basic peasants." The system was first adopted by Toyotomi Hideyoshi in the 1580s and the Bakufu continued it. If a substantial amount of debate concerning the historical significance of the *honbyakushō* system within the Marxist framework of analysis is ignored, it is possible to define the system as one in which landless agricultural laborers or adult dependents of landholders received a small amount of land from a landholding relative or a former employer in exchange for labor services and were made an independent tax-paying unit, which also became an independent farming unit. For a further discussion of the system, see Kozo Yamamura, "A Comparative Analysis of Landholding Systems: Preindustrial England and Tokugawa Japan," a paper presented at the conference "Comparative Uses of the Japanese Experience" held at Cuernavaca, Mexico, September 1974.

4. In Marxist writings, the word "contradiction" (*mujun*) is used frequently and at times loosely. At one level, *mujun* can mean contradictions in the abstract Hegelian sense and at another—in a more economic sense—merely an element or a factor that causes an economic system to collapse because of the inherent nature of the element or the factor to work against the functioning of the system.

5. Nagahara Keiji, ed., *Nihon Keizai-shi* (An economic history of Japan) (Tokyo: Yūhikaku, 1971), p. 113.

6. *Ibid.*, p. 144.

7. See Yamamura, cited in note 3 above, for an economic theoretical analysis of the *honbyakushō* system.

8. Region II obtained cash by selling agricultural, marine, and other nonmanufactured products to Region I. Here, we can compare the trading between Region I and Region II to that between an industrialized economy and an underdeveloped, raw material exporter. As the price of rice, the most important agricultural output, declined vis-à-vis processed and manufactured products during the eighteenth century, it is possible to introduce further analytical refinements by adding a discussion of the changing terms of trade between the two regions. For a discussion of Tokugawa terms of trade, see E. S. Crawcour and Kozo Yamamura, "The Tokugawa Monetary System: 1787-1868," *Economic Development and Cultural Change*, Vol. 18, No. 4, Part 1 (July 1970).

9. As will be shown in Chapters Four through Seven, economic growth also resulted from a shifting of labor out of a low productivity sector into high productivity sectors in conjunction with other growth-promoting factors described in the text.

10. This also means that income remained more in the hands of the part of the population which attempted to save and reinvest rather than in the consuming samurai class.

11. For example, see Hugh T. Patrick, "The Phoenix Risen from the Ashes: Postwar Japan," in James B. Crowley, ed., *Modern East Asia: Essays in Interpretation* (New York: Harcourt, Brace & World, Inc., 1970), especially pp. 301-302 and 328 ff.

12. See Oishi Shinzaburō, *Kyōhō kaikaku no keizai seisaku* (Economic policies of the Kyōhō Reform) (Tokyo: Ochanomizu Shobō, 1961), pp. 9-12, 255-258.

13. As the productivity of labor is a function of capital and technology as well, the marginal product of labor does not necessarily decline when capital is increasing and/or technological change is taking place. Here, the A and M curves are for a given period (comparative static). While the material presented in Chapters Four through Seven will leave little doubt that capital accumulation was taking place during the second half of the Tokugawa period much more visibly than during the first half, our study does not present quantitative evidence demonstrating that the supply of capital was increasing. Readers interested in such quantitative evidence and in discussions on principal methods of capital accumulation as well as various questions relating to financial institutions are referred to Saitō Osamu, *Tokugawa kōki ni okeru rishi ritsu to kahei kyōkū* (Interest rates and the money supply during the latter half of the Tokugawa period), in Umemura Mataji *et al.*, eds., *Nihon keizai no hatten* (The development of the Japanese economy), Vol. 1 of the Sūryō Keizaishi Ronshū (Quantitative economic history series) (Tokyo: Nihon Keizai Shinbunsha, 1976), pp. 281-297; and Yamamura, "A Comparative Analysis of Landholding Systems." Saitō's excellent article, rich in quantitative evidence, shows, for example, that the interest charged to daimyo by the merchant house of Kōnoike declined from 12.45 percent (with a standard deviation of 1.98) for the period 1707-1740 to 8.68 percent (with a standard deviation of 2.39) for the period 1861-1870 (p. 284). Saitō's article contains discussions and evidence of increased savings by the *gōnō*, the declining rate of interest, and the growth of financial institutions, as well as citations of Japanese sources containing direct or indirect evidence on capital accumulation.

14. We are maintaining here that wages corresponded to the value of the marginal product in contrast to the Marxist view whereby the wage level fails to reflect productivity changes because of increasing exploitation.

15. An important cause of the slower rate of growth in income was the slower rate of capital accumulation, an accumulation that was

necessary to increase productivity in both agriculture and the *CM* sector.

16. Richard A. Easterlin, "An Economic Framework for Fertility Analysis," *Studies in Family Planning*, Vol. 6, No. 3 (March 1975), pp. 54-63. Our Figure 2.3 has been adapted from Figure 2 (*f*) on p. 60. A major difference between Easterlin's model and that presented here is that Easterlin is working with "the reproductive career of the 'representative' household."

CHAPTER THREE

1. See the Bibliography for full citations of their major works.

2. Sekiyama concluded his first book on population with a brief section entitled "Kinsei no jinkō kara Meiji no jinkō e" (From the Tokugawa population to the Meiji population), pp. 256-262 of *Kinsei Nihon jinkō no kenkyū* (A study of the population of Tokugawa Japan) (Tokyo: Ryūginsha, 1948). In this section he discussed the problem of the discrepancies between the two surveys opening with the statement:

> The population of the Tokugawa period was, of course, not something that disappeared with the termination of the Tokugawa Bakufu. . . . In spite of the fact that this is extremely clear, respectable scholars as it were understand this as two separate phenomena. (p. 256)

In a private conversation Hanley had with Professor Sekiyama on October 11, 1965, he stated that he believed studies had proceeded as far as they could using the national data, and that further understanding of demographic change in Tokugawa Japan would result only from analysis of local documents.

3. Nomura Kanetarō, *On Cultural Conditions Affecting Population Trends in Japan* (Tokyo: Nihon Gakujitsu Shinkōkai, 1953). This is No. 2 of the Economic Series published in English by the Science Council of Japan, Division of Economics and Commerce. The quotations are from p. 8.

4. Nomura Kenkyūkai, Kōmi Mura Kyōdō Kenkyūhan, "Ogaki hanryō Mino no kuni Motosu no kōri Kōmi mura no koko tōkei" (Population statistics on Kōmi village, Motosu district, Mino province in the domain of Ogaki), *Mita Gakkai Zasshi*, Vol. 53, Nos. 10-11 (1960), pp. 166-208.

5. Some of Hayami's studies will be discussed in Chapter Eleven. See the Bibliography for a list of some of his numerous publications and those cited in this book.

6. Honjō Eijirō, "The Population of Japan in the 'Tokugawa' Era," in *Tokugawa Bakufu no beika chōsetsu* (The control of the rice price by the Tokugawa Bakufu) (Tokyo: Kōbundō Shobō, 1924), p. 12. The intent of this survey is not known. Sekiyama specifically states that "there are no materials now that let us decide the motive in making the first population survey." Sekiyama Naotarō, *Kinsei Nihon no jinkō kōzō* (The population structure of Tokugawa Japan) (Tokyo: Yoshikawa Kōbunkan, 1958), p. 63. However, the advantages to any government of knowing the size and location of its population, particularly in an agrarian-based society, are obvious.

7. Sekiyama Naotarō, "Tokugawa jidai no zenkoku jinkō ni kansuru gimon to kōsatsu" (An examination of and problems concerning the national population of the Tokugawa period), *Shakai Keizai Shigaku*, Vol. 11, Nos. 11-12, p. 172.

8. Honjō, "The Population of Japan in the 'Tokugawa' Era," p. 12.

9. For the result of these enumerations see Sekiyama, *Kinsei Nihon no jinkō kōzō*, pp. 137-139.

10. *Ibid.* The figures quoted on the national population of Japan during the Tokugawa period are all from the data quoted in Sekiyama.

11. *Ibid.*, p. 2. The first century B.C. belongs to Japan's prehistorical period. The "history" of the earliest emperors was first set down centuries later according to Chinese historical traditions and Japanese oral and mythological traditions.

12. The seventh-century surveys were based on households. The records contained the name, age, status, and relationship to head of household of the head, the family, and other persons living in the household. Sekiyama, *Kinsei Nihon no jinkō kōzō*, p. 3.

13. *Ibid.*, p. 5. The information on Hideyoshi's survey is also found here.

14. A discussion and analysis of these records can be found in Hayami Akira, "The Population at the Beginning of the Tokugawa Period," *Keiō Economic Studies*, Vol. 4 (1966-1967); and "Kokura han jinchiku aratame-chō no bunseki to Tokugawa shoki zenkoku jinkō suikei no kokoromi" (An analysis of the investigations of men and animals of Kokura domain and an attempt to estimate the total population of the early Tokugawa period), *Mita Gakkai Zasshi*, Vol. 59, No. 3 (1966).

15. For detailed discussions of the history and contents of the *shūmon-aratame*, see Sekiyama, *Kinsei Nihon no jinkō kōzō*, and Hayami Akira, "Thank You Francisco Xavier: Using the Legacy of Anti-Christian Oppression in Demographic History," a paper presented at the CISS-CSNA Workshop on "The Sources of Asian His-

tory and the Generation of Quantifiable Historical Indicators," held in Toronto, February 28-29, 1976.

16. There is disagreement among scholars as to the difference between these two surveys in the latter half of the Tokugawa period with regard to their reliability and method of registration. This disagreement seems to have arisen in large part because of the numerous differences between method, content, and title, in various regions and locales throughout Japan. Sekiyama, who provides the most detailed discussion of these points, concluded that the two systems and two registers eventually became mixed. *Kinsei Nihon no jinkō kōzō*, p. 33. Hayami concurs with this view in "The Demographic Analysis of a Village in Tokugawa Japan: Kando-shinden of Owari Province, 1778-1871," *Keiō Economic Studies*, Vol. 5 (1968), p. 51. For the various discussions of these points, see Sekiyama, *Kinsei Nihon no jinkō kōzō*, pp. 31-39; Nomura, *On Cultural Conditions Affecting Population Trends in Japan*, pp. 6-8; Honjō, "The Population of Japan in the 'Tokugawa' Era," pp. 21-23; and Hayami Akira, "Tokugawa kōki Owari ichi nōson no jinkō tōkei" (Demographic statistics of one farming village in Owari in the late Tokugawa period), *Mita Gakkai Zasshi*, Vol. 59, No. 1 (1966), pp. 58-62.

17. Honjō, "The Population of Japan in the 'Tokugawa' Era," p. 12.

18. Sekiyama, *Kinsei Nihon no jinkō kōzō*, pp. 33-34.

19. Sekiyama Naotarō, "Wakayama han no jinkō chōsa to jinkō jōtai" (The population surveys and population conditions of Wakayama domain) *Keizai Riron*, Vols. 15-18 (1953), p. 189.

20. See the *shūmon-aratame-chō* for Fujito and Fukiage villages located in Okayama University Library, Okayama, Japan. An analysis of these villages appears in Chapters Eight to Ten.

21. See Honjō, "The Population of Japan in the 'Tokugawa' Era," pp. 32-33; Honjō Eijirō, *Jinkō oyobi jinkō mondai* (Population and population problems) (Tokyo: Nihon Hyōronsha, 1930), pp. 43-46; and Irene B. Taeuber, *The Population of Japan* (Princeton: Princeton University Press, 1958), pp. 20-21.

22. Hayami, "The Population at the Beginning of the Tokugawa Period," pp. 4-6; and Taeuber, *The Population of Japan*, p. 20.

23. For example, the Bakufu provided an adult samurai with 5 *gō* of rice per day, which amounted to 1.8 *koku* per year. Half that amount was usually considered adequate for a woman.

24. The use of the word "rapid" in the context of premodern populations must be qualified. Rapid growth in the twentieth century usually refers to an annual average rate of increase of 2 percent or above. With growth rates so low throughout most of the world prior to the

Industrial Revolution, a population increase averaging even half of 1 percent per year could, in the authors' opinion, be termed rapid if it extended over a considerable period of time, because a 50 percent increase in population within a century was unusual and difficult for most premodern nations to even feed. For a discussion of various population growth rates, see Joseph J. Spengler, "Demographic Factors and Early Modern Economic Development," *Daedalus* (Spring 1968), pp. 433-446.

25. See Hayami, "The Population at the Beginning of the Tokugawa Period" for the first estimates; and Shimbō Hiroshi, Hayami Akira, and Nishikawa Shunsaku, eds., *Sūryō keizaishi nyūmon* (An introduction to quantitative economic history) (Tokyo: Nihon Hyōronsha, 1975), pp. 47-49, for the newer estimates.

26. Sawada's estimate is for the free population, exclusive of slaves. Sawada Gōichi, *Nara-chō jidai minsei keizai no sūteki kenkyū* (A quantitative study of public administration and the economy during the Nara period) (Tokyo: Kashiwa Shobō, 1972 reprint; original 1927), p. 152.

27. Shinmi Kichiji, *Kakyū shizoku no kenkyū* (A study of lower-class samurai) (Tokyo: Maruzen, 1965), pp. 63-64.

28. See Sekiyama, *Kinsei Nihon no jinkō kōzō*, pp. 211-242.

29. The figures are those cited in Sekiyama, *Kinsei Nihon no jinkō kōzō*, p. 139.

30. The difficulties in determining the samurai population and the Kosekiryō (Office of Registry) figures are discussed in Kozo Yamamura, *A Study of Samurai Income and Entrepreneurship* (Cambridge: Harvard University Press, 1974), pp. 119-120. See also Robert K. Sakai, "Feudal Society and Modern Leadership in Satsuma-han," *Journal of Asian Studies*, Vol. 16, No. 3 (1957), pp. 365-366.

31. Sekiyama, *Kinsei Nihon jinkō no kenkyū*, pp. 256-262.

32. Honjō Eijirō, "The Population and Its Problems in the Tokugawa Era," *Bulletin de l'Institut International de Statistique*, Vol. 25, No. 2 (1931), pp. 60-82.

33. Takahashi Bonsen, *Nihon jinkō-shi no kenkyū* (A study on the history of the population of Japan) Vol. 1 (Tokyo: Sanyūsha, 1941), p. 105.

34. Honjō, "The Population of Japan in the 'Tokugawa' Era," p. 12.

35. Katsu Kaishū, "Jinkō oyobi kokudaka no bu" (Section on population and output), *Suijinroku*, Vol. 1 (1890). These statistics were compiled by Kaishū in the late nineteenth century. Because he cites sources for only three of the years for which he has data, Takahashi considers the remaining data unreliable. Takahashi, *Nihon jinkō-shi no kenkyū*, p. 105.

36. Hayami, "The Population at the Beginning of the Tokugawa Period," p. 3.

37. Estimates of the Meiji population include those made by the Naikaku Tōkei-kyoku (Bureau of Statistics, the Cabinet), M. Yasukawa, Y. Morita, K. Asakawa, Y. Okazaki, and H. Ohbuchi.

38. In *Kinsei Nihon no jinkō kōzō*, Sekiyama gives as the reason for the decline in the population of some of the *kuni* the fall in the large urban populations they contained, and thus the reader assumes the urban populations have been included in the data. See the section "Chihō-betsu jinkō no sūsei" (Population trends by region), pp. 136-150. On the other hand, in discussing the population of the cities, it is nowhere made explicit that the city populations are included in the domain populations to which he is comparing them. "Toshi jinkō no gaikan" (A survey of urban populations), pp. 224-239.

39. See the section on cities in Sekiyama, *Kinsei Nihon no jinkō kōzō*. This subject is discussed in English in J. W. Hall, "The Castle Town and Japan's Modern Urbanization," in John W. Hall and Marius B. Jansen, eds., *Studies in the Institutional History of Early Modern Japan* (Princeton: Princeton University Press, 1968), pp. 182-183.

40. Sekiyama, *Kinsei Nihon no jinkō kōzō*, pp. 137-139.

41. Trend lines have been calculated both for the eleven observations from 1721-1872, in which the 1872 data were compiled by a different method of survey and included groups in the population excluded from the Tokugawa surveys, and for the ten observations from 1721 to 1846. A comparison of these results leads to the observations that: (1) The coefficient of determination tends to improve by dropping the 1872 Meiji observation because of discontinuities in the data. (2) For both positive and negative slopes, the absolute value of the slope is smaller without the eleventh observation because there was a significant increase in population in nearly all *kuni* after the Tempō famine, and because of the inclusion in the Meiji data of previously unenumerated population, such as samurai, *rōnin*, and unregistered commoners. Satsuma (No. 66 on Table 3.3), for example, had a slope over twice as steep for the 1721-1872 data as for the 1721-1846 data, partly because of the large proportion of samurai in the population who went unenumerated until 1872, and possibly because of underreporting during the Tokugawa period. However, the slope of both trend lines is positive and significant at the 0.01 level.

For comparative purposes, the 1721-1872 data have been used in this chapter. First, these data are most comparable to the rice output data discussed in the next chapter, for which the final observation is also early Meiji. Second, it is not known how much of the increase between the 1846 and 1872 figures is due to an increase in the population and how much to the inclusion of groups formerly omitted from the surveys. However, except for the qualifications made above, the differences observed in calculated trend lines are such that they do not materially affect the conclusions based on them. It should be noted that eleven of the slopes changed signs, all from positive to negative, when the eleventh observation was dropped. However, six of the results were statistically insignificant in both trend lines, four went from statistically insignificant to significant at the 0.05 level, and one became statistically significant at the 0.10 level when the eleventh observation was omitted. Since the slopes for all these *kuni* were statistically insignificant when the 1872 data is included, no entry was made for them in Figure 3.1 in any case.

42. As all Japanese authors confess, any detailed discussion of these provinces is extremely difficult, for various reasons. To begin with, the population of these cities did not follow national patterns. The population of Osaka rose until 1760 but, because of the development of rural trade that began to reduce Osaka's importance as the major commercial entrepôt of Japan, its population declined after that year. The population pattern of Edo was the opposite of Osaka's. From 1720, the first year for which usable data exist, the population declined from a peak of about 1 million and reached its eighteenth-century low during the Temmei famine, which severely affected the Kanto region. But the population increased steadily after this famine, to a point where the Bakufu had to bring in "back to the village" measures and disperse the samurai quarters to the outskirts of Edo in an attempt to reduce numbers. During the early nineteenth century the major problem facing Edo was the rising level of prices caused by a relatively large demand for all types of goods, inadequate distribution facilities, and the continued debasement of the value of coins.

However, these large cities are known to have had a large number of transients (*mushuku-mono* and *rōnin*) who were not all accounted for in the city records. Because of the lack of precise knowledge of the magnitude of the total economic activities in these cities, and of more reliable population data on which to base estimates of migration into and out of the cities, the effects of epidemics, and changing demographic trends (particularly in the birth and death rates of the urban population), at this stage of the research on historical demography the population changes in these provinces must be left as questions in need of further examination.

For useful literature on Tokugawa urban development see Sekiyama, *Kinsei Nihon no jinkō kōzō*; Toyoda Takeshi, *Nihon no hōken toshi* (Feudal cities of Japan) (Tokyo: Iwanami Shoten, 1952); Hall, "The Castle Town and Japan's Modern Urbanization"; Thomas C. Smith,

"Pre-modern Economic Growth: Japan and the West," *Past and Present*, No. 60 (August 1973), pp. 127-160; and Gilbert Rozman, *Urban Networks in Ch'ing China and Tokugawa Japan* (Princeton: Princeton University Press, 1973).

43. Sekiyama did not specify which date he is talking about, but presumably he meant the latter half of the Tokugawa period. Included in his estimate are samurai, their families, and servants, and the population of post towns and the towns that grew up around temples (*monzen-machi*) as well as the castle towns and the metropolises of Edo, Osaka, and Kyoto. Sekiyama, *Kinsei Nihon no jinkō kōzō*, pp. 238-239. For a discussion of Tokugawa urbanization in English, see Hall, "The Castle Town and Japan's Modern Urbanization," pp. 169-188.

44. Rozman, *Urban Networks*, p. 6.

45. See E. A. Wrigley, *Population and History* (New York: McGraw-Hill Book Company, 1969), pp. 150, 173-174; E. A. Wrigley, "A Simple Model of London's Importance in Changing English Society and Economy 1650-1750," *Past and Present*, No. 34 (1967), p. 44. Wrigley finds that London was not able to maintain its population without a constant influx of migrants because of a "shortfall" of births to deaths. D. V. Glass found that in the nineteenth century, for which we have census statistics for England, male life expectancy at birth for all of England and Wales was 40 in 1841, but for London it was only 35; for Manchester, 25; and Liverpool, 24. D. V. Glass, "Some Indicators between Urban and Rural Mortality in England and Wales and Scotland," *Population Studies*, Vol. 17 (1963-1964), pp. 263-267.

Hayami Akira believes the same was true for Japan, and cites the results of a survey in Edo that was carried out a number of times between 1843 and 1867 showing that 21.7 to 29.5 percent of the population was born elsewhere. Sekiyama, *Kinsei Nihon no jinkō kōzō*, pp. 220-221. Since the population of the city changed almost not at all during this period, it would not have been maintained were it not for this migration. See Hayami Akira, "Tokugawa kōki jinkō hendō no chiiku-teki tokusei" (The regional characteristics of population change in the second half of the Tokugawa period), *Mita Gakkai Zasshi*, Vol. 64, No. 8 (1971), pp. 588-591.

Sasaki Yōichirō, in an analysis of the *shūmon-aratame-chō* for a much smaller city, Takayama in Hida Province (Gifu Prefecture), found that the death rate of 26.2 exceeded the birth rate of 25.5 for the period 1773-1871, but that the population rose from 2,614 to 3,333 during the same period because of an influx of migrants. Sasaki Yōichirō, "Hida-no-kuni Takayama no jinkō kenkyū" (A demographic study of Takayama in Hida Province), *Keizai-shi ni okeru jinkō* (Population in economic history), Proceedings of the 37th meeting of the Shakai Keizai-shi Gakkai (Tokyo: Keiō Tsūshin Kabushiki Kaisha, 1969), pp. 95-117.

46. See Hayami Akira, "Labor Migration in a Preindustrial Society: A Study Tracing the Life Histories of the Inhabitants of a Village," *Keiō Economic Studies*, Vol. 10, No. 2 (1973), pp. 1-17.

47. In our analysis of economic and demographic growth in the Kinai in Chapter Five, we will discuss both the rural and urban population trends in this area.

48. Phyllis Deane and W. A. Cole, *British Economic Growth, 1688-1959* (Cambridge: Cambridge University Press, 1967), pp. 96-97.

CHAPTER FOUR

1. Kikuchi Toshio, *Shinden kaihatsu* (The reclamation of fields) (Tokyo: Shibundō, 1964), pp. 2-3. See also Takayanagi Mitsutoshi, *Toyotomi Hideyoshi no kenchi, 17* (The cadastral survey of Toyotomi Hideyoshi, Vol. 17), Vol. 6 of the series Iwanami kōza Nihon rekishi (Tokyo: Ochanomizu Shobō, 1957); and Miyakawa Mitsuru, *Taikō kenchiron* (A study on Hideyoshi's cadastral survey) (Tokyo: Ochanomizu Shobō, 1957). Conducted between 1582 and 1598, the survey measured the amount of arable land. However, little is known about the productivity of the land; no known records of total output exist. Three others were made but the figures are not extant.

2. Kikuchi Toshio, *Shinden kaihatsu* (The reclamation of fields) Vol. 1 (Tokyo: Kokon Shoin, 1958), p. 137.

3. While Bakufu officials compiled the rice output figures, the village headmen made the necessary adjustments in the area of land under cultivation and reported the figures to the domain and Bakufu officials when changes were made in the standard measures of land in the Jōkyō era (1684-1687). The defined area of the *tan* was 10.25 percent greater in the 1645 survey than in the 1697 survey, but adjustments were made so that the rice output surveys are comparable. See Kikuchi, *Shinden kaihatsu* (1958), Vol. 1, pp. 208-209 for detailed information on adjustments made, and James I. Nakamura, *Agricultural Production and the Economic Development of Japan, 1873-1922* (Princeton: Princeton University Press, 1966), p. 75, for changes in the land measure. Kikuchi, *Shinden kaihatsu* (1964), pp. 125-148, also contains a detailed discussion of these points.

4. The Tokugawa survey data were obtained from Kikuchi, *Shinden kaihatsu* (1958), Vol. 1, p. 137.

5. The Meiji data were obtained from Meiji Zaiseishi Hensankai,

Meiji zaisei-shi (A financial history of the Meiji period), Vol. 5 (Tokyo: Maruzen Shoten, 1905), pp. 361-378.

6. From the *Nihon teikoku tōkei nenkan* as quoted in James I. Nakamura, "Growth of Japanese Agriculture, 1875-1920," in William W. Lockwood, ed., *The State and Economic Enterprise in Japan* (Princeton: Princeton University Press, 1965), p. 249.

7. For a discussion of this controversy and a review of the Nakamura book cited in note 3, see Henry Rosovsky, "Rumbles in the Rice-fields: Professor Nakamura vs. the Official Statistics," *Journal of Asian Studies*, Vol. 27, No. 2 (February 1968), pp. 347-360.

8. In addition to what is cited in the Kikuchi volumes, the major works are: Furushima Toshio, *Nihon nōgyō gijitsu-shi* (A history of Japanese agricultural technology) (Tokyo: Jichōsa, 1949); Matsu-yoshi Sadao, *Shinden no kenkyū* (A study of "new fields") (Tokyo: Yūhikaku, 1926); Kimura Motoi, *Kinsei no shinden mura* (*Shinden* villages of the Tokugawa period) (Tokyo: Yoshikawa Kōbunkan, 1964); and Nōrinshō Nōmukyoku, *Kyūhan jidai no kōchi kakuchō kairyō jigyō ni kansuru chōsa* (A survey on works to expand and improve the cultivated land in the Tokugawa period) (Tokyo: Nōrinshō, 1927). The articles written on this subject have been contributed by a wide spectrum of historians, geographers, and economists.

9. Kimura, *Kinsei no shinden mura*, pp. 5-6.

10. For details, see Vol. 2 of Doboku Gakkai (Civil Engineering Society), ed., *Meiji izen Nihon doboku-shi* (A history of civil engineering before Meiji) (Tokyo: Doboku Gakkai, 1936).

11. Kimura, *Kinsei no shinden mura*, p. 6. The measures have been adjusted so that the *chō* are comparable here. What differed was the survey method.

12. Mori Katsumi and Takeuchi Rizō, eds., *Nihon-shi gaisetsu* (A general history of Japan) (Tokyo: Hanawa Shobō, 1970), p. 190.

13. Endō Moto'o *et al.*, *Nihon-shi tsūron* (An introductory history of Japan) (Tokyo: Asakura Shoten, 1959), p. 165.

14. Rekishigaku Kenkyūkai and Nihon-shi Kenkyūkai, eds., *Kōza Nihon-shi 4: Bakuhan-sei shakai* (Kōza Japanese history, Vol. 4: The Bakuhan society) (Tokyo: Tokyo University Press, 1971), p. 186.

15. See Naitō Jirō, *Honbyakushō taisei no kenkyū* (A study of the *honbyakushō* system) (Tokyo: Ochanomizu Shobō, 1968); Takeyasu Shigeji, *Kinsei Kinai nōgyō no kōzō* (The structure of Kinai agriculture during the Tokugawa period) (Tokyo: Ochanomizu Shobō, 1969); Hayama Teisaku, *Kinsei nōgyō hatten no seisanryoku bunseki* (An analysis of productivity in the development of Tokugawa agriculture) (Tokyo: Ochanomizu Shobō, 1966); Shimbō Hiroshi, *Hōkenteki shō-nōmin no bunkai katei* (The process of the disintegration of the feudal

petty farmer) (Tokyo: Shinseisha, 1967); Sasaki Jun'nosuke, *Bakuhan kenryoku no kiso kōzō* (The basic structure of the Bakuhan authority) (Tokyo: Ochanomizu Shobō, 1964); and numerous articles in Japanese journals. Takeyasu found, in his intensive study of the records of a peasant family in Kōchi province (not included in our case studies in later chapters), that the output per male labor unit increased by 27 percent in the period between 1822/23 and 1865/67. *Kinsei Kinai nōgyō*, pp. 197-203.

16. Thomas C. Smith, "The Land Tax in the Tokugawa Period." The quotation is from p. 293.

17. Naramoto Tatsuya, *Chōnin no jitsuryoku* (The real power of the merchants) (Tokyo: Chūō Kōronsha, 1966), p. 332. This is Vol. 17 of the Chūō Kōron's series, *Nihon no rekishi*.

18. *Ibid.*, pp. 315-316.

19. For evidence on the increasing commercial, manufacturing, and market-oriented agricultural activities during the Tokugawa period, see the following sources, which were used as the basis for evaluating the patterns of economic growth in Japan: Toyoda Takeshi and Kodama Kōta, eds., *Ryūtsū-shi 1* (A history of commerce, Vol. 1), Vol. 13 of Taikei Nihonshi sōsho (Japanese history series) (Tokyo: Yamakawa Shuppansha, 1969); Hayashi Reiko, *Edo tonya nakama no kenkyū* (A study of wholesale guilds in Edo) (Tokyo: Ochanomizu Shobō, 1967); and Honjō Eijirō, ed., *Kinsei no Osaka* (Osaka in the Tokugawa period) (Osaka: Kansai Keizai Dōyūkai, 1959). In English, E. S. Crawcour's "Changes in Japanese Commerce in the Tokugawa Period," in John W. Hall and Marius B. Jansen, eds., *Studies in the Institutional History of Early Modern Japan* (Princeton: Princeton University Press), pp. 189-202 is useful.

20. Kodama Kōta, ed., *Sangyō-shi 2* (A history of industry, Vol. 2), Vol. 11 of Taikei Nihonshi sōsho (Japanese history series) (Tokyo: Yamakawa Shuppansha, 1955); and Toyoda and Kodama, eds., *Ryūtsū-shi*, pp. 132-176. Indicating the degree of development in market networks, Yonezawa *han* in the north suffered an economic recession when some of the *kuni* in the Chūgoku region in western Honshu developed in the eighteenth century a kind of wax superior to that formerly produced on a wide scale in Yonezawa.

21. Yagi Akihiro, *Kinsei no shōhin ryūtsū* (Commerce in Tokugawa Japan) (Tokyo: Hanawa Shobō, 1962), p. 149.

22. For further discussion, see E. S. Crawcour and Kozo Yamamura, "The Tokugawa Monetary System: 1787-1868," *Economic Development and Cultural Change*, Vol. 18, No. 4, Part I (July 1970), pp. 489-518. Also, readers interested in monetary aspects of the Tokugawa economy are referred to the following articles by Shimbō who,

unlike many earlier Japanese authors, made extensive use of data to test explicitly stated hypotheses derived from modern (non-Marxist) economic theory. Shimbō Hiroshi, "Kinsei kōki ni okeru bukka, kin-sōba, kawase uchigin sōba—1787-1867" (Commodity prices, gold prices, and discounts on silver bills during the second half of the Tokugawa period) in Umemura Mataji *et al.*, eds., *Nihon keizai no hatten* (The development of the Japanese economy), Vol. 1 of the Sūryō Keizaishi Ronshū (Quantitative economic history series) (To-kyo: Nihon Keizai Shinbunsha, 1976), pp. 261-279; "Bakumatsu-ki no bukka hendō—1830-67" (Price fluctuations during the Bakumatsu period: 1830-67), *Keizai Kenkyū*, Vol. 26, No. 4 (October, 1975), pp. 289-301; and "Kahei, bukka, chingin" (Money, prices, and wages) in Shimbō Hiroshi, Hayami Akira, and Nishikawa Shunsaku, eds., *Sūryō keizaishi nyūmon* (An introduction to quantitative economic history) (Tokyo: Nihon Hyōronsha, 1975), pp. 169-253.

23. "Most of the servants of the samurai living in the cities and employees of the commercial and manufacturing establishments once had been peasants who were absorbed into the cities." Kodama Kōta, *Kinsei nōmin seikatsu-shi* (A history of the life of peasants in the Tokugawa period) (Tokyo: Yoshikawa Kōbunkan, 1957), pp. 269-270.

24. Harada Toshimaru, "Bakumatsu-ki Gōshū no nōson ni okeru shōhin no seisan to ryūtsū ni kansuru ichi kōsatsu" (A study on the trade and production of commercial goods in the farming villages of Gōshū in the Bakumatsu period), in Miyamoto Mataji, ed., *Shōhin ryūtsū no shiteki kenkyū* (A historical study of commerce) (Kyoto: Minerva Shobō, 1967), p. 49.

25. Thomas C. Smith, "Farm Family By-employments in Preindustrial Japan," *The Journal of Economic History*, Vol. 29, No. 4 (December 1969).

26. *Ibid.*, pp. 694-695.

27. A series of recent articles on the Chōshū economy by Nishikawa Shunsaku and other members of the newly organized study group for quantitative economic history (described in note 12, Chapter One) not only support Smith's findings but add several important new ones. To date (August 1976), the articles published using the source used by Smith, the *Bōchō fudo chushin'an*—a detailed and comprehensive survey of more than 300 villages in the domain of Chōshū—as their principal source for data, include Akimoto Hiroya and Nishikawa Shunsaku, "19-seiki chūyō Bōchō ryōkoku no nōgyō seisan kansū" (Agricultural production functions of Chōshū domain during the mid-nineteenth century), *Keizai Kenkyū*, Vol. 26, No. 4 (October 1975), pp. 302-311; Nishikawa Shunsaku, "1840-nendai Bōchō ryōkoku ni okeru hinō-seisanbutsu sanpin no seisandaka to tōnyū keisū" (Input

coefficients and output of three nonagricultural products in the domain of Chōshū during the 1840s), *Mita Shōgaku Kenkyū*, Vol. 19, No. 1 (April 1976), pp. 1-31; Nishikawa Shunsaku and Ishibe Shōko, "1840-nendai Mitajiri saiban no keizai keisan" (Income accounting of the Mitajiri district in the 1840s), Part 1 of which is in *Mita Gakkai Zasshi*, Vol. 68, No. 9 (September 1975), pp. 17-38, and Part 2 in *Mita Gakkai Zasshi*, Vol. 68, No. 10 (October 1975), pp. 1-26; Akimoto Hiroya, "Bakumatsu-ki Bōchō ryōkoku no seisan to shōhi" (Production and consumption in the domain of Chōshū during the Bakumatsu period), in Umemura *et al.*, eds., *Nihon keizai no hatten*, pp. 137-158; Nishikawa Shunsaku, "Seisan, shōhi to shotoku katoku" (Production, consumption, and income earned), in Shimbō, Hayami, and Nishikawa, eds., *Sūryō keizai nyūmon*, pp. 119-168; and Akimoto Hiroya, "19-seiki chūyō Suō Ōshima saiban no shōhi kansu" (Consumption functions in the Ōshima district of Suō during the mid-nineteenth century), *Mita Gakkai Zasshi*, Vol. 68, Nos. 11-12 (1975), pp. 31-50.

Though it is a brave undertaking, given the analytical complexity of their arguments and the carefully stated qualifications that accompany their findings, if one is to summarize a few of the findings directly relevant to our study, they are: (1) The importance of by-employments in augmenting peasant income, which Smith suggested in his study of the Kaminoseki district, is confirmed in the studies of Akimoto and Akimoto-Nishikawa, who examined most of the districts in the domain. Akimoto's article on Ōshima in the same domain also provides evidence of a high propensity to save. (2) By the 1840s the saving ratio—surplus over disposable income—of the peasant households in the Mitajiri districts (2 towns and 29 villages) was in the neighborhood of 20 percent, according to the two articles by Nishikawa and Isobe. These "conservatively estimated" savings were used by the upper-income class "to improve housing" and by the rest of the peasant class to improve their living standard. (3) The major findings made in Nishikawa's article in *Suryō keizai nyūmon* and in the Akimoto-Nishikawa article are that the estimated value of the marginal product of agricultural labor in the villages located in the plains exceeded, by about 45 percent, that of labor in the mountain villages. Since the estimated value of the marginal product in the latter virtually coincided with the level of income the domain officials then considered a subsistence income, one inference is clearly that the living standard, both for peasants working in villages located in the plains and for most of those living in the mountainous villages where by-employments were readily available, exceeded the subsistence level. Interested readers may note that a special issue, to be published in 1978, on Japanese economic development is planned by *Explorations in Economic History*, and will include a discussion of these articles by Yamamura and an article by Nishikawa on Chōshū *han*.

28. All quotations in this paragraph are from Saga Prefecture, *Saga kenshi* (A history of Saga prefecture) (Saga: Saga Prefecture, 1968), p. 304.

29. Mori Kahei, *Nihon hekichi no shiteki kenkyū* (A historical study of the remote regions in Japan) Vol. 2 (Tokyo: Hōsei University Press, 1970), pp. 953-954.

30. Naramoto, *Chōnin no jitsuryoku*, pp. 310-311.

31. Quoted in Hayami Akira, *Nihon keizai-shi e no shikaku* (A [new] perspective on Japan's economic history) (Tokyo: Tōyō Keizai Shimpōsha, 1968), p. 143.

32. Naramoto, *Chōnin no jitsuryoku*, p. 320.

33. Takenaka Yasukazu and Sakudō Yōtarō, *Nihon keizai-shi* (An economic history of Japan) (Tokyo: Gakubundō, 1972), p. 95.

34. Mori and Takeuchi, eds., *Nihon-shi gaisetsu*, p. 191.

35. Saga Prefecture, *Saga kenshi*, p. 304. Also see Watanabe Norifumi and Sasaki Jun'nosuke, "Shosangyō no gijitsu to rōdō keitai" (Technology and employment structure in several industries) in Asao Naohiro *et al.*, *Nihon rekishi* (A history of Japan), Iwanami Kōza Series, Vol. 11, Kinsei 3 (Tokyo: Iwanami Shoten, 1976), p. 198. In discussing the workers at the salt fields in Aki (modern Hiroshima prefecture) during the early decades of the nineteenth century, the authors describe the difficulties employers faced from workers who "disappear without notice," "change employment frequently," and "no longer pay heed to employers despite the higher wages being paid."

36. *Ibid.*, p. 305; and the first few chapters of Hayami Akira, *Nihon keizai-shi e no shikaku* (A [new] perspective on Japan's economic history) (Tokyo: Keizai Shimpōsha, 1968).

37. Hayami, *Nihon keizai-shi*, p. 165.

38. Smith, "Farm Family By-employments," p. 709.

39. *Ibid.*, p. 713.

40. Hayami, *Nihon keizai-shi*, pp. 165-166. For a good example of data for domains not included in our case studies in later chapters, see Watanabe and Sasaki, "Shosangyō no gijitsu to rōdō keitai," pp. 193-199. The table on p. 196 presents data leaving little doubt that wages of nine categories of workers employed in salt making in Takehara in the province of Aki (Hiroshima) more than doubled between 1726 and 1848. The authors also note that by the beginning of the nineteenth century the economic position of these employees had risen to the point of requiring admonitions for "buying too many goods"

and "dressing in a manner fitting only to those above their status in life" (p. 198).

41. Sano Yōko, "The Changes in Real Wages of Construction Workers in Tokyo, 1830-1894," *Management and Labor Studies*, English series, No. 4, published by the Institute of Management and Labor Studies, Keiō University, January 1963.

42. Kodama, *Kinsei nōmin*, pp. 184-190.

43. Quoted in *ibid.*, p. 185.

44. J. R. McEwan, *The Political Writings of Ogyū Sorai* (Cambridge: Cambridge University Press, 1962), p. 44.

45. See the section on the rises in the living standard in Chapter Seven.

CHAPTER FIVE

1. For the geographical distribution of various administrative units, see Nishioka Toranosuke and Hattori Shisō, eds., *Nihon rekishi chizu* (Historical maps of Japan) (Tokyo: Zenkoku Kyōiku Tosho K.K., 1956), p. 185.

2. Toyoda Takeshi and Kodama Kōta, eds., *Ryūtsū-shi 1* (A history of commerce, Vol. 1), Vol. 13 of Taikei Nihonshi sōsho (Japanese history series) (Tokyo: Yamakawa Shuppansha, 1969), pp. 133-134.

3. Takenaka Yasukazu and Sakudō Yōtarō, eds., *Nihon keizai-shi* (An economic history of Japan) (Tokyo: Gakubunsha, 1972), pp. 60-61.

4. Toyoda and Kodama, eds., *Ryūtsū-shi*, pp. 184, 239; and Kōda Naritomo, *Edo to Osaka* (Edo and Osaka) (Tokyo: Toyamabō, 1934), pp. 26-27.

5. Toyoda and Kodama, eds., *Ryūtsū-shi*, p. 173.

6. E. S. Crawcour, "Changes in Japanese Commerce in the Tokugawa Period," in John W. Hall and Marius B. Jansen, eds., *Studies in the Institutional History of Early Modern Japan* (Princeton: Princeton University Press, 1968), p. 194.

7. Takenaka and Sakudō, eds., *Nihon keizai-shi*, p. 62.

8. *Ibid.*, p. 62.

9. Yagi Akihiro, *Kinsei no shōhin ryūtsū* (Commerce in Tokugawa Japan) (Tokyo: Hanawa Shobō, 1962), pp. 22-26.

10. Hayama Teisaku, *Kinsei nōgyō hatten no seisanryoku bunseki* (An analysis of productivity in the development of Tokugawa agriculture) (Tokyo: Ochanomizu Shobō, 1969), pp. 256-257.

11. For a good summary discussion of the *sake* industry in the Kinai, see Kodama Kōta, ed., *Sangyō-shi 2* (History of industry, Vol.

2), Vol. 11 of Taikei Nihonshi sōsho (Japanese history series) (Tokyo: Yamakawa Shuppansha, 1955), pp. 365-388.

12. Nakabe Yoshiko, "Genroku-Kyōhō-ki ni okeru nōgyō keiei to shōhin ryūtsū" (Agricultural management and commerce during the Genroku-Kyōhō periods), in Kimura Takeo, ed., *Kinsei Osaka heiya no sonraku* (Villages in the Osaka plain in the Tokugawa period) (Kyoto: Minerva Shobō, 1970), p. 24.

13. *Ibid.*, p. 62.

14. Yagi, *Kinsei no shōhin ryūtsū*, p. 31.

15. *Ibid.*, pp. 35-37.

16. Kodama Kōta, *Genroku jidai* (The Genroku period) (Tokyo: Chūō Kōronsha, 1971), p. 268.

17. Shimbō Hiroshi, *Hōken-teki shōnōmin no bunkai katei* (The process of the disintegration of the feudal petty farmer) (Tokyo: Shinseisha, 1967), p. 110.

18. Nakabe, "Genroku-Kyōhō-ki ni okeru nōgyō," p. 38.

19. There exist no reliable estimates for the population of Osaka for the seventeenth century. See Takenaka and Sakudō, eds., *Nihon keizai-shi*, p. 42, which contains estimates of the population of Osaka, Sakai, and Kyoto; and Arai Eiji, *Bakuhan-sei shakai no tenkai katei* (The process of the development of society within the Bakuhan system) (Tokyo: Shinseisha, 1965), p. 318.

20. The best sources from which to judge the degree of the commercialization of agriculture achieved by the end of the Tokugawa period is the *Zenkoku nōsan-hyō* (A table of national agricultural products) compiled by the Meiji Government. According to this data, which Furushima believes show "somewhat less" than the actual figures for the end of the Tokugawa period, commercial crops (excluding rice marketed) accounted for 26 percent of the total agricultural output in the Kinai in contrast to the 15 percent that was the average for all other regions. Cotton and rapeseed alone accounted for 20 percent. The lowest among the five provinces in the Kinai was Yamato with 20 percent, and the highest was Kawachi with 33 percent. The cotton produced in the Kinai accounted for 30 percent of the national total, rapeseed 17 percent, and tea 10 percent. As Furushima noted, the commercialization of agriculture "in the Kinai continued as a trend" and "even accelerated." Furushima Toshio, *Kinsei Nihon nōgyō no tenkai* (The development of Japanese agriculture during the Tokugawa period) (Tokyo: Tokyo University Press, 1968), pp. 293, 296.

21. Kodama, ed., *Sangyō-shi*, p. 79.

22. Hayama, *Kinsei nōgyō hatten*, p. 294.

23. *Ibid.*, p. 298.

24. Takahashi Kamekichi, *Tokugawa hōken keizai no kenkyū* (A

study of the Tokugawa feudal economy) (Tokyo: Senshinsha, 1932), p. 317.

25. Furushima Toshio, *Kinsei Nihon nōgyō no kōzō* (The structure of agriculture in Tokugawa Japan) (Tokyo: Tokyo Daigaku Shuppan-kai, 1967), pp. 284-302; Takahashi, *Tokugawa hōken keizai*, pp. 328-331; and Kodama, ed., *Sangyō-shi*, pp. 85-90.

26. Takahashi, *Tokugawa hōken keizai*, p. 329.

27. Furushima, cited in note 25, contains excellent descriptions of these activities.

28. Takahashi, *Tokugawa hōken keizai*, p. 318.

29. Kodama, ed., *Sangyō-shi*, p. 90.

30. Furushima Toshio, *Kinsei ni okeru shōgyō-teki nōgyō no tenkai* (The development of commercial agriculture in the Tokugawa period) (Tokyo: Nihon Hyōronsha, 1950), p. 56.

31. Takahashi, *Tokugawa hōken keizai*, p. 319.

32. Furushima, *Kinsei Nihon nōgyō no kōzō*, pp. 382-419.

33. All quotations are from Kodama, ed., *Sangyō-shi*, p. 74.

34. Furushima, *Kinsei Nihon nōgyō no kōzō*, p. 314.

35. *Ibid.*, pp. 207-237, 361-377.

36. The well-known Okamoto data are cited in Arai, *Bakuhan-sei shakai*, p. 452. Also see Takeyasu Shigeji, *Kinsei Kinai nōgyō no kōzō* (The structure of Kinai agriculture in the Tokugawa period) (Tokyo: Ochanomizu Shobō, 1969), pp. 141-146.

37. Henry Rosovsky, *Capital Formation in Japan* (Glencoe: The Free Press, 1961), pp. 80-81.

38. Mori Sugio, "Shōhin seisan to nōmin-sō no dōkō" (The production of commercial crops and changes in the peasant class) in Kimura, ed., *Kinsei Osaka heiya*, pp. 195, 199.

39. Furushima Toshio and Nagahara Keiji, *Shōhin seisan to kisei jinushi-sei* (The production of commercial goods and the parasitic landlord system) (Tokyo: Tokyo University Press, 1954), p. 173.

40. Wakita Osamu, "Jinushi-sei no hatten o megutte—Sekka men-saku chitai no ba'ai" (On the development of the landlord system— The case of the cotton-growing areas in Settsu and Kawachi), *Rekishi-gaku Kenkyū*, No. 181 (April 1954), p. 15.

41. Nakabe Yoshiko, "Settsu zaigō-chō no tenkai" (The develop-ment of the Settsu rural towns), in Chihō-shi Kenkyū Kyōgi-kai, ed., *Hōken toshi no shomondai* (Problems of the feudal cities) (Tokyo: Yūzankaku, 1959), pp. 320-321.

42. *Ibid.*, p. 325.

43. For a discussion of the relative size of the *sake* makers in these towns, see Wakita Osamu and Kobayashi Shigeru, *Osaka no seisan to*

361

kōtsu (Production and transportation in Osaka) (Osaka: Mainichi Hōsō, 1973), pp. 381-386.

44. The *sake* data are from *ibid.*, p. 385. Also see Kodama, ed., *Sangyō-shi*, pp. 371-373 for a description of the relative advantage enjoyed by the Nada *sake* producers. A similar development also took place in other industries. In cotton weaving, for example, the size of establishments—even in Izumi, which tended to lag behind Kawachi—was quite large by the beginning of the nineteenth century.

In the weaving industry in Izumi, which grew because of the cotton output of the Kinai region, some organized establishments were in fact manufacturing industries. Already in the Bunka-Bunsei period [1804-1829], some, who once were jobbers, had a large number of weavers under them. In weaving *monhaori*, 20 such weaving masters had 420 households under them to weave the cloth. And by the Tempō period, 40 weaving masters had nearly 1,000 households working for them. It is known that in 1837 one Sawada Matabei in Izumi-Otsu had a workshop containing 80 weaving machines.

Kodama, ed., *Sangyō-shi*, pp. 260-261.

45. Wakita and Kobayashi, *Osaka no seisan to kōtsu*, pp. 403-416; and William B. Hauser, *Economic Institutional Change in Tokugawa Japan* (London: Cambridge University Press, 1974), pp. 86-116.

46. Wakita and Kobayashi, *Osaka no seisan to kōtsu*, p. 374.

47. Nakabe Yoshiko, *Kinsei toshi no seiritsu to kōzō* (The formation and structure of cities during the Tokugawa period) (Tokyo: Shinseisha, 1967), p. 640.

48. Sasaki Yōichiro, "Tokugawa jidai kōki toshi jinkō no kenkyū: Settsu-no-kuni Nishinari-no-kōri Tennōji-mura" (A study on the city population during the late Tokugawa period: Tennōji village in Nishinari district, Settsu province), *Shikai*, Vol. 14 (1967).

49. Tsuda Hideo, *Hōken shakai kaitai katei kenkyū josetsu* (An introduction to a study of the process of the disintegration of a feudal society) (Tokyo: Hanawa Shobō, 1970), pp. 257-305.

50. Matsuura Akira, "Kinsei kōki rōdō idō no ichi keitai—Settsu no kuni Hanakuma-mura no jinkō idō o chūshin to shite" (One form of labor movement in the latter half of the Tokugawa period—with a focus on population movement in the village of Hanakuma in Settsu Province), *Shakai Keizai Shigaku*, Vol. 38, No. 6 (February 1973), pp. 640-664.

51. Quoted in the English summary to Matsuura, "Kinsei kōki rōdō idō no ichi keitai."

52. Saitō Osamu, "Tokugawa kōki kara Taishō zenki ni itaru nōgyō chingin no chōki-teki sūsei" (Long-run trends in agricultural wages

from the late Tokugawa period to the early Taisho period), *Shakai Keizai Shigaku*, Vol. 39, No. 2 (June 1973), pp. 170-189.

53. *Ibid.*, p. 177.

54. Takeyasu, *Kinsei Kinai nōgyō*, pp. 207, 213-214.

55. Yamasaki Ryūzō, "Settsu ni okeru nōgyō rōdō-koyō keitai no hatten" (The development of the patterns of agricultural employment in Settsu), in Rekishigaku Kenkyūkai, ed., *Hōken shakai no hatten* (The development of a feudal society) (Tokyo: Aoki Shoten, 1961), p. 216.

56. Furushima, *Kinsei Nihon nōgyō no tenkai*, p. 382.

57. *Ibid.*, p. 384.

58. Takeyasu Shigeji, *Kinsei kosakuryō no kōzō* (The structure of Tokugawa tenant rents) (Tokyo: Ochanomizu Shobō, 1968).

59. *Ibid.*, p. 8.

60. *Ibid.*, p. 45.

61. *Ibid.*, p. 8.

62. *Ibid.*, p. 47.

63. Takeyasu, in the postscript to his book, accuses unnamed Japanese scholars of the tendency to indulge in "theoretical expositions developed in abstract." *Ibid.*, p. 272.

64. Also see Takeyasu Shigeji, *Kinsei hōken-sei no tochi kōzō* (The structure of land under Tokugawa feudalism) (Tokyo: Ochanomizu Shobō, 1966). For example, on p. 278 of this study, he went as far as to say that the result of his study "presents sufficient evidence with which to reconsider the tendency to emphasize the lowness of the position of tenant cultivators."

65. Takeyasu, *Kinsei kosakuryō*, p. 62.

66. *Ibid.*, p. 118.

67. *Ibid.*, pp. 145-146.

68. Furushima and Nagahara, *Shōhin seisan*, p. 245.

69. See Mizuhara Masataka, "Kinsei ni okeru suiden tantō shūryō" (Paddy yields per *tan* during the Tokugawa period), *Kinsei-shi Kenkyū*, No. 45 (April 1970); and Thomas C. Smith, "The Japanese Village in the Seventeenth Century," in John W. Hall and Marius B. Jansen, eds., *Studies in the Institutional History of Early Modern Japan* (Princeton: Princeton University Press, 1968).

70. Most Japanese scholars closely follow the Marxist analysis in examining the changes in landholding patterns and, even when the relative profitability of various sizes of farming units is discussed, the analyses are not followed through from our point of view because of the ideological commitment to emphasize conflicts of interest existing between landholder and tenant cultivator. A concise summary of Japanese works on changes in the landholding pattern in Tokugawa Japan

is found in Oishi Shinzaburō, "Gōnō to kisei jinushi-sei" (The wealthy peasants and the parasitic landlord system), in Kodama Kōta, ed., *Kinsei-shi handobukku* (A handbook for Tokugawa history) (Tokyo: Kondō Shuppansha, 1972), p. 223. For an extended analysis of the reasons for the changes in the size of the landholding and the farming unit, and for a critique of the Japanese literature, see Kozo Yamamura, "A Comparative Analysis of the Landholding Systems: Preindustrial England and Tokugawa Japan," paper presented at the Social Science Research Council conference on "Comparative Uses of the Japanese Experience" held at Cuernavaca, Mexico, September 1974.

71. Shimbō, *Hōken-teki shōnōmin*, p. 192.

72. Mori, "Shōhin seisan to nōmin-sō," p. 265.

73. Kimura Takeo, "Kinsei chūki ni okeru tochi shoyū no dōkō" (The changes in landholding during the mid-Tokugawa period) in Kimura, ed., *Kinsei Osaka heiya*, pp. 19-20.

74. Takeyasu, *Kinsei Kinai nōgyō*, p. 40. Also see pp. 105-106.

75. Hayama, *Kinsei nōgyō hatten*, pp. 328-330.

76. Arai, *Bakuhan-sei shakai*, pp. 459-460.

77. Nakabe, "Genroku-Kyōhō-ki ni okeru nōgyō," p. 98.

78. Mizuhara, "Kinsei ni okeru suiden tantō shūryō," p. 98.

79. See Nakabe, "Genroku-Kyōhō-ki ni okeru nōgyō," p. 72, for tax rates in the *tenryō*. For changes in the price level during the last century of the Tokugawa period, see E. S. Crawcour and Kozo Yamamura, "The Tokugawa Monetary System: 1787-1868," *Economic Development and Cultural Change*, Vol. 18, No. 4, Part 1 (July 1970), pp. 489-518.

80. Mori, "Shōhin seisan to nōmin-sō," p. 261.

81. Yagi, *Kinsei no shōhin ryūtsū*, pp. 105-125; and Takeyasu, *Kinsei Kinai nōgyō*, p. 229.

82. Yamaguchi Yukio, "Kinsei hōken shakai ni okeru kahei-jidai ikō e no shomondai" (Several problems concerning the change toward the cash payment of land rent in the Tokugawa feudal society) in Kimura, ed., *Kinsei Osaka heiya*, p. 306.

83. Shimbō, *Hōken-teki shōnōmin*, p. 156.

84. Andō Seiichi, *Edo jidai no nōmin* (Farmers in the Edo period) (Tokyo: Shibundō, 1966), pp. 194-195.

85. Tsuda, *Hōken shakai kaitai katei*, p. 293.

86. Furushima, *Kinsei Nihon nōgyō no tenkai*, pp. 358-359.

87. For information on income distribution among the low-ranking samurai, required expenditures, and their living standard, see Kozo Yamamura, *A Study of Samurai Income and Entrepreneurship* (Cambridge: Harvard University Press, 1974), pp. 119-133.

88. *Ibid.*, p. 59.

89. Tamura Eitarō, *Edo jidai chōnin no seikatsu* (The life of merchants during the Edo period) (Tokyo: Yūzankaku, 1966), p. 220.

90. Morimatsu Yoshiaki, Hōgetsu Keigo, and Kimura Motoi, eds., *Seikatsu-shi 2* (A history of life-style, Vol. 2), Vol. 16 of Taikei Nihonshi sōsho (Japanese history series) (Tokyo: Yamakawa Shuppansha, 1969), p. 314. "Seikatsu" cannot be rendered into one English word. It connotes the standard, style, and other economically and socially significant aspects of daily life.

91. *Ibid.*, p. 352.

92. Kitajima Masamoto, *Bakuhan-sei no kumon* (The agonies of the Bakuhan system) (Tokyo: Chūō Kōronsha, 1966), pp. 448-449.

CHAPTER SIX

1. Though there are many books that enlist Morioka *han* as an example *par excellence* of their point of view, the book that expresses the traditional pessimistic views with the fewest qualifications is Takahashi Bonsen, *Nihon jinkō-shi no kenkyū* (A study of the history of the population of Japan), Vol. 3 (Tokyo: Nihon Gakujutsu Shinkōkai, 1962).

2. This refers to Mori Kahei, *Nihon hekichi no shiteki kenkyū* (A historical study of the remote regions of Japan), Vols. 1 and 2 (Tokyo: Hōsei University Press, 1969 and 1970). This 2,650-page study incorporates most of the findings of Mori's life-long study, which were previously published in numerous articles. Except for the first 130 pages on the pre-Tokugawa period, occasional references to neighboring *han*, and some observations on social change, both volumes are devoted to the economic aspects of Morioka *han* and Hachinohe *han* (a branch *han* of Morioka). Perhaps 20 percent of the total space is devoted to citing original sources. Mori also edited the useful fifth volume of Iwate-ken, *Iwate kenshi* (The history of Iwate prefecture) (Morioka: Iwate Prefecture, 1962), which allocated approximately 1,100 pages out of the total 1,590 to economic and demographic aspects of Morioka and Hachinohe *han*. In the following footnotes, Mori's two-volume study will be denoted as MK-1 and MK-2.

3. For a discussion and critical bibliography of some of the most important of these studies, see Susan B. Hanley and Kozo Yamamura, "A Quiet Transformation in Tokugawa Economic History," *Journal of Asian Studies*, Vol. 30, No. 2 (February 1971), pp. 373-384.

4. For a good political history of the domain during the period 1590-1621, see *Iwate kenshi*, Vol. 5, pp. 3-240.

5. *Ibid.*, p. 934.

6. *Ibid.*, pp. 737, 921-930; and Chapter 6, entitled "Nōgyō keiei no kōzō to tenkai" (The development and structure of agricultural management), in MK-1, pp. 665-751. The latter includes detailed discussions of changing irrigation techniques, farm implements, crop rotations, etc., covering the entire Tokugawa period.

7. *Iwate kenshi*, Vol. 5, p. 933.

8. Mori Kahei, *Kyū-Nambu han ni okeru hyakushō ikki no kenkyū* (A study of the peasant uprisings in the former Nambu *han*) (Sendai: Saito Hō'on-kai, 1935), p. 9. This work will be referred to as Mori, *Hyakushō ikki*.

9. *Iwate kenshi*, Vol. 5, p. 1086.

10. *Ibid.*, pp. 1087-1088.

11. *Ibid.*, pp. 1090-1091.

12. *Ibid.*, pp. 1118-1119.

13. Ninohe-gun, *Ninohe gunshi* (A history of the Ninohe district) (Morioka: Ninohe-gun, 1968), p. 375.

14. *Ibid.*, 374; and *Iwate kenshi*, Vol. 5, p. 1056.

15. *Iwate kenshi*, Vol. 5, p. 1138. This page also has a description of the active shipping trade, though no data are provided.

16. Iwamoto Yoshiteru, *Kinsei gyoson kyōdōtai no hensen katei* (The process of the transformation of fishing village communities during the Tokugawa period) (Tokyo: Hanawa Shobō, 1970). During the latter part of the seventeenth century, the trading of the "marine products of this region accelerated from the level of the 1640s, during which a total annual tax of 5,000 *ryō* was paid," (pp. 25, 35). Iwamoto's study is on the fishing villages on the Pacific coast of Morioka *han*.

17. *Iwate kenshi*, Vol. 5, p. 1148. The output of marine products was increasing as a trend, though there were, of course, years in which the harvest was poor.

18. *Ibid.*, pp. 1010-1011.

19. *Ibid.*, pp. 1021-1039.

20. MK-2, p. 106 on salt; and *Iwate kenshi*, Vol. 5, pp. 1106-1116 on lead. The latter gives the output of and taxes paid on several (presumably the largest) lead mines for sixteen years between 1667 and 1684. Though there were fluctuations in output (thus on the tax paid, which was one-tenth of the value of sales), the data clearly indicate a rapid increase in output during even this short period.

21. We believe that this observation for the seventeenth century would be acceptable to most Japanese economic historians, even if applied to this region.

22. *Iwate kenshi*, Vol. 5, pp. 715-716, 725-726. These data are based on the calculations made by the authors of the prefectural history from data contained in domain and local records.

23. MK-1, p. 267.

24. *Iwate kenshi*, Vol. 5, p. 724 for an estimate of a tax burden of 50 percent. Also see pp. 716-730 for related discussions.

25. *Ibid.*, p. 549.

26. Watanabe Nobuo, *Bakuhan-sei kakuritsu-ki no shōhin ryūtsū* (Commodity flows during the period of the formation of the Bakuhan system) (Tokyo: Kashiwa Shobō, 1966), p. 113.

27. *Iwate kenshi*, Vol. 5, p. 1218.

28. *Ibid.*, p. 730.

29. *Ibid.*, p. 733.

30. *Ibid.*, pp. 716, 733.

31. The savings, called *moyohi*, amounted to at least 1,000 *ryō* per year. *Ibid.*, p. 731. If we assume that the economizing daimyo took with him 300 samurai (about one-tenth of all retainers during this time) and that each of them spent, on the average, 25 *ryō*, the total expenditure would amount to 7,500 *ryō*. Since it is well known that by the beginning of the nineteenth century many daimyo spent a sum equal to all of their income on the *sankin kōtai* and many samurai undoubtedly spent more than 25 *ryō*, the data in this paragraph should be considered only a "guesstimated" minima of these expenditures.

32. A total taxable yield of 230,000 *koku* for the mid-seventeenth century could be expected to contribute about the same value in cash, if we use the convention that 1 *koku* equals 1 *ryō*. Though the total value contributed by all other economic activites (nonrice agricultural output, commerce, and manufacturing) is next to impossible to estimate, the best "guesstimate" we can make on the strength of tax records, descriptive evidence, and educated guesses is that it was more than that contributed by rice and even in excess of 300,000 *ryō*. Given fluctuations in prices and harvests and the incomplete descriptions of some economic activities, the estimate is offered only as a very crude approximation.

33. As will be noted in the text, a continuing increase in the need for cash to meet the costs of the *sankin kōtai* also became a part of the reason for the domain's policies restricting commerce.

34. Mori, *Hyakushō ikki*, p. 20.

35. *Iwate kenshi*, Vol. 5, p. 938.

36. For the price of rice in Osaka see Kozo Yamamura, *A Study of Samurai Income and Entrepreneurship* (Cambridge: Harvard University Press, 1974), pp. 49-53.

37. Mori, *Hyakushō ikki*, pp. 21-27.

38. *Iwate kenshi*, Vol. 5, pp. 1033-1044; and MK-1, pp. 482-483.

39. *Iwate kenshi*, Vol. 5, p. 1129. For an excellent description of the growth of the iron-mining industry, see MK-2, pp. 285-316.

40. MK-1, p. 369.

41. MK-2, p. 283.

42. *Ibid.*, pp. 460-467, 607-608.

43. *Ibid.*, pp. 622, 629.

44. *Ibid.*, pp. 608, 721.

45. *Ibid.*, p. 603.

46. *Ibid.*, pp. 603-604.

47. *Ibid.*, p. 603.

48. About a dozen large mines together were known to have employed around 15,000 persons, and many others from 300 to 500 persons. Among the eighty to ninety mines in operation, the average number of employees, judged from output, must have been around 300. Even on the strength of these observations alone, the total number of persons in the iron industry must have been about 50,000. Though productivity of labor rose, the total output also increased, that is, a net reduction in labor was unlikely. We must also add at least a few thousand more persons who were employed in the lead-mining operations to obtain a total for the mining industry as a whole. If we assume that the total population of the domain at the end of the Tokugawa period was in the neighborhood of 350,000, the 50,000-plus figure comes to a little over 14 percent. It is highly unlikely that this high a percentage of the total population was employed in the mining industry but, even if the estimates are adjusted downward radically, a considerable proportion of the gainfully employed must have been in mining. And when we adjust employment estimates for mining, we thereby raise productivity figures. For scattered data on employment in the mining industries, see MK-2, pp. 552-604.

49. Otsuchi-chō (The town of Otsuchi), *Otsuchi chōshi* (A history of the town of Otsuchi) (Morioka: Otsuchi-chō, 1966), p. 844.

50. *Iwate kenshi*, Vol. 5, p. 1149.

51. Iwamoto, *Kinsei gyoson kyōdōtai*, p. 186.

52. *Iwate kenshi*, Vol. 5, p. 1151.

53. MK-2, p. 29; and *Otsuchi chōshi*, p. 973.

54. MK-2, p. 71.

55. *Otsuchi chōshi*, p. 980.

56. *Iwate kenshi*, Vol. 5, pp. 1155, 1030.

57. *Ibid.*, p. 1161.

58. *Ibid.*, pp. 1011-1015.

59. MK-1, p. 1113.

60. *Iwate kenshi*, Vol. 5, p. 1064.

61. *Ninohe gunshi*, pp. 337-338.

62. *Ibid.*, p. 376.

63. MK-1, p. 376.

64. *Ibid.*, p. 212.

65. *Ibid.*, p. 374.

66. *Ibid.*, p. 954.

67. *Ibid.*, pp. 950, 960.

68. When the domain government collected the tax by means of *unjō-kin* (thank money) imposed on a lump-sum basis, because of the difficulties involved in enforcing its tax rule (10 percent of sales value), the effective tax rate declined, although the total volume of sales continued to rise. *Iwate kenshi*, Vol. 5, pp. 733, 1151-1155.

69. MK-1, p. 961.

70. *Ibid.*, p. 968.

71. Watanabe, pp. 189, 343; and *Iwate kenshi*, Vol. 5, pp. 890-891.

72. Mori, *Hyakushō ikki*, p. 61.

73. *Ibid.*, p. 61.

74. *Ibid.*, p. 34.

75. *Ibid.*, p. 63.

76. Mori Kahei, *Konohe chihō-shi* (A local history of Konohe) (Tokyo: Hōsei University Press, 1969), pp. 333-350.

77. Mori, *Hyakushō ikki*, p. 98.

78. *Ibid.*, pp. 38-39.

79. Iwamoto, *Kinsei gyoson kyōdōtai*, pp. 120-121.

80. Mori, *Hyakushō ikki*, p. 36.

81. *Ibid.*, p. 39.

82. *Ibid.*, pp. 214-215.

83. *Ibid.*, p. 97.

84. *Iwate kenshi*, Vol. 5, pp. 795-796. As many as 1,000 samurai were dispatched to Hokkaido.

85. Mori, *Hyakushō ikki*, pp. 118-119.

86. *Iwate kenshi*, Vol. 5, pp. 324, 329.

87. Mori, *Hyakushō ikki*, p. 117.

88. *Ibid.*, p. 118.

89. Mori, *Konohe chihō-shi*, p. 316.

90. Mori, *Hyakushō ikki*, pp. 331-333.

91. Though both *Iwate kenshi* and MK-2 also contain good descriptions of these rebellions, the best source is Mori, *Hyakushō ikki*, pp. 213-301. A bibliography of historical sources and articles on these rebellions is found on p. 300.

92. *Ibid.*, p. 194.

93. All of the demands are listed in *ibid.*, pp. 245-255.

94. *Ibid.*, p. 234.

95. *Ibid.*, pp. 335-336.

96. *Ibid.*, p. 67.

97. Mori chose to state his conclusion in the following words:

In a closed society, if one depends solely on agriculture, it is not possible to cope with harvest failures. In order to cope, economic activities must include trade that is not limited by the domain borders. The exploited and oppressed peasants realized this, and they continued to expand their commercial activities so that they would not be at the mercy of nature. What stood in the way of such an effort for an expansion of commerce was the power of the domain. To destroy this impediment, the peasants united to cause the two largest peasant rebellions in Japan.

Mori, *Konohe chihō-shi*, p. 995.

98. *Iwate kenshi*, Vol. 5, p. 676.

99. Takahashi, *Nihon jinkō-shi*, Vol. 3, p. 125.

100. *Ibid.*, p. 149.

101. *Iwate kenshi*, Vol. 5, p. 675.

102. *Ibid.*, pp. 676, 712.

103. *Ibid.*, p. 707.

104. MK-1, p. 978. The diary is extensively quoted on pp. 976-977.

105. The official data contain the number of births and deaths by sex, and the amount of out- and in-migration by sex. No description is available of the method by which these data were collected. See Takahashi, *Nihon jinkō-shi*, Vol. 3, a table appended to Part I.

106. See Chapters Three and Eight to Eleven of this book.

107. Takahashi Bonsen, *Datai mabiki no kenkyū* (A study on abortion and infanticide) (Tokyo: Chūō Shakai Jigyō Kyōkai Shakai Jigyō Kenkyūjo, 1936).

108. Population figures for the castle town and three other towns in Morioka can be found in *Iwate kenshi*, Vol. 5, pp. 689-692.

109. Sekiyama Naotarō, *Kinsei Nihon no jinkō kōzō* (The population structure of Tokugawa Japan) (Tokyo: Yoshikawa Kōbunkan, 1958), p. 138.

110. Mori, *Konohe chihō-shi*, p. 995.

111. *Ibid.*, p. 929.

112. *Ibid.*, pp. 965-966.

113. Mori, *Konohe chihō-shi*, p. 508.

114. *Iwate kenshi*, Vol. 5, pp. 787-789.

115. Refer back to Chapter Five.

116. Mori, *Konohe chihō-shi*, pp. 523-524.

117. *Ibid.*, p. 524.

118. *Iwate kenshi*, Vol. 5, p. 660.

119. Mori, *Konohe chihō-shi*, p. 768.

120. MK-1, pp. 524, 536-540, 572.

121. *Ibid.*, p. 540.

122. *Ibid.*, p. 519.

123. *Iwate kenshi*, Vol. 5, pp. 787-789.

124. Watanabe Nobuo, "Murakata jinushi no seiritsu to sono kōzō"

(The formation and structure of village landholders), *Kiyō* (of Tohoku University), Vol. 2 (March 1960), p. 79.

125. MK-1, p. 817.

126. *Ibid.*, p. 856.

127. Mori, *Konohe chihō-shi*, pp. 857-858.

128. Mori, *Hyakushō ikki*, p. 119.

129. Mori, *Konohe chihō-shi*, p. 497.

130. *Iwate kenshi*, Vol. 5, p. 998.

131. Mori, *Konohe chihō-shi*, p. 544.

132. *Ibid.*, 551.

133. *Ibid.*, p. 843.

CHAPTER SEVEN

1. For histories of this domain see John W. Hall, *Government and Local Power in Japan, 500-1700. A Study Based on Bizen Province* (Princeton: Princeton University Press, 1966); Taniguchi Sumio, *Okayama han* (The domain of Okayama) (Tokyo: Yoshikawa Kōbunkan, 1964); and Taniguchi Sumio, *Okayama hansei-shi no kenkyū* (A study of the history of the administration of Okayama domain) (Tokyo: Hanawa Shobō, 1964).

2. Hall, *Government and Local Power*, p. 403.

3. In 1853 there were sixteen daimyo whose fiefs were assessed by the Bakufu at over 300,000 *koku*, which was a reflection of their position vis-à-vis the Bakufu, although by that date the official assessment usually was not a true indicator of the actual yield or income of the domain. See Toshio G. Tsukahira, *Feudal Control in Tokugawa Japan. The Sankin Kōtai System* (Cambridge: East Asian Research Center, Harvard University, 1966), pp. 140-173.

4. Taniguchi, *Okayama han*, p. 172.

5. See Taniguchi, *Okayama hansei-shi no kenkyū*, Part 2, Chapter 4, pp. 392-420, for a discussion of reclamation and water control projects.

6. Okayama Shiyakusho, *Okayama shishi* (A history of Okayama City), *Sangyō keizai hen* (Volume on industry and the economy) (Okayama: Okayama Shiyakusho, 1966), p. 109, and Mihashi Tokio, "Kinsei zenki no nōgyō" (Agriculture in the first half of the Tokugawa period), in Kodama Kōta, ed., *Sangyō-shi* (A history of industry), Vol. 2 (Tokyo: Yamakawa Shuppansha, 1955), p. 46.

7. *Okayama shishi*, p. 98; Furushima Toshio, *Kinsei Nihon nōgyo no kōzō* (The structure of Japanese agriculture during the Tokugawa period) (Tokyo: Tokyo Daigaku Shuppankai, 1967), pp. 313-314.

8. *Okayama shishi*, p. 98.

9. While Taniguchi emphasizes the accelerated production of cot-

ton and cotton goods during the late Tokugawa period from the 1830s on, Andō commented that the output of cotton must have been considerable as early as 1708, the year the first cotton guild was formed. Tawa also stressed the importance of this industry in the early part of the period. While there was undoubtedly a tremendous spurt in production in the Bakumatsu period, cotton was certainly an important product of this domain much earlier. See Taniguchi, *Okayama hansei-shi no kenkyū*, pp. 631ff; Andō Seiichi, *Kinsei zaikata shōgyō no kenkyū* (A study on rural commerce in the Tokugawa period) (Tokyo: Yoshikawa Kōbunkan, 1958), p. 192; and Tawa Kazuhiko, *Kojima sangyō-shi no kenkyū* (A study on the history of commerce in Kojima) (Kyoto: Kojima no Rekishi Kankōkai, 1959), p. 162.

10. Taniguchi, *Okayama hansei-shi no kenkyū*, p. 173.

11. *Ibid.*, p. 174.

12. *Ibid.*

13. See Edwin L. Neville, Jr., "The Development of Transportation in Japan: A Case Study of Okayama *Han*, 1600-1868" (unpublished Ph.D. dissertation, University of Michigan, 1959), especially pp. 49, 56-57.

14. Okayama-ken, *Okayama-ken no rekishi* (A history of Okayama Prefecture) (Okayama: Okayama-ken, 1962), p. 414. This is a list for the years 1661-1672.

15. *Ibid.*

16. Taniguchi, *Okayama hansei-shi no kenkyū*, p. 174.

17. Taniguchi, *Okayama han*, p. 107.

18. Taniguchi, *Okayama hansei-shi no kenkyū*, p. 472.

19. *Okayama shishi*, p. 232.

20. *Okayama-ken no rekishi*, p. 358.

21. *Ibid.*, p. 372.

22. Tawa, *Kojima sangyō-shi*, p. 135.

23. *Hōreishū*, Section 12, "Chihō fushin" (Local repairs), in the possession of the Okayama University Library, Okayama.

24. Mihashi Tokio, "Kinsei kōki no nōgyō" (Agriculture in the second half of the Tokugawa period), in Kodama, ed., *Sangyō-shi*, Vol. 2, pp. 81-82.

25. *Hōreishū*, Section 1, "Denchi no bu" (Section on rice paddies).

26. *Okayama shishi*, pp. 262-263. And in the villages of Fujino and Shakusho in Wake, cotton took 30-50 percent of the land during the second half of the eighteenth century. *Okayama-ken no rekishi*, p. 371.

27. *Okayama-ken no rekishi*, p. 392.

28. *Okayama shishi*, p. 263.

29. Ono Masao, "Okayama-han ni okeru Kokura orimono no ryūtsū keitai—Kaei-Ansei-ki o chūshin to shite" (The form of the trade in Kokura-ori in the domain of Okayama, with a focus on the Kaei

and Ansei periods), in Hōgetsu Keigo Sensei Kanreki Kinenkai, ed., *Nihon shakai keizai-shi kenkyū, Kinsei hen* (Studies on the social and economic history of Japan, Volume on the Tokugawa period) (Tokyo: Yoshikawa Kōbunkan, 1967), p. 442.

30. Ōta Ken'ichi, "Bakumatsu-ki Okayama-han no men senbai-sei" (The cotton monopoly system in the domain of Okayama during the Bakumatsu period), *Shigaku Zasshi*, Vol. 70, No. 7 (July 1961), p. 63.

31. Tawa, *Kojima sangyō-shi*, p. 168.

32. *Okayama shishi*, pp. 265-266.

33. Tawa, *Kojima sangyō-shi*, pp. 58-65, 99-101. The growth of the industry from the beginning of the eighteenth century is described, with quantitative data on the number of salt fields by size and of the large "salt pots" used to boil sea water, in Shibata Hajime, "Bizen Kojima ni okeru shinkai enden no keiei keitai" (The management of newly opened salt fields in Kojima, Bizen), *Okayama Shigaku*, No. 5 (November 1959), pp. 33-51.

34. *Okayama-ken no rekishi*, p. 371; and Matsuo Keiko, "Bakumatsu-Meiji chūki ni okeru igyō no tenkai katei" (The development of the *igusa* [rush] industry from the Bakumatsu to mid-Meiji period), *Okayama Shigaku*, No. 9 (July 1961), pp. 54-73.

35. *Okayama-ken no rekishi*, p. 379.

36. *Okayama shishi*, p. 267.

37. Tawa, *Kojima sangyō-shi*, pp. 131-133.

38. *Ibid.*, p. 186.

39. Ono, "Okayama-han ni okeru Kokura orimono," p. 461.

40. Taniguchi, *Okayama han*, p. 249.

41. Taniguchi, who cites all fifteen figures available, sees a fall in population in the nineteenth century to around 340,000, but his 1834 figure of 346,866 does not include the urban population, and we do not know how the post-Restoration figure of 341,235 for 1869 was obtained. Taniguchi also starts from a lower figure: 250,096 for 1655, but it is unlikely that the population of the domain grew by 22.3 percent in the decade between 1655 and 1665. The 1655 source is Mitsumasa's diary, and again we do not know how it was calculated. See Taniguchi, *Okayama hansei-shi no kenkyū*, p. 458.

42. The data on migration and employment for these three villages are presented in tabular form in Susan B. Hanley, "Migration and Economic Change in Okayama during the Tokugawa Period," *Keiō Economic Studies*, Vol. 10, No. 2 (1973), pp. 19-35.

43. All descriptions contained here are from the *Tempō nendo kikin jōkyō torishirabe-chō* (Report on the famine conditions in the Tempō period), compiled by the Okayama District Administration in 1888 and located in the Kurashiki Municipal Library, Kurashiki, Okayama. The description of the consequences of the Tempō famine in

Okayama sounds remarkably like Louis Simond's contemporary description of Switzerland during the famine of 1816-1817: "Many distressed people are dead, if not absolutely of hunger, yet of the consequences. After supporting for some time a miserable existence, on scarcely any thing but boiled nettles and other herbs, their organs became impaired, and when too late assisted by better food, they could not digest it; their extremities swelled, and they perished in a few days." Quoted on p. 29 of John D. Post, "Famine, Mortality, and Epidemic Disease in the Process of Modernization," *Economic History Review*, Second Series, Vol. 29, No. 1 (February 1976). Thus, one can conclude that Japan's inability to avoid harsh incidences of poor harvests and crop failure was a problem shared by Europe even in the nineteenth century.

44. Ōta Ken'ichi and Matsuo Keiko, "Bakumatsu-Meiji shoki ni okeru jinushi-sei no tenkai—Okayama-han Kojima-no-kōri Hikasa-ke o chūshin to shite" (The development of the landlord system in the Bakumatsu and early Meiji periods—with a focus on the Hikasa house of the Kojima district in the domain of Okayama), *Okayama Shigaku*, Nos. 7-6 (June 1960), p. 53.

45. These figures compiled from the *Nengumai sanyō-chō* of Fujitomura are graphically shown in Ota and Matsuo, "Bakumatsu-Meiji shoki ni okeru jinushi-sei," p. 63. The authors of the *Okayama-ken no rekishi* stated: "That such large landholders as the Hikasa could increase their economic power was due to the fact that the land tax (*nengu*) did not rise *pari passu* with agricultural productivity. This meant that the land tax was low and the tenants worked efficiently on their tenant farms." p. 374.

46. Naitō Jirō, *Honbyakushō taisei no kenkyū* (A study of the honbyakushō system) (Tokyo: Ochanomizu Shobō, 1968).

47. Taniguchi, *Okayama han*, p. 244.

48. Setonaikai Sōgō Kenkyūkai, Okayama University, ed., *Sanson no seikatsu—Okayama-ken Tomata-gun Tōmi-mura-Ō* (Life in a mountain village—Tōmi-mura-Ō of the district of Tomata in Okayama Prefecture), No. 3 of the Sonraku sōgō chōsa hōkoku series (Okayama: Setonaikai Sōgō Kenkyūkai, 1955), p. 46.

49. Naitō, *Honbyakushō*, p. 154.

50. *Ibid.*, p. 147.

51. Taniguchi, *Okayama han*, p. 238.

52. Naitō, *Honbyakushō*, p. 148.

53. Tamano Shiyakusho, *Tamano shishi* (The history of Tamano City) (Okayama: Tamano Shiyakusho, 1960), p. 370.

54. *Okayama-ken no rekishi*, p. 330.

55. Naitō, *Honbyakushō*, p. 168.

56. *Ibid.*, pp. 134, 143-145.

57. *Ibid.*, p. 128.

58. See Ōta and Matsuo, "Bakumatsu-Meiji shoki ni okeru jinushi-sei."

59. *Okayama shishi*, p. 220.

60. *Ibid.*, pp. 219-220.

61. Kozo Yamamura, *A Study of Samurai Income and Entrepreneurship* (Cambridge: Harvard University Press, 1974), pp. 54-60.

62. *Okayama-ken no rekishi*, p. 383.

63. The relative prices of copper to silver over time are to be found in E. S. Crawcour and Kozo Yamamura, "The Tokugawa Monetary System, 1787-1868," *Economic Development and Cultural Change*, Vol. 18, No. 4, Part 1 (July 1970).

64. *Okayama shishi*, p. 149.

65. Yamamura, *A Study of Samurai*, p. 125. More than 1,500 out of nearly 3,500 samurai received less than this between 1840 and 1844.

66. *Okayama shishi*, p. 263. *Okayama ken no rekishi* cites the same example, adding that "during the nineteenth century, the [supply of] agricultural laborers was depleted and only by paying high wages could *hōkōnin* be employed." p. 345.

67. *Okayama-ken no rekishi*, p. 348.

68. *Okayama shishi*, p. 157.

69. Naitō, *Honbyakushō*, p. 120.

70. *Ibid.*

71. *Ibid.*, p. 121. Note that the real yield listed here for Numa is 2.1 *koku*. Instead of using his own estimate of 2.2 *koku* per *tan*, here Naitō used the output recorded in the records of the leading family.

72. Nagayama Usaburō, *Kurashiki shishi* (A history of Kurashiki City) (Kurashiki: Kurashiki Shishi Kankō Iinkai, 1963), pp. 127-134.

73. *Okayama-ken no rekishi*, p. 374.

74. Taniguchi, *Okayama han*, pp. 144-145.

75. Taniguchi, *Okayama hansei-shi no kenkyū*, pp. 335-336.

76. *Ibid.*, pp. 145-147.

77. Andō, *Kinsei zaikata shōgyō no kenkyū*, pp. 125-128.

78. *Ibid.*

79. *Okayama shishi*, pp. 164-165.

80. *Ibid.*

81. Taniguchi, *Okayama hansei-shi no kenkyū*, p. 531.

82. This list of items comes from Andō, *Kinsei zaikata shōgyō no kenkyū*, p. 95 and has been translated into English in E. Sydney Crawcour, "The Tokugawa Heritage," in William W. Lockwood, ed., *The State and Economic Enterprise in Japan* (Princeton: Princeton University Press, 1965), p. 41.

83. *Okayama-ken no rekishi*, pp. 392-395.
84. Andō, *Kinsei zaikata shōgyō no kenkyū*, pp. 95, 125.
85. *Okayama-ken no rekishi*, p. 392.

CHAPTER EIGHT

1. See Chapter Three for further discussion of these documents.

2. For documentation and examples of superstitions, see Yoshiko Ikeda, "Parental Attitude Toward Twins in Japan," in Takie Sugiyama Lebra and William P. Lebra, eds., *Japanese Culture and Behavior: Selected Readings* (Honolulu: The University Press of Hawaii, 1974), pp. 313-322; and Edward Norbeck, *Changing Japan* (New York: Holt, Rinehart, and Winston, 1965), p. 28. In one family in Fujito one twin was kept and the other given for adoption, a practice similar to the postwar custom of having grandparents or other relatives rear one twin.

3. See Susan B. Hanley, "Migration and Economic Change in Okayama During the Tokugawa Period," *Keiō Economic Studies*, Vol. 10, No. 2 (1973), Table 3, pp. 32-33.

4. The Chi-square test was made on the registration of births by day of month. The expected number of births to be recorded each day of the month was 20.8, that is, the daily mean. The null hypothesis that births were evenly distributed by day was rejected at the 0.01 level. The Chi-square test was next made on the number of births by day, smoothed out by the use of moving averages of the third order to eliminate some of the obvious clustering in the reporting resulting from avoidance of unlucky numbers and the usual human failing of thinking in terms of fives and tens. Even with the smoothing, the large number of births on the fifth, fifteenth, and last day of the month, made it necessary to reject the null hypothesis that births were randomly distributed.

5. If two years are subtracted, then women who were born in the first month of the year and married in the last would be nearly two years older at marriage than the age reported here.

6. For example, a man who spent several weeks at a temple in Fujito was listed on the *shūmon-aratame-chō*, but visits by family members—brides for example—to parents or relatives were not recorded.

7. Births to and deaths of persons included in the population at the beginning of the year have been included in the analysis here. Births to and deaths of persons temporarily employed in the village under analysis were theoretically excluded, but in fact none were reported. The reason can be attributed primarily to the fact that most temporary in-migrants were single adults in the age groups with the lowest mor-

tality rates. If a temporary out-migrant died and it was so recorded, he was listed as a death. Many of the persons who dropped out of the registers were listed as employed outside the village in the last register in which they appeared. Most probably became permanent out-migrants but without official permission to do so, which would explain the lack of information. Some may have died, however, which is why the estimated death rates in Table 8.7 were calculated in three ways.

8. Most contracts in the villages studied were for one year, starting on the fifth day of the first month and terminating on the twentieth day of the twelfth month. Even employees on long-term contracts usually went home for the New Year's holidays, and nearly all eventually returned to their home villages. Persons working in the village on a permanent basis were listed under different categories from contract laborers, and the very few who were found were included in the permanent population.

9. See Chapters Nine and Eleven for a discussion of the average interval between births in sample villages.

10. Ansley J. Coale and Paul Demeny, *Regional Model Life Tables and Stable Populations* (Princeton: Princeton University Press, 1966).

11. This number was so small as to be statistically insignificant with the exception of young women who left to marry, the majority of whom were in their early 20s. These women were balanced by an almost equal number of women who married into the village but, since they would not be counted for this analysis if they came in during the five-year period, there is a bias present in that these age groups of females with low death rates are undercounted here.

12. The method used is described in United Nations, Department of Economic and Social Affairs, *Manual IV: Methods of Estimating Basic Demographic Measures from Incomplete Data* (New York: United Nations, 1967). The "West" model life tables were selected because Japan was one of the "Western" countries whose data fit these life tables.

13. Another method for testing birth rates for Tokugawa villages may become possible in the future, depending on the availability of the records. This is through the use of the *kainin kakiage-chō* (record of pregnancies), which purport to record all pregnancies and their outcome, whether spontaneous abortion, stillbirth, live birth, or live birth but subsequent death during early infancy. Kitō Hiroshi has analyzed the *kainin kakiage-chō* for two villages in the northern Kanto region for the 21-year period 1851-1871. According to these records, of a total of 239 pregnancies, 1.9 percent ended in spontaneous abortion, 16.4 percent in stillbirths, and 7.4 percent in death during an undetermined period after birth. Since less than 75 percent of the

pregnancies resulted in live births, Kitō argues that the Tokugawa birth rates calculated from the *shūmon-aratame-chō* should be revised upward by 20 to 30 percent. However, since the usual percentage of stillbirths is considered to be 2 or 3 percent, it could be argued that most of the stillbirths reported were in fact infanticide. Since the recording of pregnancies was initiated by the domain in order to prevent infanticide, we believe it is more reasonable to presume that the unrealistically high rate of stillbirths in fact included illegal infanticide. If this presumption is correct, the 7.4 percent death rate plus a 3 percent stillbirth rate would necessitate revising upward the birth rate by only 10 percent, or 2 to 3 per thousand for a crude birth rate of just over 20. Because of the difficulties inherent in interpreting these records, and because this small sample comes from a different part of Japan, a region with different demographic and economic characteristics from our samples, we have not attempted to make use of these records in our analysis. For Kitō's analysis, see Kitō Hiroshi, "Kainin kakiage-chō ni miru shussan to shibō—Bakumatsu-Meiji shotō no kita Kantō ni okeru jirei" (Births and deaths as seen in the records of pregnancy—an example from the northern Kanto during the late Tokugawa and early Meiji periods), *Mita Keizaigaku Kenkyū*, No. 6 (September 1972), pp. 8-17.

CHAPTER NINE

1. Irene B. Taeuber, *The Population of Japan* (Princeton: Princeton University Press, 1958), p. 33.

2. See Kozo Yamamura, *A Study of Samurai Income and Entrepreneurship* (Cambridge: Harvard University Press, 1974), pp. 79-83.

3. For a discussion of "ancestor worship" and the care of tablets for the dead, see Robert J. Smith, "*Ihai*: Mortuary Tablets, the Household and Kin in Japanese Ancestor Worship," *Transactions of the Asiatic Society of Japan*, 3rd Series, Vol. 9 (May 1966); and Robert J. Smith, *Ancestor Worship in Contemporary Japan* (Stanford: Stanford University Press, 1974), pp. 164 ff.

4. Takahashi Bonsen, *Datai mabiki no kenkyū* (A study on abortion and infanticide) (Tokyo: Chūō Shakai Jigyō Kyōkai Shakai Jigyō Kenkyūjo, 1936), pp. 121-122.

5. Various methods of abortion are vividly described in *ibid.*, pp. 27-31; and in Ōta Tenrei, *Datai kinshi to yūsei hogo-hō* (The prohibition of abortion and the Eugenic Protection Law) (Tokyo: Keieisha Kagaku Kyōkai, 1967), pp. 71 ff. The 1692 publication was a book by Kazuki Gyūzan entitled *Fujin jusō* (literally, Women's happy plant),

referring to a plant that made women happy by preventing children they did not want.

6. Ōta gives the Latin names for *goshitsu* as *Achyranthes japonica Nakai* and *Achyranthes bidentata Bivar. japonica Mig. Datai kinshi,* p. 99.

7. *Ibid.,* pp. 83 ff. Kagawa's work referred to is *Sanka hiyō okujitsuben* (Notes on the true secrets of gynecology).

8. Honjō Eijirō, *Jinkō oyobi jinkō mondai* (Population and population problems), Tokyo: Nihon Hyōronsha, 1930), p. 116.

9. *Kōjiruien,* Hogibu 12, Ijutsu 3, pp. 882-883.

10. Nishijima Minoru, *Edo jidai no sei seikatsu* (Sex life in the Edo period) (Tokyo: Yūzankaku, 1969), pp. 241-242.

11. Takahashi, *Datai Kinshi,* pp. 100, 102.

12. Cited in Takahashi, *Datai mabiki no kenkyū,* p. 15.

13. It is possible that there was more *mabiki* (infanticide) than would show up in a statistical test for sex bias. Robert Y. Eng and Thomas C. Smith, "Peasant Families and Population Control in Eighteenth-Century Japan," *Journal of Interdisciplinary History,* Vol. 6, No. 3 (Winter 1976), suggest that infanticide may have been done selectively to obtain a balance of boys and girls. It is possible that the villagers in our samples were similarly balancing the sex ratios in their families but, given the preference for boys shown statistically and the child-bearing pattern in our sample, there seems to be no way to statistically support this hypothesis for Fujito, the village in our sample for which the most data exist. For example, for the cohort group of women married between 1825 and 1841, the sex composition of their children is as follows:

| | | | | Sex of Last Child Different from All Others | |
| | Sex Composition | | | | |
No. of Children	All Girls	All Boys	Both Before Last Birth	Last Boy	Last Girl
1	5	7			
2	2	1	1	0	0
3	3	4	8	1	1
4	2	2	14	1	2
5	0	0	13	1	1
6	0	0	8	0	0

It should also be noted that there seems to be little evidence that births were restricted in the Hinoeuma year of the sixty-year calendar cycle, a year considered extremely unlucky for girls born during it. Neither does there seem to be evidence of sex-selective infanticide during these years. However, the small size of the samples in most of the villages precludes statistical testing. For example, in Nishikata, which was affected by the Temmei famine, after several years in which boys predominated in births and two years in which no girls were born, in 1786 there were three boys born and seven girls. Statistics compiled by Suda Keizō for a population numbering 2,500 to 2,900 during the late Tokugawa period also show no evidence of either hiding the births of girls by having them registered the year before or after birth, or of infanticide. In fact, according to Suda, the first year for which there is any evidence of people acting on this superstition is in 1966. See Suda Keizō, *Hida O. jiin kakochō no kenkyū* (A study of the death records of *O.* temple in Hida) (Takayama: privately published, 1973), pp. 76 ff. (The author uses the designation of the English letter *O* in order to protect the privacy of everyone connected with these records.)

14. Rose E. Frisch, "Demographic Implications of the Biological Determinants of Female Fecundity," *Social Biology*, Vol. 22 (Spring 1975), p. 19. The quotations in this and the following paragraph are all from pp. 19-20.

15. For a discussion of the effectiveness of raising the age of marriage for women in controlling fertility, see J. William Leasure, "Malthus, Marriage and Multiplication," *The Milbank Memorial Fund Quarterly*, Part 1, Vol. 16, No. 4 (October 1963), pp. 419-435.

16. See Dan Fenno Henderson, " 'Contracts' in Tokugawa Villages," *The Journal of Japanese Studies*, Vol. 1, No. 1 (Autumn 1974).

17. For discussions of regulations on movement, see Taniguchi Sumio, *Okayama hansei-shi no kenkyū* (A study on the history of the administration of Okayama domain) (Tokyo: Hanawa Shobō, 1964), pp. 635 ff.; and Edwin L. Neville, Jr., "The Development of Transportation in Japan: A Case Study of Okayama *Han*, 1600-1868" (unpublished Ph.D. dissertation, University of Michigan, 1959), pp. 94-102.

18. See the discussion on village migration in Chapter Seven.

19. Hayami Akira, "Shūmon-aratame-chō o tsūjite mita Shinshū Yokouchi-mura no chōki jinkō tōkei (Long-term demographic statistics on Yokouchi village of Shinshū seen through religious investigation registers), *Management and Labor Studies Series No. 202* (Tokyo: Keiō Gijuku Daigaku Sangyō Kenkyūjo, 1967-1968).

20. See Joseph J. Spengler, "Demographic Factors and Early Modern Economic Development," *Daedalus* (Spring 1968), pp. 441-444. In contrast to the Japanese and modern industrial pattern, the countries of Africa, Asia, and Latin America today have percentages well below 60.

21. Kodama Kōta, *Kinsei nōmin seikatsu-shi* (A history of the life of peasants in the Tokugawa period) (Tokyo: Yoshikawa Kōbunkan, 1957), p. 227.

22. *Ibid.*, pp. 227-228.

23. For discussions in English of status and how it was determined, see Thomas C. Smith, *The Agrarian Origins of Modern Japan* (Stanford: Stanford University Press, 1959), Chapter 5; and Harumi Befu, "Duty, Reward, Sanction, and Power: Four-cornered Office of the Tokugawa Village Headman," in Bernard S. Silberman and Harry D. Harootunian, eds., *Modern Japanese Leadership: Transition and Change* (Tucson: University of Arizona Press, 1966), pp. 25-50.

24. Kodama, *Kinsei nōmin*, pp. 226-227.

25. Robert J. Smith, "The Japanese Rural Community: Norms, Sanctions, and Ostracism," *American Anthropologist*, Vol. 63, No. 3 (1961), p. 523. Smith's example of the village submitting grain requisitioned by the government for two widows comes from the 1950s, and thus it could be argued that it would not be applicable. But by the twentieth century the village cohesiveness was breaking down, and it is far more likely that such examples would have been common in the Tokugawa period.

26. Iwamoto Yoshiteru, *Kinsei gyoson kyōdōtai no hensen katei* (The process of the transformation of fishing village communities during the Tokugawa period) (Tokyo: Hanawa Shobō, 1970), pp. 201, 204.

27. Ōtake Hikeo, *Hōken shakai no nōmin kazoku* (Farm families in a feudal society) (Tokyo: Sōbunsha, 1962), pp. 63-73.

28. R. P. Dore, *Land Reform in Japan* (London: Oxford University Press, 1959), p. 206.

29. *Ibid.*

30. Sekiyama Naotarō, *Kinsei Nihon no jinkō kōzō* (The population structure of Tokugawa Japan) (Tokyo: Yoshikawa Kōbunkan, 1958), p. 301.

31. Information on social pressures against having large families can be found in Tsuge Takeshi, "Nōson mondai no ichi to shite no mabiki ni tsuite [sic]" (Concerning infanticide as one of the problems of farming villages), *Keizai-shi Kenkyū*, Vol. 15, No. 2 (February 1936).

CHAPTER TEN

1. The history of Fujito was published in 1955 and, despite crucial gaps in information, it is very useful for understanding both the history of this village and its surrounding area. See Fujito Chōshi Henshū

Iinkai, ed., *Fujito chōshi* (The history of the town of Fujito) (Okayama: Fujito Chōshi Henshū Iinkai, 1955).

2. See Ōta Ken'ichi and Matsuo Keiko, "Bakumatsu-Meiji shoki ni
okeru jinushi-sei no tenkai—Okayama-han Kojima-no-kōri Hikasa-ke
o chūshin to shite" (The development of the landlord system in the
Bakumatsu and early Meiji periods—with a focus on the Hikasa
house of the Kojima district in the domain of Okayama), *Okayama
Shigaku*, Nos. 6-7 (June 1960), p. 76.

3. The records maintained by the Hikasa family have been donated
to the Okayama University Library. The family no longer lives in
Fujito, and the family home, too large to be maintained by any but the
very wealthy, has fallen into disrepair and is now used only occasionally by vagrants. The size, location, and architecture of the various
buildings give ample testimony to the wealth of this family and the
leading role it played in the history of Fujito-mura.

4. *Fujito chōshi*, p. 127.

5. The *Nengumai toritate sanyō-chō* (Records for the collection of
the rice tax) available for the years 1804, 1809, 1828, 1851, 1857, and
1863. These records also provide a breakdown of the landholdings of
individuals within the village in units of *koku*. The Hikasa house records are also available. These records are all in the Okayama University Library in Okayama.

6. From the entries on Fujito-mura in the *Kojima gunson mura
meisai-chō*, collected and copied by Nagayama Usaburō and now located in the Kurashiki Municipal Library, Kurashiki, Japan.

7. *Fujito chōshi*, pp. 120-121. The percentage is an estimate as no
data were provided.

8. Okayama Shiyakusho, *Okayama shishi* (A history of Okayama
City), *Sangyō keizai hen* (Volume on industry and the economy)
(Okayama: Okayama Shiyakusho, 1966), p. 286.

9. Ono Takeo, *Nihon kinsei kikinshi* (A history of Japanese famines
in the Tokugawa period) (Tokyo: Gakugeisha, 1935), p. 460.

10. *Ibid.*, p. 454.

11. From the *shūmon-aratame-chō* and *nengumai toritate sanyō-chō*
of Fujito comes the information that a branch family was established
by the adopted son of Sukeuemon, only 3 years younger than he. The
adopted son's holdings amounted to 15.5 *koku*, testifying to the wealth
of the Hikasa family.

The Hikasa managed to limit its main line to direct descendants and
inheritors of the headship by establishing branch households for younger sons and their families whenever they did not send them out to be
adopted. The forming of branch lines is documented in Ōta and Matsuo, "Bakumatsu-Meiji shoki ni okeru jinushi-sei no tenkai," p. 58.

12. *Shōya* was the term usually used for *nanushi* west of Owari.

However, after the early Tokugawa years, the headman of Fujito was known as *nanushi*. The equivalent of 1 *koku* is 4.96 bushels. The measuring system is on a decimal basis, so that 10 *to* equal 1 *koku*, 10 *shō* equal 1 *to*, and 10 *gō* equal 1 *shō*.

13. *Hangashira* was an official position in the village administration. The principal duties of this office were to verify the accuracy of village reports and be responsible for the contents of them. The titles of the three types of village office after 1689 were *nanushi*, *kumigashira*, and *hangashira*.

14. For the coefficients of variation for changes in family size over time by household in Fujito, see Table 15 in Susan B. Hanley, "The Influence of Economic and Social Variables on Marriage and Fertility in Eighteenth and Nineteenth Century Japanese Villages," in Ronald Lee *et al.*, eds., *Population Patterns in the Past* (New York: Academic Press, 1977).

15. At least one adoption in the village took place solely for the purpose of transferring property. One household head adopted during the Tempō period an entire family, and a year after the adoption moved out of the village, leaving his house and property to the adopted family.

16. A discussion of diseases prevalent in the Tokugawa period can be found in Fujikawa Yū, *Nihon Shitsubyō-shi* (A history of epidemic diseases in Japan) (Tokyo: Heibonsha, 1969), pp. 54-59, and a list of diseases categorized by their symptoms is in *ibid.*, pp. 294-296.

CHAPTER ELEVEN

1. Sasaki Yōichirō, "Hida-no-kuni Takayama no jinkō kenkyū" (A demographic study of Takayama in Hida Province), *Keizai-shi ni okeru jinkō* (Population in economic history), Proceedings of the 37th meeting of the Shakai Keizai-shi Gakkai (Tokyo: Keiō Tsūshin Kabushiki Kaisha, 1969), p. 113.

2. *Ibid.*, pp. 113-114.

3. The information on this village comes from Hayami Akira, "Shū-mon-aratame-chō o tsūjite mita Shinshū Yokouchi mura no chōki jinkō tōkei" (Long-term demographic statistics on Yokouchi village of Shin-shū seen through religious investigation registers) *Management and Labor Study Series No. 202* (Tokyo: Keiō Gijuku Daigaku Sangyō Kenkyūjo, 1967-1968); Hayami Akira and Yasumoto Minoru, "Jinkō-shi kenkyū ni okeru Family Reconstitution" (Family reconstitution in studies on demographic history), *Shakai Keizai Shigaku*, Vol. 34, No. 2 (1968); both the above are also included in Hayami Akira, *Kinsei nōson no rekishi jinkōgakuteki kenkyū* (A historical demographical study of Tokugawa villages) (Tokyo: Tōyō Keizai Shimpōsha, 1973).

4. English summary of Hayami, "Shūmon-aratame-chō o tsūjite mita Shinshū Yokouchi mura no chōki jinkō tōkei."

5. The information on Kando-shinden comes from Hayami Akira: "The Demographic Analysis of a Village in Tokugawa Japan: Kando-shinden of Owari Province, 1778-1871," *Keiō Economic Studies*, Vol. 5 (1968); "Tokugawa kōki Owari ichi nōson no jinkō tōkei" (Demographic statistics of one farming village in Owari in the late Tokugawa period), *Mita Gakkai Zasshi*, Vol. 59, No. 1 (1966); and "Tokugawa kōki Owari ichi nōson no jinkō tōkei zokuhen" (A sequel to the above article), *Management and Labor Studies Series No. 213* (Tokyo: Keiō Gijuku Daigaku Sangyō Kenkyūjo, 1967-1968).

6. Hayami, "The Demographic Analysis," p. 56.

7. The information on Nishijō was drawn from Hayami Akira, "Labor Migration in a Preindustrial Society: A Study Tracing the Life Histories of the Inhabitants of a Village," *Keiō Economic Studies*, Vol. 10, No. 2 (1973); and Hayami Akira and Uchida Nobuko, "Kinsei nōmin no kōdō tsuiseki chōsa" (A survey tracing the behavior of Tokugawa farmers), *Kenkyū Kiyō* (Tokyo: Tokugawa Rinsei-shi Kenkyūjo, 1971).

8. Copies of the *shūmon-aratame-chō* for Shimoyuda were supplied to the authors of this book by Professor Iwamoto Yoshiteru of Yamagata University, and were analyzed by the same methods used for the sample villages in Chapter Eight.

9. The information on the Suwa Region presented in the chapter was all taken from Hayami, *Kinsei nōson no rekishi jinkōgakuteki kenkyū*.

10. Hayami, "Labor Migration in a Preindustrial Society," p. 17.

11. See note 1.

12. Robert Y. Eng and Thomas C. Smith, "Peasant Families and Population Control in Eighteenth-Century Japan," *Journal of Interdisciplinary History*, Vol. 6, No. 3 (Winter 1976), pp. 417-445.

13. Hayami Akira, "Kishū Owashi-gumi no jinkō sūsei" (Population trends in Owashi villages of Kishū), *Kenkyū Kiyō* (Tokyo: Tokugawa Rinseishi Kenkyūjo, 1969), Vol. 62, No. 3.

14. U.S. Bureau of the Census, *World Population: 1973, Recent Demographic Estimates for the Countries and Regions of the World* (Washington, D.C.: U.S. Department of Commerce).

15. Joseph J. Spengler, "Demographic Factors and Early Modern Economic Development," *Daedalus* (Spring 1968), p. 441.

16. *Ibid.*, p. 443.

17. *Ibid.*, p. 440.

18. United Nations, Department of Economic and Social Affairs, *The Aging of Populations and Its Economic and Social Implications* (New York: United Nations, 1956), p. 54.

19. E. A. Wrigley, *Population and History* (New York: McGraw-Hill Book Company, 1969), p. 90.

20. There has been a series of articles dealing with infanticide in the new journal *History of Childhood Quarterly: The Journal of Psychohistory* edited by Lloyd deMause, the first issue of which appeared in the summer of 1973. deMause also discusses this subject in his *The History of Childhood* (New York: The Psychohistory Press, 1974). William L. Langer has also worked on this topic and his most widely read article is undoubtedly "Checks on Population Growth: 1750-1850," *Scientific American*, Vol. 226, No. 2 (February 1972).

21. John F. Embree, *Suye Mura: A Japanese Village* (Chicago: The University of Chicago Press, 1939), pp. 182-183. See also Yanagita Kunio, *About Our Ancestors: The Japanese Family System*, trans. Fanny Hagin Mayer and Ishiwara Yasuyo (Tokyo: Japan Society for the Promotion of Science, 1970), especially pp. 172 ff.

22. Allen C. Kelley and Jeffrey G. Williamson, "Writing History Backwards: Meiji Japan Revisited," *The Journal of Economic History*, Vol. 31, No. 4 (December 1971), p. 750. Italics are Kelley and Williamson's.

23. *Ibid.*, p. 774.

CHAPTER TWELVE

1. E. P. Thompson, *The Making of the English Working Class* (Middlesex: Penguin Books, Ltd., 1963), p. 231.

2. Allen C. Kelley and Jeffrey G. Williamson, "Writing History Backwards: Meiji Japan Revisited," *The Journal of Economic History*, Vol. 31, No. 4 (December 1971), pp. 729-776.

3. For example, with regard to China, Mark Elvin writes:

Broadly speaking, it seems likely that technological change in late traditional China was a stabilizing factor. As population grew and pressure on resources became sharper, it helped to keep output per person from sinking or sinking too rapidly. A lesser or a greater measure of change would probably have provoked a social and political crisis. This conclusion, if it is correct, is a significant one, for it helps to explain both the immobility and the resilience of the last few centuries of the empire.

Mark Elvin, "Skills and Resources in Late Traditional China" in Dwight H. Perkins, ed., *China's Modern Economy in Historical Perspective* (Stanford: Stanford University Press, 1975), pp. 112-113.

4. This figure was calculated by aggregating the figures of Suo, Nagato, Ōsumi, Satsuma, Tosa, and Hizen, and thus is weighted by the size of the *kuni* population. We calculated the increase from 1721 to 1846 in order to use figures compiled by the same methods.

BIBLIOGRAPHY

Akimoto Hiroya, "19-seiki chūyō Suō Ōshima saiban no shōhi kansu" (Consumption functions in the Ōshima district of Suō during the mid-nineteenth century), *Mita Gakkai Zasshi*, Vol. 68, Nos. 11-12 (1975).

Akimoto Hiroya and Nishikawa Shunsaku, "19-seiki chūyō Bōchō ryōkoku no nōgyō seisan kansū" (Agricultural production functions of Chōshū domain during the mid-nineteenth century), *Keizai Kenkyū*, Vol. 26, No. 4 (October 1975).

Andō Seiichi, *Edo jidai no nōmin* (Farmers in the Edo period) (Tokyo: Shibundō, 1966).

———, *Kinsei zaikata shōgyō no kenkyū* (A study on rural commerce in the Tokugawa period) (Tokyo: Yoshikawa Kōbunkan, 1958).

Arai Eiji, *Bakuhan-sei shakai no tenkai katei* (The process of the development of society within the Bakuhan system) (Tokyo: Shinseisha, 1965).

Arakawa Hidetoshi, *Kikin no rekishi* (A history of famines) (Tokyo: Shibundō, 1967).

———, *Kinsei kishō saigaishi* (A history of natural disasters in the Tokugawa period) (Tokyo: Chijin Shokan, 1963).

Araki Moriaki, *Bakuhan taisei shakai no seiritsu to kōzō* (The formation and structure of society within the Bakuhan system) (Tokyo: Ochanomizu Shobō, 1969).

Richard K. Beardsley *et al.*, *Village Japan* (Chicago: University of Chicago Press, 1959).

W. G. Beasley, "Feudal Revenue in Japan at the Time of the Meiji Restoration," *The Journal of Asian Studies*, Vol. 19, No. 3 (1960).

Harumi Befu, "Duty, Reward, Sanction, and Power: Four-cornered Office of the Tokugawa Village Headman," in Bernard S. Silberman and Harry D. Harootunian, eds., *Modern Japanese Leadership: Transition and Change* (Tucson: University of Arizona Press, 1966).

Ansley J. Coale and Paul Demeny, *Regional Model Life Tables and Stable Populations* (Princeton: Princeton University Press, 1966).

E. S. Crawcour, "Changes in Japanese Commerce in the Tokugawa Period," in John W. Hall and Marius B. Jansen, eds., *Studies in the Institutional History of Early Modern Japan* (Princeton: Princeton University Press, 1968).

———, "The Tokugawa Heritage," in William W. Lockwood, ed., *The*

State and Economic Enterprise in Japan (Princeton: Princeton University Press, 1965).

E. S. Crawcour and Kozo Yamamura, "The Tokugawa Monetary System: 1787-1868," *Economic Development and Cultural Change*, Vol. 18, No. 4, Part 1 (July 1970).

Phyllis Deane and W. A. Cole, *British Economic Growth, 1688-1959* (Cambridge: Cambridge University Press, 1967).

Doboku Gakkai (Civil Engineering Society), ed., *Meiji izen Nihon doboku-shi* (A history of civil engineering before Meiji), Vol. 2 (Tokyo: Doboku Gakkai, 1936).

R. P. Dore, *Land Reform in Japan* (London: Oxford University Press, 1959).

Michael Drake, ed., *Population in Industrialization* (London: Methuen & Co., Ltd., 1969).

Garrett Droppers, "The Population of Japan in the Tokugawa Period," *Transactions of the Asiatic Society of Japan*, Vol. 22, Part 2 (1894).

Cora A. Dubois, "Socio-Cultural Aspects of Population Growth," in Roy O. Greep, ed., *Human Fertility and Population Problems* (Cambridge: Schenkman Publishing Company, Inc., 1963).

Richard A. Easterlin, "An Economic Framework for Fertility Analysis," *Studies in Family Planning*, Vol. 6, No. 3 (March 1975).

Endo Moto'o *et al.*, *Nihon-shi tsūron* (An introductory history of Japan) (Tokyo: Asakura Shoten, 1959).

Robert Y. Eng and Thomas C. Smith, "Peasant Families and Population Control in Eighteenth-Century Japan," *Journal of Interdisciplinary History*, Vol. 6, No. 3 (Winter 1976).

Rose E. Frisch, "Demographic Implications of the Biological Determinants of Female Fecundity," *Social Biology*, Vol. 22 (Spring 1975).

Fujikawa Yū, *Nihon Shitsubyō-shi* (A history of epidemic diseases in Japan) (Tokyo: Heibonsha 1969).

Fujito Chōshi Henshū Iinkai, ed., *Fujito chōshi* (A history of the town of Fujito) (Okayama: Fujito Chōshi Henshū Iinkai, 1955).

Furushima Toshio, *Kinsei Nihon nōgyō no tenkai* (The development of Japanese agriculture during the Tokugawa period) (Tokyo: Tokyo University Press, 1968).

———, *Kinsei Nihon nōgyō no kōzō* (The structure of Japanese agriculture during the Tokugawa period) (Tokyo: Tokyo Daigaku Shuppankai, 1967).

———, *Kinsei ni okeru shōgyō-teki nōgyō no tenkai* (The development of commercial agriculture in the Tokugawa period) (Tokyo: Nihon Hyōronsha, 1950).

———, *Kisei jinushi-sei no seisei to tenkai* (The emergence and development of parasitic landlordism) (Tokyo: Iwanami Shoten, 1952).

——, *Nihon nōgyō gijitsu-shi* (A history of Japanese agricultural technology) (Tokyo: Jichōsa, 1949).

Furushima Toshio and Nagahara Keiji, *Shōhin seisan to kisei jinushi-sei* (The production of commercial goods and the parasitic landlord system) (Tokyo: Tokyo University Press, 1954).

E. Gautier and L. Henry, *La population de Crulai, paroisse normande* (Paris: Presses Universitaires de France, 1958).

Paul Gebhard *et al.*, *Pregnancy, Birth and Abortion* (New York: John Wiley & Sons, Inc., 1958).

D. V. Glass, "Some Indicators between Urban and Rural Morality in England and Wales and Scotland," *Population Studies*, Vol. 17 (1963-1964).

D. V. Glass and D. E. C. Eversley, eds., *Population in History* (London: Edward Arnold, Ltd., 1965).

D. V. Glass and Roger Revelle, eds., *Population and Social Change* (London: Edward Arnold, 1972).

John W. Hall, "The Castle Town and Japan's Modern Urbanization," in John W. Hall and Marius B. Jansen, eds., *Studies in the Institutional History of Early Modern Japan* (Princeton: Princeton University Press, 1968).

——, *Government and Local Power in Japan, 500-1700: A Study Based on Bizen Province* (Princeton: Princeton University Press, 1966).

Susan B. Hanley, "Migration and Economic Change in Okayama during the Tokugawa Period," *Keiō Economic Studies*, Vol. 10, No. 2 (1973).

——, "Population Trends and Economic Development in Tokugawa Japan" (unpublished Ph.D. dissertation, Yale University, 1971).

Susan B. Hanley and Kozo Yamamura, "A Quiet Transformation in Tokugawa Economic History," *Journal of Asian Studies*, Vol. 30, No. 2 (February 1971).

Harada Toshimaru, *Shōhin ryūtsū no shiteki kenkyū* (A historical study of commerce) (Kyoto: Minerva, 1967).

William B. Hauser, *Economic Institutional Change in Tokugawa Japan* (London: Cambridge University Press, 1974).

Hayama Teisaku, *Kinsei nōgyō hatten no seisanryoku bunseki* (An analysis of productivity in the development of Tokugawa agriculture) (Tokyo: Ochanomizu Shobō, 1969).

Hayami Akira, "The Demographic Analysis of a Village in Tokugawa Japan: Kando-shinden of Owari Province, 1778-1871," *Keiō Economic Studies*, Vol. 5 (1968).

Hayami Akira, "Kinsei nōmin no kōdō tsuiseki chōsa," *Kenkyū Kiyō* (Tokyo: Tokugawa Rinseishi Kenkyūjo, 1971).

———, *Kinsei nōson no rekishi jinkōgakuteki kenkyū* (A historical demographical study of Tokugawa villages) (Tokyo: Tōyō Keizai Shimpōsha, 1973).

———, "Kinsei Okujima no jinkō kōzō" (The population composition of Okujima during the Tokugawa period), *Kenkyū Kiyō* (Tokyo: Tokugawa Rinseishi Kenkyūjo, 1967).

———, "Kinsei Shinshū Suwa chihō no jinkō susei" (Population trends in the Suwa region of Shinano Province during the Tokugawa period), *Management and Labor Studies Series No. 220* (Tokyo: Keiō Gijuku Daigaku Sangyō Kenkyūjo, 1967-1968).

———, "Kinsei Suwa chihō ni okeru setai kibo no jinkōshi-gaku kenkyū (A demographical-historical study of household size in the Suwa region during the Tokugawa period), *Mita Gakkai Zasshi* (Tokyo: Keiō University), Vol. 62, Nos. 10-11 (1969).

———, "Kishū Owashi-gumi no jinkō sūsei" (Population trends in Owashi villages of Kishū), *Kenkyū Kiyō* (Tokyo: Tokugawa Rinseishi Kenkyūjo, 1969), Vol. 62, No. 3.

———, "Kokura han jinchiku aratame-chō no bunseki to Tokugawa shoki zenkoku jinkō suikei no kokoromi" (An analysis of the investigations of men and animals of Kokura domain and an attempt to estimate the total population of the early Tokugawa period), *Mita Gakkai Zasshi*, Vol. 59, No. 3 (1966).

———, "Labor Migration in a Preindustrial Society: A Study Tracing the Life Histories of the Inhabitants of a Village," *Keiō Economic Studies*, Vol. 10, No. 2 (1973).

———, *Nihon keizai-shi e no shikaku* (A [new] perspective on Japan's economic history) (Tokyo: Tōyō Keizai Shimpōsha, 1968).

———, "Nōbi chihō jinkō-shi kenkyū joron" (An introduction to research on the demographic history of the Nōbi region), *Kenkyū Kiyō* (Tokyo: Tokugawa Rinseishi Kenkyūjo, 1969).

———, "The Population at the Beginning of the Tokugawa Period," *Keiō Economic Studies*, Vol. 4 (1966-1967).

———, "Shūmon-aratame-chō o tsūjite mita Shinshū Yokouchi-mura no chōki jinkō tōkei" (Long-term demographic statistics on Yokouchi village of Shinshū seen through religious investigation registers), *Management and Labor Studies Series No. 202* (Tokyo: Keiō Gijuku Daigaku Sangyō Kenkyūjo, 1967-1968).

———, "Tokugawa kōki jinkō hendō no chiiku-teki tokusei" (The regional characteristics of population change in the second half of the Tokugawa period), *Mita Gakkai Zasshi*, Vol. 64, No. 8 (1971).

———, "Tōnō ichi sanson no jinkō tōkei" (Population statistics for a

mountain village in eastern Mino), *Kenkyū Kiyō* (Tokyo: Tokugawa Rinseishi Kenkyūjo, 1970).

———, "Tokugawa kōki Owari ichi nōson no jinkō tōkei" (Demographic statistics of one farming village in Owari in the late Tokugawa perod), *Mita Gakkai Zasshi*, Vol. 59, No. 1 (1966).

———, "Tokugawa kōki Owari ichi nōson no jinko tōkei zokuken—
Family Reconstruction-hō no tekiyō" (Demographic statistics of one
farming village in Owari in the late Togukawa period, a sequel—An
application of the family reconstruction method), *Management and
Labor Studies Series No. 213* (Tokyo: Keiō Gijuku Daigaku Sangyō
Kenkyūjo, 1967-1968).

Hayami Akira and Uchida Nobuko, "Kinsei nōmin no kōdō tsuiseki
chōsa" (A survey tracing the behavior of Tokugawa farmers), *Kenkyū Kiyō* (Tokyo: Tokugawa Rinseishi Kenkyūjo, 1971).

———, "Size of Household in a Japanese County throughout the
Tokugawa Era," in Peter Laslett, ed., *Household and Family in
Past Time* (Cambridge, Cambridge University Press, 1972).

Hayami Akira and Yasumoto Minoru, "Jinkō-shi kenkyū ni okeru
Family Reconstitution" (Family reconstitution in studies on demographic history), *Shakai Keizai Shigaku*, Vol. 34, No. 2 (1968).

Hayashi Reiko, *Edo tonya nakama no kenkyū* (A study of wholesale
guilds in Edo) (Tokyo: Ochanomizu Shobō, 1967).

Dan Fenno Henderson, "'Contracts' in Tokugawa Villages," *The
Journal of Japanese Studies*, Vol. 1, No. 1 (Autumn 1974).

Honjō Eijirō, *Jinkō oyobi jinkō mondai* (Population and population
problems) (Tokyo: Nihon Hyōronsha, 1930).

———, "The Population and Its Problems in the Tokugawa Era,"
Bulletin de l'Institut International de Statistique, Vol. 25, No. 2
(1931).

———, "The Population of Japan in the 'Tokugawa' Era," *Tokugawa
Bakufu no beika chōsetsu* (The control of the rice price by the
Tokugawa Bakufu) (Tokyo: Kōbundō Shobō, 1924).

———, "Population Problems in the Tokugawa Era," *Kyoto University Economic Review*, Vol. 2, No. 2 (1927).

———, *The Social and Economic History of Japan* (Kyoto: Institute
for Research in Economic History of Japan, 1935).

Honjō Eijirō, ed., *Kinsei no Osaka* (Osaka in the Tokugawa period)
(Osaka: Kansai Keizai Dōyūkai, 1959).

Hōreishū (Compilation of laws), in the possession of the Okayama
University Library, Okayama.

Inoue Kazuo and Gotō Kazuo, eds., *Mikawa no kuni Hōi chihō shū-
mon nimbetsu aratame-chō* (Toyohashi: Aichi-ken Hōi Chihō-shi
Hensan Iinkai, 1961).

Ishihara Akira, *Nihon no igaku* (Medical science in Japan) (Tokyo: Shibundō, 1965).

Iwamoto Yoshiteru, *Kinsei gyoson kyōdōtai no hensen katei* (The process of the transformation of fishing village communities during the Tokugawa period) (Tokyo: Hanawa Shobō, 1970).

Iwate-ken, *Iwate kenshi* (The history of Iwate prefecture), Vol. 5 (Morioka: Iwate Prefecture, 1962).

Kagoshima-ken, *Kagoshima-ken nōji chōsa* (A survey of agriculture in Kagoshima Prefecture) (Kagoshima, 1955).

Kajinishi Mitsuhaya *et al.*, *Nihon shihonshugi no hatten* (The development of Japanese capitalism) (Tokyo: Tokyo Daigaku Shuppankai, 1957).

Katsu Kaishū, "Jinkō oyobi kokudaka no bu" (Section on population and output), *Suijinroku*, Vol. 1 (1890).

Allen C. Kelley and Jeffrey G. Williamson, "Writing History Backwards: Meiji Japan Revisited," *The Journal of Economic History*, Vol. 31, No. 4 (December 1971).

Barbara A. Kellum, "Infanticide in England in the Later Middle Ages," *History of Childhood Quarterly: The Journal of Psychohistory*, Vol. 1, No. 3 (Winter 1974).

Kikuchi Toshio, *Shinden kaihatsu* (The reclamation of fields), 2 vols., (Tokyo: Kokon Shoin, 1958).

————, *Shinden kaihatsu* (The reclamation of fields) (Tokyo: Shibundō, 1964).

Kimura Motoi, *Bakuhan taisei-shi josetsu* (An introduction to the history of the Bakuhan system) (Tokyo: Bungadō Shoten, 1961).

————, *Kinsei no shinden mura* (*Shinden* villages of the Tokugawa period) (Tokyo: Yoshikawa Kōbunkan, 1964).

Kimura Takeo, ed., *Kinsei Osaka heiya no sonraku* (Villages in the Osaka plain in the Tokugawa period) (Tokyo: Minerva Shobō, 1970).

Kitajima Masamoto, *Bakuhan-sei no kumon* (The agonies of the Bakuhan system) (Tokyo: Chūō Kōronsha, 1966).

Kitayama Shigeo, *Manyō no seiki* (The century of Manyō) (Tokyo: Tokyo University Press, 1953).

Kitō Hiroshi, "Kainin kakiage-chō ni miru shussan to shibō—Bakumatsu-Meiji shotō no kita Kantō ni okeru jirei" (Births and deaths as seen in the records of pregnancy—an example from the northern Kanto during the late Tokugawa and early Meiji periods), *Mita Keizaigaku Kenkyū*, No. 6 (September 1972).

Kobayashi Kazumasa, "Edo jidai nōson jūmin no seimei-hyō" (Life tables for inhabitants of a rural village of Japan from 1812 to 1815), *Jinkō Mondai Kenkyū*, No. 65 (August 1956), pp. 12-23.

Kōda Naritomo, *Edo to Osaka* (Edo and Osaka) (Tokyo: Toyamabō, 1934).

Kodama Kōta, *Genroku jidai* (The Genroku period) (Tokyo: Chūō Kōronsha, 1971).

———, *Kinsei nōmin seikatsu-shi* (A history of the life of peasants in the Tokugawa period) (Tokyo: Yoshikawa Kōbunkan, 1957).

Kodama Kōta, ed., *Sangyō-shi 2* (A history of industry, Vol. 2), Vol. 11 of Taikei Nihonshi sōsho (Japanese history series) (Tokyo: Yamakawa Shuppansha, 1955).

Kojima gunson mura meisai-chō (Detailed village records on the villages in the district of Kojima), compiled by Nagayama Usaburō. Located in the Kurashiki Municipal Library, Kurashiki, Okayama.

James Kokoris, "The Economic and Financial Development of Okayama Prefecture, Japan" (unpublished Ph.D. dissertation, University of Michigan, 1956).

William L. Langer, "Infanticide: A Historical Survey," *History of Childhood Quarterly: The Journal of Psychohistory*, Vol. 1, No. 3 (Winter 1974).

J. William Leasure, "Malthus, Marriage and Multiplication," *The Milbank Memorial Fund Quarterly*, Part 1, Vol. 16, No. 4 (October 1963).

J. R. McEwan, *The Political Writings of Ogyū Sorai* (Cambridge: Cambridge University Press, 1962).

Matsuo Keiko, "Bakumatsu-Meiji chūki ni okeru igyō no tenkai katei" (The development of the *igusa* [rush] industry from the Bakumatsu to mid-Meiji period), *Okayama Shigaku*, No. 9 (July 1961).

Matsuura Akira, "Kinsei kōki rōdō idō no ichi keitai—Settsu no kuni Hanakuma-mura no jinkō idō o chūshin to shite" (One form of labor movement in the latter half of the Tokugawa period—with a focus on population movement in the village of Hanakuma in Settsu Province), *Shakai Keizai Shigaku*, Vol. 38, No. 6 (February 1973).

Matsuyoshi Sadao, *Shinden no kenkyū* (A study of "new fields") (Tokyo: Yūhikaku, 1926).

Meiji Zaiseishi Hensankai, *Meiji zaisei-shi* (A financial history of the Meiji period), Vol. 5 (Tokyo: Maruzen Shoten, 1905).

Miyakawa Mitsuru, *Taikō kenchiron* (A study on Hideyoshi's cadastral survey) (Tokyo: Ochanomizu Shobō, 1957).

Miyamoto Mataji, ed., *Kinai nōson no chitsujo to henbō* (The [social] order and transformation of the villages in the Kinai) (Tokyo: Yūhikaku, 1957).

———, *Shōhin ryūtsū no shiteki kenkyū* (A historical study of commerce) (Kyoto: Minerva Shobō, 1967).

Mizuhara Masataka, "Kinsei ni okeru suiden tantō shūryō" (Paddy yields per *tan* during the Tokugawa period), *Kinsei-shi Kenkyū*, No. 45 (April 1970).

Mori Katsumi and Takeuchi Rizō, eds., *Nihon-shi gaisetsu* (A general history of Japan) (Tokyo: Hanawa Shobō, 1970).

Mori Kahei, *Konohe chihō-shi* (A local history of Konohe) (Tokyo: Hōsei University Press, 1969).

————, *Kyū-Nambu han ni okeru hyakushō ikki no kenkyū* (A study of the peasant uprisings in the former Nambu *han*) (Sendai: Saitō Hō'on-kai, 1935).

————, "Meiji shonen ni okeru Iwate-ken no ikuji seido," *Shakai Keizai Shigaku*, Vol. 4, No. 1 (April 1934).

————, *Nihon hekichi no shiteki kenkyū* (A historical study of the remote regions of Japan), Vols. 1 and 2 (Tokyo: Hōsei University Press, 1969 and 1970).

Morimatsu Yoshiaki, Hōgetsu Keigo, and Kimura Motoi, eds., *Seikatsu-shi 2* (A history of life-style, Vol. 2), Vol. 16 of the Taikei Nihonshi sōsho (Japanese history series) (Tokyo: Yamakawa Shuppansha, 1969).

Morita Yūzo, "Estimated Birth and Death Rates in the Early Meiji Period of Japan," *Population Studies*, Vol. 17, No. 1 (July 1963).

Nagahara Keiji, ed., *Nihon Keizai-shi* (An economic history of Japan) (Tokyo: Yūhikaku, 1971).

Nagai Isaburō, *Kome no rekishi* (The history of rice) (Tokyo: Shibundō, 1965).

Nagai Masatarō, "Ugo-Tobishima no jinkō mondai" (The population problems of Ugo-Tobishima), *Yamagata Daigaku Kiyō*, Vol. 1 (March 1950).

Nagayama Usaburō, *Kurashiki shishi* (A history of Kurashiki City) (Kurashiki: Kurashiki Shishi Kankō Iinkai, 1963).

Naitō Jirō, *Honbyakushō taisei no kenkyū* (A study of the honbyakushō system) (Tokyo: Ochanomizu Shobō, 1968).

Nakabe Yoshiko, "Genroku-Kyōhō-ki ni okeru nōgyō keiei to shōhin ryūtsū" (Agricultural management and commerce during the Genroku-Kyōhō periods), in Kimura Takeo, ed., *Kinsei Osaka heiya no sonraku* (Villages in the Osaka plain in the Tokugawa period) (Kyoto: Minerva Shobō, 1970).

————, *Kinsei toshi no seiritsu to kōzō* (The formation and structure of cities during the Tokugawa period) (Tokyo: Shinseisha, 1967).

————, "Settsu zaigō-chō no tenkai" (The development of the Settsu rural towns), in Chihō-shi Kenkyū Kyōgi-kai, ed., *Hōken toshi no shomondai* (Problems of the feudal cities) (Tokyo: Yūzankaku, 1959).

James I. Nakamura, *Agricultural Production and the Economic Devel-*

opment of Japan, 1873-1922 (Princeton: Princeton University Press, 1966).

——, "Growth of Japanese Agriculture, 1875-1920," in William W. Lockwood, ed., *The State and Economic Enterprise in Japan* (Princeton: Princeton University Press, 1965).

Nakamura Kichiji, *Kinsei-shoki nōsei-shi kenkyū* (A study of the history of agricultural policy during the early Tokugawa period) (Tokyo: Iwanami Shoten, 1938).

Naramoto Tatsuya, *Chōnin no jitsuryoku* (The real power of the merchants) (Tokyo: Chūō Kōronsha, 1966).

Edwin L. Neville, Jr., "The Development of Transportation in Japan: A Case Study of Okayama *Han*, 1600-1868" (unpublished Ph.D. dissertation, University of Michigan, 1959).

Ninohe-gun, *Ninohe gunshi* (A history of the Ninohe district) (Morioka: Ninohe-gun, 1968).

Nishijima Minoru, *Edo jidai no sei seikatsu* (Sex life in the Edo period) (Tokyo: Yūzankaku, 1969).

Nishikawa Shunsaku, "1840-nendai Bōchō ryōkoku ni okeru hinō-seisanbutsu sanpin no seisandaka to tōnyū keisū" (Input coefficients and output of three nonagricultural products in the domain of Chōshū during the 1840s), *Mita Shōgaku Kenkyū*, Vol. 19, No. 1 (April 1976).

Nishikawa Shunsaku and Ishibe Shōko, "1840-nendai Mitajiri saiban no keizai keisan" (Income accounting of the Mitajiri district in the 1840s) Part 1 in *Mita Gakkai Zasshi*, Vol. 68, No. 9 (September 1975), and Part 2 in *Mita Gakkai Zasshi*, Vol. 68, No. 10 (October 1975).

Nishimura Makoto and Yoshikawa Ichirō, eds., *Nihon kyōkō shikō* (Historical notes on Japanese famines) (Tokyo: Maruzen Kabushiki Kaisha, 1936).

Nishioka Toranosuke and Hattori Shisō, eds., *Nihon rekishi chizu* (Historical maps of Japan) (Tokyo: Zenkoku Kyōiku Tosho K.K., 1956).

Nishiyama Matsunosuke, "Osaka, Hyōgo, Nishinomiya, Shiakujima jinkō tōkei hyō" (Statistical tables on the population of Osaka, Hyōgo, Nishinomiya, and Shiakujima), *Rekishigaku Kenkyū*, No. 157 (1952).

Nōmukyoku, ed., *Dainihon nōsei ruihen* (A compilation of agricultural policies of Greater Japan) (Tokyo, 1893), reprinted as *Dainihon nōseishishi* (Tokyo: Bungei Shunjūsha, 1932).

Nomura Kanetarō, "Edo jidai ni okeru jinkō chōsa" (Population surveys in the Edo period), *Mita Gakkai Zasshi*, Vol. 42, No. 3 (1949).

——, *On Cultural Conditions Affecting Population Trends in Japan*

(Tokyo: Nihon Gakujitsu Shinkōkai, 1953), No. 2 of the Economic Series published in English by the Science Council of Japan, Division of Economics and Commerce.

Nomura Kenkyūkai, Kōmi Mura Kyōdō Kenkyūhan, "Ogaki hanryō Mino no kuni Motosu no kōri Kōmi mura no kokō tōkei" (Population statistics on Kōmi village, Motosu district, Mino province in the domain of Ogaki), *Mita Gakkai Zasshi*, Vol. 53, Nos. 10-11 (1960).

Edward Norbeck, *Changing Japan* (New York: Holt, Rinehart and Winston, 1965.

Nōrinshō Nōmukyoku, *Kyūhan jidai no kōchi kakuchō kairyō jigyō ni kansuru chōsa* (A survey on works to expand and improve the cultivated land in the Tokugawa period) (Tokyo: Nōrinshō, 1927).

Goran Ohlin, "Mortality, Marriage, and Growth in Pre-Industrial Populations," *Population Studies*, Vol. 14 (1961).

————, "The Positive and the Preventive Check: A Study of the Rate of Growth of Pre-Industrial Populations" (unpublished Ph.D. dissertation, Department of Economics, Harvard University, 1955).

Oishi Shinzaburō, "Gōnō to kisei jinushi-sei" (The wealthy peasants and the parasitic landlord system), in Kodama Kōta, ed., *Kinsei-shi handobukku* (A handbook for Tokugawa history) (Tokyo: Kondō Shuppansha, 1972).

————, *Kinsei sonraku no kōzō to ie seido* (The structure and family system of the Tokugawa villages) (Tokyo: Ochanomizu Shobō, 1968).

————, *Kyōhō kaikaku no keizai seisaku* (Economic policies of the Kyōhō Reform) (Tokyo: Ochanomizu Shobō, 1961).

Oishi Shinzaburō et al., *Nihon keizaishi-ron* (A study of Japanese economic history) (Tokyo: Ochanomizu Shobō, 1967).

Oka Chōhei, *Okayama keizai bunka-shi* (An economic and cultural history of Okayama) (Okayama: Matsushima Sadaichi, 1939).

Okasaki Ayanori, *Histoire du Japon, L'economie et la population* (Paris: Presses Universitaires de France, 1958).

Okayama-ken, *Okayama-ken no rekishi* (A history of Okayama Prefecture) (Okayama: Okayama-ken, 1962).

Okayama Shiyakusho, *Okayama shishi* (A history of Okayama City), *Sangyō keizai hen* (Volume on industry and the economy) (Okayama: Okayama Shiyakusho, 1966).

Omori Shirō, *Kome to jinkō to rekishi* (Rice and population and history) (Tokyo: Gengensha, 1955).

O-nengumai toritate sanyo-chō (Records for the collection of the rice tax) for 1804, 1809, 1828, 1851, 1857, and 1863 for Fujito village in Kojima. Located in the Okayama University Library, Okayama.

Ono Masao, "Okayama-han ni okeru Kokura orimono no ryūtsū keitai

—Kaei-Ansei-ki o chūshin to shite" (The form of the trade in Koku-ra-ori in the domain of Okayama with a focus on the Kaei and Ansei periods), in Hōgetsu Keigo Sensei Kanreki Kinenkai, ed., *Nihon shakai keizai-shi kenkyū, Kinsei hen* (Studies on the social and economic history of Japan, volume on the Tokugawa period) (Tokyo: Yoshikawa Kōbunkan, 1967).

Ono Takeo, *Nihon kinsei kikinshi* (A history of Japanese famines in the Tokugawa period) (Tokyo: Gakugeisha, 1935).

Ōtake Hideo, *Hōken shakai no nōmin kazoku* (Farm families in a feudal society) (Tokyo: Sōbunsha, 1958).

Ōta Ken'ichi, "Bakumatsu-ki Okayama-han no men senbaisei" (The cotton monopoly system in the domain of Okayama during the Bakumatsu period), *Shigaku Zasshi*, Vol. 70, No. 7 (1961).

Ōta Ken'ichi and Matsuo Keiko, "Bakumatsu-Meiji shoki ni okeru jinushi-sei no tenkai—Okayama-han Kojima-no-kōri Hikasa-ke o chūshin to shite" (The development of the landlord system in the Bakumatsu and early Meiji periods: With a focus on the Hikasa house of the Kojima district in the domain of Okayama), *Okayama Shigaku*, Nos. 6-7 (June 1960).

Ōta Tenrei, *Datai kinshi to yūsei hogo-hō* (The prohibition of abortion and the Eugenic Protection Law) (Tokyo: Keieisha Kagaku Kyō-kai, 1967).

Otsuchi-chō (The town of Otsuchi), *Otsuchi chōshi* (A history of the town of Otsuchi) (Morioka: Otsuchi-chō, 1966).

Robert G. Potter, Jr., "Birth Intervals: Structure and Change," *Population Studies*, Vol. 17 (1964).

Orest and Patricia Ranum, *Popular Attitudes toward Birth Control in Pre-Industrial France and England* (New York: Harper & Row, 1972).

Rekishigaku Kenkyūkai and Nihon-shi Kenkyūkai, eds., *Kōza Nihon-shi 4: Bakuhan-sei shakai* (Lectures in Japanese history, Vol. 4: The Bakuhan society) (Tokyo: Tokyo University Press, 1971).

J. L. Riallin, *Economie et Population au Japon* (Paris, n.d.).

Henry Rosovsky, *Capital Formation in Japan* (Glencoe: The Free Press, 1961).

———, "Rumbles in the Ricefields: Professor Nakamura vs. the Official Statistics," *Journal of Asian Studies*, Vol. 27, No. 2 (February 1968).

Gilbert Rozman, *Urban Networks in Ch'ing China and Tokugawa Japan* (Princeton: Princeton University Press, 1973).

Ryōchi tahata chōbu ninzu-chō (Registers of paddy and upland holdings), in the possession of the Okayama University Library, Okayama, Japan.

Saga kenshi (A history of Saga prefecture) (Saga: Saga Prefecture, 1968).

Saitō Osamu, "Tokugawa kōki kara Taishō zenki ni itaru nōgyō chingin no chōki-teki sūsei" (Long-run trends in agricultural wages from the late Tokugawa period to the early Taisho period), *Shakai Keizai Shigaku*, Vol. 39, No. 2 (June 1973).

Sakudō Yōtarō, *Nihon kahei kinyūshi no kenkyū* (A study on the history of Japanese currency and finance) (Tokyo: Miraisha, 1961).

Sano Yōko, "The Changes in Real Wages of Construction Workers in Tokyo, 1830-1894," *Management and Labor Studies*, English series, No. 4, published by the Institute of Management and Labor Studies, Keio University, January 1963.

Sasaki Jun'nosuke, *Bakuhan kenryoku no kiso kōzō* (The basic structure of the Bakuhan authority) (Tokyo: Ochanomizu Shobō, 1964).

Sasaki Yōichirō, "Bakumatsu-Meiji shoki Musashi-no-kuni jinkō sūsei ni kansuru ichi kōsatsu" (An examination of population in the province of Musashi in the Bakumatsu and early Meiji periods), *Mita Gakkai Zasshi*, Vol. 59, No. 3 (1966).

———, "Hida-no-kuni Takayama no jinkō kenkyū" (A demographic study of Takayama in Hida Province), *Keizai-shi ni okeru jinkō* (Population in economic history), Proceedings of the 37th meeting of the Shakai Keizai-shi Gakkai (Tokyo: Keiō Tsūshin Kabushiki Kaisha, 1969).

———, "Tokugawa jidai kōki toshi jinkō no kenkyū: Settsu-no-kuni Nishinari-no-kōri Tennōji-mura" (A study on the city population during the late Tokugawa period: Tennōji village in Nishinari district, Settsu province), *Shikai*, Vol. 14 (1967).

Sawada Gōichi, *Nara-chō jidai minsei keizai no sūteki kenkyū* (A quantitative study of public administration and the economy during the Nara period) (Tokyo: Kashiwa Shobō, 1972 reprint; original 1927).

Sekiyama Naotarō, *Kinsei Nihon jinkō no kenkyū* (A study of the population of Tokugawa Japan) (Tokyo: Ryūginsha, 1948).

———, *Kinsei Nihon no jinkō kōzō* (The population structure of Tokugawa Japan) (Tokyo: Yoshikawa Kōbunkan, 1958).

——— *Nihon no jinkō* (The population of Japan) (Tokyo: Shibundō, 1962).

———, "Tokugawa jidai no zenkoku jinkō ni kansuru gimon to kōsatsu" (An examination of and problems concerning the national population of the Tokugawa period), *Shakai Keizai Shigaku*, Vol. 11, Nos. 11-12.

———, "Wakayama han no jinkō chōsa to jinkō jōtai" (The population surveys and population conditions of Wakayama domain), *Keizai Riron*, Vols. 15-18 (1953).

Setonaikai Sōgō Kenkyūkai, ed., *Gyoson no seikatsu—Okayama-ken Kojima-shi Shimotsui Tanoura* (Life in a fishing village—Tanoura of Shimotsui in Kojima City, Okayama Prefecture) (Okayama: Setonaikai Sōgō Kenkyūkai, 1954).

——, *Nōson no seikatsu* (Life in a farming village) (Okayama: Setonaikai Sōgō Kenkyūkai, 1951).

Setonaikai Sōgō Kenkyūkai, Okayama University, ed., *Sanson no seikatsu—Okayama-ken Tomata-gun Tomi-mura-Ō* (Life in a mountain village: Tomi-mura-Ō of the district of Tomata in Okayama Prefecture), No. 3 of the Sonraku sōgō chōsa hōkoku series (Okayama: Setonaikai Sōgō Kenkyūkai, 1955).

Shakai Keizai Shigakkai, ed., *Keizaishi ni okeru jinkō* (Population in economic history) (Tokyo: Keiō Tsūshin, 1969).

Shibata Hajime, "Bizen Kojima ni okeru shinkai enden no keiei keitai" (The management of newly opened salt fields in Kojima, Bizen), *Okayama Shigaku*, No. 5 (November 1959).

Shimbō Hiroshi, *Hōkenteki shōnōmin no bunkai katei* (The process of the disintegration of the feudal petty farmer) (Tokyo: Shinseisha, 1967).

Shimbō Hiroshi, Hayami Akira, and Nishikawa Shunsaku, eds., *Sūryō keizaishi nyūmon* (An introduction to quantitative economic history) (Tokyo: Nihon Hyōronsha, 1975).

Shinmi Kichiji, *Kakyū shizoku no kenkyū* (A study of lower-class samurai) (Tokyo: Maruzen, 1965).

Shiozawa Kimio and Kawaura Kōji, *Kisei jinushi-sei ron* (A theory of the parasitic landlord system) (Tokyo: Ochanomizu Shobō, 1957).

Neal Skene Smith, ed., "Materials on Japanese Social and Economic History: Tokugawa Japan," *Transactions of the Asiatic Society of Japan*, 2nd Series, Vol. 14 (1937).

Robert J. Smith, *Ancestor Worship in Contemporary Japan* (Stanford: Stanford University Press, 1974).

——, "*Ihai*: Mortuary Tablets, the Household and Kin in Japanese Ancestor Worship," *Transactions of the Asiatic Society of Japan*, 3rd Series, Vol. 9 (May 1966).

——, "The Japanese Rural Community: Norms, Sanctions, and Ostracism," *American Anthropologist*, Vol. 63, No. 3 (1961).

——, "Town and City in 'Pre-modern' Japan: Small Families, Small Households, and Residential Instability" in Peter Laslett, ed., *Household and Family in Past Time* (Cambridge: Cambridge University Press, 1972).

Thomas C. Smith, *The Agrarian Origins of Modern Japan* (Stanford: Stanford University Press, 1959).

399

————, "Farm Family By-employments in Preindustrial Japan," *The Journal of Economic History*, Vol. 29, No. 4 (December 1969).

————, "The Japanese Village in the Seventeenth Century," *The Journal of Economic History*, Vol. 12, No. 1 (1952). Reprinted in John W. Hall and Marius B. Jansen, eds., *Studies in the Institutional History of Early Modern Japan* (Princeton: Princeton University Press, 1968).

————, "The Land Tax in the Tokugawa Period," *Journal of Asian Studies*, Vol. 18, No. 1 (November 1958). Reprinted in John W. Hall and Marius B. Jansen, eds., *Studies in the Institutional History of Early Modern Japan* (Princeton: Princeton University Press, 1968).

————, "Pre-modern Economic Growth: Japan and the West," *Past and Present*, No. 60 (August 1973).

Joseph J. Spengler, "Demographic Factors and Early Modern Economic Development," *Daedalus* (Spring 1968).

Irene B. Taeuber, "Japan's Demographic Transition Re-examined," *Population Studies*, Vol. 14 (1961).

————, *The Population of Japan* (Princeton: Princeton University Press, 1958).

Takahashi Bonsen, *Datai mabiki no kenkyū* (A study on abortion and infanticide) (Tokyo: Chūō Shakai Jigyō Kyōkai Shakai Jigyō Kenkyūjo, 1936).

————, "Mito han no jinkō seisaku" (Population policies in Mito domain), *Jinkō Mondai*, Vol. 5, No. 1 (1942).

————, *Nihon jinkō-shi no kenkyū* (A study of the history of the population of Japan), Vol. 1 (Tokyo: Sanyūsha, 1941), Vol. 2 (Tokyo: Nihon Gakujutsu Shinkōkai, 1955), and Vol. 3 (Tokyo: Nihon Gakujutsu Shinkōkai, 1962).

Takahashi Kamekichi, *Tokugawa hōken keizai no kenkyū* (A study of the Tokugawa feudal economy) (Tokyo: Senshinsha, 1932).

Takayanagi Mitsutoshi, *Toyotomi Hideyoshi no kenchi* (The cadastral survey of Toyotomi Hideyoshi), Vol. 17, No. 6 of the series *Iwanami kōza Nihon rekishi* (Tokyo: Ochanomizu Shobō, 1957).

Takenaka Yasukazu and Sakudō Yōtarō, eds., *Nihon keizai-shi* (An economic history of Japan) (Tokyo: Gakubunsha, 1972).

Takeyasu Shigeji, *Kinsei hōken-sei no tochi kōzō* (The structure of land under Tokugawa feudalism) (Tokyo: Ochanomizu Shobō, 1966).

————, *Kinsei Kinai nōgyō no kōzō* (The structure of Kinai agriculture during the Tokugawa period) (Tokyo: Ochanomizu Shobō 1969).

——, *Kinsei kosakuryō no kōzō* (The structure of Tokugawa tenant rents) (Tokyo: Ochanomizu Shobō, 1968).

Takigawa Seijirō, *Ritsuryō jidai no nōmin seikatsu* (The life of peasants during the Ritsuryō period) (Tokyo: Tōkō Shoin, 1969).

Tamano Shiyakusho, *Tamano shishi* (The history of Tamano City) (Okayama: Tamano Shiyakusho, 1960).

Tamura Eitarō, *Edo jidai chōnin no seikatsu* (The life of merchants during the Edo period) (Tokyo: Yūzankaku, 1966).

Taniguchi Sumio, "Kinsei ni okeru Bizen minami Kojima no shōhin seisan to ryūtsū" (The production and trading of commercial goods in southern Kojima of Bizen in the Tokugawa period), in *Naikai sangyō to suiun no shiteki kenkyū* (Tokyo: Yoshikawa Kōbunkan, 1966).

——, *Okayama han* (The domain of Okayama) (Tokyo: Yoshikawa Kōbunkan, 1964).

——, *Okayama hansei-shi no kenkyū* (A study of the history of the administration of Okayama domain) (Tokyo: Hanawa Shobō, 1964).

Taniguchi Sumio and Shibata Hajime, "Kinsei ni okeru kazoku kōsei no henshitsu katei" (The process of change in the family composition in the Tokugawa period), *Kenkyū Shūroku* (Bulletin of the School of Education, Okayama University), No. 1 (1955).

Tawa Kazuhiko, *Kojima sangyō-shi no kenkyū* (A study on the history of commerce in Kojima) (Kyoto: Kojima no Rekishi Kankōkai, 1959).

Tempō nendo kikin jōkyō torishirabe-chō (Report on the famine conditions in the Tempō period), compiled by the Okayama District Administration in 1888. Located in the Kurashiki Municipal Library, Kurashki, Okayama.

E. P. Thompson, *The Making of the English Working Class* (Middlesex: Penguin Books, Ltd., 1963).

Toyoda Takeshi, *Nihon no hōken toshi* (Feudal cities of Japan) (Tokyo: Iwanami Shoten, 1952).

Toyoda Takeshi and Kodama Kōta, eds., *Ryūtsū-shi* (A history of commerce Vol. 1), Vol. 13 of Taikei Nihonshi sōsho (Japanese history series) (Tokyo: Yamakawa Shuppansha, 1969).

Tsuchiya Takao, "Shūmon-aratame-chō no shakai keizai shiteki kōsatsu" (A socioeconomic historical examination of the religious investigation registers), *Shakai Keizai Shigaku*, Vol. 3, No. 8 (1933).

Tsuda Hideo, *Hōken keizai seisaku no tenkai to shijō kōzō* (The development of feudal economic policies and the market structure) (Tokyo: Ochanomizu Shobō, 1961).

Tsuda Hideo, *Hōken shakai kaitai katei kenkyū josetsu* (An introduction to the study of the process of the disintegration of a feudal society) (Tokyo: Hanawa Shobō, 1970).

Tsuge Takeshi, "Nōson mondai no ichi to shite no mabiki ni tsuite [sic]" (Concerning infanticide as one of the problems of farming villages), *Keizai-shi Kenkyū*, Vol. 15, No. 2 (February 1936).

Toshio G. Tsukahira, *Feudal Control in Tokugawa Japan. The Sankin Kōtai System* (Cambridge: East Asian Research Center, Harvard University, 1966).

G. S. L. Tucker, "English Pre-Industrial Population Trends," *The Economic History Review*, 2nd Series, Vol. 16, No. 2 (1963).

Ueda Tōjirō, *Kinsei no kōsei* (The harsh policies of the Tokugawa period) (Tokyo: Daigadō, 1947).

Umemura Mataji *et al.*, "Tokugawa jidai no jinkō sūsei to sono kisei yōin" (Population trends and their major determining factors in the Tokugawa period), *Keizai Kenkyū*, Vol. 16, No. 2 (1965).

Umemura Mataji *et al.*, eds., *Nihon keizai no hatten* (The development of the Japanese economy), Vol. 1 of the Sūryō Keizaishi Ronshū (Quantitative economic history series) (Tokyo: Nihon Keizai Shinbunsha, 1976).

United Nations, Department of Economic and Social Affairs, *The Aging of Populations and Its Economic and Social Implications* (New York: United Nations, 1956).

————, *Manual IV: Methods of Estimating Basic Demographic Measures from Incomplete Data* (New York: United Nations, 1967).

Wakita Osamu, "Jinushi-sei no hatten o megutte—Sekka mensaku chitai no ba'ai" (On the development of the landlord system—The case of the cotton-growing areas in Settsu and Kawachi), *Rekishigaku Kenkyū*, No. 181 (April 1954).

Wakita Osamu and Kobayashi Shigeru, *Osaka no seisan to kōtsu* (Production and transportation in Osaka) (Osaka: Mainichi Hōsō, 1973).

Watanabe Nobuo, *Bakuhan-sei kakuritsu-ki no shōhin ryūtsū* (Commodity flows during the period of the formation of the Bakuhan system) (Tokyo: Kashiwa Shobō, 1966).

————, "Murakata jinushi no seiritsu to sono kōzō" (The formation and structure of village landholders), *Kiyō* (of Tohoku University), Vol. 2 (March 1960).

Watanabe Norifumi and Sasaki Jun'nosuke, "Shosangyō no gijitsu to rōdō keitai" (Technology and employment structure in several industries) in Asao Naohiro *et al.*, *Nihon rekishi* (A history of Japan),

Iwanami Kōza Series, Vol. 11, Kinsei 3 (Tokyo: Iwanami Shoten, 1976).

E. A. Wrigley, "Family Limitation in Pre-Industrial England," *The Economic History Review*, 2nd Series, Vol. 19, No. 1 (1966).

————, *Industrial Growth and Population Change* (Cambridge: Cambridge University Press, 1962).

————, "Mortality in Pre-Industrial England: The Example of Colyton, Devon, Over Three Centuries," *Daedalus* (Spring 1968).

————, *Population and History* (New York: McGraw-Hill Book Company, 1969).

————, "A Simple Model of London's Importance in Changing English Society and Economy, 1650-1750," *Past and Present*, No. 34 (1967).

E. A. Wrigley, ed., *An Introduction to English Historical Demography* (New York: Basic Books, Inc. 1966).

Yagi Akihiro, *Kinsei no shōhin ryūtsū* (Commerce in Tokugawa Japan) (Tokyo: Hanawa Shobō, 1962).

Yamada Tadao, "Kaikyū tōsō, seiji katei" (Class struggles [and] the political process), in Rekishigaku Kenkyūkai and Nihonshi Kenkyūkai, eds., *Bakuhan-sei shakai* (Society under the Bakuhan system) (Tokyo: Tokyo University Press, 1971). This is Vol. 4 of *Kōza Nihon-shi*.

Yamaguchi Yukio, "Kinsei hōken shakai ni okeru kahei-jidai ikō e no shomondai" (Several problems concerning the change toward the cash payment of land rent in the Tokugawa feudal society) in Kimura, ed., *Kinsei Osaka heiya*.

Kozo Yamamura, "A Comparative Analysis of Landholding Systems: Preindustrial England and Tokugawa Japan," paper presented at the Social Science Research Council conference "Comparative Uses of the Japanese Experience" held at Cuernavaca, Mexico, September 1974.

————, *A Study of Samurai Income and Entrepreneurship* (Cambridge: Harvard University Press, 1974).

Yamasaki Ryūzō, "Settsu ni okeru nōgyō rōdō-koyō keitai no hatten" (The development of the patterns of agricultural employment in Settsu), in Rekishigaku Kenkyūkai, ed., *Hōken shakai no hatten* (The development of a feudal society) (Tokyo: Aoki Shoten, 1961).

Yasukichi Yasuba, *Birth Rates of the White Population in the United States, 1800-1860* (Baltimore: The Johns Hopkins Press, 1961).

Yoshida Yoshinobu, *Chishi minshū seikatsushi* (A history of the life of the populace in Chishi) (Yamagata: Yamagata-ken, 1958).

INDEX

abortion. *See* birth control

adoption, 109, 227, 228-233, 259, 265, 281-283

age, 42-43, 209; calculation of Western equivalent, 43, 209; at childbearing, 235, 246; composition, 308; distribution, 236, 293; at marriage, 246, 299

agriculture: productivity, 9, 20, 23, 96, 98, 118, 163-164, 168; commercialization, 360; growth rates, 74-77; implements used in, 99, 102; improvements in methods of, 75, 99-103, 127, 163-164. *See also* rice output; landholding patterns

Ajino, 170, 186, 247

Akasaka, 181, 195

Akasaka-shuku, 307-308

Asakusanaka, 293, 310; life expectancy in, 295-296

Andō Seiichi, 5, 372

birth control, 25-26, 38, 215, 226-228, 233; abortion as means of, 38, 215, 233-234, 265, 287; biological determinants of, 244-246; compared with Europe, 315-316; infanticide as means of, 24, 26, 38, 215, 233, 237-241, 244, 265, 287, 290, 314, 378; influence of status on, 264; through regulation of marriage, 246-252. *See also* population control

birth intervals. *See* childbearing

birth rates, 151, 210-211, 216-217, 223-224, 256-259, 293, 296-306

births, registration of, 201-204; for Morioka, 148; frequency by day, month, for Fujito, 207-208

Bizen, 48, 162, 181, 183; exports from, 197; landholding in, 190-191; population figures for, 49, 172-173

by-employments, 83-85, 135, 158, 176, 186-188, 253-255, 357

census, 41-43. *See also* population surveys

childbearing: age at, 216, 235-236, 241, 251; birth intervals in, 216, 241-243

cities. *See* urban population

commerce, growth of, 78-80, 136, 164-165, 196-198, 263, 344; reasons for, 20, 23, 26; regional specialization in, 79. *See also* Kinai; Morioka; Okayama

Crawcour, E. Sydney, 6, 94, 344

death rates, 108, 151, 210-211, 213-214, 218, 293, 296-305, 313-314; during famines, 256-259; estimates for four sample villages, 219-220; frequency of deaths in four sample villages, 207-208, 306; for Morioka, 148. *See also* life expectancy

dekasegi. See migration

demographic histories. *See* family histories; death rates; fertility

demographic transition, 47, 314, 317

Dore, R. P., 264

Easterlin, Richard, 34, 346

economic growth, 3, 5, 6-7, 15, 28, 78, 91, 98-99, 126-137, 183, 254, 266, 290, 344. *See also* Kinai; Morioka; Okayama

Edo, population of, 351

Elvin, Mark, 385

Embree, John, 316

epidemics, 256, 280, 284-285, 289, 304, 311; as means of population control, 256; birth and death rates during, 257

family histories, 270-274, 280-282, 382

family reconstitution, 39, 296. *See also* family histories

family size: biological determinants of, 245; in Fukiage and Numa, 230; in Fujito, 229; pressures to limit, 250

LIBRARY OF CONGRESS CATALOGING
IN PUBLICATION DATA

Hanley, Susan B.   1939-
    Economic and demographic change in preindustrial Japan,
1600-1868.

    Bibliography: p.
    Includes index.
    1.   Japan—Economic conditions—To 1868.
2.   Japan—Population—History.   I.   Yamamura,
Kōzō, joint author.   II.   Title.
HC462.6.H27   330.9′52′025   77-71983
ISBN 0-691-03111-8
ISBN 0-691-10055-1 pbk.